Teachers and the Law

Teachers and the Law

Louis Fischer
David Schimmel
Cynthia Kelly

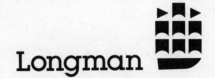

Longman
New York & London

TEACHERS AND THE LAW

Longman Inc.; 19 West 44th Street; New York, N.Y. 10036. Associated companies, branches, and representatives throughout the world.

Developmental Editor: Lane Akers
Editorial and Design Supervisor: Joan Matthews
Interior and Cover Design: Patricia M. Smythe
Manufacturing and Production Supervisor: Maria Chiarino
Composition: Americomp
Printing and Binding: Fairfield Graphics

Figure 1, on p. 184, reprinted from David Schimmel and Louis Fischer, *The Rights of Parents in the Education of Their Children*, pp. 42–43. Copyright © 1977 by the National Committee for Citizens in Education, Columbia, Maryland. Reprinted by permission of the publisher.

Figure 2, on p. 308, courtesy of West Publishing Company, St. Paul, Minnesota.

Figure 3, on p. 309, and Figure 4, on p. 310, reprinted from David Schimmel and Louis Fischer, *The Civil Rights of Students*, p. 293. Copyright © 1975 by Harper & Row, Publishers, Inc. Reprinted by permission of the publisher.

Library of Congress Cataloging in Publication Data

Fischer, Louis, 1924–
  Teachers and the law.

  Bibliography: p.
  Includes index.
  1. Teachers—Legal status, laws, etc.—United
States. 2. Teachers—Legal status, laws, etc.—United
States—States. 3. Students—Legal status, laws, etc.—
United States. 4. Students—Legal status, laws, etc.—
United States—States. I. Schimmel, David, joint
author. II. Kelly, Cynthia, joint author.
III. Title.
KF4175.Z9F55   344.73'078   80-23394
ISBN 0-582-28135-0 (cased)
ISBN 0-582-28134-2 (pbk.)

Manufactured in the United States of America
9 8 7 6 5 4 3 2 1

Contents

Preface

Americans are a highly litigious people. This attitude is not a recent development; well over one hundred years ago, a sensitive French visitor, Alexis de Tocqueville, observed that in the United States of America all issues become "sooner or later a subject of judicial debate."

Today's schools exist and function in the midst of a complex legal environment, and it is difficult not to be aware of a wide range of legal issues that influence the lives of teachers, students, parents, and administrators. It is increasingly clear that educators ignore the law at their own peril! In fact, the U.S. Supreme Court ruled in 1975 that teachers and administrators may be held personally liable in money damages for violating students' clearly established constitutional rights.

This book is about teachers and the law that affects them, law established by state and federal statutes, constitutions, and court decisions. This law will have little significance, however, unless educators know about it and are willing to make the effort to see that it is carried out.

It is not the purpose of this book to encourage teachers to go to court. On the contrary, its goal is to help resolve educational conflicts without going to lawyers or resorting to courts. How? By helping teachers become legally literate—by providing them with information about the law that affects them, about the way the legal system works, and about the way this system can work for them in the public school. With this information, teachers can practice "preventive law." This does not mean that they will be able to be their own lawyers but rather that they will know their legal rights and responsibilities and will assume responsibility for educating other members of the school community about the law. Underlying this premise is our belief that unlawful school practices are generally not intentional but result from a misunderstanding of the law. Because most school officials are anxious to avoid lawsuits, when teachers are able to show that certain school policies are illegal, administrators usually prefer to change them voluntarily rather than as the result of a court order. In addition, we believe that students' educational experiences will be improved when all members of the school community model behavior that is consistent with basic constitutional principles such as due process of law.

Why are educators so poorly informed about the law that affects schools? The answer may be in the fact that much of this law did not exist when they were students, and as a result, they learned almost nothing about this subject during their education. Consequently they have had little training in applying education law to their professional lives. This book can help fill the gap. In addition, we hope in this book to demystify the law for teachers—to break through the barrier of professional jargon and legalese that lawyers use among themselves and translate the language into everyday English.

In short, the purpose of this book is to enable teachers to constructively take the law into their own hands—to provide them with the knowledge necessary to comply with the law, assert their rights, and bring violations to the attention of administrators and colleagues.

The focus of each part of the book is as follows. Part I, "The Legal Aspects of Teaching," addresses questions related to teacher contracts, dismissals, tenure, collective bargaining, liability, defamation, and copyright law. Part II, "Teachers' and Students' Rights," explores legal issues related to personal freedom: of expression, religion and conscience, association, personal appearance, due process, and privacy. It also includes the right to be free from racial and sexual discrimination and rights related to school records, compulsory schooling, and handicapped and bilingual students. At the start of every chapter in the book, there is a list of the principal questions covered in the chapter, with the page on which each discussion begins.

Books about law often begin with a description of the judicial system and the court structure. For some readers, this is a helpful introduction. Others become bored with such descriptions because they do not yet care about these matters. But as readers become involved with legal questions, they begin to wonder why cases go to federal or state courts, when a case can be appealed to the U.S. Supreme Court, and how to find a case record in the library. Because different readers will ask these questions at different times, we have put our explanation of how the legal system works in appendixes. These appendixes also contain relevant sections of the U.S. Constitution, excerpts from state and federal laws relating to education, a glossary of common legal terms, a list of legal resources, a bibliography, and edited Supreme Court cases on education.

No single volume can address all the issues involving school law; this book covers only those issues most central in the daily lives of teachers. It does not, for example, address legal issues related to the use of school property, school boundaries, liabilities of school districts, certification of teachers, school board procedures, and teacher retirement. School law is a broad and burgeoning field, and only portions of it are directly relevant to the professional roles of teachers.

Much of the law examined in this book is neither simple nor unchanging. Many of the cases are as difficult to resolve for lawyers and judges as they are for educators. This is so because cases involving school law often do not address simple conflicts of right against wrong but complex issues encompassing the conflicting interests of teachers, parents, administrators, and students.

Moreover, education law is constantly changing. New legislation is passed, regulations are changed, school boards revise their practices, and the Supreme Court may declare a policy unconstitutional. Because of this diversity and change, our discussion of the cases and laws in each chapter is intended to be illustrative, not exhaustive. We have chosen to highlight major cases and legislation of general interest to teachers rather than focus on legal details.

To summarize, this book is designed to promote legal literacy for public school teachers. It examines a wide range of constitutional, statutory, and case law that directly affects their work. Since no two cases are alike, and since the law is constantly changing, the book can neither be comprehensive nor a substitute for legal advice.

If you contemplate legal action, you should first consult with your professional association and/or a knowledgeable lawyer. But since judicial resolution of an educational dispute is often an unhappy, expensive, difficult, and time-consuming process, bringing suit should be the *last* resort. We hope this book will help you resolve disputes through discussion and negotiation rather than litigation.

We wish to acknowledge and thank those who helped us in writing this book: Lane Akers, of Longman Inc., who initiated, encouraged, and supported this effort; Joan Matthews, Kris Becker, and Nicole Benevento, for helping us transform our manuscript into its final form; Irene Glynn, for excellent editorial work; Gail Sorenson, for critically reviewing the manuscript; Rick Mondschein, for bringing recent cases to our attention; Meyer Weinberg, who made the resources of the Horace Mann Bond Center for Equal Education available to us; and Rich Morrill, for assisting us in finding and checking case citations.

Louis Fischer
David Schimmel
Cynthia Kelly

Teachers and the Law

PART ONE

The Legal Aspects of Teaching

1

Do I have a contract?

OVERVIEW

Most school districts have written contracts with their teachers. The contract outlines teacher and school board rights, although the actual provisions of contracts vary widely from district to district. For example, the 1977–79 contract between the Chicago Board of Education and the Chicago Teachers Union ran to 144 pages and listed 49 separate articles. Contract provisions included salary schedules for teachers, maximum class size, length of the school day, insurance, student discipline, sick pay, transfer policies, and the grievance procedure for teachers who wished to complain of contract violations. Because the contract was the result of collective bargaining negotiations, it also included a provision requiring the board to recognize the union as the bargaining agent for the teacher. (Chapter 4 gives a detailed survey of collective bargaining.)

In contrast, the 1979–80 contract between the Greencastle, Indiana, school board and the Greencastle Classroom Teachers Association was only 28 pages long. This contract, too, provided for recognition of the association as the exclusive bargaining representative of the teachers, and it described teaching hours and assignments. It also outlined policies concerning leaves of absence, the grievance procedure, and the teacher salary schedule.

Although length and wording may vary in teaching contracts, certain basic legal principles are common to all. It is these principles that we discuss in this chapter.

CREATING A CONTRACT

The *Wilson* Case[1]

On January 20, 1969, Jessie Wilson applied for a position as a principal in the District of Columbia summer school program. She later received a form letter advising her that she had been selected for this position. The letter went on to state that the appointment was subject to full funding of the summer school program and the return of an attached acceptance form within five days. The acceptance form stated that the applicant's acceptance was "subject to the approval of the board of education."

Mrs. Wilson returned the acceptance form within the required time. Before the board approved her appointment, however, the selection criteria for summer positions were revised, and the board decided that Mrs. Wilson no longer qualified for the position as principal. After the board notified her that they could not approve her appointment, Mrs. Wilson sued school officials for the loss of income following their withdrawal of the offer of appointment as principal. Mrs. Wilson argued that a contract was created when the summer school program received full funding and that school officials broke the contract when they refused to hire her.

The District of Columbia Court of Appeals disagreed. The court pointed out that the acceptance form specified that the position was subject to approval by the District Board of Education. (The court also noted that such approval was required by law in the District of Columbia.) Since the board never gave its approval, "no binding contract of employment existed before Mrs. Wilson was notified that she did not meet the criteria for appointment." Because no contract was ever created, Mrs. Wilson did not have any legal right to the position as principal and was not entitled to any money for loss of income from the board of education.

When is a contract created?

As the *Wilson* case demonstrates, certain requirements must be met before a contract is legally binding on both the teacher and school officials. Like all other contracts, a teacher's contract must have

1. A meeting of the minds of both parties
2. Valid consideration
3. Legal subject matter
4. Competent parties
5. Definite terms

In contract law, "a meeting of the minds" refers to a mutual assent to the terms of the contract. This mutual agreement is usually reached through the process of offer and acceptance. This requirement was the issue in *Wilson;* the court was asked to decide whether there was a valid offer and acceptance. The court concluded that because the board did not follow proper procedures, there was no valid acceptance and thus no contract.

"Consideration" refers to the promises bargained for and exchanged between the parties. To have valid consideration to support a contract, each party must give up something of value, or, in legal terms, "suffer some legal detriment"; that is, the parties to the contract must promise to do something they are not legally obligated to do or promise to refrain from doing something they are legally privileged to do. In the case of a teaching contract, consideration consists of the exchange of promises between the teacher and the school: the teacher promises to perform certain teaching services, and the school officials promise to pay the teacher a certain salary.

"Legal subject matter" means that the contract cannot require the parties to do something that is a crime or against public policy (e.g., an Illinois teacher contracted to have a student murder his principal). "Competent parties" means that the people contracting must be of legal age (a concept that varies according to state law) and must have the mental capacity to understand the terms of the contract. The "definite terms" requirement means that the contract must be clear enough so that each party knows what is required by it. Like other employment contracts, a teaching contract that does not state either salary or teaching duties is too indefinite to be legally enforced. Thus, an Indiana court ruled that a contract to pay a teacher "good wages" was too indefinite to be valid.[2]

When does a contract become legally binding?

As Mrs. Wilson discovered, a contract is not created until the school board approves the proposed contract. Because school boards act as public bodies, they cannot accept ("ratify") a contract without taking official action. Thus, one teacher's contract was not valid when the board of education did not follow the required roll-call procedure in voting on whether to offer her a teaching position.[3] In addition, state law may provide that the school board must ratify a contract before it is legally binding, as in the *Wilson* case.

EXPRESS AND IMPLIED CONTRACTS

Does a contract have to be in writing?

No. Unless state law requires that a teacher's employment contract be in writing, an oral contract that has all the necessary legal requirements will be legally binding.

Does a contract contain all the relevant information regarding terms and conditions of employment?

Not necessarily. As with other contracts, a teacher's contract also includes the provisions of any relevant state laws, such as laws concerning teacher tenure and dismissal procedures. In addition, the contract includes any rules and regulations adopted by the school board that are in effect at the time the contract is signed. Thus, an Oregon court ruled that a teacher could be dismissed for not performing his contractual duties when he did not follow a state board of education rule that "teachers in the public schools shall . . . inculcate in the minds of their pupils correct principles of morality and a proper regard for the laws of society. . . ."[4] In addition, where the teacher's contract includes a statement that the teacher agrees to abide by all rules and regulations adopted by school officials, or where the contract specifically states that it includes the provisions of a particular rule or regulation, the teacher's contract includes even those rules and regulations adopted after the contract has taken effect. For example, a California teacher's contract stated that the teacher was elected "under section 1609 [of the Political Code] in accordance with salary schedule adopted by the Board."[5] When a teacher challenged the school board's legal authority to lower her salary, the court ruled that this provision in her contract gave the board the power to modify the salary schedule in effect at the time she signed her teaching contract. The court noted, however, that any new schedule would have to be adopted prior to the beginning of the school year.

How long does a contract last?

The contract itself states how long it is to be in effect. Nontenured teachers generally hold their positions under annual contracts. Teachers may also be employed under "continuing contracts," which provide that they will be reemployed unless school officials give notice by a certain date that their contracts will not be renewed. Most states also allow school boards to enter into multiyear employment contracts with teachers.

Can a teacher work without a contract?

A teacher can certainly work without a contract, but may have difficulty proving that a certain amount of money is owed as compensation for teaching services. In an Illinois case, for example, the court ruled that tenured teachers did not have to sign contracts.[6] Nevertheless, when a group of tenured teachers refused to sign new contracts, the court held that they should be paid on the basis of the preceding year's salary and denied the benefits given to teachers who had signed the new contract. A nontenured teacher who works without a contract will have more difficulty than a tenured teacher in collecting money from school officials. The nontenured teachers may be able to recover the reasonable value of teaching services under a theory of "quasi-contract," also known as a contract "implied in law."

A quasi-contract is not a contract at all, but "an obligation imposed by law to do justice even though it is clear that no promise was ever made or intended."[7] In order for the court to impose such an obligation, the following must occur: (1) one person must confer a benefit on another, (2) the person conferring the benefit must have a reasonable expectation of compensation, (3) the person conferring the benefit must not have volunteered, and (4) the person receiving the benefit must not be unjustly enriched if the person performing the service is not paid. A teacher who worked without a contract would generally meet these requirements and thus be entitled to be compensated for teaching services.

BREACH OF CONTRACT

How can a contract be broken by school officials?

A contract is binding on both parties, and either party who fails to meet obligations under the contract has "breached" (broken) the contract. For example, Bertrand Russell sued the Barnes Foundation for breach of contract after his services as a lecturer were terminated.[8] Russell had entered into an oral agreement with the Barnes Foundation in which he promised to deliver lectures. This agreement was confirmed in letters between the Barnes Foundation and Russell, copies of which are reprinted here:

Dear Mr. Russell:
We confirm herewith the verbal agreement made with you on August 8, 1940.

We agree to engage you as a member of the teaching staff of the Barnes Foundation at a salary of eight thousand ($8,000) dollars per year, payable in twelve (12) equal monthly installments, on the fifteenth day of each month.

The agreement is to extend for a period of five (5) years, dating from January 1, 1941. If, during the period of the aforesaid agreement, your personal affairs should make it necessary or advisable to terminate the contract, we agree that such a termination may be effected at the end of our school year; namely May 31st.

Your service to the Foundation will consist of one lecture each week during the school year, which extends from October 1st to May 31st inclusive, each lecture to be delivered in the gallery of the Barnes Foundation, at Merion, Pennsylvania.

Yours very truly,
The Barnes Foundation
Albert C. Barnes
President (Corp. Seal)
N. E. Mullen
Secretary-Treasurer

Paul Hogan, Witness
Sarah M. Cleaver, Witness

I, Bertrand Russell, hereby agree to the terms and conditions of the above agreement entered into between myself and the Barnes Foundation.
Bertrand Russell

Mary Mullen, Witness
Cynthia F. Stone, Witness[9]

After he had delivered lectures for two years, Russell was informed by the Barnes Foundation that his contract was to be terminated on December 31, 1942. Russell successfully sued the foundation for breach of contract and was able to collect damages for the money he should have received under the contract. (Chapter 5 contains a detailed discussion of damages.)

In addition to refusing to employ a teacher, a school board can breach a contract by violating one of its provisions. In Maine, for example, the school board voted to dismiss a tenured teacher who also served as a principal, citing a state law that provided the school committee could terminate a contract "when changes in local conditions warrant the elimination of the teaching position for which the contract was made."[10] The court found, however, that there was no evidence that local conditions had changed. In fact, the teacher's position was not eliminated; the teacher was merely replaced by another teacher who performed exactly the same teaching duties. The school officials had eliminated only the extra duty as principal, for which, in previous years, there had been a separate contract. Since the school board had not followed the proper statutory procedures in dismissing the teacher, the court found that the board had breached the contract.

School officials can also breach a contract if they attempt to change the terms of a contract after it is in effect. In Oregon, for example, Mr. George, a teacher, was hired under the following three-year contract:

> THIS AGREEMENT made this 22nd day of April, 1968, by and between School District No. 8R of Umatilla County, Oregon, hereinafter referred to as the district, and Robert George, hereinafter referred to as the teacher.
> WITNESSETH:
> 1. The district agrees to employ the teacher for a period of 3 year(s), commencing on the first day of July, 1968, and ending on the 30th day of June, 1971, and to pay the teacher therefor an annual salary of $11,300, together with any compensation programs established by the district.
> 2. In consideration of the compensation paid hereunder, the teacher agrees to teach Secondary grades in the schools of the district during the period of the regular school year as established by the district
>
> . . .
>
> 5. Additional terms of the contract are as follows:
>
> | | |
> |---|---|
> | Base salary 1968–69 | $ 9,300 |
> | Extra duties: Athletics | 2,000 |
> | Total salary 1968–69 | $11,300[11] |

In the middle of the first school year, the school board fired Mr. George as the football coach. In March 1969 school officials informed him that his salary for the 1969–70 school year would be $2,000 less than expected because of the elimination of his "extra duty" for football coaching. The teacher claimed that, under his contract, he was still entitled to the full salary of $11,-300. School officials treated his response as a refusal to teach and hired another teacher to replace him. Mr. George sued, claiming that the school board had breached the contract. The school board defended its actions by arguing that the teacher was actually employed under two separate contracts:

(1) a three-year contract to teach for $9,300, plus any raises; and (2) a one-year contract to coach football for $2,000. In the school board's view, Mr. George had breached his contract when he refused to teach at the $9,300 salary level.

In order to resolve this dispute the court had to interpret the contract to find out what the parties actually intended their words to mean. Under the law of contracts, a written agreement between two parties is assumed to include all the relevant information about the subject matter; the court cannot look at any prior agreements or conversations that may modify what the written contract says. The court can *interpret* the words of the contract, and in its efforts to find the true meaning of the words, the court *can* look at the circumstances surrounding the making of the contract as well as the past practices and policies of the school district concerning teaching contracts.

After examining such evidence, the Oregon court agreed with the teacher that the contract was not divisible into two parts. First, the court noted that the minutes of the school board meeting at which the teacher's contract was authorized showed that the football and basketball coaches were to be given three-year contracts. Second, after listening to testimony from a number of school officials, the court found that, although a teacher's extra-duty assignments could be changed in the middle of a contract, it was not customary for a teacher's salary to be reduced. The court therefore ruled that the school board had breached the teacher's contract by insisting that the teacher accept a $2,000 salary reduction for the remaining two years of his three-year contract.

How can a teacher break a contract?

Of course, the same principles that apply to school officials also apply to teachers. A teacher who has signed an employment contract and then refuses to accept the teaching position or abandons the position in midyear has breached the contract.

A teacher who does not abide by its terms also breaches a contract. In Texas, for example, a music teacher was employed by the Mission public schools under a contract that stated that she would not teach anywhere else in Texas during the contract period.[12] When the teacher left this job to teach music and direct the band in the Cisco, Texas, public schools, the court ruled that she had breached her contract. Similarly, an Arkansas court found that a teacher had breached her employment contract when she took a leave of absence without following the procedure outlined in the school board's regulations.[13]

What are the legal consequences of breaking a contract?

When one party breaches a contract, the other party to the contract is entitled to a legal remedy that will compensate for the injury the breaching party has caused. In most situations this remedy will be an award of some amount of money, or "damages." The specific amount of money to be awarded is determined by the court according to the particular facts in each case.

In general, when a school board breaks an employment contract, the injured teacher is entitled to damages that equal the salary owed under the contract minus any money the teacher actually earned or might have earned had another teaching position been obtained. In order to understand this rule, it helps to examine a particular case.

In the case described earlier, when Bertrand Russell's teaching contract was breached, the court awarded him $20,000. To reach this figure, the court engaged in the following analysis: First, the court turned to the contract itself to determine how much money Russell would have received if he had been permitted to lecture; under the terms of the contract, the Barnes Foundation had agreed to pay $8,000 a year, or $24,000 for the remaining three-year period. The court then explained that it was up to the Barnes Foundation (the defendant) "to show, in mitigation of this amount, the extent of plaintiff's [Russell's] earnings or ability to obtain other employment."[14] The evidence showed that, during the two years he was teaching for the Barnes Foundation, Russell had earned $2,145.00 and $3,195.68 from other sources, principally his writing and radio addresses. Russell also testified that his earning prospects from these sources for the next three years were slight, and that "his advanced age and the drastic curtailment of courses in philosophy in college curricula" made it impossible for him to obtain other employment. Given this evidence, the court found that Russell could expect to earn only $4,000 from outside sources for his teaching activities during the next three years and thus ordered the Barnes Foundation to pay him $20,000 as damages for breach of contract.

In suing for breach of contract, a teacher can also collect as damages any other expenses incurred as a result of the school board's action. For example, a Montana teacher collected the value of the living quarters supplied rent free under her contract after she was wrongfully dismissed.[15] The courts have also held that teachers who are wrongfully discharged can recover expenses that they can show were incurred in seeking another teaching position.[16] Although teachers are generally not awarded money to cover attorney's fees, such expenses may be awarded as damages under state or federal laws.[17]

The same principles apply when a teacher breaks a contract: school officials are entitled to collect money damages that will cover the school's costs in hiring a replacement.* Thus, if a teacher who is under contract quits in the middle of the school year, school officials can sue this teacher for expenses incurred in finding a teacher who can assume the same responsibilities. If the district is forced to pay a higher salary to find a replacement, school officials can sue the leaving teacher for the difference between that teacher's salary and the replacement teacher's salary.

---

* In a time of teacher surplus, when it is relatively easy for school boards to replace teachers, money damages are apt to be minimal; the teacher is more likely to be damaged in terms of professional reputation.

Some employment contracts include provisions that require teachers who break their contracts to pay a specific amount as damages to the school district. In North Dakota, a teacher's contract stated that a teacher who asked to be released from her contract within two weeks before she was scheduled to begin teaching was required to pay damages in the amount of 4 percent of her salary under the contract.[18] These contractual provisions are known as "liquidated damages clauses," and the courts will enforce them when it is difficult for the parties to a contract to determine the monetary value of a breach of contract. The courts will not enforce such contractual provisions when they feel that the party who breaks the contract has to pay such a large amount of money that this provision is really a penalty or punishment for breaching the contract.

In the North Dakota case, six days before she was to begin teaching, Marcia Walker notified her district superintendent that her husband was moving from the area and that she would be unable to meet her contractual obligations. The school district found a replacement before school started but maintained that Mrs. Walker was still required to pay damages. Mrs. Walker argued that the fixed-damages provision of her contract constituted a penalty and therefore was void under North Dakota law. The court disagreed. Although the court explained that an employer could generally recover only the costs of replacing an employee who breaches a contract, it noted that liquidation damages provisions were valid when it was difficult to ascertain the exact amount of damages. The court found that teacher replacement was such a situation:

> Thus, when we consider the damages caused by a teacher's breach of an employment contract, we cannot ignore the interruption to the school system and the resultant debilitating effect such interruption has upon the learning process of students in the school system. The possibility that the replacement teacher who was obtained may be less experienced or less qualified and, thus, a less effective instructor must also be considered in the assessment of damages. Even if known, it would be extremely difficult to evaluate these damages on a monetary basis. . . . Such damages are not legally compensable but constitute a public injury which the school district was entitled to consider.[19]

When the school board breaches a contract, must the teacher look for another teaching position to collect damages?

A teacher who is wrongfully discharged generally has the duty to look for a similar teaching position in order to "mitigate the damages." If the school board can show that other teaching jobs were available, the board can reduce the amount of money owed as damages by the salary the teacher could have earned. Nevertheless, a teacher does not have to accept a job in another locality or a job that is inferior to the denied position. A federal court found, for example, that a principal was not required to mitigate damages by accepting a position as a teacher.[20] Even though the teaching job paid as much as the principalship, the court concluded that the demotion to teacher might cast doubt on the principal's competence as an administrator and affect later career opportunities. In a Maine case the court ruled that a teacher-principal whose contract was improperly terminated had tried to mitigate damages when he investigated employment opportunities within a "reasonable area" of the school district for a teacher holding a master's degree.[21] Similarly, a federal court held that a teacher had successfully mitigated damages when she applied for ten teaching and nonteaching positions during a two-year period after her position was wrongfully terminated.[22]

If the school board breaches a contract some time before the teacher is to start working, the teacher is not required to look for another teaching position at once. Instead, the teacher has the right to wait until the contract was to begin before looking for another job. In Michigan, for example, the court ruled that a teacher whose contract was wrongfully withdrawn over the summer did not have to abandon her vacation to seek other employment but could notify the school district that she was still prepared to teach. She could wait to look for another job until after school started in the fall.[23]

Can the court order a school board to rehire a teacher?

Yes. Although the courts generally do not order people to return to work or perform certain services, they will do so when an award of money will not adequately compensate the party who has been the victim of a breach of contract. Where a teacher has tenure, for example, the courts can order reinstatement if a teacher has been wrongfully discharged. In one instance, a university failed to follow its own regulations dismissing a professor, and the court ordered that the professor be reinstated. The court explained: "In view of the uncertainty in measuring damages because of the indefinite duration of the contract and the importance of the status of plaintiffs in the milieu of the college teaching profession it is evident that the remedy of damages at law would not be complete or adequate. . . . The relief granted herein is appropriate to achieve equity and justice."[24]

Some courts have even ordered reinstatement when teachers did not have tenure. For example, in Michigan, two probationary teachers were discharged with insufficient notice. The court ruled that the teachers had the option of choosing to be reinstated or reimbursed for the salary they lost (deducting any amount of money they earned otherwise).[25]

Are other remedies available when one party breaches a contract?

Yes. The courts have the power to issue orders (known as "writs of mandamus") to force school officials to comply with the terms of a contract. When one school board was guilty of racial discrimination in refusing to renew a teacher's employment contract, the court ordered the board to renew the teacher's contract.[26] In addition, courts can issue injunctions (court orders) to require the parties to meet their contractual obligations. For example, a court issued an injunction to prevent a teacher from breaching a contractual provision that prohibited her from teaching music in any other school district in the state.[27] In another case, a court issued an injunction preventing the school board from dismissing a superintendent when the school officials had no legal power to do so.[28]

Are there other ways that a contract can end?

Yes. Under the doctrine of "impossibility of performance," a party to a contract is excused from meeting the obligations under that contract if it is impossible to do so. In Washington, for example, a teacher was discharged from his contractual obligation because of his deteriorating eyesight.[29] The court explained that when it is impossible for the teacher to meet contractual duties, the contract to teach is said to be discharged "by operation of law."

A contract can also be terminated by mutual agreement of the parties. In Kansas, a court held that a teacher's employment contract had been terminated by mutual agreement with the school board after the teacher submitted a letter of resignation and the board voted to accept her resignation.[30] Although there was some question whether the teacher had in fact resigned, the court noted that "mutual assent to abandon a contract may be inferred from the conduct of the parties and the attendant circumstances." The court found that there was sufficient evidence to indicate that both the teacher and the school board had intended to end the contract; the court thus concluded that the contract was terminated.

SUMMARY

Most teachers are employed under contracts that outline their rights and responsibilities in employment. A contract becomes effective legally when the following conditions are met: the contract has a legal subject matter, there is a meeting of the mind of both parties, there is valid consideration, the parties are competent, and the contract has definite terms. In addition, school officials must act to officially ratify a teacher's contract.

A contract is binding on both parties; either the teacher or the school officials will be legally liable if obligations under the contract are not met. A school board that breaks a contract to employ a teacher will be required to pay that teacher monetary damages to compensate for loss of salary. In such a situation, however, the teacher has the duty to mitigate these damages by attempting to secure another teaching position. In breach-of-contract situations, the teacher may be entitled to other legal remedies as well, such as reinstatement or an injunction or other order requiring the school board to perform its duties under the contract.

Of course, a teacher who breaks a contract will also be liable to the school district. Under traditional contract law principles, the teacher will be liable for the school district's costs in finding a replacement and for any additional salary that might have to be paid. Today, however, teachers' contracts may describe the specific amount of damages a teacher will have to pay in this situation.

NOTES

1. *Board of Education of D.C.* v. *Wilson,* 290 A.2d 400 (D.C. App. 1972).

2. *Fairplay School Township* v. *O'Neal,* 26 N.E. 686 (Ind. 1891).

3. *Board of Education* v. *Best,* 39 N.E. 694 (Ohio 1894).

4. *Bump* v. *Union High School District No. 3,* 24 P.2d 330 (Or. 1933), at 331.

5. *Rible* v. *Hughes,* 150 P.2d 455 (Cal. 1944), at 458.

6. *Davis* v. *Board of Education of Aurora Public School Dist. No. 131,* 312 N.E.2d 335 (Ill. App. 1979).

7. John D. Calamari and Joseph M. Perillo, THE LAW OF CONTRACTS (St. Paul, Minn.: West, 1970), p. 11.

8. *Russell* v. *Barnes Foundation,* 50 F.Supp. 174 (E.D. Pa. 1943) (establishing liability), 52 F.Supp. 827 (E.D. Pa. 1943) (awarding damages).

9. 50 F.Supp., at 175–76.

10. *Kenaston* v. *School Administrative District No. 40,* 317 A.2d 7 (Me. 1974), at 9.

11. *George* v. *School District No. 8R of Umatilla County,* 490 P.2d 1009 (Or. App. 1971), at 1011.

12. *Mission Independent School District* v. *Diserens,* 188 S.W.2d 568 (Tex. 1945).

13. *Special School District of Fort Smith* v. *Lynch,* 413 S.W.2d 880 (Ark. 1967).

14. 52 F.Supp., at 829.

15. *Wyatt* v. *School District No. 104, Fergus County,* 417 P.2d 221 (Mont. 1966).

16. *Sams* v. *Board of Com'rs. of Creek County,* 178, P. 668 (Okla. 1919); *McBeth* v. *Board of Ed. of DeValls Bluff School District No. 1, Ark.,* 300 F.Supp. 1270 (E.D. Ark. 1969).

17. *People* v. *Parker,* 240 N.E.2d 475 (Ill. App. 1968); *Moore* v. *Knowles,* 333 F.Supp. 53 (N.D. Tex. 1971); *Ward* v. *Kelly,* 515 F.2d 908 (5th Cir. 1975).

18. *Bowbells Public School District No. 14* v. *Walker,* 231 N.W.2d 173 (N.D. 1975).

19. *Id.* at 176.

20. *Williams* v. *Albemarle City Board of Education,* 508 F.2d 1242 (4th Cir. 1974).

21. *Kenaston, supra,* at 11.

22. *Ayers* v. *Western Line Consolidated School District,* 404 F.Supp. 1225 (N.D. Miss. 1975).

23. *Farrell* v. *School District,* 56 N.W. 1053 (Mich. 1893).

24. *AAUP* v. *Bloomfield College,* 322 A.2d 846 (N.J. Super. 1974), *aff'd* 346 A.2d 615 (1975), at 618.

25. *Ajluni* v. *Board of Ed. of the West Bloomfield School District,* 229 N.W.2d 385 (Mich. App. 1975).

26. *Johnson* v. *Branch*, 364 F.2d 177 (4th Cir. 1966).

27. *Mission Independent School District, supra.*

28. *Lemasters* v. *Willman*, 281 S.W.2d 580 (Mo. App. 1955).

29. *Oneal* v. *Colton Consolidated School District No. 306*, 557 P.2d 11 (Wash. App. 1976).

30. *Brinson* v. *School Dist. No. 431*, 576 P.2d 602 (Kan. 1978).

2

Can I be fired?

OVERVIEW

State laws generally give school boards the right to employ teachers; with the power to hire comes the right to fire teachers who are not performing their jobs as required by their teaching contract. The power to fire teachers is limited in a number of ways, however. First, state laws may describe specific grounds for dismissal (see chapter 3), as well as certain procedures that must be followed. In addition, teachers' contracts may include provisions concerning dismissal procedures. Finally, the Due Process Clause of the U.S. Constitution prohibits school boards from exercising their power to fire in an arbitrary or discriminating manner.

State laws commonly list a number of specific reasons why teachers can be dismissed. In Illinois, for example, the board has the power to fire teachers for "incompetency, cruelty, negligence, immorality or other sufficient cause and . . . whenever, in its opinion, the interests of the schools require it. . . ."[1] The grounds for dismissal most frequently mentioned in state laws include insubordination, incompetency, immorality, and unprofessional conduct. In states that have laws listing the grounds for teacher dismissal, a teacher cannot be fired unless school officials can prove that the teacher's actions violated state law.

INSUBORDINATION

When can a teacher be fired for insubordination?

Can a teacher who breaks a school rule be fired for insubordination? Can a teacher who feels that a rule is unreasonable refuse to follow that rule without risking dismissal? What if a teacher is honestly trying to follow a principal's order but makes a mistake? Can the teacher be fired for insubordination? The case that follows provides a typical example of how the courts have answered these questions.

The *Ray* Case[2]

In September 1970, Glenn Ray began his sixth year teaching Russian and social studies at Edison High School in Minneapolis. During that year, the North Central Association of Colleges and Secondary Schools conducted an evaluation of the foreign language and social studies departments in Minneapolis and St. Paul high schools. As part of this study, all teachers in both departments were required to fill out an eight-page form.

Mr. Ray received this form in the fall but did not complete it. In January, after he was again requested to fill out this form, Ray responded to only some of the questions. In addition, he attacked the person in charge of the evaluation for requiring this procedure. A month later, Ray told the North Central evaluation team that he would leave the room if they attended his class. As a result, the team did not visit his class. When the principal again asked Ray to complete the social studies form, he again did not fill it out completely, adding that he did not want his supervisor to harass him any further. Finally, after the assistant superintendent warned Ray that his refusal to fill out the form would be legal grounds for dismissal, the school board fired Ray for insubordination.

In reviewing the case, the Supreme Court of Minnesota concluded that Ray was indeed guilty of insubordination. The court first defined insubordination as "constant or continuing intentional refusal to obey a direct or implied order, reasonable in nature, and given by and with proper authority." The court noted that school officials both had the authority and had acted properly in ordering Ray to comply with the evaluation study, which was part of the educational program of the Minneapolis schools. The court then examined Ray's actions, and concluded that they constituted insubordination: "There is no question but that appellant [Mr. Ray] had ample opportunity to fill out the evaluation forms and that his responses were purposely and intentionally incomplete, uncooperative, unresponsive, and argumentative. The decision of the school board . . . that such conduct was insubordination is a proper determination. . . ."

Can teachers who mistakenly fail to follow a school rule be dismissed for insubordination?

No. Teachers cannot be dismissed for insubordination unless they willfully and deliberately defy school authorities or violate school rules. A West Virginia court ruled that a teacher could not be dismissed for insubordination simply because he left school without permission in order to register for a university class.[3] In finding for the teacher, the court noted that the teacher had tried unsuccessfully to contact the assistant principal and also emphasized that the students did not suffer from his absence. The court concluded that, while the teacher was guilty of "an error of judgment," his actions did not constitute insubordination.

Can a teacher refuse to obey an unreasonable rule or an order from a school supervisor without being insubordinate?

Yes. Teachers can be dismissed for insubordination only when they violate a reasonable rule or order. For the order to be reasonable, school officials must have the legal authority to issue it. In Wisconsin, a court ruled that a teacher could not be dismissed for insubordination because he refused to resign in person at a school board meeting.[4] The court explained that the school board had no legal power to force the teacher to submit his resignation at the meeting and concluded that the board's order was merely an unreasonable effort to save face.

In addition, teachers cannot be dismissed for failing to follow school rules that violate their constitutional rights. For example, school rules prohibiting teachers from using certain materials in the classroom may interfere with a teacher's right to academic freedom. School rules limiting what teachers can say or write may also violate their First Amendment rights to free speech. (Academic freedom and First Amendment rights are discussed in detail in chapter 8.)

How can school officials prove that a teacher has been insubordinate?

First, school officials have to show that the teacher has violated a valid school rule. This rule must not only be reasonable but must be clear enough for the teacher to understand. A Kentucky court ruled that a teacher could not be dismissed for insubordination on the ground that he refused to "cooperate" with the principal.[5] The court stated that the school board had not charged the teacher with violating any specific rule nor had the board claimed that the teacher had refused to obey school authorities. Concluding that a charge of noncooperation could be asserted against almost anyone, the court declared that the school board had not proved insubordination.

Second, school officials must show that the teacher was acting deliberately and/or defiantly. In many cases, a teacher's actions speak for themselves. For example, a Utah court found a teacher to be insubordinate when he flatly refused to accept a transfer to another school, even though his contract required that he do so.[6] In less obvious cases, courts look at a teacher's pattern of behavior in order to decide whether the teacher is acting willfully. In Connecticut, a teacher's contract was terminated on the basis of insubordination when he was late to class and failed to cooperate with the administration.[7] In upholding the teacher's dismissal, the court cited a number of actions that supported its conclusion that the teacher was defiant and contemptuous of authority, among them that the teacher did not prepare the required outlines for the high school evaluation and failed to supervise his classes as the principal required. In addition, the court noted that when the principal confronted the teacher in the school office at a time when he was supposed to be in class, the teacher told the principal "to write him another letter" and that he wouldn't return to class until he checked his mailbox and had a cup of coffee. The court concluded that this pattern of behavior threatened working relationships that were vital to maintaining school operations and thus constituted insubordination.

INCOMPETENCY

When can a teacher be fired for incompetency?

All teachers have bad days, but how many bad days does it take to be fired for incompetency? How can a school board prove that a teacher is incompetent? Is failure to maintain classroom discipline a sign of incompetence? Is failure to get along with other teachers evidence of incompetence? The case that follows presents a typical example of how the courts have answered these questions.

The *Blunt* Case[8]

Hattie Blunt was a second-grade teacher at the Fessenden School in Marion County, Florida. Mrs. Blunt had been teaching in the Marion County school system for twenty-five years and was employed under a continuing contract that provided that she could be dismissed only for "good and sufficient reasons." During the 1968–69 school year, school officials became concerned about Mrs. Blunt's performance in the classroom. In November, Mrs. Keeney, the early childhood coordinator for the Marion County school system, observed Mrs. Blunt's teaching and submitted a critical written evaluation, which was reviewed by both the principal and assistant principal. On November 12, 1968, Mr. Broxton, the principal, sent Mrs. Blunt a letter detailing the problems Mrs. Keeney had identified and offering assistance in helping Mrs. Blunt improve her teaching techniques. After further negative evaluations on November 20 and December 5, Mr. Broxton notified Mrs. Blunt that she would be dismissed if her teaching did not improve.

When Mrs. Blunt continued to be hostile toward any offers of assistance,

Mr. Broxton recommended that she be fired. On May 2, 1969, school officials sent Mrs. Blunt the following specific list of her teaching deficiencies:

1. Academics
   a. Unable to teach students of varying abilities.
   b. Poor planning, both daily and long range.
   c. Improper grammar, both written and spoken.
   d. Numerous spelling errors, which students copy.
   e. Communication with students is poor.
   f. Inadequate use of audiovisual aids.
   g. Handwriting style is inadequate.
   h. Mathematics, English, and reading teaching styles are inadequate.
   i. Refuses aid and assistance from principal, assistant principal, other teachers, and supervisors.
2. School Regulations
   a. Records are not kept properly, including planning books and student records.
   b. Student records are not accurate.
   c. Refuses to sign evaluation sheets.
   d. Allows teacher's aide to conduct actual classroom teaching.
   e. School reports are submitted late.[9]

On May 7, a hearing was held before the school board to decide whether Mrs. Blunt should be dismissed. The principal, assistant principal, and early childhood coordinator testified about their observations of Mrs. Blunt. Taken together, their testimony included the following criticisms:

> ... that Mrs. Blunt exhibited poor teaching techniques, that her speech was difficult to understand, that she made grammatical errors, that she exhibited instructional deficiencies in the teaching of math, phonics, and spelling, and that she failed to keep up to date in handling administrative matters such as grading papers and maintaining a plan book.

These witnesses concluded:

> As a probable result of Mrs. Blunt's instructional deficiencies, many of her students were placed in lower ability groups when they were advanced to the third grade and even to the fourth grade. Her students were unable to keep up with those students who had other second grade teachers at Fessenden, when they were promoted to higher grades.[10]

The school board voted to dismiss her, and Mrs. Blunt brought suit, claiming that the evidence presented against her indicated only minor teaching deficiencies and did not constitute incompetence. The court disagreed. After examining the evidence, the court concluded that "the testimony of Mrs. Blunt's supervisors at the school board hearing was not only substantial, it was devastating." The court explained that the only question facing the school board was who to believe: the administrators or Mrs. Blunt. Since ample evidence supported the charges made by the administrators, the court upheld the board's decision to dismiss.

What constitutes an incompetent teacher?

An incompetent teacher is one who cannot perform the duties required by the teaching contract. As the *Blunt* case demonstrates, however, a teacher who merely has an "off day" in the classroom cannot be dismissed for incompetency. In order to be fired, school officials generally have to present a number of examples of a teacher's inability to meet contractual responsibilities.

The clearest example of an incompetent teacher is one who lacks knowledge about the subject he or she is supposed to teach. For example, a Louisiana third-grade teacher was dismissed for incompetency when her supervisor "noted many mistakes in her grammar and in her punctuation."[11] A Pennsylvania second-grade teacher was dismissed for incompetency after her supervisors observed that "she showed very little evidence of technical knowledge and skill . . . that she made errors in the geography lesson; that her spoken English was poor . . . and that [she] mispronounced words."[12]

Teachers may also be physically unable to teach. One principal was found to be incompetent as both a principal and a teacher when his hearing became so poor that he could not hear ordinary conversation.[13] The court noted that his defective hearing made it impossible for him to make corrections in students' recitations and prevented him from hearing the vile and obscene language being used in the classroom.

Courts have also upheld the dismissal of teachers who are mentally disabled. In a New York case, a junior high school industrial arts teacher was found to be unfit to perform his duties after psychiatrists testified that he was "unable to render consistent and effective service as a teacher."[14] In California, a court similarly upheld the dismissal of a primary school teacher hospitalized twice for mental illness.[15] The court found the psychiatric testimony that she was unable to engage in teaching because of a schizophrenic-paranoid mental illness justified her dismissal, regardless of the fact that school authorities did not prove that her illness interfered with her work as a teacher.

Can a teacher who has problems maintaining classroom discipline be fired for incompetency?

Yes. As noted in *Blunt*, teachers are rarely found to be incompetent for one reason alone. Rather, as with Mrs. Blunt, the incompetent teacher usually has a number of deficiencies in teaching performance. Nevertheless, while a teacher can be found to be incompetent for many reasons, failure to maintain classroom discipline is one of the most commonly cited problems. Reasoning that even the best-prepared teacher cannot be effective in a chaotic classroom, the courts have emphasized that the inability to maintain discipline is a characteristic of an incompetent teacher. In Indiana, for example, the court found that a teacher had such serious discipline problems that students could not pursue their school work.[16] One witness testified that "the disturbance in the room was general; the pupils doing whatever they pleased. . . . I went in once or twice and their conduct was something furious." The court went on to note that the teacher had admitted his inability to maintain order in the classroom on one occasion when he had to threaten to call the police in order to regain control. Concluding that this evidence showed the teacher "wanting in practical efficiency and discipline," the court upheld his dismissal on the ground of incompetency.

Can a teacher who has poor relations with other staff members be fired for incompetency?

Yes. Teachers have been dismissed for incompetency because they did not cooperate with administrators. For example, a Pennsylvania teacher was dismissed after he distributed a questionnaire during school hours that asked students whether they favored his retention as a teacher.[17] The court stated that incompetency was not limited to a teacher's academic ability but included the ability to meet the demands of a position. The court concluded that his decision to distribute such a questionnaire without asking the principal's permission disregarded the proper relationship between a teacher and his administrative superior and constituted incompetency. In a more recent case, however, an Illinois court stated that a teacher could not be dismissed for incompetency merely because she did not get along with other teachers.[18] In addition, the Supreme Court has ruled that teachers have a constitutional right to criticize the actions of administrators (see chapter 8).

IMMORAL CONDUCT

When can a teacher be fired for immoral conduct?

In recent decades, teachers have been dismissed for any conduct that violated the moral standards of their community. Teachers were expected to teach morality through their actions as well as in their classrooms. When teachers violated community norms, they usually resigned quietly or were fired quickly. In the past, teachers have been fired for obesity, cheating, and making false statements; for talking about sex, using "obscene" language, and expressing disbelief in God; for public drinking, smoking marijuana, and working in a bar; for heterosexual conduct, homosexual conduct, and rumors of an affair. Thus what was considered immoral conduct has varied from place to place, and the definition has changed over time.

Today, teachers may still be fired for immoral conduct, but in many states such conduct must be linked to teacher effectiveness. Moreover, courts rule differently if the immoral conduct is discreet or public, and if it involves another adult or a student. (Chapter 13 examines this topic in detail. It illustrates the range of conduct communities continue to consider immoral for teachers. It also examines the criteria courts use to determine whether such dismissals are legal or illegal.)

When can a teacher be fired for "conduct unbecoming a teacher"?

Conduct unbecoming a teacher, or "unprofessional conduct," as some states define it, is a broad reason for dismissal and can include a wide variety of actions by teachers. In general, unprofessional conduct refers to any actions that violate the rules or ethical code of the teaching profession. Despite the apparent vagueness of this term, courts have ruled that it is a valid ground for dismissing teachers.

The following statement by a California court is typical of the reasoning used to support the large amount of discretion in teacher dismissal that this language gives to school boards: ". . . the teacher is intrusted with the custody of children and their high preparation for useful life. His habits, his speech, his good name, his cleanliness, the wisdom and propriety of his unofficial utterances, his associations, all are involved. . . . How can all of these things be provided for and offenses against them be particularly specified in a single statute?"[19]

Teachers who have attempted to use the classroom for purposes other than teaching have been found guilty of unprofessional conduct. In one such case, a Sacramento high school teacher used his classroom as a forum to advocate that his students' friends and relatives support a certain candidate who was running for superintendent of schools.[20] (Chapter 10 contains a detailed discussion of teachers and partisan politics.) The court ruled that the teacher could be dismissed for unprofessional conduct, reasoning that his behavior was beyond the scope of the purposes for which teachers were employed: "Such conduct certainly is in contravention not only of the spirit of the laws governing the public school system, but of that essential policy according to which the public school system should be maintained in order that it may subserve in the highest degree its purposes."[21]

Teachers who deliberately violate school rules and regulations can also be dismissed for unprofessional conduct. For example, a teacher who left her position without first obtaining an official leave of absence was dismissed for unprofessional conduct. In the words of the court: "She left her position after her attention had been called to the rules and regulations of the board which prohibited leaves of absence until the superintendent of schools had ascertained that a competent substitute . . . was available. . . . Disregarding this warning, plaintiff [teacher] left her position, and by so doing immediately became guilty of unprofessional conduct. . . ."[22]

Are there any other reasons why teachers can be dismissed?

Yes. Many state laws provide that teachers can be dismissed for "good and just cause." This catchall phrase gives school boards wide discretion, effectively allowing them to dismiss teachers for reasons not specifically listed under state law. Indeed, as a Massachusetts court explained, "good cause includes any ground which is put forward by the [school] committee in good faith and which is not arbitrary, irrational, unreasonable, or irrelevant to the committee's task of building up and maintaining an efficient school system."[23] Using this reasoning, an Indiana court upheld the dismissal of a teacher/principal who had been dismissed for good and just cause when he failed to cooperate with school officials.[24] The teacher/principal had opposed a plan under which seventh- and eighth-grade students were to be taught by the high school faculty; after the plan had been in operation for a year, he had discontinued it without consulting the superintendent or county officials. In addition, he refused to fill out necessary administrative papers and catalogue the school library as required by orders from the state's Department of Public Instruction. In upholding his dismissal, the court concluded that his actions had a negative effect on his fitness as a teacher/administrator and thus constituted good and just cause for dismissal: "A court cannot say as a matter of law that ability and willingness to co-operate are not reasonably related to the fitness or capacity of a teacher for the performance of his duties."

The courts have imposed limits on school officials' power to dismiss teachers for "good and just cause." Recently, courts have emphasized that the teacher's action must bear a reasonable relationship to fitness or capacity to discharge the duties of the teaching position. Thus a Michigan court ruled that a tenured elementary school teacher could not be dismissed merely because the school board disagreed with her teaching philosophy.[25] The court noted that the focus of evidence supporting dismissal "must be the effect of the questioned activity on the teacher's students." Here the evidence showed that some educators approved of Mrs. Beebee's teaching techniques and some did not; what was not shown was that her students suffered either mentally or physically in relation to other students. The court concluded that the board had not met its burden of proving "good and just cause," concluding with the following remarks: "Should we require tenured teachers to teach alike and to be liked by everyone? We think not. . . . It would be similarly unreasonable to require all teachers to teach alike or lose their tenure."

Similarly, an Ohio court ruled that a teacher fined for hitting another car and leaving the scene of the accident could not be dismissed for good and just cause.[26] In interpreting this phrase, the court concluded that it must refer to actions as serious as the other grounds for teacher dismissal, including "gross inefficiency or immorality." The court concluded that the teacher's action in leaving the scene of an accident might adversely reflect upon his character and integrity, but that this was not serious enough to constitute grounds for dismissal. When only a single crime is involved, "the crime would either have to be a more serious one or involve a more serious fact situation than that here involved" to constitute grounds for teacher dismissal.

SUMMARY

School officials who have the power to employ teachers also have the power to fire them. Nevertheless, this power to dismiss teachers may be limited by constitutional and statutory provisions. Most state laws provide that teachers can be dismissed only for specific reasons. The most common reasons include incompetency, immorality, insubordination, and unprofessional conduct. (What constitutes immoral conduct is discussed in chapter 13.) When state laws include such a list, a school board can dismiss a teacher only for one of the grounds specified. In each case, the school board has the burden of proving that the teacher has violated the law.

When school boards can present evidence to show that a teacher is not fulfilling teaching responsibilities, however, the courts are likely to uphold their decision to dismiss. Courts recognize that school boards have the legal authority to set educational policy and standards, and the courts are wary of substituting their judgment for that of school authorities. In general, if school officials can demonstrate that the teacher's actions will impair effectiveness in the classroom, the administration's ability to operate the school, or both, the courts will support their judgment that the teacher should be dismissed.

NOTES

1. ILL. ANN. STAT. chap. 122, §10–22.4 (Smith-Hurd. Supp. 1979).
2. *Ray* v. *Minneapolis Board of Education,* 202 N.W.2d 375 (Minn. 1972).
3. *Beverlin* v. *Board of Education,* 216 S.E.2d 554 (W.Va. 1975).
4. *Millar* v. *Joint School District No. 2,* 86 N.W.2d 455 (Wis. 1957).
5. *Osborne* v. *Bullitt County Board of Education,* 415 S.W.2d 607 (Ky. Ct. App. 1967).
6. *Brough* v. *Board of Education,* 460 P.2d 336 (Utah 1969).
7. *Simard* v. *Board of Education,* 473 F.2d 988 (2d Cir. 1973).
8. *Blunt* v. *Marion County School Board,* 515 F.2d 951 (5th Cir. 1975).
9. *Id.* at 954, n. 4.
10. *Id.* at 955–56.
11. *Singleton* v. *Iberville Parish School Board,* 136 So.2d 809 (La. App. 1962).
12. *Appeal of Mulhollen,* 39 A.2d 283 (Pa. Super. 1944).
13. *Alexander* v. *Manton Joint Union School District,* 255 P. 516 (Cal. App. 1927).
14. *Coriou* v. *Nyquist,* 304 N.Y.S.2d 486 (1969).
15. *Alford* v. *Department of Education,* 91 Cal. Reptr. 843 (1970).
16. *Biggs* v. *School City of Mt. Vernon,* 90 N.E. 105 (Ind. App. 1909).
17. *Fenstermacher's Appeal,* 36 Pa.D.&C. 373 (1939).
18. *Compton* v. *School Directors,* 131 N.E.2d 544 (Ill. App. 1955).
19. *Goldsmith* v. *Board of Education,* 225 P. 783 (Cal. App. 1924), at 787.
20. *Id.*
21. *Id.* at 789.
22. *Evard* v. *Board of Education of City of Bakersfield,* 149 P.2d 413 (Cal. App. 1944), at 416.
23. *Rinaldo* v. *Dreyer,* 1 N.E.2d 37 (Mass. 1936), at 38.
24. *Stiver* v. *State,* 1 N.E.2d 1006 (Ind. 1936).
25. *Beebee* v. *Haslett Public Schools,* 239 N.W.2d 724 (Mich. App. 1976).
26. *Hale* v. *Board of Education, City of Lancaster,* 234 N.E.2d 583 (Ohio 1968).

3

How secure is my tenure?

OVERVIEW

Teachers who are granted tenure have a right to continued employment and can be dismissed only for a cause set out by law. Tenured teachers do not have a right to a particular position in a school district nor the right to be employed indefinitely. Before tenured teachers can be dismissed, however, school boards have to show cause why they are not fit to teach.

Teacher tenure laws were passed to protect teachers from arbitrary actions by school officials. In the words of the Supreme Court of Pennsylvania: "Time and again our courts have stated that the purpose of the tenure provisions of the School Code is the maintenance of an adequate and competent teaching staff, free from political or arbitrary interference, whereby capable and competent teachers might feel secure, and more efficiently perform their duty of instruction."[1] In addition, tenure laws seek to provide a better educational system by ensuring the stability and security of good teachers and outlining orderly procedures for the dismissal of unsatisfactory teachers.

This chapter examines the state laws and constitutional provisions that protect a teacher's right to tenure. It explores such questions as How do teachers acquire tenure? What rights come with tenure? When may tenure be broken? and When can a tenured teacher be fired?

ACQUIRING TENURE

The *Sindermann* Case[2]

From 1959 to 1969, Robert Sindermann was a teacher in the Texas state college system. After teaching for two years at the University of Texas and for four years at San Antonio Junior College, in 1965 he became a professor of government and social science at Odessa Junior College. He was employed at the college for four successive years, under a series of one-year contracts.

During the 1968–69 academic year, Sindermann was elected president of the Texas Junior College Teachers Association and became involved in public disagreements with the college's Board of Regents. In May 1969, Sindermann's one-year employment contract came to an end, and college officials decided not to offer him a new contract for the next academic year. They did not provide him with any stated reasons for the nonrenewal of his contract, nor did they allow him a hearing at which to challenge the nonrenewal. Sindermann brought a suit against the college authorities, arguing that their failure to provide him an opportunity for a hearing violated the Fourteenth Amendment's guarantee of procedural due process.

In considering his claim that he was entitled to a hearing, the Supreme Court examined the teacher's argument that he had a right to continued employment. The teacher alleged that, while the college had no official tenure program, it actually operated a *de facto* tenure program. To support his claim, Sindermann stated that he had relied on the following provision, which had been in the college's official faculty guide for many years:

> *Teacher Tenure:* Odessa College has no tenure system. The Administration of the College wishes the faculty member to feel that he has permanent tenure as long as his teaching services are satisfactory and as long as he displays a cooperative attitude toward his co-workers and his superiors, and as long as he is happy in his work.[3]

In addition, Sindermann stated that he had relied on guidelines put out by officials of the state college system, which provided that a person employed as a teacher in the system for seven years or more had some form of job tenure.

The Court explained that a written contract with an explicit tenure provision would clearly be "evidence of a formal understanding that supports a teacher's claim of entitlement to continued employment unless sufficient 'cause' is shown." However, the Court went on to state that the absence of such a provision would not always foreclose the possibility that a teacher had a "property" interest in reemployment. Although the Court did not decide whether Mr. Sindermann was entitled to tenure, it did state that a teacher "who has held his position for a number of years, might be able to show from the circumstances of this service—and from other relevant facts—that he has a legitimate claim of entitlement to job tenure." The Court noted that proof of such a property interest in reemployment would not automatically entitle Mr. Sindermann to reinstatement as a teacher. Nevertheless, such proof would obligate college officials to grant a hearing at his request, at which he could be informed of the grounds for his nonretention and challenge their sufficiency.

Can teachers acquire tenure by custom?

As the Supreme Court explained in *Sindermann,* a teacher may acquire tenure "by custom." In such a situation, a teacher's right to tenure is not formalized in a written contract but is implied from the circumstances of employment. When a teacher can prove an expectancy of continued employment, the teacher has a property interest in job tenure that is protected by the Due Process Clause of the Fourteenth Amendment.

How can teachers acquire tenure by law?

In most situations, a teacher's right to tenure is established by state law. Most states have laws that outline the requirements for tenure, and these laws generally require teachers to undergo a period of probationary service before they can become tenured, or "permanent," teachers. In Virginia, for example, a teacher must teach for a probationary period of three years in the same county or city school system before attaining tenure status.[4] During the probationary period, the teacher is employed under a yearly contract and usually can be dismissed by school officials at the end of a contract period for any reason whatsoever. (See Chapter 12 for a discussion of teachers' due process rights to notice and a hearing prior to dismissal or failure to renew a contract.)

In order to acquire tenure status by law, the teacher must comply with the specific requirements of his or her state's law. In some states, tenure becomes permanent as soon as the teacher completes the required probationary period. In other states, the school board may have to take some positive action for the teacher to achieve tenure.

Whether the school board has to take some affirmative step to ensure that a teacher achieves tenure also depends on the nature of the teacher's employment contract. Some teachers are employed under yearly contracts. When this is the case, the board must act to renew the contract at the close of the school year before the teacher can be reemployed and thus achieve tenure status. Teachers may also be employed under continuing contracts, which are automatically renewed if the school board does not act by a certain date to inform particular teachers that their services will not be needed during the coming year.

Because each state has developed its own requirements, teachers must consult the statutes and court decisions in their own state to determine what specific procedures must be followed to achieve tenure status. Nevertheless, a number of general approaches are common. First, a statute may require that the school board take affirmative action to elect a teacher to tenure status. In Texas, for example, the law reads as follows:

> Any teacher employed by a school district who is performing his third, or where permitted fourth, consecutive year of service with the district under probationary contract, and who is elected to employment by the board of trustees of such district for the succeeding year, shall be notified in writing of his election to continuing contract status with such district. . . .[5]

The Texas tenure statute also provides that probationary teachers must be notified on or before April 1 whether their contracts will be renewed during the coming year.[6] Irene Carl, a teacher in her last year of probationary employment, was notified on March 15 that she would not be recommended for reemployment; however, the board decided to withhold a final decision pending evaluation of her teaching during the rest of the school year. The board finally notified Mrs. Carl on September 1 that her contract would not be renewed. She argued that the board's actions were too late and that she had achieved tenure status. In interpreting the statute, the Texas court concluded that the board had to act affirmatively to elect a teacher to tenure status, and since it had not done so, she was not accorded tenure.[7]

Similarly, a New Jersey teacher was denied tenure when the board failed to act affirmatively to offer him a new contract.[8] Citing the New Jersey law, which stated that a teacher could achieve tenure status after being employed for three years, Mr. Zimmerman claimed that his employment under three annual contracts entitled him to tenure. The New Jersey court disagreed, concluding: "Except for statutory conditions, a teacher is retained solely on a contract basis during his probationary employment. . . . While some states provide for automatic reemployment or renewal of contract unless contrary notice is given, our statute does not so specify." Accordingly, since the board did not execute a new contract with Zimmerman, he did not attain tenure status.

In interpreting other statutes, however, the courts have ruled that school officials do not have to take any affirmative steps to award tenure status. In California, for example, the court held that a teacher who completed the required three consecutive years of teaching and was rehired by the board automatically attained tenure status, and no affirmative action on the part of the school board was required.[9] Similarly, in interpreting New York law, a court ruled that teachers could acquire tenure in two ways: (1) by specific award of the board of education; or (2) by acquiescence, where a teacher continues to teach beyond the probationary period and the board fails to take any action.[10]

Can a teacher be awarded tenure if school officials fail to follow required legal procedures?

It depends on the state. In Kentucky, the law specifically states that a probationary teacher will achieve tenure status if the school board fails to give the teacher the proper notice concerning reemployment for the next year.[11] A federal district court interpreting a Michigan statute ruled that a teacher achieved tenure as a result of the board's failure to comply with the law.[12] The court found that the Michigan Teacher Tenure Act imposed a dual obligation on boards of education when they were deciding whether to grant tenure to probationary teachers: (1) the board must provide the teacher with notice concerning reemployment at least sixty days before the close of the school year, and (2) the board must provide a written statement as to whether the teacher's work was satisfactory. When a local school board neglected to provide a teacher with this written statement, the court ruled that the teacher achieved tenure.

Other courts have not been willing to interpret tenure laws as strictly. In Illinois, for example, a court ruled that a teacher did not achieve tenure merely because the school board did not follow the proper notice procedures in attempting to dismiss her.[13] The court did agree that, without the proper notice, she was entitled to be reemployed by the school district. However, she was not automatically entitled to tenure status. In reaching its decision, the court examined the purposes of the tenure laws, noting that the probationary period of teaching was established by the legislature in order to "impose a duty upon and to provide an opportunity for school boards to observe and evaluate the actual performance of a teacher's work for two years." The court concluded that it would be inconsistent with these purposes for it to confer tenure status on a teacher. Instead, the court ruled that the teacher should be reemployed, but only as a second-year probationary teacher. Faced with a similar situation, a Tennessee court reached the same result, ordering that a probationary teacher improperly dismissed be rehired, but only under an annual contract.[14] Again, the court looked to public policy considerations and concluded that the legislature did not intend that teachers should be entitled to tenure as a matter of right after completing their probationary service.

How else can a teacher acquire tenure?

In addition to a right to tenure under state law, a teacher may also have a right to tenure under an employment contract. The contract may specifically describe the teacher's rights to continued employment and set out specific procedures that must be followed before a teacher can be dismissed. For example, a professor at Montana State University achieved "permanent appointment" status under the terms of his employment contract.[15] In that case, university regulations provided that the initial appointment of a professor could be for a limited term but that "reappointment after three years of service shall be deemed a permanent appointment." After teaching for six years under a series of annual contracts, the professor claimed permanent appointment status. The court agreed, finding that the university regulations were made part of the professor's contract by language in the contract, which stated: "This appointment is subject to the regulations governing tenure printed on the reverse side of this sheet."

Can the state do away with tenure?

Yes. When state law creates a right to tenure, it can usually also take this right away. Many teachers' contracts specifically recognize this fact, including a provision stating that the teacher's tenure status is subject to change or termination according to any changes in the state law. Even if a teacher's contract does not include such a provision, most courts have ruled that state legislatures have the power to modify their teacher tenure laws, thus possibly depriving a teacher of tenure.

In Wisconsin, for example, the court upheld the legislature's power to repeal the Teachers' Tenure Act.[16] In examining the tenure law, the court concluded that the legislators had not intended to give teachers a contractual right to tenure, so the law could be changed at will: "... we discover no intent to create a statutory contract, and nothing to overcome the very strong presumption that this act simply declared a public policy in the important field of education—a policy to be pursued 'until the Legislature shall ordain otherwise.'"

In the rare situation where the state law does create a contractual right to tenure, however, the legislature cannot deprive a teacher of tenure status. In an early case, the Supreme Court held that Indiana's teacher tenure law created a contractual right to tenure and that a teacher who had attained tenure status under this law had a continuing contract that could not be broken by a new law passed by the legislature.[17] Thus the Court ruled that the teacher was entitled to maintain her tenure status even though the Indiana legislature had repealed its teacher tenure law.

RIGHTS OF TENURE

What rights does a tenured teacher have?

A teacher who achieves tenure status has the right to continued employment subject only to dismissal "for cause." The teacher does not have the right to be employed in a particular position, however. School boards retain the authority to transfer and reassign tenured teachers, provided that such teachers are assigned to positions of equal status and that school officials are acting to meet the current needs of the district and are not acting arbitrarily or unreasonably. A Louisiana court, for example, ruled that a tenured teacher who taught biology at one New Orleans high school could be reassigned to another high school to teach biology.[18] The school authorities had requested that the teacher be transferred because her grading practices were at odds with those of other teachers at the high school. The court ruled that the teacher could be transferred despite her tenure status.

The court noted that state law prohibited tenured teachers from being removed from office without formal charges and a hearing; nevertheless, the court explained that a teacher could not be considered "removed from office" unless

1. A reduction in salary is involved.
2. The new position requires the teaching of subjects for which the teacher is not qualified.
3. The teacher must undergo additional training, at his expense, in order to obtain permanent certification in his new post.
4. The transfer follows a dismissal without formal charges, or a hearing, and thus leaves a blot on the teacher's record.[19]

Since the teacher in this situation was assuming a similar teaching position and was being compensated at the same rate, her tenure rights were not being violated.

Courts have also ruled that tenured teachers can be reassigned as part of desegration plans. In cases of school districts under desegregation orders, the courts have stated that school boards could not use tenure laws as an excuse to resist transferring teachers to achieve an appropriate racial balance.[20] (See chapter 14 for a detailed discussion of school desegregation and teachers' rights.)

In addition, the courts have ruled that achieving tenure status does not ensure that a teacher's salary can never be reduced. School boards have the authority to fix teachers' salaries, and they retain the power to reduce them. Any reductions in salary must be applied uniformly to all teachers, however, and salary schedules cannot be changed in the middle of a school year.[21]

TENURE AND DISMISSAL

When can tenure be broken?

School officials can only dismiss a tenured teacher for "cause." Teacher tenure laws generally list specific offenses that constitute legal cause for dismissal, and school officials can dismiss a teacher only for one of these stated reasons. In Illinois, the law provides that the school board has the power "to dismiss a teacher for incompetency, cruelty, negligence, immorality or other sufficient cause and to dismiss any teacher, whenever, in its opinion, he is not qualified to teach, or whenever, in its opinion, the interests of the schools require it...."[22] In general, courts have held that tenured teachers can be dismissed only for a cause "which specifically relates to and affects the administration of the office ... something of a substantial nature directly affecting the rights and interests of the public ... one touching ... his performance of his duties, showing he is not a fit or proper person to hold the office."[23] (See chapter 2 for a detailed discussion of what constitutes legal cause for dismissal.)

In addition to being dismissed for "cause," teachers can lose the right to tenure by their own actions. For example, a teacher may lose a tenured position by resignation. A tenured teacher in Kentucky lost his right to continued employment when he voluntarily left his teaching position to work full-time for the American Federation of Teachers.[24] Before leaving, the teacher had requested an indefinite leave of absence, but the school board had denied his request. The court ruled that "the school board was under no obligation to take [the teacher] back after he voluntarily absented himself from his position." A teacher can also lose tenure status by accepting a teaching position in another school district. In California, for example, a teacher taught for two years in the Long Beach city school district and then taught for two years as a teacher in the Long Beach high school district.[25] The teacher's four years of continuous teaching would have given her tenure status if she had been teaching in the same school district. Because the city and high school districts operated separately, however, the teacher had no right to tenure in either district.

What procedures have to be followed before a tenured teacher can be dismissed?

Most states provide for a specific procedure before tenured teachers can be dismissed. (See Appendix E for an example of a typical state statute.) Typically these statutes require that teachers be given specific notice of the charges against them and an opportunity for a hearing where they can respond to those charges. In Wisconsin, for example, the law provides that a teacher is entitled to a written statement of the charges, the right to a public hearing before the school board within 30 days of receiving this notice, and the right to be represented by counsel.[26]

When the state law describes a specific procedure, it must be followed exactly. In a Pennsylvania case, a court ordered a teacher reinstated when school officials did not follow dismissal procedures required by the state's Teachers' Tenure Act.[27] The Pennsylvania law stated that a teacher could not be dismissed until the secretary of the school district had furnished "a detailed written statement of the charges upon which his or her dismissal . . . is based, together with a written notice . . . of a time and place when and where such professional employe will be given an opportunity to be heard either in person or by counsel, or both, before the Board of School Directors. . . ."[28] As it happened, the school board had merely notified the teacher that she had been dismissed and had given her an opportunity to meet with the board to "show cause why [she] should continue to hold [her] teaching position under the Act." Since the board did not give proper written notice of charges prior to dismissal, the court ordered that the teacher be reinstated in her previous teaching position.

What notice must be provided to a tenured teacher prior to dismissal?

The courts have stated that tenured teachers must be given clear statements of the charges against them so that they can answer those charges. Thus, a Kentucky court found that a teacher had not been given adequate notice when he was merely informed that he was guilty of the following act: "insubordination based upon fact that you refuse to co-operate with the principal of your school."[29] The court found that this statement was insufficient because it did not inform the teacher of facts on which he could reasonably formulate a defense: "It gives no date of his actions, nor does it indicate in any way the specific nature of his acts." Similarly, an Alabama court ruled that a teacher could not be dismissed because the board had notified her only that her services "had been unsatisfactory and incompetent" over the past year.[30] The court concluded that " 'incompetency' is a relative term which may be employed as meaning disqualification, inability or incapacity." Since the board did not give the teacher any specific information about her "incompetency," she could not be dismissed. A Kentucky court ruled that a teacher *was* provided with sufficient notice when the school board informed her that she would not be reemployed for the following reasons:

1. Poor relationship with other teachers
2. Lack of cooperation with the principal and the guidance staff
3. Poor attitude and disruptive influence
4. Not in harmony with the educational philosophy of the school
5. Not in the best interest of the school to award a continuing contract[31]

What kind of hearing must be provided before a tenured teacher can be dismissed?

When state laws require a hearing before a tenured teacher can be dismissed, they generally describe that hearing. In Illinois, for example, an impartial hearing officer (selected from a list provided by the state board of education) presides at a hearing that will be public at the request of either the teacher or the school board.[32] Both teacher and board can subpoena witnesses. The teacher also has the right to be present with counsel at the hearing, can call and cross-examine witnesses, and can present a defense to the charges. All testimony is given under oath, and the state board of eduction must pay a reporter to make a written record of the hearing.

Do teachers without tenure have a right to notice and hearing prior to dismissal?

State laws vary in the extent to which they give nontenured teachers any procedural rights prior to dismissal. (See Appendix E for an example of such a law.) In Illinois, state law requires that a probationary teacher be given notice of the reasons for dismissal.[33] In Connecticut, a nontenured teacher must make a special written request in order to receive a statement of the reasons for which the board decided not to renew the contract.[34] State laws typically do not give nontenured teachers the right to a hearing prior to dismissal.

Whether or not a nontenured teacher is guaranteed certain procedural rights under state law, however, the U.S. Supreme Court has ruled that nontenured teachers are entitled to notice and a hearing if their termination deprives them of "property" or "liberty" interests under the Due Process Clause of the Fourteenth Amendment to the Constitution. In *Board of Regents* v. *Roth*[35] and *Perry* v. *Sindermann*,[36] the Court defined these terms: "To have a property interest in a benefit, a person clearly must have more than an abstract need or desire for it. He must have more than a unilateral expectation of it. He must, instead, have a legitimate claim of entitlement to it." The Court went on to explain that property interests are not created by the Constitution. "Rather, they are created and their dimensions are defined by existing rules or understandings that stem from an independent source such as state law—rules or understandings that secure certain benefits and that support claims of entitlement to those benefits." In *Roth*, the teacher involved had been hired under a one-year contract, and the Court concluded that he had absolutely no such interest in reemployment as to establish a property right that would entitle him to procedural rights under the Fourteenth Amendment.

The most obvious example of deprivation of a property interest occurs when a school board dismisses a teacher with whom it has a contract in the middle of the term of employment. The courts have stated, however, that other factors may create a "property interest." In *Sindermann*, for example, the Court stated that if the customary practices of the institution created a *de facto* tenure system, a teacher would have a property interest in reemployment and would be entitled to due process protection prior to dismissal. In another case,[37] a federal court found that a teacher who had taught in the schools of Russell County, Virginia, for twenty-nine years had a property interest in continued employment. Although Virginia law had procedures for attaining tenure and procedures for dismissing tenured teachers, this law was passed long after this teacher assumed her position, and she was therefore not covered by it. The court found that her years of continuous service raised such an expectancy of continued employment as to constitute a property interest under the Fourteenth Amendment and that the teacher was entitled to notice and a hearing prior to the nonrenewal of her teaching contract.

In *Roth*, the Supreme Court also held that teachers were entitled to due process protection if their dismissal deprived them of a "liberty" interest under the Fourteenth Amendment. In interpreting this term, the Court included "not merely freedom from bodily restraint but also the right of the individual to contract, to engage in any of the common occupations of life." In addition to actions that would foreclose a teacher's opportunities for employment, the Court stated that a liberty interest would be involved whenever the school board, in declining to rehire a teacher, made a charge that might seriously damage the teacher's standing and associations in the community (e.g., charges such as dishonesty or immorality). In the Court's words: "Where a person's good name, reputation, honor, or integrity is at stake because of what the government is doing to him, notice and an opportunity to be heard are essential."

In the *Roth* case itself, the Court did not find any violation of a liberty interest. The state university had merely refused to renew Roth's one-year teaching contract; university officials did nothing that would have "stigmatized" Mr. Roth so as to reduce his chances of obtaining future employment. In general, the courts have found that a liberty interest is not affected when a teacher who is not rehired is free to seek another job. For example, a court held that a nontenured teacher who was not rehired because of her failure to coordinate her teaching with that of other teachers was not entitled to a hearing, even though her nonretention "unquestionably made plaintiff [the teacher] less attractive to other employers."[38] Similarly, a court ruled that no liberty interest was involved when a principal described a teacher as "anti-establishment" in a rating report.[39] In general, the courts have not required hearings when the charges against teachers have related to their inability to perform. Charges that have been held to involve a liberty interest and entitle a teacher to a hearing prior to dismissal include an allegation of manifest racism,[40] mental illness,[41] fraud,[42] and moral unfitness.[43]

In *Roth* and *Sindermann*, the Supreme Court did not describe the notice and hearing that must be given when a teacher is deprived of a property or liberty interest under the Fourteenth Amendment. The Court did note in *Sindermann* that the teacher must be given the opportunity to request a hearing "where he could be informed of the grounds for his nonretention and challenge their sufficiency." In applying these principles in particular cases, various courts have set out more specific requirements. For example, the Fifth Circuit Court of Appeals has held that due process requires that nontenured teachers be given the names of witnesses against them.[44] The Seventh Circuit Court has stated that the president of a junior college was constitutionally entitled to present witnesses at a dismissal hearing.[45] Another federal court has concluded that the right to counsel is a necessary component of due process under the Fourteenth Amendment.[46]

Can a teacher be dismissed for economic reasons (riffing)?

Student enrollments are declining in many school districts, and teachers may face dismissal on the grounds that a reduction in teaching staff is necessary for financial reasons, a procedure commonly known as "riffing." Such teachers are not dismissed for any behavior that affects their ability to teach. Rather, in a general "reduction in force," both tenured and nontenured teachers may be dismissed in order to accommodate changing staff requirements.

Some state laws specifically provide that tenured teachers can be dismissed for economic reasons. Alabama law states: "Cancellation of an employment contract with a teacher on continuing service status may be made for incompetency, insubordination, neglect of duty, immorality, justifiable decrease in the number of teaching positions or other good and just cause. . . ."[47] Other state laws provide more detailed guidelines about when teachers can be dismissed for economic reasons. For example, an Oregon law states that a tenured teacher can be dismissed in the following situations:

> Reduction in permanent teacher staff resulting from the district's inability to levy a tax sufficient to provide funds to continue its educational program at its anticipated level or resulting from the district's elimination of classes due to decreased student enrollment or reduction of course due to administrative decision. School districts shall make every effort to transfer teachers of courses scheduled for discontinuation to other positions for which they are qualified. Merit and seniority shall be considered in determination of a teacher for such transfer.[48]

Even if the state law is silent on this matter, the courts have ruled that school boards have the authority to dismiss tenured teachers for economic reasons. School boards may include such provisions in teachers' contracts. An Iowa teacher was employed in a small, rural elementary school under a nine-month contract that provided "that in case the enrollment of said school becomes less than six, this contract becomes null and void."[49] After she had been teaching only a month, the student enrollment fell below six, and the board of directors closed the school. The teacher sued, claiming that she could be dismissed only for specific reasons stated in Iowa law. The court, however, ruled that a provision in the state law that permitted teachers' contracts to be "terminated by mutual agreement" gave school officials the authority to dismiss the teacher when enrollment dropped to only four students.

Even when there is no relevant state law or contractual provision, the courts have held that school officials have the authority to dismiss teachers for economic reasons. A Pennsylvania kindergarten teacher was dismissed when the school board recommended that the entire kindergarten department be abolished "as a matter of good school business administration and instructional efficiency."[50] The teacher argued that her tenure status prevented the board from dismissing her. The court disagreed, reasoning that the Teacher Tenure Act was not designed to inhibit school officials from acting to operate the schools in the most economical manner: "When an entire department is lawfully abolished for valid reasons, which may include financial ones, in the interest of a more efficient system, the teachers in that department can be dismissed. Economy is desirable in any governmental function, and we cannot so view the present legislation as to prevent the abolition of a department for this purpose."

What situations commonly qualify as economic reasons for teacher dismissal?

The most common situation in which the courts have upheld the school board's right to dismiss tenured teachers for economic reasons is *decline in student enrollment*. For example, Pennsylvania state law gave school authorities the power to suspend teachers whenever there was a substantial decrease in pupil enrollment in a district.[51] Examining past, present, and projected student enrollments in one district, the school board voted to dismiss four teachers. The teachers argued that they could not be dismissed because the

board's statistics actually showed a slight increase in secondary school enrollment in two years of a six-year period. Nevertheless, the court noted that
the overall trend in the statistics indicated a decrease in student enrollment
and upheld the dismissals. The court emphasized that enrollment was an
area in which school boards must exercise discretion and concluded that
courts should not intervene unless school officials were clearly acting arbitrarily.

Courts have also ruled that teachers can be dismissed when school officials decide on *curriculum reorganization* for economic reasons. In Pennsylvania, for example, a tenured teacher was dismissed after the high school curriculum was reorganized.[52] Although there had been no overall decrease in
student enrollment, the number of students taking this teacher's academic
courses had decreased after the school had instituted a commercial course of
studies. The court ruled that school authorities had the power to dismiss the
teacher, emphasizing that the Teacher Tenure Act was not intended to prohibit school officials from making administrative decisions necessary to operate the schools: "It is the administrative function of the school directors and
superintendents to meet changing educational conditions through the creation of new courses, reassignment of teachers, and rearrangement of curriculum." To deny the board this power "would transfer much of the discretion
accorded to these administrative boards to the teachers, that they might preserve their positions in perpetuity."

The courts have also stated that school officials can dismiss teachers as the
result of a decision to abolish a particular position. In a New Jersey case,[53] the
board of education decided to abolish the position of a full-time physical
education instructor and create a new position that would require teaching
both physical education and English. Because the current physical education
teacher was not qualified to teach English, she was dismissed. Despite the
fact that she had tenure, the court ruled that the board could dismiss her because its decision was based on "public economy" and because "the action of
the local board was in good faith and not the result of prejudice or discrimination."

Are there any limitations on a school board's power to dismiss a tenured teacher for economic reasons?

Yes. A school board has considerable discretion in deciding whether to dismiss a teacher for economic reasons, but there are limits on its power. State
laws may define which teachers can be dismissed. For example, many state
laws provide that probationary teachers must be dismissed before tenured
teachers. California state law provides not only that tenured teachers have
priority but that teachers with more seniority must be given preference.[54] In
addition, the law requires school officials to provide teachers who request it
with a list of the criteria used in deciding which teachers to dismiss. (See Appendix E for the actual langue of this statute.) Individual or collective bargaining contracts also may specify criteria for selecting teachers who will be
dismissed in reduction-in-force situations.

In the absence of contractual or statutory guidelines, the courts have generally required that school boards give preference to tenured over nontenured teachers. For example, an Indiana court ruled that school authorities could not dismiss a tenured elementary school teacher while they retained a nontenured teacher on staff.[55] The court concluded that to allow such a practice would make the tenure law completely ineffective:

> The principal purpose of the Act was to secure permanency in the teaching force. If a justifiable decrease in the number of teaching positions should be held to give the trustee the power to choose between tenure and nontenure teachers, both of whom are licensed to teach in the teaching position which remains, he is thereby given the power to nullify the Teachers' Tenure Act, and to discharge without cause a teacher who has, by reason of having served satisfactorily as a teacher during the specified period, secured a tenure status and an indefinite permanent contract. To countenance such an interpretation of the law would be to permit the trustee to do indirectly that which the law expressly forbids him to do directly.[56]

Beyond these restrictions, the courts generally have stated that, in the absence of contractual or statutory guidelines, school boards can use whatever reasonable standards they wish in deciding which teachers to dismiss in reduction-in-force situations.[57] For example, courts have ruled that school boards do not have to make their selections on the basis of seniority.[58] As long as the school board is not acting arbitrarily or discriminating against particular individuals, the courts are likely to uphold their decision in identifying teachers who are to be dismissed.

SUMMARY

Most states have passed tenure laws that give teachers the right to continued employment, subject only to dismissal for "cause." These laws describe the procedures teachers must follow to achieve tenure, generally satisfactory completion of a stated number of years of probationary service. State laws generally do *not* give teachers a contractual right to tenure, and state legislatures have the power to change or repeal these laws. In addition, the courts have ruled that teachers enjoy tenure of employment and not position, leaving school boards with the authority to reassign and transfer tenured teachers.

State laws generally describe specific procedures to be followed before a tenured teacher can be dismissed. These laws require that teachers be given notice of the charges against them and some form of hearing. The specific procedures required vary among states. In addition to these requirements under state law, the U.S. Supreme Court has ruled that the Due Process Clause of the Fourteenth Amendment requires that all teachers are entitled to notice and a hearing prior to dismissal whenever they are deprived of a "liberty" or "property" interest. Tenured teachers have such a property interest in continued employment, which entitles them to constitutional rights to due process prior to dismissal. Nontenured teachers are also entitled to constitutional protections when they can demonstrate that they have been deprived of a "liberty" interest (damage to reputation) or a "property" interest (an expectation of continued employment created by a contract or the customary employment practices at an educational institution).

Even when teachers have achieved tenure, however, school boards retain the power to dismiss them for economic reasons. Courts have upheld reduction in force (or "riffing") for tenured teachers in situations of declining student enrollment and curriculum reorganization. Where state laws are silent on this matter, school boards have wide discretion in deciding which teachers will be dismissed. Many states limit this power by listing criteria that must be followed, such as requiring that school boards consider seniority. In addition, collective bargaining contracts may impose similar restrictions on school officials.

NOTES

1. *Smith* v. *School District of Township of Darby*, 130 A.2d 661 (Pa. 1957), at 667.

2. *Perry* v. *Sindermann*, 408 U.S. 593 (1972).

3. *Id.* at 600.

4. VA. CODE §22–21.3 (Cum. Supp. 1979).

5. TEX. EDUCATION CODE ANN. tit. 2, §13.106 (Vernon 1972).

6. *Id.*, §13.103.

7. *Carl* v. *South San Antonio Independent School District*, 561 S.W.2d 560 (Tex. App. 1978).

8. *Zimmerman* v. *Board of Education of Newark*, 183 A.2d 25 (N.J. 1962).

9. *Vittal* v. *Long Beach Unified School District*, 87 Cal. Rptr. 319 (Cal. App. 1970).

10. *McCarthy* v. *Board of Education of Union Free School District No. 3*, 340 N.Y.S.2d 679 (1973).

11. KY. REV. STAT. §161.750 (1980).

12. *Morse* v. *Wozniak*, 398 F.Supp. 597 (E.D. Mich. 1975).

13. *Bessler* v. *Board of Education of Chartered School District*, 356 N.E.2d 1253 (Ill. App. 1976).

14. *Snell* v. *Brothers*, 527 S.W.2d 114 (Tenn. 1975).

15. *State* v. *Ayers*, 92 P.2d 306 (Mont. 1939).

16. *State* v. *District No. 8 of Town of Milwaukee*, 10 N.W.2d 155 (Wis. 1943).

17. *Indiana ex rel. Anderson* v. *Brand*, 303 U.S. 95 (1938).

18. *Rosenthal* v. *Orleans Parish School Board*, 214 So.2d 203 (La. App. 1968).

19. *Id.* at 207.

20. *United States* v. *Board of Education of City of Bessemer*, 396 F.2d 44 (5th Cir. 1968).

21. *Rible* v. *Hughes*, 150 P.2d 455 (Cal. 1944).

22. ILL. ANN. STAT. chap. 122 §10–22.4 (Smith-Hurd Supp. 1979).

23. *State* v. *Board of Regents*, 261 P.2d 515 (Nev. 1953), at 517.

24. *Miller* v. *Noe,* 432 S.W.2d 818 (Ky. App. 1968).

25. *McKee* v. *Edgar,* 30 P.2d 999 (Cal. App. 1934).

26. WIS. STAT. ANN. §118.23 (Wis. 1973).

27. *In re Swink,* 200 A. 200 (Pa. Super. 1938).

28. *Id.* at 203.

29. *Osborne* v. *Bullitt County Board of Education,* 415 S.W.2d 607 (Ky. App. 1967), at 608.

30. *County Board of Education of Clarke County* v. *Oliver,* 116 So.2d 566 (Ala. 1959).

31. *Sparks* v. *Board of Education of Ashland Independent School District,* 549 S.W.2d 323 (Ky. App. 1977), at 325.

32. ILL. ANN. STAT. chap. 122 §24–12 (Smith-Hurd Supp. 1979).

33. ILL. ANN. STAT. chap. 122 §24–11 (Smith-Hurd Supp. 1979).

34. CONN. STAT. ANN. §10–151 (West Supp. 1980).

35. 408 U.S. 564 (1972).

36. 408 U.S. 593 (1972).

37. *Johnson* v. *Fraley,* 470 F.2d 179 (4th Cir. 1972).

38. *Shirck* v. *Thomas,* 486 F.2d 691 (7th Cir. 1973), at 693.

39. *Lipp* v. *Board of Education of City of Chicago,* 470 F.2d 802 (7th Cir. 1972).

40. *Wellner* v. *Minnesota State Junior College Board,* 487 F.2d 153 (8th Cir. 1973).

41. *Lombard* v. *Board of Education of City of New York,* 502 F.2d 631 (2d Cir. 1974).

42. *Huntley* v. *North Carolina State Board of Education,* 493 F.2d 1016 (4th Cir. 1974).

43. *McGhee* v. *Draper,* 564 F.2d 902 (10th Cir. 1977).

44. *Ferguson* v. *Thomas,* 430 F.2d 852 (5th Cir. 1970).

45. *Hostrop* v. *Board of Junior College District No. 515,* 471 F.2d 488 (7th Cir. 1972).

46. *Ortwein* v. *Mackey,* 358 F.Supp. 705 (M.D. Fla. 1973).

47. ALA. CODE tit. 16, §16–24–8 (1975).

48. OR. REV. STAT. §342.865 (1977).

49. *Ashby* v. *School Township of Liberty,* 98 N.W.2d 848 (Iowa 1959).

50. *Ehret* v. *School District of Borough of Kulpmont,* 5 A.2d 188 (Pa. 1939).

51. *Tressler* v. *Upper Dublin School District,* 373 A.2d 755 (Pa. 1977).

52. *Jones* v. *Holes,* 6 A.2d 102 (Pa. 1939).

53. *Weider* v. *Board of Education,* 170 A. 631 (N.J. 1934).

54. CAL. EDUCATION CODE §44955 (West Supp. 1980).

55. *Watson* v. *Burnett,* 23 N.E.2d 420 (Ind. 1939).

56. *Id.* at 423.

57. *Williams* v. *Board of Education of Lamar County,* 82 So.2d 549 (Ala. 1955).

58. *Unruh* v. *Piedmont High School District,* 41 P.2d 212 (Cal. App. 1935); *Woods* v. *Board of Education of Walker County,* 67 So.2d 840 (Ala. 1953).

4

How does collective bargaining affect me?

OVERVIEW

The American labor union movement began in response to poor working conditions in industry but has spread to involve even workers employed in the public sector. Today, over 80 percent of all public school teachers belong to the National Education Association (NEA), which has about 2 million members, or the American Federation of Teachers (AFT), which has approximately half a million members. As a result, almost two-thirds of the states have passed laws outlining school boards' responsibilities in collective bargaining with these groups. This chapter examines the impact of these laws and relevant court cases that have considered such questions as Does a teacher have a right to join a union? Can a teacher be forced to join a union? What is collective bargaining all about? What duties does a union have to perform for it members? and Are teachers allowed to go on strike?

THE RIGHT TO ORGANIZE

The *Norwalk Teachers' Association* Case[1]
Do teachers have the right to organize?

In 1946, all but two of the three hundred teachers in the Norwalk, Connecticut, school system were members of the Norwalk Teachers' Association (NTA). In April of that year, a dispute broke out between the NTA and the Board of Education of the City of Norwalk concerning teachers' salaries. After protracted negotiations, 230 NTA members rejected their contracts of employment and refused to return to their teaching duties. After further negotiations, the NTA and the Norwalk Board of Education entered into a contract that gave the NTA the exclusive right to represent Norwalk teachers in collective bargaining over teachers' working conditions. The contract also established a grievance procedure and a salary schedule.

Even with a contract negotiated, the NTA and the board of education continued to disagree about its interpretation and about a number of state education laws that seemed to be inconsistent with the contract's provisions. Fearful of another teachers' strike, the NTA went to court to ask for an order declaring the rights of both parties to the contract. Specifically, the NTA wanted answers to the following:

   a. Is it permitted to the plaintiff [NTA] under our laws to organize itself as a labor union for the purpose of demanding and receiving recognition and collective bargaining? . . .
   e. May the plaintiff [NTA] engage in concerted action such as strike, work stoppage, or collective refusal to enter upon duties?

In a decision that was to be followed by courts in other states, the Connecticut court ruled that the teachers did have the right to organize a labor union. The court noted that the laws in Connecticut were completely "silent on the subject" of teacher unions. After pointing out that "union organization in industry is now the rule rather than the exception," the court upheld this right for teachers: "In the absence of prohibitory statute or regulation, no good reason appears why public employees should not organize as a labor union." The court warned that the NTA did not have unlimited bargaining rights, however; teacher associations could only "organize and bargain collectively for the pay and working conditions which it may be in the power of the board of education to grant." The NTA's salary demands, for example, had to be subject to the board's taxation power.

Turning to the second question, the court held that the teachers had no right to strike. In reaching its decision, the court explained: "It should be the aim of every employee of the government to do his or her part to make it function as efficiently and economically as possible. The drastic remedy of the organized strike to enforce the demands of unions of government employees is in direct contravention of this principle." The court stated that government employees occupy a different status from those who work in private enterprise because they "serve the public welfare," and concluded that allowing teachers to strike would "deny the authority of government and contravene the public welfare."

Do all teachers have a right to join a union and engage in collective bargaining?

At the time *Norwalk* was decided, none of the states had passed laws permitting boards of education to engage in collective bargaining with teacher organizations, and the courts had to resolve questions that arose in this area. Today, almost two-thirds of the states have passed such laws. (See Appendix E for a list of state laws concerning collective bargaining for teachers.) Only North Carolina specifically prohibits public employees from engaging in collective bargaining.

The state laws vary considerably. Some states merely require boards of education to "meet and confer" with teacher organizations. In some states with these general statutes, it is up to the courts to resolve any disputes concerning what are the proper subjects of collective bargaining. See page 55 for a more detailed discussion of how the courts decide. The Rhode Island law is an example:

> *Right to organize and bargain collectively.*—The certified teachers in the public school system in any city, town or regional school district, shall have the right to negotiate professionally and to bargain collectively with their respective school committees and to be represented by an association or labor organization in such negotiation or collective bargaining concerning hours, salary, working conditions and all other terms and conditions of professional employment. For purposes of this chapter, certified teachers shall mean certified teaching personnel employed in the public school systems in the state of Rhode Island engaged in teaching duties. Superintendents, principals and assistant principals are excluded from the provisions of this chapter.[2]

After stating that the association or organization selected by the teachers shall be the exclusive bargaining agent, the law provides for:

> *Obligation to bargain.*—It shall be the obligation of the school committee to meet and confer in good faith with the representative or representatives of the negotiating or bargaining agent within ten (10) days after receipt of written notice from said agent of the request for a meeting for negotiating or collective bargaining purposes. This obligation shall include the duty to cause any agreement resulting from negotiations or bargaining to be reduced to a written contract, provided that no such contract shall exceed the term of three (3) years. Failure to negotiate or bargain in good faith may be complained of by either the negotiating or bargaining agent or the school committee to the state labor relations board which shall deal with such complaint in the manner provided in chapter 7 of this title.[3]

Other state laws are much more detailed and require boards of education to meet with the teacher organization selected as the exclusive agent to represent the teachers to negotiate about specific topics. Such laws also generally include more detailed procedures for resolving negotiating impasses that may arise during the bargaining process. The California law, for example, provides that the board and the teachers' representative must negotiate about health and welfare benefits, leave transfer and reassignment policies, safety conditions of employment, class size, procedures to be used for the evaluation of employees, procedures for processing grievances, and the layoff of probationary certificated school district employees.[4]

TEACHERS' RIGHTS

How are collective bargaining laws enforced?

In order to enforce collective bargaining and other laws affecting public employees, many states have established labor relations boards. These boards attempt to ensure that both school officials and teachers' organizations comply with the law. For example, the Rhode Island law quoted in the preceding question provides that either party to collective bargaining negotiations can complain to the state's labor relations board if the other party fails to negotiate or bargain in good faith.

Are there any federal laws concerning teachers' unions?

No. There is still no federal law that regulates collective bargaining for teachers. Federal laws that outline the rights of unions and management (the National Labor Relations Act of 1935 and the Taft-Hartley Act of 1977) do not apply to public employees, and no other federal laws have been enacted. (Public employees in the federal government were given the right to join a union and engage in collective bargaining concerning matters affecting their working conditions in an executive order issued by President Kennedy in 1962.) Moreover, a recent Supreme Court case[5] suggests that such a federal law would be unconstitutional because it would involve Congress in legislating in education, which the Tenth Amendment reserves as a state function.

Is there a constitutional right to organize?

Yes. In addition to state laws giving teachers the right to join unions, the courts have ruled that the U.S. Constitution gives teachers the right to organize. In Illinois, two probationary teachers were dismissed because of their work for the American Federation of Teachers. A federal court ruled that "teachers have the right of free association, and unjustified interference with teachers' associational freedom violates the Due Process Clause of the Fourteenth Amendment."[6]

Is there a constitutional right to bargain?

No. Most states have statutes that provide for collective bargaining for teachers. But in the absence of such laws, teachers do not have a constitutional right to bargain collectively. This issue was confronted in 1974 when the North Carolina legislature passed a law abolishing collective bargaining between public employees and any state or city agency. The state education association sued to have the law declared unconstitutional. But a federal court ruled that there was no such constitutional right.[7] "The Constitution," wrote the court, does not require that the government "be compelled to talk to or contract" with any organization. Although the teachers' union "may someday persuade state government of the asserted value of collective bargaining agreements," this is a political and not a judicial matter. While the First Amendment protects the right of teachers to associate and advocate, it does not guarantee that their advocacy will be effective or that government bodies must bargain with them.

Who decides who will represent teachers in the collective bargaining process?

State laws that provide for collective bargaining for teachers generally also establish a procedure to decide who will represent the teachers in negotiations with the school board. Typically the laws state that the board must bargain with the organization that a majority of teachers in the district (or other "bargaining unit") designates as exclusive representative. This organization is generally elected. In Oklahoma, for example, the law states that teachers shall choose an employee organization to serve as their exclusive representative through the following procedure:

1. Twenty-five percent or more of the employees in the bargaining unit petition for an election to be held.
2. An election by secret ballot shall be held.
3. The local board of education shall certify the employee organization which received a majority of votes in the election.
4. If none of the choices on the ballot receives a majority of votes, a runoff election shall be held between the two choices with the largest number of votes.[8]

   In addition, state laws usually define who the union will represent as part of the "bargaining unit." This unit, or group of teachers, may include all teachers in a city or school district or all teachers under the same salary schedule. Decisions about the size of such a unit and whether it is appropriate for a particular group of teachers to be represented by only one union are often made by the state's employment relations board.

Do all teachers have to join the employee organization selected as the exclusive bargaining representative?

No. Public employees cannot be forced to join a union as a condition of their employment (the so-called union shop or closed shop). Some state laws have explicitly recognized this right. In California, for example, the law provides that, although public employees have the right to join a union, they also have the right "to refuse to join or participate in the activities of employee organizations and shall have the right to represent themselves individually in their employment relations with the public school employer [as long as they are not union members]."[9]

In addition, the U.S. Supreme Court has recently ruled that the First Amendment gives teachers who are not union members the right to make public comments about matters that are the subject of collective bargaining negotiations. In *City of Madison* v. *Wisconsin Employment Relations Commission*,[10] Mr. Holmquist, a nonunion teacher, attended a public meeting of the board of education and spoke against a topic being pushed by the union in collective bargaining negotiations. The union filed a complaint with the state's employment relations board, claiming that the board of education had violated its duty under Wisconsin law to negotiate only with the teachers' exclusive collective bargaining representative when it permitted Holmquist to speak at the board meeting.

The Court, however, ruled that the First Amendment's guarantee of freedom of speech gave Holmquist the right to express his views: "Holmquist did not seek to bargain or offer to enter into any bargain with the board, nor does it appear that he was authorized by any other teachers to enter into any agreement on their behalf. . . . Moreover, the school board meeting at which Holmquist was permitted to speak was open to the public. He addressed the school board not merely as one of its employees but also as a concerned citizen, seeking to express his views on an important decision of his government."

The Court explained that, according to its decision in *Pickering* v. *Board of Education* (see chapter 8 for a detailed discussion of this case), teachers cannot be "compelled to relinquish the First Amendment rights they would otherwise enjoy as citizens to comment on matters of public interest in connection with the operation of the public schools in which they work" and concluded that "the mere expression of an opinion about a matter subject to collective bargaining, whether or not the speaker is a member of the bargaining unit, poses no genuine threat to the policy of exclusive representation that Wisconsin has adopted."

Can teachers who are not union members be required to pay dues to a union?

Yes. About one-third of the states have passed laws that permit "agency shop" or "fair share" arrangements under which employees who are not members of a union can be required to pay union dues as a condition of their employment. (See Appendix E for a list of these states.) Although such agreements are not likely to be upheld in the absence of such a state law, the U.S. Supreme Court has recently ruled that they are constitutional. In *Abood* v. *Detroit Board of Education*,[11] a group of teachers challenged the validity of an agency-shop clause in a collective bargaining agreement between the Detroit Board of Education and the Detroit Federation of Teachers. Michigan law authorized a provision whereby every teacher who had not become a union member within 60 days of hire had to pay the union an amount equal to the regular dues or face discharge. The nonunion teachers stated that they were opposed to collective bargaining and that they also did not approve of a number of the union's political activities unrelated to collective bargaining. They asked the Court to declare the agency-shop clause unconstitutional, arguing that it deprived them of their right to freedom of association protected by the First and Fourteenth amendments.

The Supreme Court ruled that the agency-shop clause was constitutional. The Court noted that such arrangements had previously been upheld in labor relations in the private sector on the ground that the union's collective bargaining activities benefited all employees and that all employees should help defray the union's expenses in these negotiations. The Court explained that a "union-shop arrangement has been thought to distribute fairly the cost of these activities among those who benefit, and it counteracts the incentive that employees might otherwise have to become 'free riders'—to refuse to contribute to the union while obtaining benefits of union representation that necessarily accrue to all employees." The Court concluded that this reasoning also made agency-shop arrangements valid for public employees:

> Public employees are not basically different from private employees; on the whole, they have the same sort of skills, the same needs, and seek the same advantages. . . . The very real differences between exclusive-agent collective bargaining in the public and private sectors are not such as to work any greater infringement upon the First Amendment interests of public employees.

Can teachers be required to support union political activities?

No. In *Abood*, the Supreme Court ruled that it was in violation of the First Amendment to require a public employee to be forced to pay dues to support a union's political activities. The Court did not attempt to define which union activities (e.g., political lobbying) need not be supported financially. Instead, the Court merely noted that there would be "difficult problems in drawing lines between collective-bargaining activities, for which contributions may be compelled, and ideological activities unrelated to collective bargaining, for which such compulsion is prohibited."

What are the union's legal responsibilities as the exclusive collective bargaining representative for teachers?

The employee organization that acts as the exclusive bargaining agent also has the legal duty to represent all teachers in that bargaining unit. This "duty of fair representation" prohibits the union from discriminating against any of its members in the negotiation and administration of collective bargaining agreements. In addition, this duty requires the union to represent the interests of all members of the bargaining unit—even those who are not union members—in the negotiation process. This duty requires the union to be honest and fair but does not deprive the union of discretion in deciding how to negotiate with the school board or how to handle teachers' grievances. Unless a union is acting out of political, racial, or other "bad faith" reason, it is not a violation of this duty for the union to take a position which some members oppose, or to decide to settle a grievance.

In addition, the union has the duty to bargain with the school board in "good faith." This duty requires that the union meet at reasonable times to negotiate with the school board and make a sincere effort to reach an agreement on the topics under discussion. The good-faith requirement means that the union cannot merely "go through the motions" of meeting with school officials; it must consider and respond to the board's proposals. It does *not* require that the union reach an agreement with the school board.

What legal responsibilities does the school board have in the bargaining process?

The school board has the same legal duty to bargain in good faith as the union does. In addition, state law may impose certain responsibilities on the school board to inform the public about the nature of the collective bargaining process. Many states have passed "open public meeting laws," which require school boards to inform the public about educational policy decisions. The California law reads as follows: "All initial proposals of exclusive representatives and of public school employers, which relate to matters within the scope of representation, shall be presented at a public meeting of the public school employer and thereafter shall be public records."[12]

CONTRACT NEGOTIATIONS

What happens during collective bargaining?

The bargaining process begins when either the teachers' union or the school board drafts a contract proposal. This procedure is typically initiated by the union, which picks a team of individuals to represent the teachers during the negotiations. This bargaining team examines the past contract and prepares a document that proposes various changes and/or additions representing the teachers' interests.

The school board generally also appoints a team of individuals to represent its interests, and these individuals develop counterproposals. After the two sides have exchanged the preliminary written statements that describe their positions, they proceed to the discussion table. Each side usually appoints one spokesperson, and bargaining sessions are held to discuss each of the proposed contract's provisions. The actual bargaining sessions involve a complicated process of give and take through which each side must evaluate the other side's demands and decide on what issues to compromise. The steps in the negotiating process vary depending on the tactics adopted by the parties involved.

What do the union and the school board bargain about?

State laws determine what the union and board can bargain about, and these laws vary widely. Some state laws are very broad and allow teachers' unions and school boards to bargain about "wages, hours, and other terms and conditions of employment." Other states require that the bargaining be restricted to specific subjects. The Tennessee law, for example, provides:

> The board of education and the recognized professional employees' organization shall negotiate in good faith the following conditions of employment:
> a. Salaries or wages
> b. Grievance procedures
> c. Insurance
> d. Fringe benefits, but not to include pensions or retirement programs of the Tennessee consolidated retirement system
> e. Working conditions
> f. Leave
> g. Student discipline procedures
> h. Payroll deductions
>
> Nothing shall prohibit the parties from agreeing to discuss other terms and conditions of employment in service, but it shall not be bad faith as set forth in this chapter to refuse to negotiate on any other terms and conditions. Either party may file a complaint in a court of record of any demands to meet on other terms and conditions and have an order of the court requiring the other party to continue to meet in good faith on the required items of this section only. . . .[13]

When the law is not this specific, the courts have had to decide the mandatory subjects for collective bargaining. In general, courts have held that those topics "directly" or "significantly" related to the teachers' working conditions are mandatory subjects for collective bargaining (e.g., salaries, sick leave, and seniority). Topics that concern major educational policies that indirectly affect teachers' working conditions and that the board must control in order to manage the schools effectively are not within the scope of bargaining (e.g., curriculum content and hiring policies).

In applying these general rules, the courts look at each individual case and balance the interests of both parties. As might be expected, different courts have reached different conclusions. The Alaska Supreme Court has ruled that salaries, fringe benefits, number of hours worked, and the amount of leave time are mandatory subjects for negotiation; class size, pupil-teacher ratio, the school calendar, and teacher representation on school board advisory committees are not.[14] The Supreme Court of Wisconsin has held that the length of the school calendar is a mandatory subject of bargaining, whereas class size is not.[15] On the other hand, the Supreme Court of Connecticut has found that the length of the school calendar is not a mandatory subject, whereas class size is.[16]

Are there other limitations on the scope of collective bargaining?

Yes. First, the parties cannot enter into any contractual negotiations that are in violation of constitutional law. For example, the U.S. Supreme Court has ruled that nonunion teachers have the right to make comments at public meetings on issues subject to collective bargaining negotiations, and so the union and school board could not agree to a contract that prohibited such activity. Similarly, the parties must abide by existing state and federal laws. If state laws establish certain certification requirements for teachers, the collective bargaining contract cannot set up conflicting standards for teacher employment. Finally, the collective bargaining contract must recognize any rights that exist under other contracts currently in effect.

What happens if the union and the school board cannot agree on a contract?

State procedures vary when the union and the school board are deadlocked in their negotiations. As noted earlier, states with laws that merely require the school board to "meet and confer" with the union do not have any procedures for resolving an impasse in negotiations. A majority of states, however, do make some provision for resolving a deadlock. Some states, such as Oklahoma, give the parties the opportunity to develop a procedure for resolving impasses.[17] The most common procedure is mediation. The parties meet with a neutral third person(s) who attempts to resolve their differences through discussion and by proposing compromise provisions. The mediator has no legal power to force the parties to accept these suggestions and merely functions as a facilitator.

If the parties reject the mediator's recommendations, the next step is usually fact finding. The fact-finding process involves a more formal discussion during which each party again presents its position and supporting facts. The fact-finding body then issues its recommendations. Unlike mediation, fact-finding recommendations are generally made public, thus placing additional pressure on the parties to come to an agreement. If the parties are still at an impasse, state law may require the union and the school board to submit to arbitration. At this point, the parties agree to abide by an impartial arbitrator's decision.

The Hawaii statute incorporates all three steps.[18] The law requires mediation within three days of the impasse in negotiations. If the dispute continues fifteen days after the date of the impasse, the Hawaii Public Employment Relations Board appoints a fact-finding board of not more than three members from a list of qualified persons maintained by the board. This board transmits its findings to the parties, and if the dispute is still unresolved five days later, these findings are made public. If the dispute continues thirty days after the date of impasse, the parties may mutually agree to arbitration; if they do not, the board appoints an arbitration panel to attempt to resolve the differences. If the parties cannot agree within fifty days of the date of impasse, the arbitration panel submits its findings, which are binding on both parties.

What does a collective bargaining contract include?

Every collective bargaining contract is different, reflecting the concerns of teachers and school officials in different districts. Nevertheless, certain provisions are generally part of all collective bargaining contracts. Provisions derived from an examination of a number of different collective bargaining contracts are described herewith:

1. *Preamble:* identifies the parties to the contract and the period for which the contract will be in effect.
2. *Recognition Clause:* identifies the union/association as the exclusive representative of the teachers in a certain bargaining unit, which is also defined. A typical recognition clause might state: "The Board of Trustees of Smalltown School District hereby recognizes the Smalltown Community Education Association as the exclusive representative of all teachers employed by the Smalltown Community Schools Corporation."
3. *Grievance Procedure:* defines "grievance" and a description of the steps to be followed if a grievance is claimed. A grievance may be defined as "a claim by a teacher or by the union that there has been a violation, a misapplication, or a misinterpretation of the agreement"; a grievance may also be defined more broadly to mean "a claim by a teacher or the union that there has been a violation, a misapplication, or a misinterpretation of any policy or administrative decision affecting employees of the school district." The procedure usually defines the steps that must be taken and the time limits that apply. It may include provisions for arbitration.
4. *Teachers' Rights Clause:* provides that teachers have the right to organize for the purpose of collective negotiations and prohibits discrimination against teachers regardless of membership or nonmembership in any employee organiation.
5. *Teacher Organizations' Rights Clause:* outlines union/association rights to communicate with members, including the right to use bulletin board

space, place mail in teachers' mailboxes, schedule meetings with teachers, and have access to certain school board documents.

6. *Representation Clause:* describes the procedure to be followed if the
   school board or any employee organization wishes to challenge the
   union/association status as the exclusive bargaining agent.

7. *Management Rights Clause:* provides that the school board does not
   "waive any rights or powers granted under the laws of the state." This
   provision merely affirms what is already the law, that school boards
   cannot be required to bargain away their rights to establish educational
   policy.

8. *Terms of the Agreement:* describes the specific contract provisions concerning teachers' employment; it generally includes provisions concerning salaries, sick leave, pregnancy leave, other leaves of absence,
   insurance, vacations, transfer policy and procedure, and teaching days
   and hours.

STRIKES

Do teachers have the right to strike?

The situation concerning teacher strikes has not changed much since the
Norwalk case was decided. Teachers have no constitutional right to strike,
and state courts have also refused to grant this right. In addition, most states
have passed laws that specifically prohibit strikes by teachers. Some states
also have laws making it illegal for a school board to engage in a lockout (a
refusal to allow teachers to work). In enforcing these laws, the courts have
defined strikes as any collective refusal to work; it is not necessary that teachers label their action a strike. For example, a New York court ruled that
teachers were actually on strike when they submitted mass resignations to
the union.[19]

In addition, courts have found that it is illegal for teachers to use sanctions
against a school board that involve urging teachers not to accept employment
in the district. Faced with such a case, the Supreme Court of New Jersey
concluded that such sanctions were just as unlawful as a strike: "The public
demand for services which makes illegal a strike against government in-
veighs against any other concerted action designed to deny government the
necessary manpower, whether by terminating existing employments in any
mode or by obstructing access to the labor market."[20]

Recognizing that teacher strikes will occur despite the laws against them, a
few states now have laws that give teachers a limited right to strike. Generally these laws provide that teachers in a union/association are allowed to
strike only after they have complied with the state's procedures for impasse
resolution, and after they have given the school board notice of their intent to
strike. In Hawaii, teachers are permitted to strike after (1) the procedures relating to dispute resolution have been followed, (2) sixty days have elapsed
since the fact-finding board has made public its findings and any recommen-

dation, and (3) the exclusive representative has given a ten-day notice of intent to strike to the public employment relations board and the employer.[21] If the school board feels that the strike will endanger public health or safety, school officials can petition the public employment relations board to make an investigation. If the board finds that there is imminent or present danger to the health and safety of the public, the board can set requirements that must be complied with to avoid or remove any such danger.

What penalties can be imposed on teachers who engage in an illegal strike?

A number of state laws describe penalties that may be imposed on teachers and/or organization officials who engage in an illegal strike. For example, Indiana law states that a striking teachers' union/association loses its dues-deduction privilege for one year; in addition, teachers will not be paid for any school day missed as the result of a strike.[22] Nevada law provides that school officials can impose any of the following sanctions on teachers who engage in a strike:

1. Dismiss, suspend, or demote all or any employees who participate in such strike or violation.
2. Cancel the contracts of employment of all or any employees who participate in such strike or violation.
3. Withhold all or any part of the salaries or wages that would otherwise accrue to all or any employees who participate in such strike or violation.[23]

In addition to the sanctions described in state laws, courts have ruled that school boards have certain remedies available in strike situations. School officials can ask the courts to issue an injunction to prohibit the strike. The union, its officers, and members can be held in contempt and fined or jailed if they remain on strike in violation of a court order to return to work.[24] The courts have ruled that the school board can fire teachers who engage in an illegal strike. In a recent Wisconsin case,[25] teachers went out on strike while the school board and the teachers' association were negotiating over the terms of the new contract. After sending letters to the striking teachers informing them that the strike was illegal, school officials scheduled disciplinary hearings for each striking teacher. The teachers then appeared before the school board, asking that they be treated as a group in any disciplinary proceedings. The board voted to fire all the teachers, and the Wisconsin Supreme Court upheld the board's decision.

Finally, the courts have ruled that school boards can impose economic sanctions on teachers who go on strike. A New York court upheld the constitutionality of a state law that allowed the board to make payroll deductions in the amount of twice the daily rate of pay for each day a teacher was on strike.[26] Similarly, a Florida court ruled that a school board had the authority under state law to require striking teachers to pay a $100 fine as a condition of reemployment.[27]

SUMMARY

Over the past twenty years, collective bargaining in the public schools has changed from a rare to a common practice. Most states have passed laws that give teachers the right to join employee organizations, and most teachers are union/association members. In addition, the courts have held that teachers have a constitutional right to organize as part of their right of free association.

Many state laws now provide procedures for teachers to select an organization as the exclusive bargaining agent to represent them in contract negotiations with the school board. The laws vary widely from state to state but generally require school boards to bargain with teacher organizations about "wages, hours, and other terms and conditions of employment." Most states also describe some procedure to be followed when there is an impasse in collective bargaining negotiations.

Despite the support for collective bargaining in education, there are limits on teachers' rights. There is no constitutional right to bargain with school boards. In addition, the vast majority of states still prohibit strikes by public school teachers and often provide that teachers who go on strike can be dismissed. In addition, the courts have been willing to issue injunctions against teachers who engage in illegal strikes, and to uphold the board's authority to impose economic sanctions on striking teachers.

NOTES

1. *Norwalk Teachers' Association* v. *Board of Education,* 83 A.2d 482 (Conn. 1951).

2. R.I. GEN LAWS §28–9.3–2 (1956, Reenactment of 1968).

3. *Id.* §28–9.3–4.

4. "The scope of representation shall be limited to matters relating to wages, hours of employment, and other terms and conditions of employment. 'Terms and conditions of employment' mean health and welfare benefits as defined by Section 53200, leave, transfer and reassignment policies, safety conditions of employment, class size, procedures to be used for the evaluation of employees, organizational security pursuant to Section 3546, procedures for processing grievances pursuant to Sections 3548.5, 3548.6, 3548.7,and 3548.8, and the layoff of probationary certified school district employees, pursuant to Section 4459.5 of the Education Code. In addition, the exclusive representative of certified personnel has the right to consult on the definition of educational objectives, the determination of the content of courses and curriculum, and the selection of textbooks to the extent such matters are within the discretion of the public school employer under the law. All matters not specifically enumerated are reserved to the public school employer and may not be a subject of meeting and negotiating, provided that nothing herein may be construed to limit the right of the public school employer to consult with any employees or employee organization on any matter outside the scope of representation." CAL. GOVT. CODE §3543.2 (West Supp. 1979).

5. *National League of Cities* v. *Usery,* 426 U.S. 833 (1976).

6. *McLaughlin* v. *Tilendis,* 398 F.2d 287 (7th Cir. 1968).

7. *Winston-Salem/Forsyth County Unit of the North Carolina Association of Educators* v. *Phillips*, 381 F.Supp. 644 (M.D. N.C. 1974).
8. The actual language of the law is as follows:

> B. 1. Within fourteen (14) days of the receipt of an employee petition filed by or on behalf of twenty-five percent (25%) or more of the employees in a unit, such petition calling for an election to determine which, if any, employee organization represents the employees in a bargaining unit, the local board of education shall verify all names appearing on the petition. The board shall verify that the names are those of bona fide members of the unit and that the challenging numbers are correct.
>
> 2. The petition calling for the secret ballot election shall contain only the names of employees of the bargaining unit who have signed and dated said petition. The time for signing the petition shall be within thirty (30) days of the first day of classes. Provided that the first day of classes shall serve as the beginning date for all subsequent petition drives.
>
> 3. Any employee in the bargaining unit shall have the right to challenge the validity of any or all names appearing on the petition. Such challenge shall be filed with the local board of education no later than five (5) days after receipt of said petition. After the challenge period expires, and the petition is validated by the local board as having the sufficient percentage of names, the local board shall call for a secret ballot election.
>
> C. 1. The election shall be held not less than thirty (30) days nor more than forty-five (45) days after the receipt of the petition, to determine which, if any, employee organization shall legitimately represent the unit. The first such election held in a bargaining unit after the effective date of this act may be held in 1978. Thereafter, no election shall be directed to be held by a local board in a bargaining unit within which a valid election was held in the preceding two (2) years.
>
> The local board shall certify the employee organization which received a majority in the election. An appropriate election ballot shall be printed for this election, which contains the names of all employee organizations seeking to represent the appropriate bargaining unit and shall also provide an option specifying that no organization shall represent the employee bargaining unit. Only those organizations which have paid a filing fee of Two Hundred Fifty Dollars ($250.00) to the local board shall be allowed on the ballot. Every organization that receives at least fifteen percent (15%) of the vote in the election shall be reimbursed the Two Hundred Fifty Dollars ($250.00) by the local board. The local board shall use any remaining filing fee money to help offset the cost of the validation process of the petition as well as any election costs incurred.
>
> 2. When none of the choices on the ballot receives a majority of the votes, a runoff election shall be conducted on the fourteenth day following the first election between the two choices which received the largest number of votes in the preceding election. . . . OKLA. STAT. ANN. tit. 70, §509.2 (West Supp. 1980).

9. CAL. GOVT. CODE §3543 (West Supp. 1979).
10. 429 U.S. 167 (1976).
11. 431 U.S. 209 (1977).
12. CAL. GOVT. CODE §3547a (West Supp. 1979).
13. TENN. CODE ANN. §49-5510 (Cum. Supp. 1979).

14. *Kenai Peninsula Borough* v. *Kenai Peninsula Education Association,* 572 P.2d 416 (Alaska 1977).
15. *City of Beloit* v. *Wisconsin Employment Relations Commission,* 242 N.W.2d 231 (Wis. 1976).
16. *West Hartford Education Association* v. *DeCourcy,* 295 A.2d 526 (Conn. 1972).
17. OKLA. STAT. ANN. tit. 70 §509.7 (West 1972).
18. *"Resolution of disputes; grievances; impasses.* (a) A public employer shall have the power to enter into written agreement with the exclusive representative of an appropriate bargaining unit setting forth a grievance procedure culminating in a final and binding decision, to be invoked in the event of any dispute concerning the interpretation or application of a written agreement. In the absence of such a procedure, either party may submit the dispute to the board for a final and binding decision. A dispute over the terms of an initial or renewed agreement does not constitute a grievance.

third and impartial arbitrator selected by the other two arbitrators. If either party fails to select an arbitrator or for any reason there is a delay in the naming of an arbitrator, or if the arbitrators fail to select a neutral arbitrator within the time prescribed by the board, the board shall appoint the arbitrator or arbitrators necessary to complete the panel, which shall act with the same force and effect as if the panel had been selected by the parties as described above. The arbitration panel shall take whatever actions necessary, including but not limited to inquiries, investigations, hearings, issuance of subpoenas, and administering oaths, in accordance with procedures prescribed by the board to resolve the impasse. If the dispute remains unresolved within fifty days after the date of the impasse, the arbitration panel shall transmit its findings and its final and binding decision on the dispute to both parties. The parties shall enter into an agreement or take whatever action is necessary to carry out and effectuate the decision. All items requiring any moneys for implementation shall be subject to appropriations by the appropriate legislative bodies, and the employer shall submit all such items agreed to in the course of negotiations within ten days to the appropriate legislative bodies.

(4) The costs for mediation and fact-finding shall be borne by the board. All other costs, including that of a neutral arbitrator, shall be borne equally by the parties involved in the dispute.

(c) If the parties have not mutually agreed to submit the dispute to final and binding arbitration, either party shall be free to take whatever lawful action it deems necessary to end the dispute; provided that no action shall involve the disruption or interruption of public services within sixty days after the fact-finding board has made public its findings of fact and any recommendations for the resolution of the dispute. The employer shall submit to the appropriate legislative bodies his recommendations for the settlement of the dispute on all cost items together with the findings of fact and any recommendations made by the fact-finding board. The exclusive representative may submit to the appropriate legislative body its recommendations for the settlement of the dispute on all cost items." HAW. REV. STAT. §89–11 (1976).

19. *Board of Education of City of New York* v. *Shanker*, 283 N.Y.S.2d 548 (1967).
20. *Board of Education* v. *New Jersey Education Association*, 247 A.2d 867 (N.J. 1968), at 872.
21. *"Strikes, rights and prohibitions.* (a) Participation in a strike shall be unlawful for any employee who (1) is not included in an appropriate bargaining unit for which an exclusive representative has been certified by the board, or (2) is included in an appropriate bargaining unit for which process for resolution of a dispute is by referral to final and binding arbitration.

(b) It shall be lawful for an employee, who is not prohibited from striking under paragraph (a) and who is in the appropriate bargaining unit involved in an impasse, to participate in a strike after (1) the requirements of section 89–11 relating to the resolution of disputes have been complied with in good faith, (2) the proceedings for the prevention of any prohibited practices have been exhausted, (3) sixty days have elapsed since the fact-finding board has made public its findings and any recommendation, (4) the exclusive representative has given a ten-day notice of intent to strike to the board and to the employer.

(c) Where the strike occurring, or is about to occur, endangers the public health or safety, the public employer concerned may petition the board to make an investigation. If the board finds that there is imminent or present danger to the health and safety of the public, the board shall set requirements that must be complied with to avoid or remove any such imminent or present danger.

(d) No employee organization shall declare or authorize a strike of employees, which is or would be in violation of this section. Where it is alleged by the employer that an employee organization has declared or authorized a strike of employees which is or would be in violation of this section, the employer may apply to the board for a declaration that the strike is or would be unlawful and the board, after affording an opportunity to the employee organization to be heard on the application, may make such a declaration.

(e) If any employee organization or any employee is found to be violating or failing to comply with the requirements of this section or if there is reasonable cause to believe that an employee organization or an employee is violating or failing to comply with such requirements, the board shall institute appropriate proceedings in the circuit in which the violation occurs to enjoin the performance of any acts or practices forbidden by this section, or to require the employee organization or employees to comply with the requirements of this section. Jurisdiction to hear and dispose of all actions under this section is conferred upon each circuit court, and each court may issue, in compliance with chapter 380, such orders and decrees, by way of injunction, or otherwise, as may be appropriate to enforce this section." HAW. REV. STAT. §89–12 (1976).

22. IND. CODE ANN. §20–7.5–1–14 (Burns 1975).

23. NEV. REV. STAT. §288.260 (1979).

24. *In re Block*, 236 A.2d 589 (N.J. 1967).

25. *Hortonville Joint School District No. 1* v. *Hortonville Education Association*, 225 N.W.2d 658 (Wis. 1975), *rev'd on other grounds*, 426 U.S. 482 (1976).

26. *Lawson* v. *Board of Education*, 307 N.Y.S.2d 333 (1970).

27. *National Education Association, Inc.*, v. *Lee County Board of Public of Public Instruction*, 299 F.Supp. 834 (M.D. Fla. 1969), *state question certified*, 448 F.2d 451 (5th Cir. 1971), *state question answered*, 260 So.2d 206 (Fla. 1972), *rev'd* 467 F.2d 447 (5th Cir. 1972).

When am I liable?

OVERVIEW

Many books and articles about education law dwell on the dangers of being held responsible for students' injuries. They emphasize the seriousness of "personal liability," the "multiplicity of hazards" in the schools, and the "possibilities of disaster" for the teacher. The result is to portray the law as a ubiquitous monster hiding in every educational shadow and ready to ensnare every innocent teacher. There emerges a sense that teaching is an especially dangerous profession in which the hazards are greater, liability is more personal, negligence is more likely, and the results of negligence are more disastrous for teachers than for other people. This is a seriously distorted impression.

It is true that teachers may be held personally liable for injuries that occur because of their negligence, but this is equally true of every citizen. And the legal principles that apply to teachers whose negligence may cause injury are the same as those that apply to anyone else. This chapter explains these principles, which lawyers refer to as the *law of torts*. It also considers the related question of educational malpractice. Should students and their parents be able to sue teachers for malpractice just as they can sue doctors and other professionals? Finally, the chapter considers when educators may be held personally liable for violating a student's constitutional rights and how the courts determine when to award money damages.

STUDENT INJURIES

When can a teacher be required to pay damages for a student's injury?

A teacher can be held liable for damages to an injured student if, and only if, the student proves four things: (1) the teacher had a duty to be careful not to injure the student and protect him from being injured, (2) the teacher failed to use due care, (3) the teacher's carelessness caused the injury, and (4) the student sustained provable damages. Usually, in cases of student injury, it is easy to prove that the teachers had a duty to be careful toward their students and that the injuries resulted in monetary damages. Sometimes there is a question about what precisely caused the injury. In most cases, however, the critical question is whether the teachers violated their duty to be careful and therefore were negligent. These are the issues examined in the following cases.

When is a teacher negligent?

The *Sheehan* Case[1]

A teacher is negligent when she fails to exercise reasonable care to protect her students from injury. Such negligence was found in the case of Margaret Sheehan, an eighth-grade student at St. Peter's School who was injured one morning during recess. The injury occurred when a teacher took Margaret and nineteen other girls to an athletic field where a group of eighth-grade boys were playing baseball. The teacher told the girls to sit on a log on the third-base line and then she returned to the school. About five minutes after the teacher left, some of the boys waiting their turn to bat began throwing pebbles at the girls. Although the girls protested, the stone throwing continued for several minutes, until Margaret was seriously injured by a pebble that struck her eye. Margaret's parents sued for damages on her behalf. They alleged that the school and the teacher were negligent in failing to supervise the children's recess. The evidence indicated that the teacher was absent from the athletic area from the time she brought the girls there until after the accident.

After both sides presented their case, the judge instructed the jury on the law to be applied. "It is the duty of a school," said the judge, "to use ordinary care and to protect its students from injury resulting from the conduct of other students under circumstances where such conduct would reasonably have been foreseen and could have been prevented by the use of ordinary care." The jury found that it was reasonable to foresee that a student might be hurt as a result of failure to supervise an athletic area. It therefore decided that the school was negligent. The school appealed on the grounds that there was no proof that this activity had been dangerous in the past or that supervision would have prevented the accident. But the Supreme Court of Minnesota ruled in Margaret's favor. It noted that children have a "known proclivity to act impulsively without thought of the possibilities of danger." It is precisely this lack of mature judgment that makes supervision so vital. "The mere presence of the hand of authority," wrote the court, "normally is effective to curb this youthful exuberance and to protect the children against their own folly."

Does this mean that a teacher is expected to anticipate every situation where one child may suddenly injure another? No, the law does not expect a teacher to prevent an unforeseen injury that could happen quickly and without warning. But this was not such a case. Here the girls protested when the pebble throwing began, and the boys continued throwing stones for several minutes before Margaret was injured. Under these circumstances, the jury concluded that a teacher using reasonable care would have put a stop to this activity and would have prevented the injury. The teacher therefore was negligent in leaving the athletic field unsupervised.

Are teachers required to constantly supervise their students?

Not always. According to a Minnesota court, there is generally "no requirement of constant supervision of all the movements of the pupils at all times."[2] However, a teacher would have a duty to provide constant supervision under dangerous conditions, especially among young children.

The *Mancha* Case[3]

In Chicago two teachers organized a field trip to the city's Natural History Museum for about fifty students, twelve to fifteen years of age. When they arrived at the museum, the students were allowed to view the exhibits without direct supervision. At a time when he was away from the teachers, Roberto Mancha was beaten by several boys not connected with the school. Roberto's parents sued, charging that the teachers who organized the trip were negligent in not supervising their students and in failing to foresee and guard against Roberto's injury.

In discussing this question, an Illinois court observed that hindsight makes every event foreseeable. But, according to the court, a teacher's duty does not depend only on foreseeability. Judges should also consider the likelihood of the injury, the magnitude of the burden of guarding against it, and the consequences of placing that burden on teachers. The court regarded the risk that a twelve-year-old boy would be assaulted in the museum as "minimal." The burden of constantly supervising children in cases such as this would be extremely heavy and would discourage teachers from planning many useful extracurricular activities. The court pointed out that even a game of hopscotch could suddenly break into a fight resulting in serious injury. And it would be practically impossible to require a teacher to watch each student at all times. Moreover, the judge noted that the museum in this case had been a "great educational enterprise," not a place of danger. Under these circumstances, the court ruled that the teachers did not have a duty to anticipate an assault or directly supervise the entire museum trip.

Similarly, a California district was not held liable when a twelve-year-old student was fatally injured playing a dangerous skateboard game at an elementary school playground about 5:30 P.M. The student's parents sued the school for negligent supervision and for maintaining grounds that were not locked. The court said that schools do *not* have a duty to supervise their grounds at all times. On the contrary, the duty of supervision is limited to school-related or encouraged functions and activities taking place during school hours. "To require round-the-clock supervision or prison-tight security for school premises," wrote the court, "would impose too great a financial burden on the schools."[4]

On the other hand, the judge in the *Mancha* case did acknowledge that constant supervision would be required on some field trips (e.g., where dangerous machinery is used or where there is reason to believe an assault might take place). Similarly, it might be reasonable to require teachers to provide close supervision for students working with dangerous equipment in school. This was the ruling in a 1979 Indiana case in which Tom Peters, a ninth-grade student, lost four fingers while working with a circular saw in an industrial arts class.[5] Peters was cutting wood; one of the saw guards was broken, and his teacher was supervising another class in an adjacent room. A state appeals court found it reasonable to hold the school liable for the damage to Peters because it allowed him to use improperly guarded machinery without the personal supervision of the teacher.

When do teachers have a duty to warn students?

Teachers always have a duty to instruct students concerning the proper use of equipment and facilities and to warn them of the dangers of improper use. This applies to all teachers and all school activities whether in a classroom, shop, gym, laboratory, or swimming pool. Failure to warn of known or foreseeable dangers constitutes negligence.

For example, a physical education instructor in New York told two students to box for three rounds without teaching them how to defend themselves. While the teacher sat in the bleachers, the students engaged in a "slugging match." As a result, one of the students suffered a cerebral hemorrhage. The teacher was found negligent for failing to warn the students about the dangers involved in boxing and for failing to provide instructions on how to box properly.[6]

A California high school student was welding a metal plate to the floor of his car when his gas tank exploded. The explosion was caused by the torch igniting gas vapors from an open tank, killing the student. As a result, a state court ruled that the teacher could be found guilty of negligence in allowing the student to weld the floor of his car without warning him of the dangers involved.[7] In an earlier California case, a student was injured in a high school chemistry class as a result of a teacher-conducted experiment requiring the use of explosive gases. The court ruled that the teacher could be found negligent for failing to properly warn the students about the dangers involved in the experiment and for failing to properly safeguard them from the possible results of such an experiment.[8]

How careful must teachers be?

The legal principles to be applied in cases of alleged negligence are clear: teachers have a duty to exercise reasonable care not to injure their students and to prevent them from being injured. "Reasonable care" is the degree of care a reasonable teacher of ordinary prudence would have used under the circumstances. The circumstances considered would include the age, maturity, and experience of the students and the extent of danger involved. When circumstances are more dangerous, as in shop or physical education, a teacher would be expected to exercise greater care. Failure to be more careful when dangers are greater—to provide careful instructions, clear warnings, and close supervision—would constitute negligence.

Whether a teacher exercised reasonable care is a factual issue decided by the jury or the trial judge. In *Sheehan*, the jury concluded that reasonable care was not exercised in leaving Margaret at the baseball game without supervision. In *Mancha* however, the judge did not feel that reasonable care required the teachers to provide constant supervision of twelve- to fifteen-year-old students while they visited a museum.

If teachers are careless, are they automatically liable for damages?

No. Injured students must show more than carelessness to recover; they must also show that the teacher's failure to use due care was the cause of the injury. For example, Wilmer Nash, an elementary school student from Louisiana, was waiting for the school bus to take him home. While playing with a girl, another girl struck him in the eye with a stick, leading to partial blindness. Wilmer's parents sued the school.

The court noted that the school is required to provide supervision while students are waiting for the school bus and that it failed to do so at the time Wilmer was injured. Nevertheless, the court did not find the school or the teachers liable because Wilmer's lawyer was not able to prove that careful supervision would have prevented the injury. "How," asked the judge, "could any teacher anticipate a situation where one child, while teasing another child, would be struck in the eye with a stick by a third child?" Even if educators can anticipate that accidents like this sometimes happen, there was no evidence that this injury could have been prevented if a teacher had been present. "As is often the case," concluded the judge, "accidents such as this, involving school children at play, happen so quickly that unless there was direct supervision of every child (which we recognize as being impossible), the accident can be said to be almost impossible to prevent."[9] Thus the court did not find the school liable for damages because Wilmer failed to show a causal connection between the absence of supervision and his accident.

In New York City, Alan Kaufman was critically injured when he jumped for a basketball and bumped heads with another student. Kaufman's father sued, alleging that the school failed to properly supervise the playing of this game. But the court ruled in favor of the school.[10] According to the court, even if there was an absence of supervision and even if "such absence constituted negligence, still under the circumstances, such lack of supervision was not the proximate cause of the accident." The presence of a teacher would not have prevented the boys from bumping their heads during the basketball game. "That," wrote the court, "is one of the natural and normal possible consequences or occurrences in a game of this sort which cannot be prevented no matter how adequate the supervision."

Are there defenses against liability?

Yes. Injured students who sue teachers and administrators for damages may encounter the defenses of contributory negligence, assumption of risk, or governmental immunity. Of these, contributory negligence is the most frequent and significant defense for teachers. Assumption of risk is rarely applicable except in cases of competitive athletics. And governmental immunity may protect some school districts, but it is not a defense for individual teachers.

What is contributory negligence?

If a student's own negligence contributed to the injury, the law in most states would consider the student "guilty of contributory negligence." Unless the injured student was very young, this would usually prevent him or her from recovering damages against a negligent teacher. This principle can be illustrated in the 1979 case of Jodeen Miles, a seventeen-year-old high school student from Nebraska. Jodeen was working on her senior project in Shop II when she attempted to remove a piece of wood from an operating machine with her hands, contrary to safe practice. As a result she severed two fingers and sued her instructor for negligent supervision.

Evidence indicated that the teacher had demonstrated the safe use of power tools, had assigned students to read a safety booklet, had required them to take a safety exam, and had watched Jodeen operate the machine safely. Although there was some question about whether the teacher was negligent in not directly supervising her at the time of the injury, the court ruled that Jodeen was negligent in failing to use the ordinary care that a student of her age and maturity "would have used under like circumstances." Thus the court dismissed Jodeen's claim and concluded that her contributory negligence was the "proximate cause of the injuries she sustained in this unfortunate accident."[11]

The Supreme Court of Wisconsin reached a similar finding after a high school sophomore was injured in a science class when a beaker of burning alcohol spilled on him.[12] The accident occurred when Ronald Rixman and two of his friends decided to light some heated alcohol on a table during an experiment, although they had been warned not to place any flame near alcohol. Evidence indicated that the teacher was negligent in the way he attempted to put out the fire, but the court ruled that the student was also negligent and that his negligence was a substantial factor in contributing to his injury.

A Louisiana school bus driver who negligently failed to repair a hole in the floor of his bus was not liable for damages to an injured student who was held contributorily negligent for deliberately sticking his foot through the hole, despite warnings from other students.[13] Similarly, a janitor who negligently unlocked a chemical supply room was held not liable for the injury to a seventeen-year-old high school student who carelessly experimented with some of the chemicals that were stolen from the unlocked room.[14] Thus, if students fail to exercise that degree of care usually expected of their age, knowledge, and experience, their contributory negligence might prevent or reduce recovery from a negligent teacher.

Does a student's negligence always prevent recovery?

No. The younger the student, the more difficult it is to prove contributory negligence. In most states, courts hold that very young children are incapable of contributory negligence. This means that even if the carelessness of such students contributed to their injury, this would not prevent them from recovering damages from a negligent teacher. In states such as Illinois, Michigan, North Carolina, Ohio, and Wisconsin, judges have ruled that students under seven years of age cannot be barred from recovery because of their negligence. In other states the age has been set at four, five, or six. For older children, usually those between seven and fourteen, there is often a "rebuttable presumption" that they are incapable of contributory negligence. With sufficient evidence concerning their intelligence, maturity, and the circumstances of the case, this presumption can be rebutted and the court can find them negligent.[15]

If a student is also negligent, can he or she still win?

At least thirteen states have comparative negligence statutes. These statutes have changed the common-law rule that holds contributory negligence on the part of a plaintiff prevents recovery against a negligent defendant. In states with comparative negligence statutes, a student's contributory negligence would not completely prevent him or her from recovering compensation from a negligent teacher. Thus in the Wisconsin case involving the student who lit hot alcohol and was injured when the teacher carelessly tried to put it out, a court or jury would compare the negligence of the student with that of the teacher. Since the negligence of both contributed to the student's injury, the court would reduce the amount of compensation awarded to the student by the relative proportion of his negligence. However, many comparative negligence statutes bar recovery if the plaintiff's negligence is equal to or greater than that of the defendant.[16]

When does a student assume the risk of being injured?

The doctrine of "assumption of risk" has been recognized as a defense against liability in activities such as competitive sports. It is based on the theory that people who appreciate the danger involved in an activity and voluntarily engage in it willingly expose themselves to certain predictable risks. The doctrine is illustrated by an Oregon case in which a fifteen-year-old student was seriously injured when he was tackled by two larger players in a football game. He sued, charging that it was negligent for the coach to allow an inexperienced freshman to compete against a team with older, heavier, and more experienced players. The court dismissed the charge and noted that "high school freshmen who go out for football are usually inexperienced" and have much to learn "about the intracacies of team play and not a little to learn about protecting themselves from injury to the extent that such is possible in playing the game." On every team there are some boys who are bigger and older and others who are younger and smaller. To say it is improper for inexperienced boys to play, wrote the judge, "would be the equivalent of saying that football could not properly be part of the athletic program of any high school."[17] Thus students who go out for football assume the risks inherent in the game. Similarly, golfers assume the obvious and ordinary risks involved in playing that game, such as being struck by a mishit golf ball. And the doctrine might bar recovery by a parent injured by a careless athlete or a wild throw while watching a sports event from the sidelines.

On the other hand, the Oregon court noted that "two football teams may be so disparate in size and ability that those responsible for supervising the athletic program would violate their duty in permitting the teams to play." It also acknowledged that it would be negligent for a coach to allow a student "to participate in a varsity football game without proper or sufficient instruction."[18] And a Louisiana court did not protect a coach who allowed a football player suffering from severe heatstroke to remain untreated for two hours before calling a doctor.[19] Thus, students do not assume the risk of improper coaching, gross mismatching of teams, or negligence in seeking medical treatment.

Can teachers use governmental immunity as a defense against negligence?

No. Even in states where this doctrine still can prevent negligence suits against school districts, students may sue individual teachers, who can be held personally liable for their negligence.

Governmental immunity is a common-law theory which holds that since the state and its agencies are sovereign, they cannot be sued without their consent and should not be held liable for the negligence of their employees. Some courts justify this practice on the grounds that public funds raised for schooling should not be legally diverted for noneducational purposes. But in recent years the doctrine has been widely condemned by legal writers. And an increasing number of state courts have abolished governmental immunity. According to the Pennsylvania Supreme Court, whatever may have justified the doctrine in the past, "it is clear that no public policy considerations presently justify its retention."[20] Today, governmental immunity has been abolished in most states and has been modified in others by authorizing school districts to insure their staff against possible negligence claims.[21]

Does a parental "waiver" or "release" prevent injured students from suing?

No. Parents cannot waive their children's claims for damages. While parental waivers may be important for public relations purposes, a teacher always has a duty to act with care, and a waiver does not change this duty. Therefore, even if schools require all parents to sign a waiver, release, or permission slip before allowing their children to participate in sports programs, field trips, or other special activities, this does not relieve teachers or schools of possible liability for negligence.

Might these waivers or releases bar suits by parents or adult students who sign them? Some lawyers argue that a release given before liability arises is meaningless and that it is against public policy to exempt a person or institution in advance from liability for their negligence.[22] Judges who do not consider waivers illegal are extremely strict in interpreting them, and, in practice, schools are generally unsuccessful in using waivers to prohibit negligence suits. This was illustrated by a New York case in which a student, Bruce Gross, sued a parachute training school. After breaking his leg when he landed on his first jump, Gross charged that the school was negligent in failing to instruct him properly. The school tried to block the suit on the grounds that Gross signed a responsibility release that said he would "waive any and all claims" he may have against the school "for any personal injuries . . . that I may sustain or which may arise out of my learning, practicing or actually jumping out of an aircraft."

Despite this release, the court allowed Gross to sue. According to the judge, such releases are "closely scrutinized and strictly construed" by the courts and will be enforced only when the limits of liability are "precisely defined" and any omissions plainly noted. According to the court, since the release does not contain any "specific provision which waives any claim for defendant's failure to instruct plaintiff properly," it does not release the school from negligence arising out of improper instructions.[23]

EDUCATIONAL MALPRACTICE

What is educational malpractice?

According to some lawyers and parents, schools should be held liable for negligent teaching that injures a student intellectually or psychologically just as they can be held liable for negligence that injures a student physically. They argue that teachers have a duty of care toward their students similar to the duty that doctors and lawyers have toward their patients and clients. Therefore they feel that teachers should be subject to educational malpractice suits like other professionals whose negligent practices cause injury.

Can teachers be held liable for educational malpractice?

Probably not. Despite three widely publicized educational malpractice suits decided between 1976 and 1979, students and their parents have not yet convinced the courts of the legal legitimacy of their claims. Because these suits included huge damage claims, ranging from $500,000 to $5,000,000, they often received front-page publicity when they were filed and insignificant coverage when the courts ruled against them. As a result, many teachers mistakenly believe that the sums claimed were amounts awarded, and some continue to be unreasonably fearful of malpractice suits.

The first two cases involve claims of nonfeasance, a failure to educate properly; and in these cases both the trial and appellate courts ruled in favor of the schools. The third case involved misfeasance, charges that the schools acted contrary to good professional standards. In this case two courts ruled in favor of the injured student but were finally overruled in a close vote by the New York Court of Appeals.

The *Peter Doe* Case[24]

In 1973, Peter W. Doe, a high school graduate with fifth-grade reading ability, sued the San Francisco School District for failing to provide him with adequate instruction in basic skills. A district intelligence test showed that Peter had at least an average IQ. And when Peter's mother repeatedly asked about her son's academic progress, she was assured by teachers and administrators that he was performing at or near grade level. Feeling that his poor reading ability hurt his chances to get a job, Peter charged that the school district had negligently assigned him to classes with unqualified instructors, placed him in inappropriate reading groups, failed to inform his parents about his educational problems, and advanced him through the grades without his acquiring the knowledge required.

Since schools had never been held liable for negligent teaching, this case presented three difficult questions. First, how would a court determine whether the San Francisco schools had been negligent? "Classroom methodology," wrote the judge, "affords no readily acceptable standards of care or cause or injury. The science of pedagogy itself is fraught with different and conflicting theories of how or what should be taught." Second, how can judges determine that the teacher's conduct was responsible for the student's injury? Achieving literacy in school, wrote the court, is "influenced by a host of factors which affect the pupil subjectively, from outside the formal teaching process." Besides the influence of the home and media, there are "physical, neurological, emotional, cultural, [and] environmental factors." Thus the court found no objective standard of care to use in judging a school's alleged misconduct and no way to determine a causal connection between the alleged negligence and the injury. Third, practical financial considerations also led to the rejection of Peter's claim. The court noted that in recent decades, public schools have been charged with educational failure and with responsibility for many of society's problems. Under these circumstances, "to hold them to an actionable 'duty of care' in the discharge of their academic functions would expose them to the tort [negligence] claims—real or imagined—of disaffected students or parents in countless numbers." Since schools already have so many problems, the court concluded that the ultimate consequence of permitting suits such as this "would burden them—and society—beyond calculation."

The *Donohue* Case[25]

Edward Donohue graduated from a Long Island, New York, high school in 1976. Although his teachers had passed him in every required subject, he was functionally illiterate—with the language, reading, and spelling ability of a third grader. He could not fill out a job application and had trouble finding work. Six months after graduation, he filed a $5 million lawsuit against his school system. He claimed the school negligently failed to evaluate his mental ability, failed to hire proper teachers, failed to teach him properly, failed to advise his parents of his difficulties, and failed to use accepted professional methods.

The New York courts ruled against his claim. The appellate court catalogued a series of moral, educational, economic, and administrative policy questions that would be involved in allowing such suits. Would recognizing a duty of care flood the courts with litigation? Would it lead to phony claims? Could the schools pay the damages? Would teachers be unfairly burdened in defending against malpractice suits? Would education suffer if these suits were allowed?

If malpractice suits were permitted, judges or juries would have to decide "whether one teaching method was more appropriate than another, or whether certain tests should have been administered or test results interpreted in one way rather than another, and so on, ad infinitum." According to the judge, courts are simply "inappropriate forums" to evaluate conflicting theories of how best to educate. Even if it were possible to decide the best way to teach an individual, "public education involves an inherent stress" between satisfying individual needs and the needs of the student body as a whole. And courts are not the place to decide "how best to utilize scarce educational resources to achieve these sometimes conflicting objectives." Finally, the court noted the practical impossibility of demonstrating that the school's alleged negligence caused Donohue's injury. "Failure to learn," wrote the court, "does not bespeak a failure to teach." Since there was no evidence that Donohue's classmates were illiterate, the court inferred that his illiteracy resulted from other sources. In addition to innate intelligence, the court noted that "the extent to which a child learns is influenced by a host of social, emotional, and other factors which are not subject to control by a system of public education."

On June 14, 1979, New York's highest court affirmed this decision.[26] It wrote that permitting educational malpractice suits would require the courts "not merely to make judgments as to the validity of broad educational policies—a course we have unalterably eschewed in the past—but, more importantly, to sit in review of the day-to-day implementation of these policies." The court concluded that recognizing these suits "would constitute blatant interference with the responsibility for the administration of the public school system."

The *Hoffman* Case

Danny Hoffman had a severe speech defect when he started kindergarten in 1956. When the school psychologist gave him an intelligence test that was primarily verbal, he scored 74 and was placed in a class for children with retarded mental development (CRMD). However, the school psychologist noted in his report that Danny "obviously understands more than he is able to communicate . . . and should be re-evaluated within a two-year period so that a more accurate estimation of his abilities can be made." But Danny remained in classes for the retarded for eleven years and was not retested until 1969 when he scored 94, placing him in the normal range of intelligence. As a result, he sued the school board for negligence in failing to reevaluate him within two years and for keeping him in CRMD classes, causing him diminished intellectual growth and psychological injury.

The court that ruled in favor of Danny said that by placing him in CRMD classes, the school created a duty to take reasonable steps to determine whether that placement was proper, especially since a mistake could have such serious consequences.[27] Unlike *Peter Doe* and *Donohue*, this case did not merely involve an omission of good teaching; it involved an active failure to follow sound educational practice. Thus the court said its decision would not mean that "the parents of the Johnnies who cannot read may flock to the courts and automatically obtain redress." According to the judge, this decision would not open the door to a flood of suits for nonfeasance since it only involved "*misfeasance* in failing to carry out the individualized and specific prescription" of the school's own psychologist. The court concluded that "not only reason and justice, but the law as well, cry out for [Danny's] right to a recovery," and it awarded him $500,000 as compensation for the school district's negligence.

But on December 17, 1979, the New York Court of Appeals reversed the lower courts' decisions.[28] As in *Donohue*, the judge wrote that malpractice suits should not be considered by the courts of this state. According to the court, the reasoning in *Donohue* applies with equal force to educational malpractice actions based on misfeasance or nonfeasance. In this 4–3 decision, the majority asserted that the judicial system is not the proper forum to decide the wisdom of placing a particular student in one of the many programs offered by the schools. The courts concluded that any dispute concerning proper placement can best be resolved by seeking a review of such professional educational judgment through the administrative processes that are provided by state statute.

Can a student ever win an educational malpractice suit?

Perhaps. The foregoing cases simply mean that a student could probably not win a malpractice suit in California or New York. And the policy considerations that made these courts reluctant to consider malpractice cases are likely to be given substantial weight by the courts of other states. On the other hand, even the New York court acknowledged that judges might intervene in malpractice cases under "exceptional circumstances involving gross deviations from defined public policy."[29] In other states, courts might be persuaded by the reasoning of judges who argued in favor of allowing the suits in both *Donohue* and *Hoffman*.

Justice Suozzi, for example, wrote that the question of whether Donohue's failure to learn was caused by the school system or other forces "is really a question of proof to be resolved at a trial," like any other question of fact. He pointed out that there is no reason to distinguish educational malpractice from other malpractice litigation. And he argued that dismissing Donohue's complaint without allowing him "his day in court, would merely serve to sanction misfeasance in the educational system." An alternative approach suggested by Justice Suozzi would be to sue on the grounds of intentional or fraudulent misrepresentation. If this approach were followed, teachers could be held liable for educational malpractice when they knowingly make false statements about a student's educational progress, which students and their parents then rely on. But we cannot predict whether other courts will be persuaded by Justice Suozzi's arguments.

In short, as of 1980, no educational malpractice suits have been successful. Such suits will probably be "thrown out of court" in California and New York. Whether other states will be more receptive to these suits in the future is uncertain.[30]

DAMAGES

What kinds of damages are awarded by the courts?

Courts can award several kinds of damages. The most common is *compensatory damages*. The purpose of this award is to compensate injured persons for their actual losses—for their medical expenses, lost salary, court costs, and other expenses incurred as a result of the defendant's negligence. Damages can be awarded for monetary, physical, or psychological injury. *Exemplary* or *punitive damages* are awarded where defendants have shown malice, fraud, or reckless disregard for an injured person's safety or constitutional rights. The purpose is to punish the defendants for their wrongful action and deter similar action in the future. *Nominal damages* are a small, symbolic award (e.g., one dollar), where the plaintiff has been wronged but has not been able to show actual damages. In earlier cases we have seen how students have sued for a variety of physical injuries and monetary losses. Next we look at a relatively new kind of claim, in which students sue schools for violating their constitutional rights.

Can school officials be held liable for violating a student's constitutional rights?

Yes. In the landmark case of *Wood* v. *Strickland*, two Arkansas students were unlawfully suspended for three months without due process, and their parents sued the school board for damages.[31] (See chapter 12 for a detailed discussion of due process rights of students.) In this 1975 decision, the U.S. Supreme Court ruled that school officials could be held liable "if they knew or reasonably should have known that the action they took within their sphere of official responsibility would violate the constitutional rights of the students affected."

What if school officials were honestly unaware of students' rights? The Court responded that an act violating a student's constitutional rights cannot be "justified by ignorance or disregard of settled, indisputable law on the part of one entrusted with supervision of students' daily lives." A school official, noted the Court, must be held to a standard of conduct based not only on good intentions "but also on knowledge of the basic, unquestioned constitutional rights of his charges."

These kinds of injuries have become known as "constitutional torts." Based on the *Wood* case, courts have held principals, superintendents, and school board members personally liable for damages to students or teachers whose rights they violated. Since teachers also serve as school officials, they too might be held liable under the principles of the *Wood* decision.

When a student's rights are violated, how will the amount of damages be determined?

In 1978 the Supreme Court answered this question in a case involving two Chicago students who were suspended twenty days without due process.[32] Their lawyer introduced no evidence to show any actual damages they had suffered because of their suspension, but he argued that they should receive substantial damages simply because they had been deprived of their constitutional rights.

The Court disagreed. It ruled that when a student is deprived of his constitutional rights, the amount of damages should depend on the circumstances of the case. A student should be awarded substantial sums for two reasons: (1) as punitive damages to deter or punish school officials who intentionally deprive the student of his or her rights; or (2) as compensatory damages for actual injury, which can include "mental and emotional distress" as well as financial loss. When the violation is unintentional and no actual injury is shown, the student is entitled to the award of a nominal sum of money.

In a related federal case, several Puerto Rican college students were unlawfully suspended for up to twelve days and sued for damages.[33] They were unable to prove an actual injury, such as "delay in meeting academic requirements or significant harm to plaintiff's reputation in the community or medically cognizable psychological distress." Nor were they able to show that their suspension was caused by school officials acting in bad faith or trying to harass them. Rather, the evidence indicated that the improper suspension "was nothing more than an isolated error in the administration of university discipline." Under these circumstances, the court refused to award punitive damages or compensatory damages for "general mental distress." Instead, the appeals court felt that the appropriate award in a case like this was to grant the students nominal damages plus the costs of their attorneys' fees.

Can teachers be awarded substantial damages if their constitutional rights are violated?

Yes. The same legal principles that determine the amount of damages to be awarded students also apply to teachers whose rights are violated. (See chapter 12 for a detailed discussion of due process rights of teachers.) A 1978 federal court illustrated these principles in the case of a Texas teacher.[34] Jerry Burnaman was a competent, dedicated, well-qualified educator who had taught successfully in the Bay City schools for more than a decade. Then a new principal and superintendent (the latter considered an expert in school law) were brought in to "shake up the school system and make substantial changes." Among the changes they wanted to make was to demote or remove Jerry Burnaman. They did this through a two-step process: they gave him the first unfavorable recommendation he had ever received and then recommended that his year-to-year contract not be renewed. Burnaman requested a hearing in mid-April to refute the negative recommendation. But the administration put off the hearing until late August, after which his discharge was upheld. (During this time he had further angered the administration by testifying in favor of another educator who had been fired.) As a result of these events, Burnaman sued the principal, the superintendent, and the school board, charging that they had violated his constitutional rights.

A federal judge agreed. The court found that the principal's negative evaluation was "inaccurate, nonfactual, grossly unfair," and not prepared in accordance with school policy requiring the use of objective evaluation standards. The court also found that in the evaluation the principal made statements he knew or should have known were inaccurate. The judge concluded that Burnaman's discharge violated his due process rights, was in retaliation for statements he had made that were protected by the First Amendment, and damaged his professional reputation. Therefore the jury granted him several awards: (1) compensatory damages of $16,440 for lost wages and $17,000 "for mental anguish accompanying the termination of his employment"; (2) exemplary damages of $25,000 against the superintendent and principal for acting with malice and intentionally depriving Burnaman of his constitutional rights; and (3) fees for Burnaman's attorney, which were incurred unnecessarily because of the "school board's unreasonable and obdurate obstinancy."

SUMMARY

In order to hold a teacher or administrator liable for a student's injury, the student must prove the following:

The teacher was negligent. Teachers have a duty to exercise reasonable care not to injure their students and to prevent them from being injured. "Reasonable care" is that degree of care that a reasonably prudent teacher would have exercised under the circumstances. The circumstances considered by the courts include the age, maturity, and experience of the students and the extent of danger involved. When conditions are more dangerous (e.g., in woodshop, a chemistry lab or a boxing class), a reasonable teacher would be expected to be more careful—to provide closer supervision, clear warnings, and careful instructions. If teachers do not use reasonable care, there is a breach of duty, and they are negligent.

There was no contributory negligence. If a student's own negligence contributed to his or her injury (i.e., if he or she failed to exercise that degree of care usually expected of a student of the same age, experience, and knowledge), the carelessness may prevent recovery. There are at least two limitations to this defense. In an increasing number of states, comparative negligence statutes provide that a plaintiff's contributory negligence would not prevent recovery but would reduce damages in proportion to his negligence. Second, the younger the student, the more difficult it is to prove contributory negligence. In the case of children under five or six, many courts will not even allow evidence of such negligence to be considered.

In recent years, courts have begun to hold school officials personally liable for damages if they violate the clearly established constitutional rights of students or teachers. Such awards could include compensatory damages for actual financial, physical, or psychological injury; exemplary or punitive damages for intentional violations; or nominal damages, where the violation is not intentional and no actual injuries are proven. On the other hand, courts have thus far been unwilling to allow students to sue teachers or administrators for educational malpractice as a result of negligent teaching.

In sum, the law requires teachers or administrators who carelessly cause injury to pay compensation. Teachers are subject to the same law as other citizens, who are held financially responsible for their negligence. Just as responsible drivers purchase liability insurance for their cars, so responsible teachers should purchase professional liability insurance to provide extra financial protection for their students and themselves.

NOTES

1. *Sheehan* v. *St Peters Catholic School,* 188 N.W.2d 868 (Minn. 1971).
2. *Id.*
3. *Mancha* v. *Field Museum of Natural History,* 283 N.E.2d 899 (Ill. 1972).
4. *Bartell* v. *Palos Verdes Peninsula School District,* 147 Cal. Rptr. 898 (1978).
5. *South Ripley Community School Corp.* v. *Peters,* 396 N.E.2d 144 (Ind. 1979).
6. *LaValley* v. *Stanford,* 70 N.Y.S.2d 460 (1947).
7. *Dutcher* v. *City of Santa Rosa High School District,* 290 P.2d 316 (Cal. 1955).
8. *Damgaard* v. *Oakland High School District,* 298 P. 983 (Cal. 1931).
9. *Nash* v. *Rapides Parish School Board,* 188 S.2d 508 (La. 1966).
10. *Kaufman* v. *City of New York,* 214 N.Y.S.2d 767 (1961).
11. *Miles* v. *School District No. 138 of Cheyenne County,* 281 N.W.2d 396 (Neb. 1979).
12. *Rixman* v. *Somerset Public Schools,* 266 N.W.2d 326 (Wis. 1978).
13. *Gilcrease* v. *Speight,* 6 S.2d 95 (La. 1942).
14. *Frace* v. *Long Beach City High School District,* 137 P.2d 60 (Cal. 1943).
15. 57 AM. JUR. 2d *Negligence* §363–64 (1971).
16. 57 AM. JUR. 2d *Negligence* §426, 431 (1971).
17. *Vendrell* v. *School District No. 26C Malheur County,* 376 P.2d 406 (Ore. 1962).
18. *Id.*
19. *Mogabgab* v. *Orleans Parish School District,* 239 So.2d 456 (La. 1970).
20. *Ayala* v. *Philadelphia Board of Public Education,* 305 A.2d 877 (Pa. 1973).
21. See note 8, *Davies* v. *City of Bath,* 364 A.2d 1269, 1272 (Me. 1976).
22. 66 AM. JUR. 2d *Release* §14, 33 (1971).
23. *Gross* v. *Sweet,* 407 N.Y.S.2d 254 (1978), 424 N.Y.S.2d 365 (1979).

24. *Peter W. Doe* v. *San Francisco School District,* 131 Cal. Rptr. 854 (1976).

25. *Donohue* v. *Copiague Union Free School District,* 407 N.Y.S.2d 874 (1978).

26. *Donohue* v. *Copiague Union Free School District,* 391 N.E.2d 1352 (N.Y. 1979).

27. *Hoffman* v. *Board of Education of the City of New York,* 410 N.Y.S.2d 99 (1978).

28. *Hoffman* v. *New York City Board of Education,* 424 N.Y.S.2d 376 (1979).

29. *Id.*

30. *Donohue* v. *Copiague Union Free School District,* 407 N.Y.2d 874 (1978) at 882–85; Cynthia Kelly and Bernice McCarthy, "Educational Malpractice Worrying You?" *Update on Law-Related Education,* Winter 1980, pp. 16–20.

31. *Wood* v. *Strickland,* 420 U.S. 308 (1975).

32. *Carey* v. *Piphus,* 435 U.S. 247 (1978).

33. *Perez* v. *Rodriguez Bou,* 575 F.2d 21 (1st Cir. 1978).

34. *Burnaman* v. *Bay City Independent School District,* 445 F. Supp. 927 (S.D. Tex. 1978).

6

What constitutes slander and libel?

OVERVIEW

The law of civil defamation makes it unlawful for one person to use language that tends to harm another person's reputation. Statements are defamatory if they tend to expose another person to hatred, shame, disgrace, contempt, or ridicule. When such statements are spoken, they are called *slander*; when such statements are written or communicated in some other permanent form, they are called *libel*.

Because defamation law is concerned with reputation, a statement can be defamatory only if it is communicated to a third person. For example, if a principal writes a defamatory letter to a teacher, no libel is involved unless someone besides the teacher sees the letter. In addition, a true statement cannot be defamatory.

This chapter examines how the courts have applied these principles in cases involving teachers. It addresses such questions as Can a teacher who ridicules students be found guilty of slander? Can a teacher who writes unflattering comments in a student's permanent file be guilty of libel? and Can a teacher sue a principal for slander for making critical remarks about teaching techniques?

DEFAMATORY STATEMENTS ABOUT TEACHERS

The *Pitka* Case[1]

How can teachers be libeled?

Elizabeth Pitka was a schoolteacher at North Pole, Alaska, a small community not far from Fairbanks. In August 1957 she resigned her position; a few days later, she withdrew the resignation with the consent of the North Pole School Board. On October 7, she wrote to the board saying that she wanted to resign "effective in thirty days from this date." On October 18, however, she received a letter advising her that the board had voted "to relieve you of your duties as head teacher and teacher as of October 18, 1957." After she ignored this letter, the board sent her another letter in which she was advised not to enter on school property. When she nonetheless returned to school, the board president had her arrested for disturbing the peace. That evening, the Fairbanks newspaper carried a front-page article describing Pitka's difficulties with the school board. The headline read *North Pole Teacher Fights Board*, with a subheading that stated: "Territorial Police Called to Expel Fired Schoolmarm, Dispute at Outlying Community Finds Teacher Defying School Board; She Is Arrested for Disorderly Conduct." Ms. Pitka claimed that these words were false and defamatory and sued the newspaper for libel.

The Supreme Court of Alaska ruled that the newspaper headline was libelous on its face (or libelous per se). The court explained that "for a publication to be libelous per se the words used must be so unambiguous as to be reasonably susceptible of only one interpretation—that is, one which has a natural tendency to injure another's reputation [footnote omitted]. If the publication on its face shows that it is of that type, then the judge has the right to tell the jury that the words are defamatory." Examining the specific language in the newspaper headline, the court concluded that it was libelous per se: "a statement that a school teacher was engaged in a 'fight' with her employer, that she was 'fired,' that the police were called to expel her, and that she was arrested for disorderly conduct, would have a natural tendency to diminish the esteem in which she was held and to result in a lack of confidence in her professional competency."

What kinds of statements are defamatory?

As the court pointed out in *Pitka*, some statements are automatically assumed to be defamatory. Historically, words have been held to be clearly defamatory on their face if they

1. impute a criminal offense
2. impute a loathsome disease (e.g., venereal disease, tuberculosis)
3. disparage professional competency (as in *Pitka*)
4. impute unchastity or immorality of a woman (e.g., a charge of adultery or incest)

Statements that do not fall into one of these four categories also can be defamatory. Such statements are not defamatory on their face, however, but require additional information to show that they injured someone's reputation. For example, a New York school principal sued a newspaper publisher for an article that appeared months after the principal had transferred to another school.[2] The article stated that at the school where the principal had formerly taught, a new principal had "brought harmony out of chaos," the "teachers would do anything in the world for him," and from 150 to 200 boys "used to come late to school and now the average is not more than seven or eight." Although these statements were not defamatory on their face, the former principal argued that anyone who knew he had previously been in charge of the school would interpret these statements to mean that he had lacked administrative ability.

The court did not agree that these additional facts made the statement libelous. The court concluded that no particular charge was made against the former principal, and there was no reason why readers should assume that the charges of chaos and disharmony referred to him. In addition, the court stated that there was no reason to assume that the principal was responsible for the tardiness of the boys: "He may have materially improved conditions during his administration of the school, and the parents or guardians of the pupils may have been responsible for their tardiness."

Courts in some states treat slander and libel differently. Reasoning that written statements are more likely to cause harm because they are permanent, some courts have not required that a written statement fall into one of the four categories listed above in order to be found defamatory on its face. In these states, any written words that expose a person to hatred, ridicule, or abuse are defamatory on their face; spoken words are actionable on their face only if they fall into one of the four listed categories.

What is the significance of finding that a statement is "defamatory on its face"?

If a statement is defamatory on its face, the law assumes that an individual's reputation has been injured. An individual who can prove that such a statement was made falsely will be awarded damages automatically. This individual is not required to show how he or she was injured by the false statements. The amount of the damages can vary, however, according to whether or not the statements were made maliciously.

If the false statements are not defamatory on their face, the injured party can collect monetary damages only by showing that he or she was directly harmed in some way by these statements. Examples of such harm could include physical or mental illness or loss of salary.

What are some examples of statements about teachers that have been found to be defamatory on their face?

The courts have ruled that any statements that falsely disparage a teacher's professional competence are defamatory on their face. In an early Ohio case,[3] for example, the court found the following statement about a teacher, made by the president of the board of education, was defamatory on its face: "He is not a fit person to teach any school. He is no good as a teacher and he will not get the school another year. He plays for dances and then goes to sleep in the school room during school hours." In addition, courts have held all the following charges defamatory on their face: a newspaper article that described a college professor as "illiterate, uncultivated, coarse, and vulgar" and that also conveyed the impression that he made himself ridiculous "both in his method of instruction and by his public lectures";[4] a statement before the school board that a teacher was so "intoxicated at the public dinner at Bundick's creek . . . that it was necessary that [he] be brought to the table";[5] and a teacher's statement that a principal allowed students to "pet" in the hallways without taking any disciplinary action.[6] In addition, statements falsely charging teachers with criminal activity have been held to be defamatory on their face, as when an Indiana newspaper printed an article headlined *A School Child Killed in Pike County by a Teacher.*[7]

In order to be defamatory, however, the false statements must relate to the teacher's professional performance. For example, an Iowa court ruled that a letter from a finance company to a school superintendent stating that a teacher in his district owed money on a debt was not defamatory on its face.[8] The court concluded that a statement that a teacher owed an unpaid debt did not reflect on professional ability or qualifications: "The statements allegedly made of plaintiff [teacher] do not impute insolvency or that plaintiff has failed to pay the debt from dishonest motives and from a desire to defraud the creditor. They do not relate to her profession."

When an individual is slandered or libeled, how is the amount of damages determined?

In a suit for libel or slander, the jury has the responsibility to listen to the evidence and decide if the plaintiff is entitled to any damages and, if so, how much. As noted in earlier questions, the jury can assume damage to the plaintiff's reputation when the defendant has made a statement that is defamatory on its face. The amount of damages awarded to the plaintiff will vary, however, according to how seriously the jury feels the plaintiff's reputation has been harmed. In making a decision, the jury can consider such factors as the plaintiff's general character and reputation in the community, the nature of the statements made, and the number of people who heard or read these statements. Quantifying damage to reputation is obviously a difficult task, and the size of the awards varies considerably.

For example, a South Dakota jury awarded only one dollar to a secretary after his employer falsely told others that he was a crook, that he had stolen a carpet, and that he belonged in the penitentiary.[9] A New York jury awarded an attorney damages of $100 after a woman remarked within earshot of his wife and some of his neighbors: "You're no lawyer. You're a crook. You took graft."[10] A principal and vice principal in West Virginia were each awarded $7,000 after the school superintendent charged them with willful neglect of duty at a meeting of the county board of education.[11]

In addition to injury to reputation, damage awards may include compensation for mental or physical injury or for other financial losses suffered as a result of defamatory statements. A Louisiana court awarded a customer $3,250 after she had been falsely accused of shoplifting in a clothing store.[12] Convinced that she was shoplifting, a store employee had grabbed Mrs. Levy after she left a dressing room and stopped her from leaving the store. In order to establish her innocence, Mrs. Levy emptied her purse on the floor and raised her blouse and lowered her slacks; these activities occurred in front of forty to sixty people. The jury awarded Mrs. Levy $2,500 to compensate her for the humiliation and embarrassment she suffered; it also awarded her $750 for mental pain and suffering. A District of Columbia jury awarded an attorney $15,000 in damages to compensate him for mental anguish and the business he lost after one of his clients was falsely informed that he had acted fraudulently in the past, practiced bigotry, and should be sued for malpractice.[13]

Finally, if the defendant has acted maliciously or with reckless disregard for the truth, the jury can award punitive damages. These damages are imposed to punish the defendant and deter such further behavior. In Georgia, for example, the court awarded $200,000 to a former university student after the head of the chemistry department falsely accused him of forging paychecks.[14] The award of punitive damages was based on the fact that the university professor made defamatory remarks about the student to many people not involved in the criminal investigation and that he continued the claim that the student was guilty long after the university investigation had disclosed that the discrepancy in the accounts had been caused by an embezzler in the professor's department.

Can teachers sue administrators for defamatory statements made in letters of recommendations or on evaluation forms?

The courts have ruled that school administrators generally have what is known as a "qualified privilege" to comment on matters concerning the operation of the school. Under this qualified privilege, school administrators will not be liable for defamatory statements made in good faith that they had the duty to make. This privilege extends to comments made in letters of recommendation.

For example, a Wisconsin court ruled that a school superintendent could not be sued for libel when he wrote a negative letter of recommendation about a teacher formerly employed as a speech therapist in his school district.[15] The teacher, Mr. Hett, had applied for a job at another school and had listed the superintendent as a reference. In writing a letter in reply to a request for information, the superintendent made the follow statements: "I, personally, feel that Mr. Hett does not belong in the teaching field. He has a rather odd personality, and it is rather difficult for him to gain the confidence of his fellow workers and the boys and girls with whom he works." The court ruled that the superintendent's statements were made in good faith and as part of his official responsibilities, thus Hett could not sue him for libel: "The background of the relationship of Hett and Ploetz [the superintendent] satisfactorily demonstrates that the latter's negative recommendation was grounded on the record and not upon malice. Ploetz was not an intermeddler; he had a proper interest in connection with the letter he wrote."

Similarly, a Kentucky court ruled that a college president's letter to a student's father was privileged.[16] The college president had written two letters to the student's father describing how the student had indecently exposed himself "at the open window of his room in such way as persons traveling the street saw his nude form and were embarrassed thereby," and asking him to withdraw from the college. In a suit for libel brought against the president by the student's father, the court found the statement to be protected by a qualified privilege. The court concluded that in writing the letter, the president was acting both out of duty and in good faith:

> ... the president of the school, being in charge of the student body, owed a duty to the father and family of young Baskett [the student], which he could not discharge except by faithfully, fully, and accurately reporting to the father and family the progress and deportment of the student.... In this case Dr. Crossfield [the president] appears to have done only what his duty required of him. He gently and rather apologetically wrote and sent to the father of the student the two letters of which complaint is made. That these letters were written in the utmost good faith and for the good of the father and the dismissed student is beyond cavil.[17]

School officials can lose this qualified privilege if they act in bad faith or without regard for whether the statements are true. For example, the president of a Texas commercial college incorrectly wrote a letter to a student's prospective employer stating that the student "was arrested and put in jail for stealing a typewriter."[18] Evidence showed that the president later discovered that this charge was false but did not correct it because he wanted the job filled by a graduate of the college. The court ruled that his statements in the letter were not privileged.

In some situations, courts have gone even further, ruling that school officials' statements are "absolutely privileged," under which an administrator cannot be found liable for defamation even in cases where he or she acted maliciously or in bad faith. For example, a Missouri teacher sued a school superintendent for slander, claiming that she was defamed when he falsely stated at a school board meeting in resonse to her request for the reasons for her not being reemployed: "that plaintiff [teacher] had disobeyed school rules and regulations; that plaintiff was insubordinate, and that plaintiff was insufficient and inadequate with her students."[19] In reaching its decision, the court first noted that whether a statement is subject to an absolute or a qualified privilege depends on "the occasion or circumstances surrounding the utterance of the alleged slander." The court concluded that the superintendent's statements were absolutely privileged because they were made in response to the teacher's request: ". . . the publication of false and defamatory matter of another is *absolutely* privileged if the other consents thereto. . . ." When the teacher asked the superintendent why she was not going to be reemployed the following school year, the superintendent was "absolutely protected in his explanation" and was not liable for slander.

Courts have also held that statements made by public officials during judicial, legislative, or official executive proceedings are absolutely privileged. Thus, where school officials have made comments about teachers as part of their administrative duties, some courts have ruled that these statements are also absolutely privileged. An Illinois court dismissed a suit for slander against a superintendent of schools who made statements to the board of education that a teacher's performance in the classroom was poor, that he had done poorly in certain college courses, and that he had left his room unattended.[20] The court explained that "all communications, either verbal or written, passing between public officials pertaining to their duties and in the conduct of public business are of necessity absolutely privileged and such matters cannot be made the basis of recovery in a suit at law." Finding that the superintendent was carrying out an official duty when making these comments, the court dismissed the suit against him.

In general, then, statements by school officials are subject to a qualified privilege when they are made in good faith and about matters concerning school administration. School officials are not liable for defamatory statements that fall under this qualified privilege even if such statements turn out to be false. School officials are liable if they act maliciously or with reckless disregard for the truth of their statements, or if their statements concern matters outside the scope of their official duties.

In addition, some statements by school officials are held to be absolutely privileged; in those situations, school officials can never be held liable for defamatory statements. An absolute privilege can extend to statements to which the other party consents or invites, or statements made in the course of judicial, legislative, or administrative proceedings.

DEFAMATORY STATEMENTS ABOUT STUDENTS

Can students sue teachers for written statements in students' files?

The Family Educational Rights and Privacy Act of 1974 guarantees students' rights to privacy in their educational records.[21] In general it provides that in schools receiving federal funds, students and their parents must have access to permanent school records. This right becomes the student's exclusively when she or he becomes eighteen or is attending an institution of postsecondary education. Under the act, teachers can make notes about students for their own personal use. As long as a teacher does not show these notes to any person except a substitute teacher, students and their parents have no right to see them. In addition, the act provides that students can give up their rights to have access to certain papers. (See chapter 17 for a more detailed discussion of this act.)

Teachers can be sued for defamatory statements published in students' permanent records. In an early case in Oklahoma, a teacher was found to have libeled a student after he made a note in the school register that the student was "ruined by tobacco and whisky."[22] In order to avoid being sued for defamation, teachers should be careful to accurately describe relevant, observable behavior rather than make derogatory remarks about students.

Can teachers be sued for ridiculing students in classrooms or in the teacher's lounge?

If teachers knowingly spread false gossip that harms a student's reputation, they can be found guilty of slander. Nevertheless, some court decisions suggest that a teacher's statements are subject to a qualified privilege if they are made as part of the teacher's professional responsibilities. For example, a Georgia court held that a college president's statements charging a student with theft were conditionally privileged when made during an investigation of the crime.[23] The president had accused the student of theft during a meeting with the president, the student, and the college chaplain. The court ruled that such statements were conditionally privileged because they were made by the president as part of his official responsibility to "inquire into and regulate the behavior of members of the student body." Although the state supreme court later found that there was no slander because the student had not proved that the chaplain actually heard this statement, the court discussed the privilege question.[24] This reasoning was not essential in reaching its decision, but the Supreme Court of Georgia agreed with the lower court that such statements would be conditionally privileged, invoking the concept of *in loco parentis* as support:

> This case can not be justly decided if the fact that it involves the relationship, standards and duties of a college faculty and the students is lost sight of. Does a father slander his child when he accuses it of wrong in the presence of its mother? The parent-child relationship very closely parallels that of a college faculty and students in matters of discipline, discovering misconduct and punishing therefor. Any legal restraint of either parent or faculty in the reasonable discharge of duty, not only would not be beneficial to the child or student but might well be disastrous to them.[25]

Following this reasoning, a teacher's statements may be conditionally privileged if they are made as part of the disciplinary process or administrative responsibilities.

Can students sue teachers for negative statements made in letters of recommendation?

The Family Educational Rights and Privacy Act provides that parents and students do not have the right to see letters of recommendation to colleges or prospective employers placed in students' records prior to January 1, 1975. In addition, the act states that a student can waive the right to see such letters if the student, upon request, is notified of the names of all persons making such recommendations and if the recommendations are used solely for the purpose for which they were specifically intended.

Again, however, if students gain access to these letters, teachers can be sued for any defamatory statements they may have made. The same general principles outlined regarding administrators' liability in suits by teachers apply here: a teacher's statements about a student will be at least conditionally privileged when a student lists a teacher as a reference and the teacher responds to such a request for information about the student's competence and character. Thus, unless a teacher acts maliciously by making statements he or she knows are untrue, the teacher will not be liable for any negative statements made in such letters.

Can students sue teachers for giving them low grades?

Low grades certainly may expose students to shame or ridicule, but the courts have not found that giving low grades is libelous. The courts have reasoned that they do not have the expertise to evaluate the accuracy of a teacher's grading decision and will not intervene in grading unless it can be shown that school officials acted in bad faith.

This philosophy was illustrated in an early Massachusetts case where the court ruled that it was not proper for a jury even to examine the question whether a high school student had been properly dismissed for failure to attain an adequate standard of scholarship.[26] The court explained: "So long as the school committee act in good faith, their conduct in formulating and applying standards and making decisions touching this matter is not subject to review by any other tribunal. . . . It is an educational question, the final determination of which is vested by law in the public officers charged with the performance of that important duty." In effect, this position prohibits any libel suit by students because the courts refuse to consider the "truth" or "falsity" of the grade.

A federal district court in Vermont applied the same reasoning in a more recent case in which a medical student sued the state college of medicine claiming that he should not have been dismissed for failing to attain a proper standard of scholarship.[27] The third-year medical student failed the pediatrics-obstetrics course and was not allowed to advance to the fourth year because of a college of medicine rule stating that no student could continue who had failed 25 percent or more of the third-year courses. This student's petition to repeat his third-year work was denied, and he was dismissed from school. He then sued school officials, claiming that his work was of passing quality and that he should not have been dismissed.

The court ruled that school authorities had "absolute discretion in determining whether a student [had] been delinquent in his studies" and that the court would only consider cases where the student could show that his dismissal was motivated by "arbitrariness, capriciousness or bad faith." The court explained: "The reason for this rule is that in matters of scholarship, the school authorities are uniquely qualified by training and experience to judge the qualifications of a student, and efficiency of instruction depends in no small degree upon the school faculty's freedom from interference from other noneducational tribunals. It is only when the school authorities abuse this discretion that a court may interfere with their decision. . . ."

PUBLIC OFFICIALS

Do any constitutional considerations apply in slander or libel cases?

Yes. In *New York Times* v. *Sullivan*, the Supreme Court ruled that the First Amendment guarantees of freedom of speech and press require that public officials cannot be awarded damages for libel or slander unless they can prove that such statements were made with actual malice.[28] "Actual malice" means that the defendant made the libelous or slanderous statements either knowing that they were false or with a reckless disregard for the truth of the statements. An elected official in Montgomery, Alabama, sued the *New York Times*, alleging that he had been libeled by an advertisement in that paper that included false statements about police brutality and harassment directed against students who had participated in a civil rights demonstration. Since Mr. Sullivan's duties included supervision of the police department, he claimed that these statements referred to him and were libelous.

The Alabama trial court instructed the jury that such statements were "libelous per se" since they concerned Sullivan's execution of his public duties and that injury to his reputation was assumed under the law. In a landmark decision, the Supreme Court disagreed. The Court ruled that the First and Fourteenth amendments required that public officials must meet a higher standard of proof in defamation suits. The Court first noted that the First Amendment embodied "a profound national commitment to the principle that debate on public issues should be uninhibited, robust, and wide-open, and that it may well include vehement, caustic, and sometimes unpleasantly sharp attacks on government and public officials." A rule that would require a critic of official conduct to guarantee the truth of all factual assertions or risk a suit for defamation would be inconsistent with this principle; it would make people afraid to voice their criticism, thus dampening the vigor and limiting the variety of political debate. The Court therefore protected individuals who criticized public officials by holding that such individuals would not be liable for defamation unless they acted with "actual malice."

Can teachers or students be considered "public officials"?

Yes. The *New York Times* standard would apply to any teacher or student serving as a duly elected public official. For example, an elected member of a board of education would be considered a public official.[29] This standard would also apply to an individual appointed a member of such a public body.[30]

An Arizona court has also held that elected student government representatives can be public officials.[31] The court reasoned that it would be inappropriate that there be "one law of libel in this state for 'public officials' off the campuses of our state universities and another law of libel applicable to the student government officers upon such campuses, when the systems of politics and news media are so obviously patterned after the situation off campus, and when the publication is primarily addressed in the 'interested community.'" The court therefore ruled that a law student who was a duly elected member of the Student Senate of the University of Arizona qualified as a public official under *New York Times* v. *Sullivan*.

Does the New York Times standard apply to all defamatory statements made about public officials?

No. The *New York Times* standard applies only when the defamatory statements relate to "official conduct." For example, a New York court held that this standard applied in a libel suit brought by a member of a board of education when a newspaper made charges that she was pressuring her son's math teacher to raise his grade.[32] While conceding that she was a public official, the school board member argued that the *New York Times* standard should not apply because the defamatory statements concerned private rather than official conduct. The court agreed that the *New York Times* rule would not apply to statements about conduct as a private citizen and mother. However, since these charges stated that she had used the power of her office for personal gain, the court found that they related to her duties as a public official and that the newspaper would not be liable unless she could show that the statements were made with actual malice.

Can the New York Times standard be applied to others besides public officials?

Yes. The Supreme Court has extended the *New York Times* standard to public figures. A "public figure" is one who either (1) achieves general fame or notoriety in the community or (2) "voluntarily injects himself or is drawn into a particular controversy and thereby becomes a public figure for a limited range of issues. In either case such persons assume special prominence in the resolution of public questions."[33]

Depending on the circumstances, administrators, teachers, and students could all qualify as public figures. For example, a Texas court held that a uni-

versity professor was a public figure after he led an anti-Vietnam war demonstration "which aroused a considerable amount of interest and comment
in the city of El Paso."[34] A Maryland court found that a high school principal
fell within the "public figure–public official" classification.[35] In that case, the
local newspaper had published an article entitled "Our High School Principals: How Good Are They?" When Mr. Dunn was given an "unsuited" rating
in this article, he brought a libel action against the paper. On the ground that
his suitability for the position was "a matter of public or general interest or
concern," the court ruled that the *New York Times* standard applied.

What proof is necessary to show "actual malice"?

To prove actual malice, the plaintiff must show that the defendant made the
objectionable statements either with knowledge that they were false or with
reckless disregard of whether or not they were false. In attempting to meet
this test, the plaintiff is allowed to inquire into the defendant's state of mind
at the time the statements were made and to gather other evidence to show
that the defendant knew the statements were false when made.[36] A Louisiana
court, for example, concluded that a doctor had proved that a grocery store
owner falsely accused him of being a communist when he was a candidate
for public office.[37] After the store owner testified that, on an earlier occasion,
he had defended the doctor when someone else accused him of being a communist, the trial court stated that it "was not greatly impressed with the defendant's testimony or his defense as a whole," that much of what he said
was "poppycock," and concluded that his remarks about the doctor were
completely untrue and were meant to harm, belittle, and malign the doctor.

A high school principal did not prove actual malice when he sued a black
citizens' group that published a pamphlet criticizing his supervision of the
school.[38] The pamphlet called the principal "an Uncle Tom, a traitor to his
race, a stooge, a stool pigeon, an informer and a betrayer of his people." Although the defendants testified that it was their intention to have the principal removed from his position at the school, the court ruled that this ill will
did not constitute actual malice. Since the principal offered no evidence that
the defendants knew the statements were false or that they were made with
reckless disregard for whether they were false, he did not meet his burden of
proving actual malice, and the suit was dismissed.

SUMMARY

Both teachers and administrators who make false statements that harm
teachers' and students' reputations are liable for defamation. A written comment in a student's school record can lead to a libel suit. A gossip session in
the teachers' lounge can support a charge of slander.

In many situations, however, teachers and administrators are protected in
making statements about other teachers' and students' character and ability.

The courts have ruled that educators who are acting in good faith have a "qualified privilege" to comment on matters that are within their scope of authority. For example, an educator can explain to a parent why a student was disciplined without being liable for defamation. Even if these statements actually turn out to be false, the teacher is not liable for defamation unless found to be acting maliciously (knowing that these statements were false when made) or from some improper purpose (lying to the parent because of personal animosity toward the student). This conditional privilege also protects teachers and administrators who write negative evaluations or letters of recommendation.

In some situations, the courts have also ruled that educators' statements are absolutely privileged and that they cannot be held liable even if their comments were made maliciously. An absolute privilege could apply, for example, to protect an administrator who presented the reasons for a teacher's dismissal at a board of education meeting.

Of course, teachers can also sue individuals who defame them. When teachers are falsely charged with matters relating to their professional competence, they can collect damages to compensate for injury to their reputation. If such statements are clearly related to a teacher's professional competence (e.g., a charge of brutality against students), the courts automatically assume that a teacher has been injured and entitled to some amount of damages. In other situations, a teacher may have to prove that the comments actually did harm his or her reputation in order to be awarded damages. In addition to collecting damages for injury to reputation, teachers can also be awarded monetary damages to compensate them for mental or physical injury or financial loss. Punitive damages can be awarded when false statements are made maliciously.

Teachers and administrators found to be either public officials or public figures have a higher burden of proof in defamation suits. In *New York Times* v. *Sullivan* the Supreme Court ruled that public officials/public figures can be awarded damages for libel or slander only if they can prove that the defendant made defamatory statements with actual malice. To prove actual malice, the plaintiff must show that the defendant made the statement either knowing that it was false or with reckless disregard for whether it was true or false.

NOTES

1. *Fairbanks Publishing Company* v. *Pitka*, 376 P.2d 190 (Alaska 1962).
2. *Barringer* v. *Sun Printing and Publishing Ass'n*, 145 N.Y.S. 776 (1914).
3. *Mulcahy* v. *Deitrick*, 176 N.E. 481 (Ohio App. 1931).
4. *Triggs* v. *Sun Printing and Publishing Ass'n*, 71 N.E. 739 (N.Y. App. 1904), at 742.
5. *Ford* v. *Jeane*, 106 So. 558 (La. 1925), at 558–59.
6. *Larive* v. *Willitt*, 315 P.2d 732 (Cal. App. 1957).
7. *Doan* v. *Kelley*, 23 N.E. 266 (Ind. 1890).
8. *Ragland* v. *Household Finance Corporation*, 119 N.W.2d 788 (Iowa 1963).

9. *Walkon Carpet Corporation* v. *Klapprodt*, 231 N.W.2d 370 (S.D. 1975).

10. *Kruglak* v. *Landre*, 258 N.Y.S.2d 550 (1965).

11. *Chambers* v. *Smith*, 198 S.E.2d 806 (W. Va. 1973).

12. *Levy* v. *Duclaux*, 324 So.2d 1 (La. App. 1976).

13. *Collins* v. *Brown*, 268 F.Supp. 198 (D.C. 1967).

14. *Melton* v. *Bow*, 247 S.E.2d 100 (Ga. 1978).

15. *Hett* v. *Ploetz*, 121 N.W.2d 270 (Wis. 1963).

16. *Baskett* v. *Crossfield*, 228 S.W. 673 (Ky. App. 1921).

17. *Id.* at 675–76.

18. *Lattimore* v. *Tyler Commercial College*, 24 S.W.2d 361 (Tex. Ct. App. 1930), at 362.

19. *Williams* v. *School District of Springfield R-12*, 447 S.W.2d 256 (Mo. 1969), at 267.

20. *McLaughlin* v. *Tilendis*, 253 N.E.2d 85 (Ill. App. 1969).

21. 20 U.S.C.A. §1232, *et seq.* (West 1974).

22. *Dawkins* v. *Billingsley*, 172 P. 69 (Okla., 1918).

23. *Davidson* v. *Walter*, 91 S.E.2d 520 (Ga. App. 1956).

24. *Walter* v. *Davidson*, 102 S.E.2d 686 (Ga. App. 1958), *rev'd.* 104 S.E.2d 113 (Ga. 1958).

25. *Id.* at 115.

26. *Barnard* v. *Inhabitants of Shelburne*, 102 N.E. 1095 (Mass. 1913), at 1096.

27. *Connelly* v. *University of Vermont and State Agricultural College*, 244 F.Supp. 156 (D. Vt. 1965).

28. 376 U.S. 254 (1964).

29. *Cabin* v. *Community Newspapers, Inc.*, 270 N.Y.S.2d 913 (1966).

30. *Henry* v. *Collins*, 380 U.S. 356 (1965).

31. *Klahr* v. *Winterble*, 418 P.2d 404 (Ariz. App. 1966).

32. *Cabin, supra.*

33. *Gertz* v. *Robert Welch, Inc.*, 418 U.S. 323 (1974), at 351.

34. *El Paso Times, Inc.* v. *Trexler*, 447 S.W.2d 403 (Tex. 1969), at 404.

35. *Kapiloff* v. *Dunn*, 343 A.2d 251 (Md. App. 1975).

36. *Herbert* v. *Lando*, 441 U.S. 153 (1979).

37. *Sas Jaworsky* v. *Padfield*, 211 So.2d 122 (La. App. 1968).

38. *Reaves* v. *Foster*, 200 So.2d 453 (Miss. 1967).

7

How does copyright law affect me?

OVERVIEW

Copyright law is designed to give authors and artists the right to own their creative works. Under principles that state laws adopted from the law in England (the common law), an author has the right to publish his or her writings first. In addition to this common-law "right of first publication," federal law also provides protection, giving authors the exclusive right to control who can make copies of their work. A comprehensive law[1] that became effective on January 1, 1978, describes the procedures that must be followed to obtain a federal copyright. This chapter describes this law, answering such questions as What materials can be copyrighted? How long does a copyright last? Can teachers copyright their own teaching materials? Can teachers make photocopies of published materials without violating copyright laws? and What are the penalties for violating copyright laws?

MATERIALS COVERED BY COPYRIGHT

The *Williams* Case[2]

Do teachers have a copyright on their own materials?

Operating a business known as Class Notes, Edwin Weisser published and sold outlines and notes from various courses at the University of California at Los Angeles (UCLA). Mr. Weisser obtained these materials by paying UCLA students to attend classes and turn over copies of their notes. In 1965 Mr. Weisser paid Karen Allen to attend Dr. Williams' class in Anthropology I and turn over her typed copies of his lectures. After Ms. Allen delivered her notes, Mr. Weisser put a copyright notice on them in the name of Class Notes and sold them to other students. When Dr. Williams discovered that copies of his lectures were being offered for sale by Class Notes, he sued Mr. Weisser. Dr. Williams claimed that the lecture notes were his property and that they were protected by a common-law copyright. He asked the court to prohibit Mr. Weisser from publishing the notes and to award him a sum of money as damages.

The California court agreed with Dr. Williams. First, the court found that the lectures were indeed protected by a common-law copyright. Mr. Weisser argued that the lectures were "merely lightly embellished and thinly disguised paraphrasings of the works of others, both as to form and content . . . [and were] wholly in the public domain." The court, however, found that the lectures were created by Dr. Williams and were therefore entitled to the common-law copyright protection that gave Dr. Williams the first right to publish the notes.

The court also rejected Mr. Weisser's argument that Dr. Williams lost his common-law copyright protection when he delivered his lectures. The court recognized that an author loses a copyright under common law after the material has been made generally available but concluded that Dr. Williams was not making a "general" publication when he delivered his lectures: ". . . where the persons present at a lecture are not the general public, but a limited class of the public, selected and admitted for the sole and special purpose of receiving individual instruction, they may make any use they can of the lecture, to the extent of taking it down in shorthand, for their own information and improvement, but cannot publish it. . . ."

Finally, the court considered the question whether the university owned the copyright on Dr. Williams' lecture notes. The court noted that while the common law gives the copyright to the creator of an intellectual/artistic work, employers own the copyright on materials their employees produce as part of their job. Under this doctrine of "work for hire," the employer owns the copyright only when the material is created as part of the employee's duties and when the employer has control over the employee's work product. In the case of a university professor, the court concluded that this doctrine did not apply and that Dr. Williams owned the copyright on his lectures. As the court explained: "A university's obligation to its students is to make the subject matter covered by a course available for study by various methods, including classroom presentation. . . . As far as the teacher is concerned, neither the record in this case nor any custom known to us suggests that the university can prescribe his way of expressing the ideas he puts before his students."

Finding that Mr. Weisser had indeed violated Dr. Williams' common-law copyright in his lecture notes, the court ordered Mr. Weisser to pay him $1,-500 as damages.

What material can be covered by a copyright?

As the court explained in *Williams*, a common-law copyright protects all intellectual products before publication, including writings, drawings, photographs, and musical scores. The Copyright Act of 1976 supersedes this protection, however, providing that federal copyright law covers all works that "are fixed in a tangible medium of expression."[3] Federal copyright therefore applies as soon as an author uses a pen or a typewriter to put ideas on paper or as soon as an artist puts paint on a canvas. In addition, federal law covers such other "fixed" works as sound recordings and computer programs. In fact, almost the only creative works not covered by federal copyright law are extemporaneous performances such as dances or musical compositions. In those situations, state law still applies to protect the creator's ownership of the artistic product.

What is the significance of having a copyright under federal law?

Any author or artist who has a federal copyright has, in effect, a monopoly on the materials created; the author or artist has the right to control how the materials are to be distributed to the general public. Under the new copyright act (1976), the copyright owner has the exclusive right to reproduce the work, prepare derivative works, distribute copies by sale or other transfer, and display the work publicly. Under this law, "reproduction" includes fixing a work in any form through which it can be "perceived, reproduced, or otherwise communicated, either directly or with the aid of a machine or device"[4] and therefore includes copying a work on paper or onto a magnetic tape or other recording device. An author's or artist's work protected by this federal copyright law enables the copyright owner to go to federal court to sue anyone who reproduces, distributes, or displays copies of this work without permission.

How can a teacher obtain a copyright?

As noted, federal law gives authors and artists the right to own their creative works as soon as they are "fixed" in a tangible form. In order to exercise this right, an author or artist must put a copyright "notice" on all copies of the work. The act provides that the notice must include: (1) the symbol © or the word "copyright" or "copr.," (2) the year of publication, and (3) the name of the owner of the copyright. The act also states that the notice shall be placed "in such manner and location as to give reasonable notice of the claim of copyright."[5] The act further provides that the Register of Copyrights has the authority to describe specific methods for affixing this notice.

By following these procedures an author or artist will have a copyright under federal law. An author who wishes to be fully protected, however, must also register the copyright and deposit two copies of the work with the copyright office within three months after the work is published. A registration fee of $10 is also required.[6] An author who does not register a copyright will not be able to maintain a suit against anyone who makes unauthorized copies. Registration and deposit are also necessary before a court can take certain actions against those who violate a copyright.

Is a copyright lost if the author does not follow these procedures?

Under common law, the copyright was lost as soon as there was a general publication of the work. After this public distribution, the author had to turn to federal law for copyright protection. Under prior federal law, an author who distributed a work without complying with copyright notice provisions lost all rights to copy and distribute the work. At this point, the work was said to "fall into the public domain," and anyone was free to copy, distribute, or perform the work.

The situation is different today. Federal law now provides that a copyright is not lost when an author or artist omits the copyright notice from only a "relatively small number"[7] of copies distributed to the public. In addition, the act states that even an author who distributes copies without a copyright notice will retain the copyright if he or she registers the work with the copyright office within five years of publication *and* if a "reasonable effort"[8] is made to add the copyright notice to all copies distributed to the public after the omission was discovered.

How long does a copyright last?

The "right of first publication" that existed under common law existed indefinitely. Under the prior federal law, a copyright lasted for 28 years, with an option to renew for 28 more years by following certain formal procedures. The new federal law states that all works created on or after January 1, 1978, have copyrights that last until 50 years after the death of the author. If there is more than one author, the 50-year term begins only after the death of the last surviving author.[9]

Can an author sell a copyright?

Yes. Some confusion has arisen in the law because a copyright—the right to make and/or distribute copies of a work—can be sold separately from the work itself. For example, an artist may own an original painting, while another person owns the right to make and sell copies of the painting.

In earlier decisions under both state and federal law, the courts developed rules to determine who owned the creative object and who owned the copyright. The new federal law has attempted to simplify matters by providing that the owner of a copyright can transfer this right to someone else. Merely transferring the physical object itself is not sufficient to transfer the copyright, however; the copyright owner must clearly state in writing that he or she is giving someone else the right to make copies of the work. After such transfer is made, federal law gives the new copyright owner the power to sue for violation of the exclusive right to make and distribute copies of the original work.

FAIR USE

Is it ever possible to make copies of an author's copyrighted work without first securing permission?

Yes. Under a doctrine known as "fair use," courts have ruled that it is in the public interest to allow certain uses of copyrighted materials. Generally, it is not a violation of a copyright to use the "idea" or "system" developed by an author. Although an author has a monopoly on the particular form of expression created, the author has no exclusive right to control dissemination of the theory developed. Another author can quote Einstein's theory of relativity, for example, without violating any copyright held by Einstein. In addition, the courts have held that it is a fair use of copyrighted material to make copies in news reporting, criticism, or scholarly research. For example, a scholar who as part of research copies a short quotation from an earlier writer in the field does not violate the coyright laws.

What is "fair use"?

There are no clear rules to define "fair use." Nevertheless, the new federal copyright act lists four criteria for the courts to consider in cases involving fair use:

1. The purpose and character of the use, including whether such use is of a commercial nature or is for nonprofit educational purposes
2. The nature of the copyrighted work
3. The amount and substantiality of the portion used in violation to the copyrighted work as a whole
4. The effect of the use upon the potential market for or value of the copyrighted work[10]

The general test for fair use is "reasonableness." Copying is more likely to be permitted as fair use when only part of a work is copied, when the material is not being used for a commercial purpose, and when it would not make sense to purchase the entire work.

Are there any "fair use" exceptions for teachers?

Yes. In addition to the general situations described above, the new federal law lists a number of specific exceptions for teachers. First, teachers are permitted to make *single* copies of the following copyrighted works for their own use in scholarly research or classroom preparation:

1. A chapter from a book
2. An article from a periodical or newspaper
3. A short story, short essay, or short poem
4. A chart, graph, diagram, drawing, cartoon, or picture from a book, newspaper, or periodical[11]

In addition, a teacher can make multiple copies of the following copyrighted works for use in the classroom (with the number of copies not to exceed one copy per student in the class):

1. A complete poem, if it is less than 250 words and printed on not more than two pages
2. An excerpt from a longer poem, if it is less than 250 words
3. A complete article, story, or essay, if it is less than 2,500 words
4. An excerpt from a prose work, if it is less than 1,000 words or 10 percent of the work, whichever is less
5. One chart, diagram, drawing, cartoon, or picture per book or periodical[12]

The act also prohibits certain activities. Teachers may *not* make multiple copies of any of the following:

1. Copies of a work for classroom use if another teacher at the school has already copied it for use in his or her class
2. Copies of a short poem, article, story, or essay from the same author more than once in the same term
3. Copies from the same collective work or periodical issue more than three times a term

In addition, teachers cannot make copies of "consumable"[13] materials such as workbooks or answer sheets to standardized tests. Finally, teachers are prohibited from making a copy of works to take the place of an anthology.

The act also exempts certain public performances. For example, the performance of a copyrighted dramatic work by students and teachers in the classroom is not a copyright violation.[14] If students give a "public performance" of a copyrighted work, however, they will be protected from copyright violation only when there is no admission charge and no compensation is paid to any performer or promoter. Even when students perform without pay, if the school charges admission to the performance, the copyright owner has the right to prohibit the performance by giving proper notice.[15]

COPYRIGHT VIOLATION

What are the penalties for violating a copyright?

The Copyright Act of 1976 provides that the owner of a copyright can sue anyone who "infringes" his or her exclusive right to control the distribution of literary or artistic property.[16] In a suit for copyright infringement, a court has the power to issue an order (an injunction) to prevent people from making or distributing further copies of a work. A court may also impound all copies of a work claimed to have been made in violation of the owner's copyright. If the court later finds that there has been a copyright violation, it can order that all illegal copies be destroyed or otherwise disposed of. The act also states that the copyright owner can collect *either* of the following monetary awards:

1. Any actual damages the copyright owner has sustained, as well as any profits the copyright infringer has made. *Or,*
2. An amount of money to be determined by the court, which can range from $250 to $10,000 for an infringement of any one work. If the court finds that the infringer has acted willfully, the court can increase the award to $50,000; if the infringer was unaware that he or she was violating someone else's copyright, the court can make an award as low as $100.[17]

Thus, even when the copyright owner cannot show that he or she was damaged in any specific way (such as through a loss of sales of the work), the court can still make a monetary award. For example, one author's copyright was violated when two commercial book companies published and sold copies of his book without his permission.[18] Although both publishing companies lost money on the book, and the author could not show that he had suffered any damages, the court still awarded the author ten cents for every copy that was sold. In addition, as the act allows, the court made an award to cover the costs of the author's attorney's fees in bringing the suit.

The act also provides that "any person who infringes a copyright willfully and for purposes of commercial advantage or private financial gain shall be fined not more than $10,000 or imprisoned for not more than one year, or both.[19] Moreover, any person who knowingly puts a false notice of copyright on any article, or who fraudulently alters any notice of copyright on a copyrighted work, can be fined up to $2,500.

SUMMARY

Copyright law gives authors and artists property rights in their work. Under the common law, they have the right of first publication. Once an author or artist publishes or distributes a creative work, however, this protection under the common law is lost, and the author or artist must look to federal law to protect the right to control distribution of the work.

Federal law now applies to protect all literary and artistic works from the moment that they are "fixed" in some form, whether in writing or punched on a computer card. In order to establish a copyright under federal law, an author or artist merely places the proper copyright notice on all copies of the work. In order to maintain a suit for copyright infringement, however, the copyright owner must also register and deposit copies of the work with the Copyright Office. Federal law provides various remedies for those who violate another person's copyright, including a right to monetary damages and criminal sanctions in cases of willful infringement.

NOTES

1. Copyright Act of 1976, 17 U.S.C.A. §301 *et seq.* (West 1977).
2. *Williams* v. *Weisser,* 78 Cal. Rptr. 542 (Cal. App. 1969).
3. 17 U.S.C.A. §301(a) (Supp. 1977).
4. *Id.,* §101.
5. *Id.,* §401(c).
6. For information on how to register, write to the Copyright Office, Library of Congress, Washington, D.C. 20559.
7. *Id.,* §405(a) (1).
8. *Id.,* §405(a) (2).
9. *Id.,* §302.
10. *Id.,* §107.
11. *Id.*
12. *Id.*
13. *Id.*
14. *Id.,* §110(1).
15. *Id.,* §110(4) (B).
16. *Id.,* §501.
17. *Id.,* §504.
18. *Robinson* v. *Bantam Books, Inc.,* 339 F.Supp. 150 (S.D. N.Y. 1972).
19. 17 U.S.C.A. §506 (West 1977).

PART TWO

Teachers' and Students' Rights

When can schools restrict freedom of expression?

OVERVIEW

During the first half of this century, the Bill of Rights rarely assisted teachers or students who challenged the constitutionality of school rules. Courts generally used the "reasonableness" test to judge school policies. If there was any reasonable relationship between the rule and the goals of the school, the rule would be upheld even if most judges believed it was unwise, unnecessary, or restricted constitutional rights. Courts felt that school boards should have wide discretion and that courts should not substitute their judgment for that of school officials, who were presumed to be experts in educational matters.

In 1969, the U.S. Supreme Court handed down a historic decision that challenged the reasonableness test. In *Tinker* v. *Des Moines*, the Court ruled that neither teachers nor students lose their constitutional rights to freedom of expression when they enter the public schools. The fact that the Constitution now applies to schooling, of course, does not mean that teachers and students can say or write anything they wish.

When conflicts arise between the rights of teachers or students and the authority of school administrators, it is the job of the courts to balance the legitimate rights in conflict and determine when to protect and when to limit freedom of expression. In resolving these conflicts, the courts establish legal principles that apply to similar cases. Based on these cases and principles, this chapter indicates when the Constitution protects teachers' freedom to criticize school policy, engage in partisan activities on controversial issues, and alter teaching methods; and when students' freedom of speech, academic freedom, and freedom of the press are protected.

It is worth noting here that in this chapter, and throughout Part Two, we have not separated teachers' and students' rights but have put related issues on both in the same chapter.

CRITICIZING SCHOOL POLICY

An employee of a private business who is discharged for publicly "blasting" the boss has no constitutional right to be reemployed. Should a public school teacher have more freedom than the employee in private industry? Or should a teacher have a duty of loyalty to superiors, an obligation to go through channels before making criticism public, and a greater responsibility than the average citizen to speak carefully and accurately about educational matters? And if a teacher fails to exercise this responsibility, what disciplinary actions can a school board take?

The *Pickering* Case[1]

Marvin Pickering was a high school teacher from Will County, Illinois, who published a long, sarcastic letter in the local newspaper about the way his superintendent and school board raised and spent school funds. Pickering's letter detailed his objection to the "excessive" athletic expenditures by school officials who were then allegedly unable to pay teachers' salaries. He also wrote that "taxpayers were really taken to the cleaners" by those who built one of the local schools. And he criticized the "totalitarianism teachers live in" at the high school.

Angered by the publication of the letter, the board of education charged that it contained false and misleading statements, "damaged the professional reputations" of school administrators and the board, and was "detrimental to the efficient operation and administration of the schools." Pickering argued that his letter should be protected by his right of free speech, but an Illinois court ruled against him. Since Pickering held a position as teacher, the state court wrote that he "is no more entitled to harm the schools by speech than by incompetency."

Pickering still believed his letter was protected by the First Amendment, and so he appealed to the U.S. Supreme Court. On behalf of the Court, Justice Thurgood Marshall wrote that the problem in this case is "to arrive at a balance between the interests of the teacher, as citizen, in commenting upon matters of public concern, and the interests of the state, as an employer, in promoting the efficiency of the public services it performs through its employees." The Court's examination of the issues in this case are detailed in the questions that follow.

Can a teacher be dismissed for publicly criticizing school policy?

The Court found that Pickering's letter consisted mainly of criticism of the school board's allocation of funds and of both the board's and the superintendent's method of informing (or not informing) the taxpayers of the real reasons why additional funds were sought. Since such statements were not directed toward people Pickering normally worked with, they raised no question of maintaining discipline by immediate superiors or harmony among co-workers. Pickering's relationships with the board and superintendent, wrote the Court, "are not the kind of close working relationships for which it can persuasively be claimed that personal loyalty and confidence are necessary." Thus the Court "unequivocally" rejected the board's position that critical public comments by a teacher on matters of public concern may furnish grounds for dismissal.

The question whether a school system requires additional funds is a matter of legitimate public concern in which the judgment of the school administration cannot be taken as conclusive. On such an issue, wrote the Court, "free and open debate is vital to informed decision making by the electorate. Teachers are, as a class, the members of a community most likely to have informed and definite opinions as to how funds allocated to the operation of the schools should be spent. Accordingly, it is essential that they be able to speak out freely on such questions without fear of retaliatory dismissal."

Can a teacher be dismissed for making public statements that are not accurate?

Pickering's inaccurate statements mainly consisted of exaggerated cost claims for the athletic program, the erroneous suggestion that teachers had not been paid on occasion, and a false statement regarding the cost of transporting athletes. The Court found no evidence that these inaccurate statements were intentional or that they damaged the professional reputations of the board and the superintendent. In fact, wrote the Court, "Pickering's letter was greeted by everyone but its main target, the board, with massive apathy."

According to Justice Marshall, the accusation that administrtors are spending too much money on athletics cannot be regarded as "detrimental to the district's schools." Such an accusation, wrote the Court, reflects "a difference of opinion between Pickering and the board as to the preferable manner of operating the school system, a difference of opinion that clearly concerns an issue of general public interest."

In sum, Pickering unintentionally made several incorrect statements on current issues that were critical of his employer but did not impede his teaching or interfere with the regular operation of the schools. The Court therefore concluded that "absent proof of false statements knowingly or recklessly made by him, a teacher's exercise of his right to speak on issues of public importance may not furnish the basis for his dismissal from public employment."

Can a teacher be transferred for publicly criticizing a school program?

Pickering protected a teacher from being fired, but what about a teacher who is simply transferred with no loss of pay or status? In Arizona, a guidance counselor publicly opposed the way Mexican-American children were placed in classes for the mentally retarded because they were tested in English rather than Spanish. After the teacher suggested that parents could sue to stop this practice, she was transferred to a wealthy school with very few Mexican-American children. But she felt the transfer violated her rights, and a federal appeals court agreed.[2] The court acknowledged that she had no right initially to be assigned to work with Mexican-American children. But once she was given such an assignment, officials could not constitutionally transfer her because of her public criticism. The court concluded that the schools' interest in being free from criticism "cannot outweigh the right of a sincere educational counselor to speak out against a policy she believes to be both harmful and unlawful."

In a related case, an elementary teacher, Barbara McGill, was transferred because she repeatedly complained about school procedures and was "stirring up trouble" in the teachers' lounge.[3] But there was no evidence that her speech intefered with her teaching or with school operations. A federal court wrote that the test to determine whether a transfer was legitimate is whether the school's action is "likely to chill the exercise of constitutionally protected speech." Here the court ruled that it was. According to the judge, "the threat of transfer—whether it be to a school with a less desirable reputation or one perceived as dangerous or one that is difficult to get to—could be an effective means of chilling constitutionally protected speech." Therefore, the court held McGill's transfer unconstititional.

Can a school board ever restrict teachers' rights to publicize their views?

Yes. In *Pickering,* Justice Marshall wrote: "It is possible to conceive of some positions in public employment in which the need for confidentiality is so great that even completely correct public statements might furnish a permissible ground for dismissal." Such a situation might occur, for example, if a teacher publicly played a tape recording of a confidential student interview or published personal information from student files without permission.

A related Alabama case involved James Swilley, a teacher who disseminated charges about a local principal's negligence to the news media.[4] The school board reprimanded the teacher because he refused to wait until the board's investigation was complete before publicizing his allegations. Swilley then charged the board with violating his freedom of speech. But a federal judge ruled in favor of the board. The court wrote that this case was not like *Pickering:* the possible removal of a principal is not a matter of public policy to be resolved by majority vote; it is a personnel decision of the board. The court concluded that when such problems are made public before they are investigated, they can indeed "interfere with the orderly operation of the school system."

In New Jersey, the president of a local teachers' association was dismissed as a result of a speech she gave at an orientation for new teachers. In her speech she described the district as a "snakepit for young teachers" and characterized the superintendent as a "villain" who was "intimately embroiled" in local politics. A state appeals court ruled that her speech was not protected by the First Amendment, that free speech does "not endow a teacher ... with a license to villify superiors publicly."[5] Unlike *Pickering*, the court found that this teacher did not speak directly about issues of public concern "but distorted them into a vehicle to bring scorn and abuse" on the school administration.

Can teachers be disciplined for publicly criticizing their immediate superiors?

This would depend on the circumstances. In *Pickering*, Justice Marshall wrote that "certain forms of public criticism of the superior by the subordinate would seriously undermine the effectiveness of the working relationship between them" and thus justify appropriate discipline. In an Alaska case, for example, two teachers were dismissed for publishing an "open letter" to the school board that contained a series of false charges against their immediate superior.[6] Unlike Pickering's letter, these false allegations "were not consistent with good faith and were made in reckless disregard of the truth." (For a discussion of teacher liability for slander and libel, see chapter 6.) Furthermore, the Alaska letter was not greeted with apathy but led to intense public controversy that lasted more than a year. Because this situation differed from *Pickering*, the Alaska Supreme Court upheld the dismissal of these teachers.

On the other hand, a federal court protected Haywood Lusk, a Texas teacher, after his critical statements received wide media coverage and seriously injured his relationship with his principal.[7] The teacher was dismissed after he testified before the school board and city council that his principal and co-workers were "mentally and sociologically unqualified to deal with modern, complex, multiracial student bodies." He also charged that students in his school "learn to disobey authority, run, lie, cheat and steal" in order to survive. In rejecting Lusk's dismissal, a federal court wrote that his criticism concerned "matters of vital interest to every citizen of Dallas" and that they were properly brought to the attention "of the governing bodies who had the power to act" on them. In this case the court concluded that "society's interest in information concerning the operation of its schools far outweighs any strain on the teacher-principal relationship." According to the judge, only if the exercise of a teacher's First Amendment rights "materially and substantially" interferes with his classroom performance or disrupts the operation of the school "will a restriction on his rights be tolerated."

Would the Pickering decision always protect teachers against being dismissed for unintentional false public statements?

Generally, but not always. Suppose a teacher carelessly made false statements about a school, statements that had a harmful impact and would be difficult to counter because of the teacher's presumed access to the facts. For instance, a high school teacher might carelessly charge that guidance counselors were using discredited tests as a central part of the college advising program. In this case, school officials might require that the teacher make substantial efforts to verify the accuracy of statements before publishing them. A teacher who failed to do so might be dismissed. This would be different from Pickering's erroneous reports on athletic expenditures, which were matters of public record, and which the school board could easily have refuted by publishing the facts.

A related case occurred in Hartford, Connecticut, when a tenured high school teacher was dismissed for distributing leaflets that contained a number of false statements about her principal.[8] Prepared by a radical student group at a time of racial tension, the leaflets charged the principal with imposing a "reign of terror" at the school and falsely alleged that he had refused to reinstate a militant student despite a court order and had used "military riot gas" against demonstrating students at another school. The teacher testified that she did not know the charges were false at the time she distributed them. A federal court ruled that her distribution of these leaflets was not protected by the First Amendment because their basic purpose was to cause dissension; and they contained serious, damaging, and incorrect accusations, which had an immediate and harmful impact on the school.

Is private criticism protected?

The U.S. Supreme Court confronted this question in the 1979 *Givhan* case.[9] Bessie Givhan, an English teacher, was dismissed after a series of private encounters with her principal. The principal alleged that Givhan made "petty and unreasonable demands" in an "insulting, loud and hostile" manner. The trial court found that her demands were not petty or unreasonable since they involved practices she felt were racially discriminatory. But a court of appeals ruled for the school on the grounds that private complaints were not protected by the Constitution. The Supreme Court disagreed and extended the *Pickering* ruling to apply to private as well as public criticism.

The Court rejected the notion that the First Amendment does not protect criticism of a principal simply because of the close working relationship between principal and teacher. The Court emphasized that freedom of speech is not lost when a teacher "arranges to communicate privately with his employer rather than to spread his views before the public." On the other hand, a teacher's criticism may not be protected when it specifically impedes classroom duties or the operation of the schools. In personal confrontations between an educator and an immediate superior, the Court noted that judges may also consider the "manner, time, and place" of confrontations when balancing the rights in conflict.

In a related case, Donna Johnson, a "floating" teacher from Roanoke, Virginia, complained that her lack of a permanent classroom made it difficult for her to teach effectively.[10] After two conferences about the matter, her principal said "he didn't want to hear any more about it." Despite this warning, Johnson wrote a letter of complaint to the superintendent and filed a grievance about her "floating position." As a result, her contract was not renewed. A federal court ruled that her complaints were protected by the First Amendment. According to the judge, "the right of a teacher to voice concerns about conditions which interfere with the education of her students falls squarely within the protections afforded by the Constitution."

If a court finds that constitutionally protected criticism was one of the reasons for a teacher's dismissal, does this guarantee the teacher's reinstatement?

No. Cases concerning controversial expression involve a two-step judicial analysis. First, the teacher must prove that the conduct was constitutionally protected and that it was a "substantial or motivating" factor in the dismissal. Then, according to the *Givhan* case, the burden of proof shifts, and the school board must prove "that it would have reached the same decision . . . in the absence of such protected conduct." If the board can show that it would have dismissed the teacher even if the controversial expression had not occurred, the dismissal will be upheld. If not, the teacher will be reinstated and perhaps be entitled to monetary damages. (For a more detailed discussion of this issue, see chapter 12.)

Do teachers have the right to circulate controversial petitions on school premises?

According to the California Supreme Court, they do.[11] In Los Angeles, the school board prohibited the circulation of a teachers' union petition to public officials protesting cutbacks in education funds and calling for an overhaul of the tax structure. The board prohibited the petition because it was controversial and would cause teachers to take opposing political positions, thereby creating discord and lack of harmony. However, the liberal California court strongly defended the right of teachers to petition for redress of grievances.

The court pointed out that "tolerance of the unrest intrinsic to the expression of controversial ideas is constitutionally required even in the school." According to the court: "It cannot seriously be argued that school officials may demand a teaching faculty composed . . . of thinking individuals sworn never to share their ideas with one another for fear they may disagree and, like children, extend their disagreement to the level of general hostility and uncooperativeness."

The judge noted that the union's petition in this case falls within "the desirable category of political activity," and their past conduct evidences respect for law because of their willingness to try to resolve differences in court "rather than through disruptive channels." The court concluded: "Absent a showing of a clear and substantial threat to order and efficiency in the school, such proposed First Amendment activity should not be stifled."

CONTROVERSIAL ISSUES AND ACADEMIC FREEDOM

What is academic freedom?

Academic freedom includes the right of teachers to speak freely about their subjects, to experiment with new ideas, and to select appropriate teaching materials and methods. Courts have held that academic freedom is based on the First Amendment and is fundamental to our democratic society. It protects a teacher's right to evaluate and criticize existing values and practices in order to allow for political, social, economic, and scientific progress. Academic freedom is not absolute, and courts try to balance it against competing educational values.

Does teachers' academic freedom protect the assignment of controversial books and articles?

Usually it does if the material is relevant to the subject, appropriate to the age and maturity of the students, and does not cause disruption. In Montgomery, Alabama, Marilyn Parducci assigned her eleventh-grade class a satire by Kurt Vonnegut, Jr., entitled "Welcome to the Monkey House." The next day her principal and associate superintendent advised her not to teach the story again. They described the story as "literary garbage," which condoned "the killing off of elderly people and free sex." Parducci considered the story a good literary piece and believed she had a professional obligation to teach it. Because she refused the advice of her principal and assigned "disruptive" material, she was dismissed. Parducci felt her dismissal violated her right to academic freedom.

A federal court agreed.[12] In considering this case, Judge Johnson first summarized the constitutional principles involved. The Supreme Court, he wrote, "has on numerous occasions" emphasized that academic freedom— the right to teach, to evaluate, and to experiment with new ideas—is "fundamental to a democratic society." On the other hand, academic freedom, like all other constitutional rights, is not absolute, and must be balanced against competing interests. According to the Supreme Court, school officials cannot restrict First Amendment rights unless they first demonstrate that "the forbidden conduct would *materially* and *substantially* interfere" with school discipline.

Applying these principles to this case, the court found that the school board "failed to show either that the assignment was inappropriate reading for high school juniors or that it created a significant disruption to the educational process." Therefore the court ruled that Parducci's dismissal "constituted an unwarranted invasion of her First Amendment right to academic freedom."

Can a civics teacher be prohibited from discussing controversial issues?

No, it would probably be unconstitutional for a school official to order teachers of civics or current events not to discuss any controversial questions. This was the ruling of a federal court in a case that arose in Stafford, Texas.[13] Parents objected to the way Henry Sterzing, a civics teacher, taught a unit on race relations and to his response to a question indicating that he did not oppose interracial marriage. As a result, the principal and the school board told him to teach his course "within the text and not discuss controversial issues." After Sterzing replied that it was impossible to teach current events to high school seniors and avoid controversial questions, he was dismissed for insubordination. But the court ruled that he could not be fired for discussing controversial issues. The judge acknowledged that a teacher has a duty to be "fair and objective in presenting his personally held opinions" and to ensure that different views are presented. In this case, however, the court held that Sterzing's classroom methods were "conducted within the ambit of professional standards" and that his statements in class neither substantially interfered with discipline nor subjected students to unfair indoctrination.

Do teachers have the right to preach their religious beliefs in school?

No, ruled a New York court.[14] An art teacher was dismissed for recruiting students for her religious organization under the guise of guidance and for using classroom facilities during school time to preach about her religion. Since the teacher failed to stop discussing her beliefs and recruiting for her faith in school, the court ruled that her actions violated the religion clause of the First Amendment.

Does academic freedom allow teachers to disregard the text and syllabus?

No. A federal court considered this question when a biology teacher was not rehired for overemphasizing sex in his health course.[15] The teacher explained that his students "wanted sex education and mental health emphasized," and he agreed to "only touch on the other topics covered by the assigned text and course syllabus." In rejecting the teacher's contention that his First Amendment rights had been violated, the court ruled that he had no constitutional right "to override the wishes and judgment of his superiors and fellow faculty members as to the proper content of the required health course." The court concluded that academic freedom is not "a license for uncontrolled expression at variance with established curricular content."*

Can teachers be punished for discussing topics or distributing materials that are not relevant?

Generally they can be. Academic freedom does not protect materials, discussions, or comments that are not relevant to the assigned subject. A federal case from Cook County, Illinois, illustrated this point when it upheld the dismissal of three eighth-grade teachers for distributing movie brochures about the 1969 rock festival "Woodstock."[16] These contained various pictures, articles, and poems that presented a positive viewpoint on drugs, sexual freedom, and vulgar language. The three teachers taught French, industrial arts, and language arts. The brochures were distributed to any student who wanted them ("to promote rapport"), but the teachers did not relate the brochures to what the students were studying. In addition to being irrelevant, the court found that the brochures were inappropriate for eighth-grade students and promoted a viewpoint on drug use that was contrary to what state law required students to be taught about the "harmful effects of narcotics."

Will academic freedom protect classroom comments that do not cause substantial disruption?

Not necessarily. "Substantial disruption" and "relevance" are two of the limits of academic freedom, and even relevant comments may not be protected if they cause such disruption. Similarly, even if a teacher's comments do not cause disruption, they may not be protected if they are irrelevant. This was the ruling in a case involving a St. Louis math teacher.[17] The teacher was dismissed after he told his class that army recruiters had no right to be at their high school and that the students could push the recruiters, throw apples at them, make them feel unwanted, and get them off campus. The teacher argued that he should not be dismissed because his comments did not cause substantial disruption and therefore were protected by the First Amendment. But the court ruled that his statements were not protected since they were "completely irrelevant" to his math class and "diverted the time and attention of both students and teacher from the prescribed curriculum."

The Keefe Case[18]

Robert Keefe, a high school English teacher from Ipswich, Massachusetts, wanted to expose his students to provocative contemporary writing. He gave each member of his class a recent issue of the *Atlantic* magazine and assigned

---

* In an interesting recent case, a Maryland English teacher was suspended for introducing students to Aristotle's *Politics* and Machiavelli's *The Prince*, as an aid to studying Shakespeare's *Julius Caesar*, because they were not approved for tenth graders. *Time*, Dec. 15, 1980, p. 77.

the lead article, which discussed dissent, protest, and revolt. Entitled "The Young and the Old," the article contained the term *motherfucker,* which was repeated a number of times.

Although there was no evidence of negative student reaction to the article, a number of parents found the "dirty" word offensive and protested to the school committee. Members of the committee asked Keefe if he would agree not to use the word again in class. But Keefe refused to agree (as a matter of conscience) and was dismissed.

The case raises a number of issues about controversial speech in a high school classroom. The following questions discuss the way one federal appeals court treated them.

May teachers assign articles with vulgar or "obscene" words?

It depends on the quality of the article and the way in which the language is used. In this case, the judge read the article and found it "scholarly, thoughtful, and thought-provoking." The court said it was not possible to read this article as an "incitement to libidinous conduct." If it raised the concept of incest, wrote the judge, "it was not to suggest it but to condemn it," for the word was used "as a superlative of opprobrium." (For an explanation of what makes a publication legally obscene, see page 133.)

Assuming the article had merit, couldn't the teacher have discussed it without using the controversial word?

Not in this case. Here the offending word was not artificially introduced but was important to the thesis and conclusions of the author. Therefore, no proper study of the article could avoid considering the controversial word.

Can schools prohibit offensive language?

This would depend on the specific situation—the age of the students, the word used, and the purpose of its use. Here the word was used for educational purposes among high school seniors. Under these circumstances, the judge doubted that quoting a "dirty" word in current use would be a shock to these students or that they needed to be "protected from such exposure." In a frequently quoted conclusion, the court wrote that the sensibilities of offended parents "are not the full measure of what is proper in education."

Does a teacher have the right to use "any" language in the classroom?

No. In fact, the court acknowledged that "some measure of public regulation of classroom speech is inherent in every provision of public education." But the judge ruled that the application of such a regulation in the *Keefe* case "demeans any proper concept of education."

TEACHING METHODS

Can a teacher be punished for using a controversial teaching method that is not clearly prohibited?

Not usually. If a teacher does not know that a certain method is prohibited, it would probably be a violation of due process for the teacher to be punished for using that method unless it had no recognized educational purpose. (The concept of due process for teachers is discussed more fully in chapter 12.)

A case arose in Lawrence, Massachusetts, in an eleventh-grade English class. Teacher Roger Mailloux was discussing a novel about conservative customs in rural Kentucky when a student said that the custom of seating boys and girls on opposite sides of the classroom was ridiculous. Mailloux said that some current attitudes are just as ridiculous. As an example he introduced the subject of taboo words and wrote the word *fuck* on the blackboard. He then "asked the class in general for an explanation. After a couple of minutes, a boy volunteered the word meant 'sexual intercourse.' Plaintiff [Mailloux], without using the word orally, said: 'We have two words, sexual intercourse, and this word on the board; one is accepted by society, the other is not accepted. It is a taboo word.'" After a few minutes of discussion, Mailloux went on to other matters.

As a result of this incident, a parent complained and an investigation took place; Mailloux was dismissed and took his case to court. The court found that Mailloux's method did not disturb the students, that the topic of taboo words was relevant to the subject, and that the word *fuck* was relevant to the topic of taboo words.[19] ("Its impact," wrote the judge, "effectively illustrates how taboo words function.") The court also found that eduational experts were in conflict about Mailloux's method: some thought the way he used the word was reasonable and appropriate; others did not.

With these facts in mind, the judge discussed the law in such cases. The *Keefe* case, wrote the court, upheld two kind of academic freedom: the "substantive" right of a teacher to choose a teaching method that serves a "demonstrated" educational purpose and the "procedural" right of a teacher not to be discharged for the use of a teaching method not prohibited by clear regulation. This procedural protection is afforded a teacher because he is engaged in the exercise of "vital First Amendment rights," and he should not be required to "guess what conduct or utterance may lose him his position." Since Mailloux did not know that his conduct was prohibited, the court ruled that it was a violation of due process for the school committee to discharge him.

In a related California case, Eileen Oliker, a young reading teacher, was dismissed for distributing to students material they wrote containing vulgar descriptions of sexual organs and the sex act. The material was written as part of a class assignment for poor readers, who were told that they could write about anything they chose and that their stories would be shared with the class. Oliker was dismissed after a student she had disciplined left a copy of the material in the principal's box a month after the incident.

In a 2–1 decision, a state appeals court ruled in Oliker's favor.[20] The court noted that she had been an unusually sensitive, dedicated, and effective teacher and that this one incident did not cause "any disruption or impairment of discipline." Moreover, two experts testified that Oliker's method of having students write about subjects that interested them was "a sound educational approach," although they would not have reproduced the materials. The majority concluded that teachers should not be disciplined "merely because they made a reasonable, good faith, professional judgment in the course of their employment with which higher authorities later disagreed."

When are controversial methods not protected?

When methods are inappropriate, when they are not supported by any significant professional opinion, or when they are clearly prohibited by reasonable school policy, they are not likely to be protected by academic freedom. The following cases indicate when two courts were unwilling to protect controversial methods and why.

Allen Celestine, a fifth-grade teacher from Louisiana, became increasingly concerned about the vulgar language used by his students. Therefore, when two girls in his class used the word *fuck*, he required them to write it 1,000 times. As a result, he was dismissed for incompetence. Celestine claimed that his academic freedom should protect his choice of punishment, but no educational experts defended Celestine's method, and a state court ruled against him.[21] It wrote that the First Amendment does not entitle a teacher to require young students to use vulgar words "particularly when no academic or educational purpose can possibly be served."

Frances Ahern, a high school economics teacher, attended a summer institute that led her to change her teaching methods and allow students to determine course topics and materials. She also began spending substantial time discussing classroom rules and school conflicts and policies. The principal directed her to stop discussing school politics, to teach economics, and to use more conventional teaching methods. When Ahern ignored the warning, she was dismissed. The teacher defended her action in the interest of "guarding her academic freedom to select the method of teaching to be employed in the classroom." But a federal appeals court ruled that the Constitution does not give a teacher the right to use methods which violate valid administrative requirements.[22]

Is it legal for a school to refuse to rehire a teacher because of basic disagreement over teaching methods and philosophy?

Probably. Courts distinguish controversial speech from controversial methods. As noted earlier, schools may not deny reemployment to teachers who publicly disagree with school policy. But administrators apparently can refuse to rehire a teacher who refuses to comply with a school's teaching methods and philosophy.*

For example, Phyllis Hetrick was not rehired as an English instructor at a college in Kentucky. The college expected instructors "to teach on a basic level, to stress fundamentals, and to follow conventional teaching patterns." But Hetrick emphasized student freedom and choice and failed to cover the material she had been told to teach. The issue in this case, wrote a federal court, is not which educational philosophy has greater merit but whether a school "has the right to require some conformity" to its educational philosophy and whether it may decline to hire a teacher whose methods are not conducive "to the achievement of the academic goals they espoused." In ruling for the administration, the court wrote that academic freedom "does not encompass the right of a non-tenured teacher to have her teaching methods insulated from review."[23]

Is academic freedom the same in public schools and in colleges?

Yes and no. While academic freedom applies to all teachers employed by the state, the scope of this freedom is usually broader in colleges and universities than in public schools. In *Mailloux*, Judge Wyzanski explained that this is so because in secondary schools "the faculty does not have the independent traditions, the broad discretion as to teaching methods, nor usually the intellectual qualifications, of university professors. . . . Some teachers and most students have limited intellectual and emotional maturity. . . . While secondary schools are not rigid disciplinary institutions, neither are they open forums in which mature adults, already habituated to social restraints, exchange ideas on a level of parity. Moreover . . . a secondary school student, unlike most college students, is usually required to attend school classes, and may have no choice as to his teacher."[24]

STUDENTS AND FREE SPEECH

The *Wooster* Case[25]

Earl Wooster was expelled from a California high school because he refused to apologize for a controversial speech he made during a school assembly. The speech was highly critical of the Fresno School Board for "compelling" students to use "unsafe" facilities, and it included caustic comments about some of the board's policies. School officials called Wooster's talk a "breach

---

* In a recent case, the Washington Supreme Court ruled that requiring high school history teachers to teach in a conventional manner contrary to their teaching philosophy did not violate their academic freedom. *Millikan* v. *Board of Directors of Everett*, 611 P.2d 414 (Wash. 1980).

of school discipline" that was intended to discredit the board in the eyes of the students. A state court agreed and wrote that Wooster's refusal to apologize not only "accentuated his misconduct" but also "made it necessary" to expel him to maintain school discipline.

The *Wooster* case was decided in 1915. Wooster's lawyer didn't even raise the possibility that his client's speech might be protected by the Constitution. How would the case be decided today? Even if students have freedom of speech in public schools, can't schools restrict that freedom? Can administrators, for example, limit student speech if they fear it will lead to disruption or if they know it will offend other students? Some of these questions are confronted by the Supreme Court in the following controversy.

The *Tinker* Case[26]

Does freedom of speech apply to students in the classroom?

In 1965, when the debate over American involvement in the Vietnam war was becoming heated, a group of students in Des Moines, Iowa, decided to publicize their antiwar views by wearing black armbands. On learning of the plan, principals of the Des Moines schools established a policy prohibiting armbands in order to prevent any possible disturbance. Although they knew about the policy, several students nevertheless wore armbands to school and refused to remove them. They were suspended. The students argued that the school policy was unconstitutional, and they took their case to court. After the trial, a federal judge ruled that the anti-armband policy was reasonable. But the students appealed their case all the way to the Supreme Court, presenting it with a conflict between their rights and the rules of the school.

First, the Court outlined the legal principles to be applied. While it recognized that school officials must have authority to control student conduct, it held that neither students nor teachers "shed their constitutional rights to freedom of speech or expression at the schoolhouse gate." To support this ruling, Justice Fortas noted that since school boards "are educating the young for citizenship," they should scrupulously protect the "constitutional freedoms of the individual, if we are not to strangle the free mind at its source and teach youth to discount important principles of our government as mere platitudes."

Concerning this particular case, the Court wrote that the First Amendment protects symbolic speech as well as pure speech. (See Appendix A for the wording of the First Amendment and other constitutional amendments relevant to teachers and students.) The wearing of an armband to express certain views is the kind of symbolic act protected by that amendment. After reviewing the facts, the Court found "no evidence whatsoever" that wearing armbands interfered "with the school's work or with the rights of other students to be secure or to be left alone." School officials might have honestly feared that the armbands would lead to a disturbance, but the Court said that this fear was not sufficient to violate student rights. "In our system," wrote the Court, "undifferentiated fear or apprehension of disturbance is not enough to overcome the right to freedom of expression."

While the Court recognized that free speech in the schools may cause problems, it noted that "any word spoken in class, in the lunchroom, or on the campus that deviates from the views of another person may start an argument or cause a disturbance. But our Constitution says we must take this risk: and our history says that it is this sort of hazardous freedom—this kind of openness—that is the basis of our national strength and of the independence and vigor of Americans who grow up and live in this relatively permissive, often disputatious society."

In a provocative comment about education and freedom, the Court wrote: "In our system, state operated schools may not be enclaves of totalitarianism. . . . Students in schools as well as out of school are possessed of fundamental rights which the State must respect, just as they themselves must respect their obligations to the State. In our system, students may not be regarded as closed-circuit recipients of only that which the State chooses to communicate."

In sum, the *Tinker* case held that school officials cannot prohibit a particular opinion merely "to avoid the discomfort and unpleasantness that always accompany an unpopular viewpoint." On the contrary, unless there is evidence that the forbidden expression would "materially and substantially" interfere with the work of the school, such a prohibition is unconstitutional. Thus this landmark decision established guidelines to help educators understand the scope and limits of student free speech. Since *Tinker* clearly recognized that teachers as well as students have a constitutional right to freedom of expression, it has been used as precedent by both groups in almost all subsequent cases in this area.

Does the Tinker *decision apply only to the classroom?*

No. The Court ruled that the principles of this case are not confined to the curriculum or to classroom hours. On the contrary, a student's right to freedom of expression applies equally "in the cafeteria, or on the playing field" and in all other school activities.

Can schools legally limit student expression or symbolic speech?

Yes. There are limits to all constitutional rights. In *Tinker*, the Court stated that any student conduct which "materially disrupts classwork or involves substantial disorder or invasion of the rights of others is, of course, not immunized by the Constitutional guarantee of freedom of speech." Thus, a federal appeals court upheld the rule of a Cleveland high school forbidding all buttons and badges because the wearing of some symbols had led to fighting between black students and white students.[27] Evidence indicated that if all symbols were permitted, racial tensions would be intensified and the educational process would be "significantly and substantially disrupted."

Must officials wait until a disruption has occurred?

No. In a case involving a student demonstration inside a high school, a federal judge ruled that the First Amendment does not require school officials to wait until actual disruption takes place before they may act.[28] The judge explained that an official may take reasonable action to restrict student expression when there is significant evidence to conclude that there is a "reasonable likelihood of substantial disorder."

Can officials always restrict symbols that might lead to disruption?

No, according to a Texas case where officials prohibited armbands because they expected those who opposed the armbands to cause disruption.[29] Since no one thought the armband wearers would cause trouble, the court ruled that the expectation of disruption by others was not enough to suspend the students' right of symbolic speech. What more was required? To justify the school's action, administrators should determine "based on fact, not intuition" that disruption would probably result from wearing the armbands. In addition, officials should make an effort to bring leaders of different student factions together to agree on mutual respect for each other's constitutional rights. If actions such as these had been tried and failed, the failure would have tended to justify restricting the armbands. But no attempt was made.

The court emphasized that the *Tinker* ruling is not nullified whenever a school is confronted with disruption. "Rather," concluded the judge, "the Supreme Court has declared a constitutional right which school authorities must nurture and protect, not extinguish, unless they find the circumstances allow them no practical alternative."

Can demonstrations be prohibited near the school?

If they interfere with schoolwork, they can. The Supreme Court upheld the conviction of a high school student who violated a law prohibiting demonstrations on or near school grounds that disturbed classes.[30] In upholding the law, Justice Marshall noted that the constitutionality of a restriction may depend on what is being regulated and where. Making a speech in a public park might be protected, while making the same speech in a public library might not be. "The crucial question," wrote the Court, "is whether the manner of expression is basically incompatible with the normal activity of a particular place at a particular time." Just as *Tinker* made clear that free speech is not off limits in the schools, so Marshall emphasized that "the public sidewalk adjacent to school grounds may not be declared off-limits for expressive activity." But in each case protected expression may be prohibited if it "materially disrupts classwork."

Are "fighting words" protected?

No. In a Pennsylvania case, a high school senior was punished when he loudly commented to a friend off campus that his teacher was "a prick."[31]

The court said that the student's conduct involved an invasion of the right of the teacher "to be free from being loudly insulted in a public place." The judge concluded that the use of "fighting words—those which by their very utterance inflict injury" is not protected by the constitutional guarantee of freedom of speech.

Do students have a right to remain silent?

Yes. Closely related to the right to speak is the right to remain silent—especially in relation to matters of conscience. (A detailed discussion of students' rights under freedom of conscience can be found in chapter 9.) Thus, students cannot be compelled to say the Pledge of Allegiance or salute the flag. Similarly, a court ruled in favor of a New Jersey student who refused to stand during the Pledge.[32] The judge wrote that the state cannot require a student to engage in "implicit expression" by standing at attention while the flag is being saluted. A requirement that students engage in a form of symbolic speech is unconstitutional and interferes with the students' right "not to participate" in the flag ceremony.

Do students have a right to academic freedom?

No. Although student choice in courses, curriculum materials, assignments, and even teachers is increasing in many school districts, this is a matter of educational policy and not a legal right. Courts have not ruled that students have a constitutional right to determine courses, texts, or teaching methods.*

Do students have a "right to know" or a right to read controversial material?

Courts differ in their answers to this question, and the Supreme Court has not yet ruled directly on the issue. In an Ohio case dealing with the removal from the library of Kurt Vonnegut's *Cat's Cradle* and Joseph Heller's *Catch-22*, the Sixth Circuit Court of Appeals ruled that school boards cannot censor libraries and remove books simply because they object to their social or political views.[33] In his opinion, the judge wrote that students have a First Amendment "right to know" and a right to receive information and ideas from their teachers. This decision is binding in Michigan, Ohio, Kentucky, and Tennessee. In a related Massachusetts case, brought by a group of students and faculty, a judge ruled that board members could not remove books from the library simply because they found the language of the books offensive.[34] "What is at stake here," wrote the court, "is the right to read and be exposed to controversial thoughts and language—a valuable right subject to First Amendment protection."

---

* In a recent case, for example, a federal appeals court ruled that students have no constitutional right to challenge a school board's decision not to renew a teacher's contract and to eliminate a popular course from the curriculum. *Zykan* v. *Warsaw Community School Corporation,* 49 *Law Week* 2183 (Sept. 16, 1980).

On the other hand, the Second Circuit Court of Appeals has approached this issue differently.[35] The court ruled that a local school board had the authority to take Piri Thomas's *Down These Mean Streets* off the library shelves and restrict its circulation. When a group of students, parents, and teachers argued that the removal of the book violated their rights, the court noted that "no matter what choice of books" may be made by the board, someone may dissent. However, the judge wrote that the "ensuing shouts of book burning, witch hunting, and violation of academic freedom hardly elevate this intramural strife to First Amendment constitutional proportions." The judge rejected the notion of "a book acquiring tenure by shelving" as a novel and unsupportable theory. The court concluded that "books which become obsolete or irrelevant or were improperly selected initially, for whatever reason, can be removed by the same authority which was empowered to make the selection in the first place." Because of this decision, which is binding in New York, Connecticut, and Vermont, two district courts in the second circuit upheld the authority of school boards to remove objectionable books from public school libraries.[36] (A related issue of a student's right to hear controversial speakers is considered in chapter 10.)

Do recent court decisions mean that schools cannot control the contents of their libraries?

No. Courts are divided only about whether schools can remove controversial books from the libraries after they are shelved. All courts agree that school officials have substantial control and discretion. First, they are not required to provide students with a library. Second, they are not required to purchase any particular book. Third, they can remove books that are obsolete, irrelevant, or obscene for minors or because of space limitations. Some courts have simply ruled that officials do not have total control and cannot remove books because they are offensive to the personal, political, or social views of the board.

STUDENT PUBLICATIONS

Many teachers assume that when schools finance a student newspaper, they can control its contents. Teachers usually believe that unofficial, "underground" papers, which are written and printed off campus, are different. They reason that if students pay for the newspaper, then the school cannot restrict its content or distribution. While both these assumptions may be reasonable, neither is correct. The fact that students finance an underground paper does not mean that administrators can never restrict its distribution or review its contents. Conversely, administrators do not have total control over the contents of school-sponsored publications.

Can an underground newspaper be banned for discussing highly controversial or unpopular topics?

No. In a case involving a high school underground paper, a federal appeals court wrote: "It should be axiomatic at this point in our nation's history that in a democracy 'controversy' is, as a matter of constitutional law, never sufficent in and of itself to stifle the views of any citizen."[37] The controversial subjects in the student publication included a statement about the injustice of current drug laws and an offer of information about birth control, venereal disease, and drug counseling. The court seemed surprised that an educational institution "would boggle at controversy" to such an extent that it would restrict a student publication merely because it urged students to become informed about these widely discussed and significant issues. The court commented that "our recollection of the learning process is that the purpose of education is to spread, not to stifle, ideas and views. Ideas must be freed from despotic dispensation by all men, be they robed as academicians or judges or citizen members of a board of education."[38]

Can a student newspaper be prohibited from criticizing school officials?

No, such criticism is protected by the First Amendment. In a Texas case, school officials defended their ban of a student newspaper because of its "negative attitude" and its criticism of the administration.[39] In rejecting this defense, the court explained that "aversion to criticism" is not a constitutional justification for restricting student expression. The Bill of Rights, wrote the court, protects freedom of the press precisely because those regulated "should have the right and even the responsibility" of commenting upon the actions of their regulators.

In a related Illinois case, a student was suspended for writing an editorial in an underground paper that criticized the senior dean and indicated that in the student's opinion one of the dean's statements was "the product of a sick mind."[40] The court acknowledged that the editorial reflected a "disrespectful and tasteless attitude toward authority." Nevertheless, it ruled that the statement itself did not justify suspending the student. As *Tinker* pointed out, schools cannot punish students merely because they express feelings that officials do not want to deal with. On the other hand, this ruling probably would have been different if school officials had produced evidence showing that the editorial had substantially disrupted school discipline.

Can a student newspaper be prohibited from criticizing school policies?

No. Mere criticism of school rules and policies is not enough to allow officials to ban student publications or punish the writers. To support such action, officials would have to show that the publications caused or would probably cause substantial and material disruption.

In the Illinois case mentioned in the previous question, the student editorial had strongly criticized some school procedures as "utterly idiotic and asinine" and called the school's detention policy "despicable and disgusting." The court ruled that this did not justify suspending the students responsible for the editorial. Moreover, the court noted that "prudent criticism" by high school students may be socially valuable because they possess a unique perspective on matters of school policy.

Do schools have any control over the distribution of student publications?

Yes. Officials can enforce reasonable regulations concerning the place and the manner in which student publications are distributed. But the rules cannot be so restrictive that they have the effect of preventing the distribution of student views. Similarly, administrators could probably not prohibit all "in-school" distribution or distribution "while any class is being conducted" since such rules are broader than necessary for safety or to prevent disruption of school activities.[41] Examples of appropriate restrictions might include prohibiting distribution in laboratories, on stairways, or in narrow corridors and establishing rules aimed at minimizing litter on campus.

Can schools ever restrict the content of student publications?

Yes. School officials may restrict the publication of material that is libelous, obscene, or substantially disruptive. Officials cannot restrict a publication simply based on their "fear," "intuition," or "belief" that it will cause disruption; their judgment must be supported by significant facts and evidence.

Libel is a false written statement that injures a person's reputation. A person who is libeled can sue for damages. If the person is a public figure, he or she must prove that the writer knew or should have known that the statement was untrue. Writing falsely that the principal stole $1,000 may be libelous; an editorial alleging that many teachers in a school district are incompetent probably is not. (For more on libel, see chapter 6.)

Is a publication obscene if it contains offensive, vulgar, and "dirty" language?

No. Many parents and teachers equate obscenity with offensive four-letter words. But this is not what lawyers and judges mean. To be legally obscene, material must violate three tests developed by the U.S. Supreme Court: (1) it must appeal to the prurient or lustful interest of minors; (2) it must describe sexual conduct in a way that is "patently offensive" to community standards; *and* (3) taken as a whole, it "must lack serious literary, artistic, political or scientific value."[42]

Parents, teachers, and administrators may be offended by student use of profanity in their writing. But most controversial articles about social, political, or educational issues in student newspapers, even though they may use offensive language, do not violate any of the Supreme Court tests. As Chief Justice Burger noted: "All ideas having even the slightest redeeming social importance—unorthodox ideas, controversial ideas, even ideas hateful to the prevailing climate of opinion—have full protection of the [First Amendment] guarantees."[43]

Can students be required to submit publications to the administration for review before distribution?

In most states, they can. Generally courts have held that it is not unconstitutional to require that materials for students be submitted to the administration for screening prior to distribution. The justification for allowing prior review, explained one federal court, is "to prevent disruption and not to stifle expression."[44] A publication by students can be prohibited if it is libelous or obscene or if administrators can "demonstrate reasonable cause to believe" that it would result in substantial disruption. On the other hand, courts emphasize that a student publication cannot be prohibited simply because other students, teachers, administrators, or parents may disagree with its content.[45]

In contrast, the Seventh Circuit Court of Appeals held that a rule requiring prior approval of student publications by the superintendent was "unconstitutional as a prior restraint in violation of the First Amendment."[46] This decision, which applies in Illinois, Indiana, and Wisconsin, indicated that schools could establish rules punishing students who publish or distribute literature that is obscene, libelous, or causes substantial disruption. But according to this court, schools may not require that publications be submitted to the administration for approval before distribution. Despite this ruling, most courts have indicated that schools may require prior review *if* the procedures for review have due process safeguards and clear standards.

What procedures and standards are necessary before schools can require prior review of student publications?

In a number of cases, courts have held prior review procedures unconstitutional because they lacked either clear standards or due process safeguards. In Maryland, for example, a federal court wrote that rules requiring prior review "must contain narrow, objective, and reasonable standards" by which the material will be judged.[47] Such standards are required so that those who enforce the rules are not given "impermissible power to judge the material on an *ad hoc* and subjective basis." The court emphasized that legal terms such as "libelous" or "obscene" used without explanation "are not sufficiently precise or understandable by high school students and administrators untutored in the law" to be acceptable criteria of what is prohibited. Although obscene and libelous material may be prohibited, the court wrote that there is "an intolerable danger . . . that under the guise of such vague labels, [school officials] may unconstitutionally choke off criticism, either of themselves or school policies, which they find disrespectful, tasteless or offensive." Therefore, prior review policies must contain "precise criteria sufficiently spelling out what is forbidden" so that students may clearly know what they may or may not write.

In another federal case, an appeals court declared a Texas school's prior review requirement unconstitutional because it lacked due process safeguards.[48] There was no provision for an appeal if the principal prohibited distribution, nor did the rules state how long the principal could take to make her decision. Delays in reviewing newspapers, wrote the court, "carry the inherent danger that the exercise of speech might be chilled altogether during the period of its importance." Therefore, the court held that any requirement for screening student publications before distribution must clearly state (1) how students are to submit proposed materials to the administration, (2) a brief period of time during which the administration must make its decision, (3) a clear and reasonable method of appeal, and (4) a brief time during which the appeal must be decided. Due process should also provide for some kind of informal hearing for the students affected. Because the regulations challenged in this case provided none of these procedures and violated the students' First Amendment rights, the court commented that "it would be well if those entrusted to administer the teaching of American history and government to our students began their efforts by practicing the document on which that history and government are based."

In short, before administrators can legally require screening of student publications before distribution, the school must establish precise and objective standards of review *and* clear due process safeguards.

May schools ban the sale of underground publications on campus?

Probably not. An Indiana case held that a rule prohibiting the sale of all publications except those benefiting the school was unconstitutional.[49] School officials had argued that newspaper sales and other commercial activities are "unnecessary distractions" that are "inherently disruptive." The judge acknowledged that administrators have a legitimate interest in limiting commercial activities on campus by nonstudents. But he pointed out that the reason the students sold the newspaper in this case was only to raise the money needed to publish their paper. The court rejected the notion that the sales were inherently disruptive. On the contrary, administrators have ample authority to regulate the time, place, and manner of newspaper sales to maintain order and avoid littering or interference with others without restricting First Amendment rights. In a related California case, the state supreme court wrote: "We fail to see how the *sale* of newspapers on the school premises will necessarily disrupt the work and discipline of the school, whereas their distribution free of charge will not."[50]

Can schools prohibit the distribution of material not written by a student or school employee?

Probably not. In the Indiana case mentioned in the preceding question, the court wrote that such a rule would prohibit use of materials by all sorts of people "whose views might be thought by the students to be worthy of circulation." And the judge indicated that he had "no doubt" that such a rule violated the students' First Amendment rights.[51]

May schools prohibit the distribution of anonymous publications?

Not according to a federal judge who noted that historically anonymous publications have been an important vehicle for criticizing oppressive practices and laws and that anonymous student publications can perform a similar function in schools. "Without anonymity," wrote the judge, "fear of reprisal may deter peaceful discussion of controversial but important school rules and policies."[52] The problem with this prohibition, the court explained, is that it is not limited to potentially libelous, obscene, or disruptive material but applies equally to thoughtful, responsible criticism.

Can administrators ban articles on sensitive topics in school-sponsored newspapers?

Probably not. In a recent Virginia case, a federal court ruled that a high school principal could not ban an article entitled "Sexually Active Students Fail to Use Contraception."[53] The principal defended his action on the grounds that the paper was funded by the school and the article would conflict with school policy against teaching about birth control. The judge, however, ruled that financial support of a student newspaper by a school does not mean that "any manner of state regulation is permissible." On the contrary, he noted that "the state is not necessarily the unrestrained master of what it creates and fosters." Although the schools had the authority to exclude birth control from its courses, the judge ruled that the student newspaper was not part of the curriculum but was more like the school library, which contained extensive information on contraception.

Can surveys by student newspapers be prohibited if they could cause emotional harm?

Probably. In 1976, New York administrators prohibited an anonymous survey by a high school newspaper about students' sexual attitudes, knowledge, and experience. The administrators did not want the editors to use school facilities to ask for information that would "invade the rights of other students by subjecting them to psychological pressures" that could cause emotional harm. Since there was some expert testimony that attempting to answer the questions could create anxiety among some students, a federal court ruled that school officials had authority to prohibit the survey to protect students from peer pressures which might result in emotional disturbance.[54] The court concluded that freedom of expression does not include the right to ask questions when there is reason to believe that such questions might cause harm.

Can school newspapers prohibit political ads?

Not if other ads are accepted. This issue arose in New York when a group of students challenged the policy of their school newspaper that prohibited all advertising not related to the school. The students wanted to publish an ad opposing a government policy and claimed the school rule violated their First Amendment rights. A federal judge agreed.[55] He pointed out that the student newspaper carried a number of articles and letters about controversial political issues. Therefore he wrote that "there is no logical reason" to permit news stories on these subjects and preclude student advertising.

Can a school stop funding a student newspaper because of its editorial policy?

This question was confronted by a federal appeals court when the president of a predominantly black college terminated the student newspaper's financial support after it refused to change its editorial policy opposing the admission of more white students.[56] The president explained that the newspaper's editorials were contrary to college policy and inconsistent with the constitutional guarantees of equality. But the court ruled in favor of the students. Since the newspaper did not cause disruption, reject opposing views, or incite anyone to interfere with white students, the administration could not censor or restrict the paper because of its editorial policy. In a broad summary of related cases, the court wrote: "Censorship of constitutionally protected expression cannot be imposed by suspending the editors, suppressing circulation, requiring imprimatur of controversial articles, excising repugnant material, withdrawing financial support, or asserting any other form of censorial oversight based on the institution's power of the purse."

Can schools regulate off-campus publications?

No, according to Judge Irving Kaufman. In a broad, articulate, and challenging opinion, Judge Kaufman examined the principles governing the student press and the dangers involved in administrative control.[57] The case concerned several high school students from a small, rural New York community who produced *Hard Times*, a satirical publication addressed to the school community. The language in the publication was considered "indecent," but it was probably not legally obscene. *Hard Times* was written, sold, and printed off campus. But when the president of the local school board learned about the publication, she urged administrative action. As a result, the school imposed a series of penalties on the student publishers, and they took their case to court.

Judge Kaufman acknowledged that schools had the right to punish certain student expression. "Our children could not be educated," he wrote, if school officials "were without power to punish one who spoke out of turn in class or who disrupted the quiet of the library or study hall." But this case was different. Here school officials went outside the campus to regulate free-dom of expression because board members and other citizens found a stu-dent publication objectionable. According to the court: "We may not permit school administrators to seek approval of the community-at-large by pun-ishing students for expression that took place off school property. Nor may courts endorse such punishment because the populace would approve."

Despite the good intentions of school officials, Judge Kaufman said they must be restrained in moving against student expression since they act "as both a prosecutor and a judge" and since their desire to preserve decorum gives them "a vested interest in suppressing controversy." In addition, they are "generally unversed in difficult constitutional concepts such as libel and obscenity." For these reasons, the court concluded that the First Amendment "forbids public school administrators and teachers from regulating the mate-rial to which a child is exposed after he leaves school each afternoon."

Could officials ban *Hard Times* if students tried to distribute it on campus? In a concurring opinion, Judge Newman said yes. Even though the publica-tion was not obscene, the judge felt that schools should be able to prohibit it since "by contemporary standards" it was "indecent and vulgar for school age children." The publication described itself as "vulgar." And this descrip-tion, wrote Judge Newman, "was not false advertising." He believed that school authorities could regulate indecent language because "its circulation on school grounds undermines their responsibility to try to promote stan-dards of decency" among students. Since the majority opinion only consid-ered school regulation of off-campus publications, it remains uncertain whether or to what extent school officials could legally restrict "indecent" writing that was not obscene.[58]

SUMMARY

For most of this century, the Constitution did not protect students or teachers when they spoke out on controversial issues. In 1969, however, the U.S. Su-preme Court ruled that neither teachers nor students lose their right to free-dom of expression when they enter the public schools. But freedom of ex-pression, like most constitutional rights, is not absolute; it can be limited when it conflicts with other basic values.

To decide when a teacher's statements are protected, the Supreme Court wrote that judges should balance "the interests of the teacher, as citizen, in commenting on matters of public concern and the interests of the state, as employer, in promoting the efficiency of the schools." The Court emphasized that voters should be able to hear the informed opinions of teachers about public educational issues and that teachers should not be punished merely for expressing their views on controversial topics. Other courts have held that teachers cannot be fired because they complain about teaching condi-tions, because they criticize school officials privately, or because they circu-late controversial petitions in school during their free time—unless these activities pose a serious threat to the educational process. If teachers' statements are constitutionally protected, they cannot be reprimanded, transferred, or otherwise disciplined for making them. On the other hand, the First Amendment does not protect a teacher's false and reckless accusations that cause disruption, statements to the press about a personnel matter under investigation, or scornful and abusive personal attacks on school officials.

In deciding whether to protect controversial teaching methods or materials, most courts use a "balancing test," a case-by-case inquiry that balances the teacher's right to academic freedom against the legitimate interests of the community. Judicial protection for academic freedom is based on the First Amendment, on the importance of intellectual inquiry to social progress, and on the belief that teachers and students should be free to question and challenge established concepts. Some judges have held that teachers cannot be fired simply because they assign a controversial book or article or use vulgar language in class. According to most courts, whether such methods or materials are protected depends on the circumstances of each case. The circumstances judges consider include the educational relevance of the controversial language or publication, the teacher's purpose, the age and maturity of the students, and the quality of the teaching material and its effect on the class. According to some courts, even when schools have authority to prohibit certain methods or materials, teachers have a right to use them unless they are clearly prohibited. Academic freedom, however, does not protect teaching that is incompetent or irrelevant, or that is religious or political indoctrination; nor does it give teachers the right to refuse to use required texts or ignore the established curriculum.

Courts now recognize that the First Amendment applies to students as well as teachers. In *Tinker*, the Supreme Court held that it is unconstitutional to restrict student expression unless it would "materially and substantially interfere" with school activities. According to some courts, an "expectation of disruption" is not enough to justify suspending student rights unless (1) such an expectation is based on fact, not intuition; and (2) school officials first make an honest effort to restrain those who might cause the disruption. Schools can restrict symbolic expression when such symbols have caused material disruption in the past or when there is evidence that they would probably cause substantial disorder.

Freedom of the press protects both school-sponsored newspapers and "underground" student publications. This means that even if a school finances a student newspaper, administrators do not have the right to censor it or control its contents. Thus high school students are free to discuss unpopular or controversial topics and to criticize school policies and personnel. Furthermore, one court held that students could not be prohibited from selling an underground paper or from publishing anonymous articles by nonstudents. Nor can schools regulate student publications written, printed, and distributed off campus.

On the other hand, schools are under no obligation to finance student publications. If they do sponsor such a publication, administrators can decide its level of funding, the broad goals of the publication (e.g., whether for literary, scientific, or general purposes), and whether it will be part of the academic program (such as a poetry or journalism course) or an extracurricular activity. Furthermore, schools have the right to establish reasonable rules regulating the time, place, and manner for distributing all student publications. In addition, administrators can punish students for distributing material that is legally obscene or libelous or is likely to cause substantial disruption. Moreover, most courts allow schools to screen student publications for illegal material prior to distribution if they have issued clear, objective standards and have procedural safeguards for the review process. As a minimum, due process requires a brief period of time for administrative review plus procedures for a speedy and fair appeal.

NOTES

1. *Pickering* v. *Board of Education*, 225 N.E.2d 1 (1967); 391 U.S. 563 (1968).

2. *Bernasconi* v. *Tempe Elementary School District, No. 3*, 548 F.2d 857 (9th Cir. 1977).

3. *McGill* v. *Board of Education of Pekin Elementary School*, 602 F.2d 774 (7th Cir. 1979).

4. *Swilley* v. *Alexander*, 448 F.Supp. 702 (S.D. Ala. 1978).

5. *Pietrunti* v. *Board of Education of Brick Township*, 319 A.2d 262 (N.J. 1974).

6. *Watts* v. *Seward School Board*, 454 P.2d 732 (Ala. 1969).

7. *Lusk* v. *Estes*, 361 F.Supp. 653 (N.D. Tex. 1973).

8. *Gilbertson* v. *McAlister*, 403 F.Supp. 1 (D. Conn. 1975).

9. *Givhan* v. *Western Line Consolidated School District*, 99 S.Ct. 693 (1979).

10. *Johnson* v. *Butler*, 433 F.Supp. 531 (W.D. Va. 1977).

11. *Los Angeles Teacher's Union* v. *Los Angeles City Board of Education*, 455 P.2d 827 (Cal. 1969).

12. *Parducci* v. *Rutland*, 316 F.Supp. 352 (N.D. Ala. 1970).

13. *Sterzing* v. *Ft. Bend Independent School District*, 376 F.Supp. 657 (S.D. Tex. 1972), 496 F.2d 92 (5th Cir. 1974).

14. *La Rocca* v. *Board of Education of Rye City School District*, 406 N.Y.S.2d 348 (1978).

15. *Clark* v. *Holmes*, 474 F.2d 928 (7th Cir. 1972), *cert. denied*, 411 U.S. 972 (1973).

16. *Brubaker* v. *Board of Education, School District 149, Cook County, Illinois*, 502 F.2d 973 (7th Cir. 1974).

17. *Birdwell* v. *Hazelwood School District*, 491 F.2d 490 (8th Cir. 1974).

18. *Keefe* v. *Geanakos*, 418 F.2d 359 (1st Cir. 1969).

19. *Mailloux* v. *Kiley*, 436 F.2d 565 (1st Cir. 1970).

20. *Oakland Unified School District* v. *Olicker*, 25 C.A.3d 1098 (1972).

21. *Celestine* v. *Lafayette Parish School Board*, 284 So.2d 650 (La. 1973).

22. *Ahern* v. *Board of Education of School District of Grand Island*, 456 F.2d 399 (8th Cir. 1972).

23. *Hetrick* v. *Martin*, 480 F.2d 705 (6th Cir. 1973).

24. *Mailloux, supra*, at 1392.

25. *Wooster* v. *Sunderland*, 148 P. 959 (1915).

26. *Tinker* v. *Des Moines Independent School District*, 393 U.S. 503 (1969).

27. *Guzick v. Debras*, 431 F.2d 594 (6th Cir. 1970), *cert. denied*, 401 U.S. 948 (1971).

28. *Karp* v. *Becken*, 477 F.2d 171 (9th Cir. 1973).

29. *Butts* v. *Dallas Independent School District*, 436 F.2d 728 (5th Cir. 1971).

30. *Grayned* v. *City of Rockford*, 408 U.S. 104 (1972).

31. *Fenton* v. *Stear*, 423 F.Supp. 767 (W.D. Penn. 1976).

32. *Lipp* v. *Morris*, 579 F.2d 834 (3d Cir. 1978).

33. *Minarcini* v. *Strongsville City School District*, 541 F.2d 577 (6th Cir. 1976).

34. *Right to Read Defense Committee of Chelsea* v. *School Committee of the City of Chelsea*, 454 F.Supp. 703 (Mass. 1978).

35. *President's Council, District 25* v. *Community School Board No. 25*, 457 F.2d 289 (2d Cir. 1972).

36. *Pico* v. *Board of Education Island Trees Union Free School District*, 474 F.Supp. 387 (E.D. N.Y. 1979), *Bicknell* v. *Vergennes Union High School Board of Directors*, 475 F.Supp. 615 (D. Vt. 1979). *Pico* was recently reversed by a federal appeals court, 49 *Law Week* 2274 (Oct. 28, 1980).

37. *Shanley* v. *Northeast Independent School District*, 462 F.2d 960 (5th Cir. 1972).

38. *Id.*

39. *Id.*

40. *Scoville* v. *Board of Education of Joliet Township*, 425 F.2d 10 (7th Cir. 1970).

41. *Jacobs* v. *Board of School Commissioners*, 490 F.2d 601 (7th Cir. 1973).

42. *Miller* v. *California*, 413 U.S. 15 (1973).

43. *Id.*

44. *Shanley, supra.*

45. *Id.*

46. *Fujishima* v. *Board of Education*, 460 F.2d 1355 (7th Cir. 1972).

47. *Baughman* v. *Freienmuth*, 478 F.2d 1345 (4th Cir. 1973).

48. *Shanley, supra.*

49. *Jacobs* v. *Board of School Commissioners*, 490 F.2d 601 (7th Cir. 1973).

50. *Bright* v. *Los Angeles Unified School District*, 134 Cal. Rptr. 639 (1976).

51. *Jacobs, supra.*

52. *Id.*

53. *Gambino* v. *Fairfax County School Board*, 564 F.2d 157 (4th Cir. 1977).

54. *Trachtman* v. *Anker*, 563 F.2d 512 (2d Cir. 1977).

55. *Zucker* v. *Panitz*, 299 F.Supp. 102 (S.D. N.Y. 1969).

56. *Joyner* v. *Whiting*, 477 F.2d 456 (4th Cir. 1973).

57. *Thomas* v. *Board of Education, Granville Central School District*, 607 F.2d 1043 (2d Cir. 1979).

58. A full and thoughtful discussion of this issue can be found in M. Chester Nolte, "New Pig in the Parlor: Official Constraints on Indecent Words," *NOLPE Law School Journal*, vol. 9, no. 1 (1980): 1–22.

9

When can schools limit religious freedom?

OVERVIEW

Controversies concerning the appropriate place, if any, of religion in the schools have occurred periodically since the early days of the republic. Though the First Amendment states that "Congress shall make no law respecting the establishment of religion, or prohibiting the free exercise thereof," the interpretation of these general provisions and their application to public schools have been problematic. Religion tends to be so important in the lives of people, and so surrounded by powerful emotions, that many want to use the schools to maintain and spread their religious beliefs at the same time that others insist on the complete exclusion of religion from public schools.

Some of the most bitter controversies that have embroiled America's schools have involved questions related to religion. This chapter addresses only those questions concerning religion and public education that are of greatest relevance to teachers and students. For example, must teachers and students salute the flag, or follow the curriculum even if it violates their religious beliefs? Are prayers permitted in the public schools? What about silent meditation? And may students be exempt from compulsory schooling or from certain courses in the curriculum on religious grounds?

TEACHERS' FREEDOM OF CONSCIENCE

In recent decades, although attention has focused on issues related to religion and public education, the attention of the courts and media has been primarily on students: their right and/or obligation to read the Bible in school, to pray, to salute the flag, to be exempt from objectionable parts of the curriculum, and other issues. But teachers, too, have religious beliefs and commitments. There are various important differences between teachers and students, the most salient being that teachers are adults and are paid employees hired to accomplish certain objectives for the community. Students are minors and are compelled by law to attend school. Should these differences lead to different applications of the Constitution for teachers and for students? We must look to court cases for our answers.

May teachers be excused from saluting the flag?

Yes, they may, if their objections are based on either religion or conscience. When a New York high school art teacher refused to participate in the daily flag ceremony, she was dismissed from her job. A federal circuit court upheld her right not to participate in such a ceremony and the Supreme Court denied a request to review the decision, allowing the ruling of the lower court to stand.[1] The nonparticipating teacher stood silently and respectfully while another instructor conducted the program. The teacher's objections were held a matter of conscience and not necessarily disloyal. In the words of the court of appeals, "we ought not impugn the loyalty of a citizen . . . merely for refusing to pledge allegiance, any more than we ought necessarily to praise the loyalty of a citizen who without conviction or meaning, and with mental reservation, recites the pledge by rote each morning."

What if state law requires a daily flag salute?

State law requiring a salute to the flag is superseded by the First Amendment of the Constitution. Many states mandate daily flag salutes and other patriotic exercises. For example, a Massachusetts law passed in 1977 provides that "each teacher at the commencement of the first class of each day in all public schools shall lead the class in a group recitation of the Pledge of Allegiance to the Flag."

The state supreme court advised the governor that the law violated the First Amendment rights of teachers.[2] The court based its opinion on the U.S. Supreme Court ruling in the *Barnette* case (see page 155), indicating that the reasons used to excuse students from saluting the flag apply equally to teachers. According to the Massachusetts court, "any attempt by a governmental authority to induce belief in an ideological conviction by forcing an individual to identify himself with that conviction through compelled expression of it is prohibited by the First Amendment."

May a teacher refuse to follow the curriculum if the refusal is based on religious objections?

No. This question was raised in the Chicago public schools when Joethelia Palmer, a probationary kindergarten teacher and a member of Jehovah's Witnesses, informed her principal that because of her religion she would not be able "to teach any subjects having to do with love of country, the flag or other patriotic matters in the prescribed curriculum." For example, she considered it "to be promoting idolatry . . . to teach . . . about President Lincoln and why we observe his birthday." School officials insisted that these matters were part of the regular curriculum; although *she* did not have to salute the flag, provisions should be made for students to do so. Moreover, students were to follow the prescribed curriculum including the holidays, songs, and other patriotic materials.

The U.S. Court of Appeals ruled in favor of the school board, and the Supreme Court upheld the ruling.[3] The court commented that "the First Amendment was not a teacher license for uncontrolled expression at variance with established curricular content." Furthermore, "there is a compelling state interest in the choice and adherence to a suitable curriculum for the benefit of our young citizens and society." Thus, while Palmer's right to her religious beliefs must be respected, she has no "right to require others to submit to her views and to forgo a portion of their education they would otherwise be entitled to enjoy."

Are teachers who belong to Jehovah's Witnesses unqualified to teach in public schools?

Not necessarily. Their qualifications depend on their willingness to provide the prescribed curriculum for children in their classes. For example, Ms. Bein, a New York kindergarten teacher, told the parents of her students that she could no longer lead certain activities or participate in certain projects because these were "religiously oriented" according to her newly acquired religion of Jehovah's Witnesses. She could not decorate the classroom for holidays, coordinate gift exchange during the Christmas season, sing "Happy Birthday," or recite the Pledge of Allegiance. When some parents and school officials wanted to dismiss her, the teacher insisted that she was competent to teach and that the First Amendment protected her from participating in activities forbidden by her religion. The important difference between this case and the one discussed in the previous question was that Ms. Bein made arrangements to provide the children with all the curricular activites she could not conduct. With the cooperation of parents, older students, and other teachers, all activities specified in the curriculum were conducted. Thus, Ms. Bein's religious views were not imposed on the children, and the school's objectives in connection with patriotic exercises and holiday celebrations were satisfied. The New York State Commissioner of Education ruled in Ms. Bein's favor and held that her dismissal violated the religious freedom provisions of the First Amendment.[4]

RELIGIOUS HOLIDAYS

May teachers take religious holiday leaves?

Yes they may, if they don't take too many leaves. State laws or local district policies usually allow teachers to be absent from school for the major holidays of recognized religions. Nevertheless, problems have arisen over questions of pay for religious holidays, as well as over the taking of an excessive number of days off for religious reasons.

Must schools pay teachers for religious holiday leaves?

No, they don't have to pay for such days. Payment for religious holiday leaves is within the discretion of the local school district. This question arose in California when a high school teacher requested a "personal necessity leave" to observe Rosh Hashanah, a Jewish holiday. Like many other states, California provides a certain number of paid days a year for "personal necessity leave" for teachers. It is up to local school authorities to adopt rules controlling the use of such leaves.

The teacher, Mrs. Waldman, claimed that under the First Amendment she had a right to a leave for a major religious holiday and that it should be a paid leave under the personal necessity leave policy of the state and district. The courts ruled against her, holding that it was within the discretion of the school board to decide whether or not to consider such leave a personal necessity.[5] If courts imposed such a rule on schools, said the court, "the results would be chaotic. Every school teacher belonging to every sect, whether a legitimate religious group or not, would forthwith be entitled to six days of paid holidays. It appears reasonable, therefore, to limit the definition of personal necessity in a way which allows for effective supervision."

May teachers take unpaid religious holidays at will?

Within limits, teachers' freedom of religion will be protected even if the number of special holidays taken seems excessive to some school officials. This issue arose in California, and the judges were closely divided in their attempts to balance the rights of the individual to the free exercise of his religion and the legitimate interest of the state to provide effective schooling for all children.[6] Mr. Byars was a competent teacher employed by his school district in 1969. He joined the Worldwide Church of God in 1971 and requested certain days off for religious holidays. Despite the fact that his request was denied, between 1971 and 1975 he was absent from work for thirty-one days to observe religious holidays. School officials notified him in 1973 that his absences were not approved and that if he continued them, he would be dismissed for "persistent failure to abide by the rules of the District." Byars, insisting that he had a constitutional right to practice his religion, continued to observe the religious holidays of his church and missed more classes. When the school board dismissed him, Byars went to court.

The school board claimed that continuity of instruction was very important and that the repeated use of substitutes would diminish the educational benefits of the students. The court ruled in favor of the board; recognizing the clash of interests between the individual and society, the court observed: "While the free exercise clause prevents any governmental regulation of religious beliefs, in this case we are concerned not with . . . [the teacher's] beliefs but only with his practice in leaving his teaching duties for the purpose of religious observances while under contract with the district."

Nevertheless, the Supreme Court of California, by a vote of 4–3, reversed the decision and ruled in favor of the teacher. The court based its ruling on the California Constitution's provision protecting freedom of religion. The court was influenced by the fact that the total number of days Mr. Byars was absent was approximately the same as the mandatory number of paid leave days provided for teachers by the state. Thus the majority held that this teacher's religious beliefs must be accommodated by the public schools, despite the inconvenience and disruption it might entail for the schools.[7] The U.S. Supreme Court dismissed an appeal "for want of a substantial federal question."

May teachers wear distinctively religious clothing in public schools?

Probably not, although there is no uniform law on this question applicable to the entire nation. Objections have arisen to Catholic nuns teaching in religious garb. When there was no evidence that the nuns injected religious views into their teaching, some courts did not prohibit them from wearing their religious clothing.[8] Other courts, however, even forbade nuns from teaching in public schools, on the grounds that their lives are dedicated to religion and their constant presence in the classroom violates the "establishment clause" of the First Amendment.[9] There are no recent cases on this issue, but it is probable that today nuns or ministers may teach secular subjects in public schools if they do not wear religious garb or other sectarian symbols. The fact that they may contribute their earnings to a church is their own personal and private business.[10] This principle would apply with equal force to members of, say, the Hare Krishna sect, as well as to more traditional religions.

When the issue of teaching in religious garb has arisen, most states have passed laws against the practice or forbidden it by administrative regulation. Such laws and regulations have been upheld by the courts.[11] Most educators and judges today hold the view that the wearing of religious garb introduces a sectarian influence that should not be present in the public schools. In sum, the teacher's religious *beliefs* are always protected; *actions* based on religious beliefs may be limited when a compelling state interest is at stake.

STUDENTS' FREEDOM OF CONSCIENCE

"If there is any fixed star in our constitutional constellation, it is that no official, high or petty, can prescribe what shall be orthodox in politics, nationalism, religion, or other matters of opinion or force citizens to confess by word or act their faith therein. If there are any circumstances which permit an exception, they do not now occur to us."[12] As this quote illustrates, certain social issues or conflicts are never completely resolved; they are perennial. The specific substance of the issues may change over time, but the general substance and form remain the same. They all relate to two basic principles of the First Amendment, one of which guarantees the free *exercise of religion*, while the other orders government officials not to *establish* any religion. But what do these principles mean in the daily lives of students in public schools?

Must students salute the flag?

No, they do not have to salute the flag if they have a genuine religious objection to such an act. However, most schools still require children to recite the Pledge of Allegiance at the start of each school day by virtue of state law or policy of the school board. In the 1940s, children of the Jehovah's Witnesses faith refused to participate in the official pledge and offered, instead, to recite their own religious pledge. When school officials insisted on their reciting the official pledge, the students went to court. Their refusal eventually led to a Supreme Court ruling in favor of the children.[13] In the words of the Court: "We think the action of the local authorities in compelling the flag salute and pledge transcends constitutional limitations on their power and invades the sphere of intellect and spirit which it is the purpose of the First Amendment to reserve from all official control."

The Court overruled an earlier case that did not consider saluting the flag to be a significant enough religious act to merit constitutional protection. Many people, perhaps most, do not consider flag salutes or other patriotic exercises to be religious activities; therefore they cannot understand why anyône should have religious objections to them. Nevertheless, the Court held that school administrators or other officials may not determine for a religious group whether such activities are allowed or proscribed by their religion. There is to be no official orthodoxy under the Constitution. Majority vote, or the vote of a legislature, cannot resolve this question, said the Court. "The very purpose of a Bill of Rights was to withdraw certain subjects from the vicissitudes of political controversy, to place them beyond the reach of majorities and officials and to establish them as legal principles to be applied by the courts. One's right to life, liberty, and property, to free speech, a free press, freedom of worship and assembly, and other fundamental rights may not be submitted to vote; they depend on the outcome of no elections."

The majority of the Court considered freedom of religion to be a *fundamental* or *preferred freedom*. Such freedoms can be abridged only if the state shows it has a *compelling* need to do so. This is in contrast to *ordinary freedoms*, such as the freedom to drive a car, which can be restricted or regulated if the government has some legitimate reason to do so (e.g., to reduce pollution or congestion). There was no compelling state interest requiring Jehovah's Witnesses to salute the flag, for no major public interest was threatened by their refusal, and thus their fundamental religious freedom prevailed. There have been instances of religious freedom being outweighed by a powerful public interest, however. For example, mandatory polio immunization of all schoolchildren has been upheld, despite the religious objections of some parents.

Is religion the only basis for not saluting the flag?

No. There are students, as well as people in general, who object to saluting the flag as a matter of conscience. Courts have held that a sincerely held conscientious objection to the flag salute receives the same protection from the Constitution as an objection based on religious beliefs.

A student at Coral Gables High School in Florida had a deeply felt objection to the flag salute and did not even want to stand while the salute was being conducted. A board policy allowed him not to participate but required that nonparticipating students stand quietly during the salute. The student claimed that such a requirement violated his right to free speech, and a federal district court upheld this contention.[14] The court noted that "standing is an integral portion of the pledge ceremony and is no less a gesture of acceptance and respect than is the salute or the utterance of the words of allegiance."

In a similar case, New York students challenged the rule that nonparticipating students leave the room and wait in the hall, for they considered such treatment to be a punishment for the exercise of a constitutional right. The New York court agreed with the students and upheld their right not to participate in the flag salute for reasons of conscience, as well as their right to remain quietly in the room.[15] What if the refusal becomes contagious and other students also refuse to salute the flag? The New York case noted that "the First Amendment protects successful dissent as well as ineffective protest."

May public schools start the day with prayers?

No. Historically, many public schools began each day with a required prayer, Bible reading, or both. In 1959 Pennsylvania enacted a law requiring daily Bible reading in the schools but exempting children who had written requests for exemption from their parents. The Schempp children, who were Unitarians, challenged the law. Their case eventually reached the Supreme Court, which ruled in their favor.[16]

The Court held that state-required Bible reading or prayer violates the establishment clause of the First Amendment when it is part of the curriculum in schools children are required to attend: "They [prayers] are held in the school buildings under the supervision and with the participation of teachers employed in those schools . . . such as opening exercises in a religious ceremony." The fact that students may be excused from the exercises does not change the fact that schools, which are arms of the state, are involved.

Must religion be completely excluded from schools?

The Supreme Court never mandated such exclusion. In fact, in the same case where it declared prayers and Bible reading unconstitutional, the Court made it clear that studying *about* religion is perfectly legitimate, whether it be comparative religion, the history of religion, art and music and religion, or other approaches. Religious exercises, rituals, and celebrations are against the law, whether compulsory or voluntary; an objective, scholarly study of religion has a proper place in the public schools.* †

May students receive religious instruction during school hours?

Yes. The instruction must take place away from school, however, not on school grounds, and must be conducted by teachers or religious figures independent of the schools and not paid by the schools. The so-called released time religious education is used in some communities in the country, and the Supreme Court has ruled that the arrangement does not violate the Constitution.[17]

Are silent meditations allowed?

Yes. Massachusetts passed a law that required public schools to observe a minute of silence "for meditation or prayer." The law was challenged by students and parents who claimed that it was a violation of the "establishment clause" of the First Amendment. The word "or" saved the law from being declared unconstitutional. According to the court, meditation refers to a silent reflection on any subject, religious or secular. Thus, since meditation

---

* The Supreme Court in a 5 to 4 decision declared unconstitutional a Kentucky statute requiring the posting of a copy of the Ten Commandments, purchased with private contributions, on the wall of each classroom in the public schools of the state. Though the state courts upheld the law the Supreme Court concluded that such a law served no secular legislative purpose.

    The court applied its three part test: (1) a statute must have a secular legislative purpose, (2) its principal or primary effect must be one that neither advances nor inhibits religion, and (3) the statute must not foster an excessive government entanglement with religion. (*Stone* v. *Graham*, 49 Law Week 3369, Nov. 12, 1980).

† Certain school practices and a school board policy related to Christmas programs in public schools was challenged in Sioux Falls, South Dakota in 1979. In short, the courts ruled that schools may teach about religion as a significant aspect of our culture and our history. Religious ceremonies must not be performed in schools "under the guise of 'study,' " yet the performance of religious art, literature or music does not necessarily invalidate the activity if the primary purpose served is secular and not religious. Schools should be sensitive to the "religious beliefs and disbeliefs of their constituents and should attempt to avoid conflict," according to the court, "but they need not and should not sacrifice the quality of the students' education." [*Florey* v. *Sioux Falls School Dist. 49–5*, 619 F.2d 1311 (1980), cert. filed Sept. 17, 1980].

can be on a secular subject, and the law used the disjunctive "or," there is no necessary prayer involved—only a moment of silence.[18]

Is Transcendental Meditation allowed in schools?

No, it is not, ruled a federal court in New Jersey after schools introduced a course in Transcendental Meditation (TM), claiming that it would reduce stress and produce a variety of beneficial physical effects. Some parents believed that TM was a religion and, as such, had no place in public schools. Although there was conflicting testimony on whether or not the the course was religious, the judge ruled that it was.[19] TM used a *mantra*, a special word repeated regularly by the meditating person. A mantra and a special textbook were assigned to each student at an out-of-school religious ceremony. In the estimate of the judge, the goals of TM may have been secular, but the means used were religious and therefore violated the First Amendment.

Must children attend public schools?

No, they and their parents may choose among several alternatives that include public schools, private religious or secular schools, or private military schools. (See chapter 18 for a detailed discussion of schooling and parents' rights.) The Supreme Court established this principle in 1925 when an Oregon law that required every child between the ages of eight and sixteen to attend public schools was challenged by a Catholic religious order. The Court ruled in their favor.[20]

The Court recognized the right of states to require that all children of certain ages attend school and the right of states to provide reasonable regulations for all schools, public and private, related to school buildings, teachers, and the curriculum. Nevertheless, to require that all educating be done in public schools was considered arbitrary and unreasonable. In a famous quote the Court warned against the standardization of children and recognized the parents' right to guide and nurture the young:

> The fundamental theory of liberty upon which all governments in this Union repose excludes any general power of the state to standardize its children by forcing them to accept instruction from public teachers only. The child is not the mere creature of the state; those who nurture him and direct his destiny have the right, coupled with the high duty, to recognize and prepare him for additional obligations.

May children attend church school at home?

They may do so only if the "home school" qualifies under the requirements of the particular state. (See chapter 18 for a detailed discussion of home schooling.) In most states this would mean that the parents or other adults teaching the children would have to be qualified in the eyes of the court and would have to present an acceptable educational program for the children. That a school claims to be a religious school does not exempt it from reasonable state regulation.

A court in Florida ruled on a case involving a church "school" in a home where the mother was the only teacher.[21] The parents claimed that their religious beliefs forbade "race mixing as practiced in the public schools" as "sinful." The mother was not certified to teach, nor did she meet state regulations for private tutors, and the church to which they claimed to belong was not a regularly established church in Florida. Thus the court held that the home arrangement was unacceptable and the children had to attend either the local public school or some acceptable private school.

May children avoid school attendance altogether for religious reasons?

In general, they may not, although special circumstances may lead to some exemptions. A child who lives in a state that requires school attendance must attend *some* acceptable school during the years of compulsory education. What if the family has religious objections? This question was raised by some Amish children in Wisconsin, and the Supreme Court provided some exceptions to the general rule stated above.[22] Wisconsin required school attendance until the age of sixteen. The Amish believed that the curriculum of the high school, particularly its emphasis on intellectual and scientific achievement, competition, worldly success, and social life, was inconsistent with their religious beliefs. They accepted the need for basic literacy but were convinced that schooling beyond the eighth grade would destroy their close-knit rural, religion-centered way of life. They insisted that after eighth grade, their youth should learn on their farms and in their homes all the skills relevant to the Amish way of life. The state, on the other hand, insisted that the compulsory laws applied to all children, without exception.

After reviewing all the evidence and arguments, the Court exempted the Amish children from high school attendance. The Court was impressed by the fact that this religion-based, self-sufficient community has existed successfully for over two hundred years. In effect, the Amish way of life was an "alternative to formal secondary school education" and enabled the Amish to live peacefully and successfully fulfill their economic, social, and political responsibilities without becoming burdens on the larger society. After balancing the interests of the state against the Amish interest in the preservation and practice of their religion, the Court reached a decision on behalf of religious freedom. As the Court recognized, the case involved "the fundamental interest of parents, as contrasted with that of the State, to guide the religious future and education of their children "and the primary role of parents in the upbringing of their children "is now established beyond debate as an enduring American tradition."

Are courts likely to extend the ruling regarding the Amish to other religious groups that object to school attendance? Not likely. The Court made it clear that the long history of the Amish religious way of life was important to its decision and groups "claiming to have recently discovered some 'progressive' " or other enlightened way of rearing children for a modern life will not qualify for similar exemption. Since the law is always growing and changing, however, only time will tell whether some other groups will find ways to successfully challenge state compulsory education laws.

An attempt by other parents in Wisconsin illustrates this point. When Mr. and Mrs. Kasuboski did not send their eight children to public schools, they claimed an exemption for religious reasons. They were members of the Basic Bible Church and alleged that the schools' teaching of racial equity, humanism, and "one-world government," together with the influence of communists and Jews, was offensive to their religion. Evidence showed that the particular church was not opposed to education and that some of its members sent their children to public schools. The court ruled that the Kasuboski children could not be exempt because their parents' objection was based on philosophic and ideological grounds and not on religious ones.[23] The Amish case could not be used as a precedent by them. "A personal, philosophic choice by parents, rather than a religious choice, does not rise to the level of a First Amendment claim of religious expression." (A related question appears on page 296.)

May students be exempt from certain courses for religious reasons?

That depends on the state law. Religious objections have been raised by parents and students to various parts of the curriculum. The most often heard objection is to sex education courses whether labeled family life education, human development, human sexuality, or some other title. The course itself does not violate freedom of religion, ruled a California court, particularly if the state law permits children to be excused from participating in such classes.[24] Schools usually make such courses voluntary, but the New Jersey Commissioner of Education ruled that even a required course on family living, in which some sex education was included, does not violate freedom of religion.[25]

Religious objections have also been raised against dancing in physical education classes, and courts have long protected students who have genuine religious objections to participating in dancing.[26] Similarly, courts would uphold a student's religious objection to watching movies in schools or playing with cards, though such activities were part of the curriculum. A federal appeals court also ruled in favor of a high school student who objected to ROTC training on grounds of religious freedom.[27] In his high school, ROTC was part of a required physical education course, and the court held that the student need not "choose between following his religious beliefs and forfeiting his diploma, on the one hand, and abandoning his religious beliefs and receiving his diploma on the other hand."

SUMMARY

Throughout the history of public schooling, disagreements concerning the appropriate relationship between religion and public education have resulted in spirited controversies that have had to be resolved by our courts. Although controversies still abound, there are some guiding principles for the conduct of daily schooling.

It is clear today that teachers and students may be exempt from saluting the flag if they have objections based either on religion or conscience. Teachers or students so exempt may remain in the classroom and sit or stand respectfully while others participate in the ceremony. Teachers may not, however, refuse to follow a curriculum, properly adopted by a school board, even though they may have personal religious objections to it. If parts of the curriculum are objectionable to them, they must provide acceptable alternative ways for the students to learn the materials.

Teachers may take personal leaves for religious holidays, but it is up to the local school district whether to pay them for such personal leaves. When school officials consider such leaves to be excessive and thus an interference with the continuity of instruction, provisions of the state law or state constitution must be consulted. In one such case a teacher was protected by the California Constitution, and the U.S. Supreme Court rejected an appeal on the grounds that no "substantial federal question" was involved.

Courts have ruled that prayers or Bible reading must be excluded from public schools as violations of the "establishment clause" of the First Amendment. This is the case whether such practices are mandatory or voluntary, and whether led by faculty or students. Studying *about* religion is perfectly legal, however, and so is released time religious instruction as long as it takes place away from school facilities and does not involve school personnel or other support from the schools. The provision of a period of silent meditation does not violate the Constitution because such silence may be used for secular or religious purposes, but the inclusion of Transcendental Meditation in the curriculum of public schools was declared a violation of the First Amendment.

Students have the right to attend either private or public schools, and state compulsory attendance laws may be satisfied by attending religious or secular schools. In at least one case, some students were exempt from attending school beyond the eighth grade when they could show that the high school curriculum would violate their religious beliefs and religiously based way of life. Other attempts at "home schooling" based on religious grounds succeeded only if the state laws for such alternatives were satisfied. State law may also specify whether students may be exempt from certain parts of the curriculum. For example, courses related to sex education are often made elective, though some courts have upheld their inclusion in the curriculum even when they were required. Students have been exempt from participating in ancillary parts of the curriculum such as dancing in physical education classes when they could show genuine religious objections to the activities.

Thus, while controversies still abound surrounding the issue of religion and public education, careful examination shows that both students and teachers have made significant gains in asserting their right to free exercise of religion on the one hand and being free from the states' efforts to use the schools to "establish" religion on the other.

NOTES

1. *Russo* v. *Central School District No. 1*, 469 F.2d 623 (2d Cir. 1972), *cert. denied*, 411 U.S. 932 (1973).

2. *Opinions of the Justices to the Governor*, 363 N.E.2d 251 (Mass. 1977).

3. *Palmer* v. *Board of Education of City of Chicago*, 603 F.2d 1271 (7th Cir. 1979).

4. *Matter of Bein*, 15 Educ. Dep. Rep. 407, N.Y. Comm'r. Dec. No. 9226 (1976).

5. *California Teachers Association* v. *Board of Trustees*, 138 Cal. Rptr. 817 (Cal. App. 1977).

6. *Rankins* v. *Commission on Professional Competence*, 142 Cal. Rptr. 101 (Cal. App. 1977).

7. *Rankins* v. *Commission on Professional Competence of Ducor Union School District*, 154 Cal. Rptr. 907 (Cal. App. 1979), *appeal dismissed*, 100 S.Ct. 515 (1979).

8. *Rawlings* v. *Butler*, 290 S.W.2d 801 (Ky. 1956); *New Haven* v. *Torrington*, 43 A.2d 455 (Conn. 1945).

9. *Harfst* v. *Hoegen*, 163 S.W.2d 609 (Mo. 1942).

10. *Gerhardt* v. *Heidt*, 267 N.W. 127 (N.D. 1936).

11. *Commonwealth* v. *Herr*, 78 A. 68 (Pa. 1910); *Zellers* v. *Huff*, 236 P.2d 949 (N.M. 1951).

12. Justice Jackson, in *West Virginia* v. *Barnette*, 319 U.S. 624 (1943).

13. *Id*.

14. *Banks* v. *Board of Public Instruction of Dade County*, 314 F.Supp. 285 (S.D. Fla. 1970).

15. *Frain* v. *Barron*, 307 F.Supp. 27 (E.D. N.Y. 1969).

16. *Abington School District* v. *Schempp*, 374 U.S. 203 (1963).

17. *Zorach* v. *Clausen*, 343 U.S. 306 (1952).

18. *Gaines* v. *Anderson*, 421 F.Supp. 337 (D. Mass. 1976).

19. *Malnak* v. *Yogi*, 440 F.Supp. 1284 (D. N.J. 1977).

20. *Pierce* v. *Society of Sisters*, 268 U.S. 510 (1925).

21. *T. A. F. and E. M. E.* v. *Duval County*, 237 S.2d 15 (Fla. 1973).

22. *Wisconsin* v. *Yoder*, 406 U.S. 205 (1972).

23. *State* v. *Kasuboski*, 275 N.W.2d 101 (Wis. Ct. App. 1978).

24. *Citizens for Parental Rights* v. *San Mateo City Board of Education*, 124 Cal. Rptr. 68 (Cal. App. 1975).

25. *"J. B." and "B. B." as Guardians and Natural Parents of "P. B." and "J. B."* v. *Dumont Board of Education*, Dec. of N.J. Comm'r of Education (1977).

26. *Hardwick* v. *Board of Trustees*, 205 P. 49 (1921).

27. *Spence* v. *Bailey*, 465 F.2d 797 (6th Cir. 1972).

10

When can schools limit freedom of association?

OVERVIEW

Citizens often judge teachers and students by the company they keep and the organizations they join. In the past, teachers have been fired for being members of groups considered subversive by their community or even for being active in local partisan politics. And students have been prohibited from organizing radical groups on campus if the aims of the groups were controversial or seemed to conflict with the goals of their school. Some teachers and students believed they were victims of guilt by association and that restrictions on their organizational activity violated their freedom of association. But many administrators argued that both teachers and students were in a special class and that their associational freedom should not be as broad as that of other citizens.

On the other hand, increasing numbers of teachers and students are rejecting the notion that their rights should be less or their obligations should be more than those of others. Teachers object to the practice of penalizing teachers for failure to sign loyalty oaths, for membership in unpopular or radical organizations, or for taking an active part in politics. Students want to be able to organize fraternal, religious, or political groups in school and to organize demonstrations and hear controversial speakers.

The scope and limits of teachers' and students' freedom of association is the focus of this chapter. The court cases discussed indicate how judges have been resolving conflicts on these issues.

OATHS OF ALLEGIANCE

What are the goals of loyalty oaths?

The goals of loyalty oaths have varied according to the times and the legislatures that enacted them. In the 1950s, when half the states passed such oaths, their focus was to ensure that teachers were loyal to the American form of government and that schools were free from the influence of subversive teachers. In upholding a New Jersey loyalty oath, a judge noted: "A teacher who is bereft of the essential quality of loyalty and devotion to his government and the fundamentals of our democratic society is lacking in a basic qualification for teaching."[1] Some oaths sought to promote "respect for the flag," "reverence for law and order," or "faithful" job performance. Others had procedures for investigating and firing disloyal teachers. While educators have debated whether these oaths are a good way is ensure loyal teachers, courts have considered whether they are constitutional.

Can teachers be required to swear that they will promote "respect for the flag," "reverence for law and order" and "undivided allegiance" to the government?

The state of Washington required its teachers to swear to the above until the U.S. Supreme Court declared the oath unconstitutionally vague, ambiguous, and overly broad.[2] The Court wondered about the institutions for which the teacher is expected to "promote respect." Do they include those institutions to which most Americans are loyal? If so, the oath might prevent a teacher from criticizing his state's judicial system, the Supreme Court, or the FBI. Would a teacher who refused to say the Pledge of Allegiance because of religious beliefs be charged with breaking the promise to promote respect for the flag? "It would not be unreasonable," wrote Justice White, "for the serious-minded oath taker to conclude that he should dispense with lectures voicing far-reaching criticism of any old or new [government] policy" lest he be accused of violating his oath to "promote undivided allegiance" to the U.S. government. The result of these uncertainties is that teachers who are conscientious about their "solemn oath" and sensitive to the dangers posed by the oath's indefinite language can avoid risk "only by restricting their conduct to that which is unquestionably safe." Free speech, wrote the Court, "may not be so inhibited." Whenever statutes place limits on First Amendment freedoms, they must be "narrowly drawn," and the conduct prohibited must be "defined specifically" so that the teachers affected remain secure in their rights to engage in constitutionally protected activity.

Can teachers be required to swear that they are not subversive and do not teach others to overthrow the government by force or revolution?

No. In two related cases, the Supreme Court held that "negative" oaths that prohibit "subversive activities" are unconstitutional. In the first case, the Court noted that it was not clear what "subversive" or "revolutionary" activity includes.[3] Does revolution include altering the government through any rapid or fundamental change? If so, any person supporting or teaching peaceful but far-reaching constitutional amendments might be engaged in subversive activity. In the second case, a Maryland loyalty oath law provided for the discharge of subversive persons and called for perjury action against those who violated the oath.[4] The Court wrote that "the continuing surveillance which this type of law places on teachers is hostile to academic freedom," and its "overbreadth" makes possible "oppressive or capricious applications as regimes change." Here, concluded the Court, "we have another classic example of the need for 'narrowly drawn' legislation in this sensitive and important First Amendment area."

Can teachers be required to swear that they will uphold the federal and state constitutions?

Yes. A group of Denver teachers argued that such an oath was unconstitutional, but a federal court disagreed.[5] According to the court, the oath is simply a recognition of our system of constitutional law. It is not overly broad and is not an improper invasion of a teacher's freedom of expression. On the contrary, the judge wrote that "support for the constitutions and laws of the nation and state does not call for blind subservience." This oath, explained the court, has roots as deep as the Constitution, which requires that government officials swear to uphold it. Thus the writers of the Constitution thought the requirements of a positive loyalty oath was worth whatever minor deprivation of freedom of conscience might be involved.

Is an oath that teachers will "faithfully perform" their duties constitutional?

Yes. Again, Denver teachers argued that this oath was unconstitutionally vague, and again the court disagreed.[6] It held that a state can reasonably ask teachers in public schools to subscribe to professional competence and dedication. "It is certain," wrote the court, "that there is no right to be unfaithful in the performance of duties."

Is a loyalty oath unconstitutional if it applies to teachers and not to other state employees?

No. Teachers claimed that such an oath deprived them of equal protection by arbitrarily requiring educators but not all state employees to take it. The court replied that an oath to uphold the federal and state constitutions is "an almost universal requirement of all public officials, including lawyers and judges, and it cannot be truthfully said that teachers are being picked on."[7] As long as the oath is reasonable as applied to teachers, who work in an influential area, there is no constitutional requirement that it be applied to all public employees.

May teachers be required to swear to "oppose the overthrow" of the government by any "illegal or unconstitutional method"?

Yes. Opponents of this Massachusetts oath said it raised the specter of "vague, undefinable responsibilities actively to combat a potential overthrow of the government." However, Chief Justice Burger rejected such "literal notions." On behalf of the Court, he wrote that the purpose of the oath was not to create specific responsibilities but "to assure that those in positions of public trust were willing to commit themselves to live by the constitutional process of our system," and not to use illegal force to change it.[8] The Chief Justice indicated his hope that these oaths and the intense controversy they cause might someday disappear. "The time may come," he wrote, "when the value of oaths in routine public employment will be thought not worth the candle." The Court concluded that those who fear the oath may lead to the prosecution of innocent people should bear in mind that such dire consequences will "not occur while this Court sits."

POLITICAL AND SOCIAL AFFILIATIONS

Can a teacher be fired for belonging to a communist, Nazi, or revolutionary organization?

No. A teacher cannot be punished merely for being a member of such an organization. This was the ruling of the U.S. Supreme Court in the case of a New York instructor Harry Keyishian.[9] To comply with state law, Keyishian was asked to sign a certificate stating that he was not a communist. The law disqualified any New York public school teacher or administrator who belonged to an organization that advocated the overthrow of the government by illegal means. When Keyishian refused to sign the certificate, his contract was not renewed. Administrators explained that to preserve our democracy, it was reasonable not to employ teachers who belonged to subversive organizations.

The Supreme Court disagreed. On behalf of the Court, Justice Brennan wrote: "Under our traditions, beliefs are personal and not a matter of mere association, and men in adhering to a political party or other organization do not subscribe unqualifiedly to all of its platforms or asserted principles. A law which applies to membership, without the specific intent to further the illegal aims of the organization, infringes unnecessarily on protected freedoms. It rests on the doctrine of guilt by association which has no place here."

The Court believed that the New York law would "cast a pall of orthodoxy over the classroom," encourage suspicion and distrust, and restrict academic freedom in the schools. Thus, it would have a damaging effect on educators and the nation. "Teachers and students," wrote Justice Brennan, "must always remain free to inquire, to study, and to evaluate, to gain new maturity and understanding; otherwise our civilization will stagnate and die." According to the Court, those who join an organization but do not share its unlawful purposes and do not participate in its unlawful activities pose no threat, either as citizens or as teachers. Therefore, mere membership in the Communist party or any other subversive organization, without a specific intent to further the unlawful aims of the organization, is not a constitutional basis for excluding an individual from his teaching position.

Does the Keyishian case automatically void similar state laws prohibiting membership in subversive organizations?

No. When the Supreme Court declares a state law unconstitutional, similar statutes in other states are not automatically voided. They remain "on the books" and are sometimes enforced unless the state legislature repeals them or a court specifically holds that they are unconstitutional. This was the situation in Arkansas in the 1970s when a professor who advocated "revolutionary change" was fired under a state law which prohibited any "member of a Nazi, Fascist, or Communist" organization being employed by the state. In 1975, the Supreme Court of Arkansas reluctantly ruled that the law was unconstitutional.[10] After considering *Keyishian* and related decisions of the U.S. Supreme Court, the Arkansas court indicated that it had "no choice but to follow these decisions of the Court which is the final arbiter when constitutional interpretation is in dispute."

May teachers be prohibited from sending their children to private, segregated schools?

Yes, ruled a federal appeals court, in a case involving several Mississippi teachers.[11] The teachers were not rehired when they sent their children to private, segregated academies in violation of school board policy. The policy was designed to ensure faculty support for the desegregated public schools. The court upheld the policy because of evidence that students in desegregated classes are "likely to perceive rejection . . . from a teacher whose own children attend a nearby racially segregated school." Although the policy infringed upon the teachers' freedom of association, the court ruled in favor of the school board. Because of the importance·of desegregation, the court concluded that in this case the board may restrict the exercise of these teachers' associational rights, which conflict with their effectiveness and job performance.

Can teachers be denied employment because the people they married are controversial?

No. This would violate their constitutional right of free association. So ruled a federal court in the case of a middle school teacher who was denied a job because her husband was a controversial civil rights leader who helped organize a local school boycott.[12] The court concluded that the teacher could not be punished "because she elected to become the wife" of a civil rights activist.

Nevertheless, there are limits to a teacher's freedom of association in this area. These limits were confronted by a South Carolina teacher whose contract was not renewed because of his many serious personal problems with his wife. On several occasions she had assaulted him with a bottle and a knife, and once burst into his classroom and threatened his life. A federal court noted that school officials in this case were faced with a "potentially explosive and dangerous" domestic conflict, which had disrupted school activities. The court denied that a teacher's right to marry whom he wishes gives him the right "to engage in domestic altercations in the classroom of a public high school."[13] Rights and duties, concluded the court, must be weighed; and the board's duty to protect its students is paramount under the facts of this case.

Can teachers be prohibited from promoting political candidates in class?

Yes. An early California case provides an example of an educator who was punished for such behavior.[14] In 1922, a Sacramento teacher named Goldsmith suggested to his students that their parents support one of the candidates for school superintendent. According to Goldsmith, his candidate "would be more helpful to our department than a lady, and we need more men in our schools." As a result of these comments, the administration suspended him for "unprofessional conduct," and a state court supported this action. The judge observed that a teacher's "advocacy" of the election of a particular candidate before students in a public school and his attempts to influence students and their parents "introduced into the school questions wholly foreign to its purposes and objectives." Such conduct, wrote the court, can "stir up strife" among students over a political contest, and the results would disrupt school discipline.

May teachers wear political buttons, badges, or armbands to class?

Yes, they may, as long as such symbols do not interfere with a teacher's classroom performance and are not an attempt to proselytize or indoctrinate students. A case in point occurred when a New York English teacher, Charles James, refused to stop wearing an armband to class to protest the Vietnam war. As a result he was dismissed for presenting only one point of view on an important and controversial public issue. A federal appeals court ruled in James' favor.[15] The court noted that teachers do not "shed their constitutional rights to freedom of speech or expression at the school-house gate" unless they cause substantial disruption.

On the other hand, since students may be a captive audience, there must be some restraint on the free expression of a teacher's view. Thus, if a teacher tries to persuade students that they should adopt his or her values, it is reasonable "to expect the state to protect impressionable children from such dogmatism." In James' case, however, the wearing of an armband did not interfere with his teaching, was not coercive, and was not an attempt to indoctrinate.

Can teachers be prohibited from encouraging or participating in demonstrations?

No. Such a broad prohibition would violate a teacher's constitutional rights. This was the ruling of a federal court in Alabama where the legislature barred raises to any teacher who "participates in, encourages or condones . . . any extra-curricular demonstration."[16] The court acknowledged that a state may punish a teacher who disrupts schooling. But under this vague policy teachers can be punished for encouraging a peaceful demonstration. According to the court, this policy is a "comprehensive interference with associational freedom which goes far beyond what might be justified in the protection of the state's legitimate interest." Thus the court ruled that it was "clearly unconstitutional."

Can administrators refuse to hire a teacher who participated in disruptions at another school?

Yes. Bruce Franklin, a Marxist English scholar, had his appointment rejected by the University of Colorado because of his participation in disruptions at Stanford University. Franklin argued that he never violated any criminal statutes. But a federal judge noted that schools need not tolerate political conduct "substantially disrupting school discipline even though that conduct was perhaps not unlawful."[17] The judge emphasized that he was not ruling against Franklin because of his political beliefs or his associations with radical political groups. Rather, it was because (1) there was "clear and convincing" evidence that Franklin's conduct at Stanford "materially and substantially interfered with university activities," and (2) this was a reasonable basis to conclude that he posed a "substantial threat of material disruption" at the University of Colorado.

TEACHERS AND PARTISAN POLITICS

Can a teacher elected to public office be required to resign?

Yes. In 1976, Professor Mary Jane Galer was elected to the Georgia House of Delegates and requested an unpaid leave of absence. Because a state statute prohibited members of the legislature from being employed by a state agency, Galer's request was denied. She argued that the statute was unconstitutional because it restricted her right to hold office. The Georgia Supreme Court ruled that the law was a reasonable restriction on her rights because it furthered an important governmental interest.[18] Its purpose was to "enforce the separation of powers" and prevent "the obvious conflict of interests inherent in situations where an individual serves concurrently in two of the branches of state government." Thus the court ruled that Galer may be employed by her state college or by the legislature, but may not hold both positions at the same time. Although many schools grant leaves of absence to faculty members appointed or elected to political office, the *Galer* case indicates that they are under no constitutional obligation to do so.

Can a teacher be prohibited from running for political office?

Courts are split in this issue. Some hold that it is reasonable to require a teacher to resign before campaigning for public office; others feel that a general prohibition against running for any office is unconstitutional. In resolving this issue, one judge might focus on whether the prohibition is overly broad and vague; another might focus on what is involved in campaigning for and serving in the particular office. Such judges might consider whether campaigning would interfere with the teacher's duties, whether the office is highly political or nonpartisan, or whether the position might involve a conflict of interests (e.g., a teacher running for the school board that employs her).

In Florida, for example, a law professor was dismissed after he filed to seek the nomination for circuit judge because he violated a university rule prohibiting employees from engaging in "a political campaign for public office." The professor argued that the rule was unconstitutional, but a Florida court held that it was reasonable because

—The demands on the time and energies of a candidate in a "warmly contested" political campaign would necessarily affect his efficiency as a teacher.

—Campaigning can have a detrimental effect on the students not only because of the teacher's inefficiency but also because of the political influences that might be brought to bear on them.

—The potential political involvement of a state university, which depends on public support from all political elements, is a major consideration supporting the reasonableness of the prohibition against teachers running for office.[19]

On the other hand, an Oregon court ruled that a state law prohibiting public employees from running for any political office was unconstitutional.[20] The court recognized that the state could bar some of its employees from campaigning for some offices to promote an efficient public service. But this law went much further than necessary and broadly restricted the First Amendment right of political expression. The court noted that "a revolution has occurred in the law relative to the state's power to limit federal First Amendment rights. Thirty years ago the statutes now under consideration would have been held to be constitutional." But in this case the court declared the law prohibiting public employees from running for state, federal, or nonpartisan office "unconstitutional because of overbreadth." It cannot be demonstrated, concluded the court, "that the good of the public service requires all of the prohibitions of the present statute."

Can teachers be penalized for supporting a candidate for office?

No. In 1977 a federal court ruled in favor of two Texas teachers who were not rehired because they supported an unsuccessful school board candidate.[21] In addition, the court ruled that several members of the school board could be held personally liable for damages since their failure to rehire these teachers "because of their political associations was done in disregard of the teachers' clearly established constitutional rights." In a related West Virginia case, several school employees were not rehired because they failed to support an influential board member for reelection. In this 1978 decision, the judge wrote that a non-policy-making government employee "may not be discharged from a job that he or she is satisfactorily performing upon the sole ground of his political beliefs or activities."[22]

May teachers be prohibited from taking an active part in partisan politics?

Probably. Since the U.S. Supreme Court has upheld the Hatch Act, which prevents federal employees from being active in partisan politics, it is likely that school districts could impose similar restrictions on their teachers. The purpose of the Hatch Act is to reduce the hazards to fair and impartial government, prevent political parties from using public employees for political campaigns, and prohibit selection for government employment being based on political performance. Yet the act does not bar all political activities. Employees are allowed to vote and contribute funds, to express their opinions on political subjects and candidates, to display political stickers and badges, and to take an active part in nonpartisan elections. Many school districts allow greater political freedom for their teachers. But a 1973 Supreme Court ruling concerning federal employees indicates that Hatch Act-type restrictions on teachers probably would be upheld.[23]

Can teachers be prohibited from taking part in all political activity except voting?

No, ruled a federal court in a Texas case.[24] The court acknowledged that school boards can protect their educational system from undue political activity that may "materially and substantially interfere" with their schools. But a broad ban on *all* political activity went too far and violated the teacher's constitutional rights. This prohibition, wrote the judge, threatens popular government, not only "because it injures the individuals muzzled, but also because of its harmful effect on the community" in depriving it of the political participation of its teachers.

STUDENT ORGANIZATIONS

Is freedom of association a constitutional right?

Yes, it is. Although freedom of association is not directly mentioned in the Constitution, the Supreme Court has held the right to be "implicit" in the freedoms of speech, assembly, and petition. "Among the rights protected by the First Amendment," wrote Justice Lewis Powell, "is the right of individuals to associate to further their personal beliefs."[25] While courts have broadly protected this right among teachers and other adults, it has been more narrowly applied to students in the public schools.

Can secret societies be prohibited in public schools?

Yes. As early as 1909, the California legislature declared it unlawful for any public student to become a member of any secret society or club. In defending this legislation, a state court wrote that such groups "tend to engender an undemocratic spirit of caste" and "to promote cliques" among students.[26] The judge noted that "regulations have recently been adopted by boards of education in many cities of the country" to curb the negative effects of secret organizations, and "courts have uniformly held valid reasonable rules adapted by school authorities to prevent the establishment" of such groups. This decision was written in 1912, and it is still the prevailing legal opinion on the subject.

Can schools prohibit students from belonging to fraternities, sororities, and other undemocratic organizations?

Yes. Although adults cannot be prohibited from joining undemocratic groups, courts have held that such prohibitions can apply to high school students "in their formative years." A California case concerned a former high school sorority that had given up it secret ritual, handshake, and Greek letter name and reorganized itself into the Manana Club. Despite these changes, the Sacramento School Board prohibited the Manana Club and other undemocratic organizations that perpetuate themselves by the decision of their own members. As a result, one of the members of the Manana Club went to court to have the rule declared unconstitutional. She argued that the club was not secret and submitted in evidence its constitution, which described its objectives as being "literature, charity, and democracy." But a California appeals court found that the club had different purposes than its stated objectives and upheld the school regulations.[27]

The court said that schools had authority to restrict student social organizations that try to create a membership composed of the "socially elite" by "self-perpetuation, rushing, pledging," and admitting a select few from the student body. The Manana Club rules provided that only twenty girls from the Sacramento schools could be rushed each semester; each candidate had to be sponsored by three members, and new members were chosen by a secret process. Thus the court concluded that the purpose of these prohibited organizations is "not to foster democracy (as the Manana constitution preaches) but to frustrate democracy (as the Manana Club by its admitted activities practices)."

Do many states have legislation outlawing undemocratic high school organizations, and have such laws been upheld?

Yes. Although such legislation might seem inconsistent with the principles of the *Tinker* decision, judges have pointed out that statutes in about twenty-five states have outlawed high school fraternities, sororities, and organizations such as the Manana Club and that numerous cases over the past fifty years have upheld such legislation against attack on the grounds of unconstitutionality. In the 1966 case discussed above,[28] the judge noted that the following states have legislation similar to California's, which makes it unlawful for any public school student to join "any fraternity, sorority or secret club": Arkansas, Colorado, Florida, Illinois, Indiana, Iowa, Kansas, Louisiana, Maine, Massachusetts (optional with local board), Michigan, Minnesota, Mississippi, Montana, Nebraska, New Jersey, Ohio, Oklahoma, Oregon, Pennsylvania, Rhode Island, Texas (limited), Vermont, Virginia, Washington. A 1978 report added Maryland, Missouri, and New York (optional with local board) to the list of states that prohibit public schools from setting up secret organizations.[29]

Are schools required to recognize controversial student groups?

Probably. Public schools are not required to recognize any extracurricular student organizations. But if they recognize some political groups (e.g., Young Democrats or Republicans or a United Nations Club), then they cannot discriminate against other groups (e.g., socialists or conservatives) simply because of the unpopularity or controversial quality of their ideas or goals.

In a 1972 Supreme Court case, Justice Powell ruled that college officials could not deny recognition to Students for a Democratic Society, a "leftist" organization whose philosophy was in conflict with that of the school.[30] Justice Powell wrote that "denial of recognition, without justification to college organizations," abridges their constitutional right of association. This is because nonrecognition usually restricts a group's ability to function by denying it use of school facilities such as meeting rooms, bulletin boards, and the school newspaper. The court ruled that basic disagreement with a group's philosophy was not justification for nonrecognition. Although this case did not involve precollege students, the same principles are likely to apply to public high schools.

Does recognition of an organization imply approval of its goals or programs?

No, courts generally hold that it does not.[31] The purpose of recognition is to enable school officials to be informed about the purposes and activities of an organization; to ensure that student groups understand and are willing to comply with reasonable school rules; and to establish procedure for governing the time, place, and manner in which groups may conduct their activities. If school officials used the term "registered" rather than "recognized" student organization, they might lessen the tendency of some parents and educators to erroneously believe that recognition implies approval.

Can schools regulate or restrict student organizations?

Yes. Administrators can require student groups to obey a variety of reasonable regulations governing the equitable and responsible use of school facilities. Groups that fail to comply with such regulations can be disciplined and barred from campus. Moreover, the Supreme Court ruled that school officials would be justified in refusing to recognize a proposed organization if there was evidence that the group was likely to be a disruptive influence and break "reasonable rules, interrupt classes, or substantially interfere" with other students.[32]

Are student religious groups entitled to recognition?

Probably not. In 1977, a California appeals court ruled that a public school was not required to recognize a proposed Bible study club that wanted to meet in school during lunch hour.[33] The court held that permitting the group to operate on campus during school hours would "foster excessive state entanglement with religion." The First Amendment, concluded the court, does not allow an organization to use public school facilities to proselytize their beliefs among students, who are compelled to be on campus.

Must public schools recognize gay student groups?

The answer is uncertain, although courts have generally ruled in favor of gay college groups that have been denied recognition. Judges have reasoned that college students "of whatever sexual persuasion have the fundamental right to meet [and] discuss current problems" so long as they do not advocate un-lawful activity.[34] There has not yet been an appellate court case on this topic concerning the public schools, but it is probable that judges will give admin-istrators wider latitude in denying recognition to high school student groups promoting unconventional sexual ideas or practices because such students are still in their formative years and public schools have a responsibility to guide the social and emotional development of their students.

DEMONSTRATIONS AND PROTESTS

Do students have a right to demonstrate on campus?

Yes. School officials probably could not issue a total prohibition against all demonstrations anywhere on campus without violating students' First Amendment rights. On the other hand, administrators clearly have the au-thority to protect safety, property, and normal school operations by placing reasonable, nondiscriminatory restrictions on the time, place, and manner of proposed demonstrations.

In Pennsylvania, a group of high school students were suspended for par-ticipating in a sit-in demonstration, although they attempted to conduct their protest in a peaceful and orderly fashion. The evidence indicated that some demonstrators were noisy, skipped classes, and required others to be relo-cated. Therefore, despite the students' peaceful intentions, the judge ruled against them because the evidence indicated that their protest substantially interfered with the educational process.[35] On the other hand, the court noted that the demonstration was not illegal merely because it was in school, because other students gathered to watch, or because school administrators did not attend to their regular duties. (Related questions appear on pages 128–29.)

Can controversial speakers be prohibited from public schools?

No, not simply because they are controversial or are likely to express unpop-ular views. Although public schools probably can prohibit *all* outside speak-ers, officials do not have the authority to discriminate against views with which they and most citizens or students disagree.

After a New Hampshire school official denied a socialist candidate the op-portunity to speak, a federal court wrote that the First Amendment "encom-passes the right to receive information and ideas," and its protection extends to listeners as well as speakers.[36] When a school chooses to provide a forum for outside speakers, it must do so in a way that is consistent with constitu-tional principles. According to the court, this means that (1) school officials may not influence a public forum by censoring the ideas, the speakers, or the audience; (2) the right of students to hear speakers cannot be left to the com-plete discretion of administrators; and (3) freedom of speech and assembly requires that "outside speakers be fairly selected and that equal time be given to opposing views."

Can schools bar all outside political speakers?

No. A case confronting this issue arose in Oregon when a high school teacher invited a variety of political speakers, including a communist, to his class. Before the communist was to speak, the school board banned "all political speakers" from the high school. This ban was ruled unconstitutional by a federal court.[37]

The judge acknowledged that schools might exclude all speakers, unqualified speakers, or speakers who would cause disruption. But officials could not bar only "outside political speakers," nor could they contend that "political subjects are inappropriate in a high school curriculum." On the contrary, the court noted that political subjects are frequently discussed in schools and such discussions are often "required by law."

The judge acknowledged the problem faced by school officials in a community in which many equate communism with "violence, deception and imperialism." He observed, however, that schools would eliminate much of their curriculum if they teach only about "pacifist, honest, and nonexpansionist societies." "I am firmly convinced," concluded the judge, "that a course designed to teach students that a free and democratic society is superior to those in which freedoms are sharply curtailed will fail entirely if it fails to teach one important lesson: that the power of the state is never so great that it can silence a man or woman simply because there are those who disagree."

SUMMARY

In recent decades, the Supreme Court has looked critically at teacher loyalty oaths since they tended to inhibit the exercise of First Amendment freedoms. Negative oaths (e.g., swearing that one does not belong to any subversive organization) were usually held unconstitutional. Similarly, oaths that were "overbroad," uncertain, and ambiguous were also struck down—especially when there were statutory procedures to "police" the oath and punish violators. Nevertheless, two kinds of oaths have been consistently upheld: (1) loyalty oaths drawn with precision and prohibiting clearly unlawful conduct, and (2) positive employment oaths affirming support for the state and federal constitutions or pledging to uphold professional standards.

Teachers cannot be dismissed simply because they are members of a revolutionary or subversive organization unless they have supported the organization's illegal activities. Similarly, teachers cannot be fired because they associate with political extremists or because their spouse engages in controversial activities unless competent evidence indicates that such behavior clearly impairs the teacher's effectiveness.

In recent years, teachers' organizations have become powerful political machines, and individual teachers are no longer prohibited from engaging in all political activity. Today's teachers cannot be punished merely for wearing political symbols, for supporting particular candidates, or for participating in political demonstrations. On the other hand, they have no right to use their position to campaign for candidates, to indoctrinate students, or to urge disruptive political action. While in some districts teachers may run for and hold partisan political office, this is not a constitutional right; it usually depends on state legislation or local policy.

Although adults have the right to join secret and undemocratic organizations, courts have refused to grant these rights to public school students. Statutes in over twenty states have outlawed high school fraternities, sororities, and similar groups that chose their members in a undemocratic manner. Numerous cases during the past sixty years have upheld such laws against charges of unconstitutionality.

When school officials refuse to recognize a proposed student organization without justification, such action violates the students' constitutional rights of association. This means that if administrators deny recognition to a student group, they bear a "heavy burden" to demonstrate the appropriateness of their action. On the other hand, schools may issue reasonable rules concerning the time, place, and manner by which student groups must conduct their activities; and they may deny recognition to groups that do not follow such rules.

When schools provide a forum for outside speakers, they must give equal time to opposing views and may not discriminate among proposed speakers or censor their ideas. Moreover, public schools may not ban all political speakers or all candidates for public office or prohibit views with which most students, teachers, or parents disagree. Student groups can be required to request approval of school officials before inviting an outside speaker. If a request is denied, there must be a fair and prompt hearing.

In short, the associational freedoms of students and teachers have expanded in recent years; however, their right to freedom of association has not been as broadly protected by the courts as has their right to freedom of expression.

NOTES

1. As quoted in Robert R. Hamilton, LEGAL RIGHTS AND LIABILITIES OF TEACHERS (Laramie, Wyo.: School Law Publications, 1956), p. 84.
2. *Baggett* v. *Bullitt*, 377 U.S. 360 (1964).
3. *Id.*
4. *Whitehall* v. *Elkins*, 389 U.S. 54 (1967).
5. *Ohlson* v. *Phillips*, 304 F.Supp. 1152 (D. Col. 1969), aff'd, 397 U.S. 317 (1970).
6. *Id.*
7. *Id.*
8. *Cole* v. *Richardson*, 405 U.S. 676 (1972).
9. *Keyishian* v. *Board of Regents of New York*, 385 U.S. 589 (1967).
10. *Cooper* v. *Henslee*, 522 S.W.2d 391 (Ark. 1975).

11. *Cook* v. *Hudson*, 511 F.2d 744 (5th Cir. 1975).

12. *Randle* v. *Indianola Municipal Separate School District*, 373 F. Supp. 766 (N.D. Miss. 1974).

13. *Mescia* v. *Berry*, 406 F.Supp. 1181 (D. S.C. 1974).

14. *Goldsmith* v. *Board of Education*, 225 Pac. 783 (Cal. 1924).

15. *Charles James* v. *Board of Education of Central District No. 1*, 461 F.2d 566 (2d Cir. 1972).

16. *Alabama Education Association* v. *Wallace*, 362 F.Supp. 682 (M.D. Ala. 1973).

17. *Franklin* v. *Atkins*, 409 F.Supp. 439 (Colo. 1976).

18. *Galer* v. *Board of Regents of the University System*, 236 S.E.2d 617 (Ga. 1977).

19. *Jones* v. *Board of Control*, 131 So.2d 713 (Fla. 1961).

20. *Minielly* v. *State*, 411 P.2d 69 (Ore. 1966).

21. *Guerra* v. *Roma Independent School District*, 444 F.Supp. 812 (S.D. Tex. 1977).

22. *Miller* v. *Board of Education of the County of Lincoln*, 450 F.Supp. 106 (S.D. W.Va. 1978).

23. *United States Civil Service Commission* v. *National Association of Letter Carriers, AFL-CIO*, 413 U.S. 548 (1973).

24. *Montgomery* v. *White*, 320 F.Supp. 303 (E.D. Tex. 1969).

25. *Healy* v. *James*, 408 U.S. 169 (1972).

26. *Robinson* v. *Sacramento City Unified School District*, 53 Cal. Rptr. 781 (1966).

27. *Id.*

28. *Id.*

29. STATE LEGAL STANDARDS FOR THE PROVISION OF PUBLIC EDUCATION (Washington, D.C.: National Institute of Education, 1978), p. 32.

30. *Healy, supra.*

31. *Gay Alliance of Students* v. *Matthews*, 544 F.2d 162 (4th Cir. 1976).

32. *Healy, supra.*

33. *Johnson* v. *Huntington Beach Union High School District*, 137 Cal. Rptr. 43 (1977).

34. *Gay Alliance of Students, supra.*

35. *Gebert* v. *Hoffman*, 336 F.Supp. 694 (E.D. Pa. 1972). For a more restrictive decision, see *Sword* v. *Fox*, 446 F.2d 1091 (4th Cir. 1971).

36. *Vail* v. *Board of Education of Portsmouth*, 354 F.Supp. 592 (D. N.H. 1973).

37. *Wilson* v. *Chancellor*, 418 F.Supp. 1358 (D. Ore. 1976).

11

When can schools restrict personal appearance?

OVERVIEW

During the 1950s, teachers and students rarely questioned a school's dress and grooming codes. Had students or teachers thought of challenging these codes in court, they would have uniformly lost. Few imagined that personal appearance would become a constitutional issue. But during the late 1960s and 1970s, it did. Little more than a decade ago, teachers were expected to be adult models of neatness and good taste to their students; teachers were to conform to the dress and grooming standards of other professionals in the community. And for the most part they did. In the late 1960s teachers began to challenge dress and grooming codes, and many school districts abandoned them. As a result many teachers came to believe that such codes were unconstitutional. But this is far from true. An issue that seemed buried in the 1970s has reemerged in the 1980s.

Controversy over student dress and grooming was especially intense a decade ago. In fact, long hair and unconventional clothes were among the hottest students' rights issues of the time.* And they were often viewed as important symbols of protest and dissent by teachers as well as students.

Unlike most constitutional controversies that bombard the courts, judges have been deeply divided over the question of grooming in the public schools. Although they are less divided about appropriate school clothing, the law concerning personal appearance still differs among the

---

* Grooming controversies did not begin in the 1960s. Disputes about hair length have been taking place on this continent at least since 1649 when the magistrates of Portsmouth decried "the wearing of long hair, after the manner of ruffians" and declared their "dislike and detestation against wearing such long hair, as against a thing uncivil and unmanly."[1]

states. The constitutional and educational reasons underlying these differences and the current state of the law on the subject are examined in this chapter.

GROOMING STANDARDS FOR TEACHERS

Can teachers be punished without due process for violating a school's grooming code?

No. What constitutes due process in cases such as this was explained by a federal court in a Massachusetts controversy.[2] A teacher named David Lucia grew a beard one winter vacation. This conflicted with an unwritten school policy explained to Lucia by the superintendent after the vacation. When Lucia failed to shave his beard following a meeting with the school committee, he was suspended because of "insubordination and improper example set by a teacher." He was not invited to a subsequent meeting at which the committee voted to dismiss him, and he took his case to court.

The court did not decide whether a teacher had a constitutional right to wear a beard. However, it did rule that Lucia's freedom to wear a beard could not be taken from him without due process. The court noted several deficiencies in the procedure used to dismiss Lucia: prior to this case, there was no written or announced policy against teachers wearing beards; the committee did not explain to Lucia the charges against him; and it did not indicate that failure to remove his beard would result in the dismissal. After criticizing the committee's lack of due process, the court observed: "The American public school system, which has a basic responsibility for instilling in its students an appreciation of our democratic system, is a peculiarly appropriate place for the use of fundamentally fair procedures."

From this case we can conclude that a teacher cannot be lawfully dismissed for wearing a beard or sideburns unless (1) there is a clear school policy outlawing such grooming, (2) teachers are given adequate notice of the policy and the consequences of not adhering to it, and (3) teachers are given the right to request a hearing if specific facts are in dispute.

Can schools require teachers to be clean-shaven?

Judges are divided over this issue. A few courts have held that grooming for teachers is a constitutional right. In the case of a Pasadena school teacher, Paul Finot, a California appeals court explained why it ruled this way.[3] When Finot arrived at school one September wearing a recently grown beard, his principal asked him to shave it off. After he refused, the board of education transferred him to home teaching because he violated the teacher handbook requirement that teachers conform to acceptable standards of dress and grooming and set an example of neatness and good taste. This was related to the student handbook, which prohibited beards and mustaches. The administrators were concerned that Finot's beard might attract undue attention, interfere with education, and make the prohibition of beards for students more difficult to enforce.

The court was not persuaded by these arguments. It ruled that Finot's right to wear a beard was guarded by two constitutional provisions. It was one of the liberties protected by the Fourteenth Amendment, and it was a form of symbolic expression protected by the First Amendment. The court noted that some people interpret a beard as a symbol of masculinity, authority, or wisdom; others see it as a symbol of nonconformity or rebellion. In either case, the court felt that such symbols "merit constitutional protection." Thus the court ruled that beards on teachers "cannot constitutionally be banned from the classroom" unless the school can show that the beard had an adverse effect on the educational process.

Have most courts ruled that teachers have a constitutional right to wear beards and sideburns?

No. Although courts are divided over this issue, the trend of recent decisions seems to be against granting constitutional protection to teacher grooming. While an increasing number of school districts have abolished detailed grooming codes for teachers, this is often because of administrative willingness to allow greater freedom in this area rather than because constitutional law requires it.

In the case of an Illinois math teacher, a federal appeals court reflected the view of many judges who do not believe teacher grooming is a major constitutional issue.[4] When Max Miller's contract was not renewed because of his beard and sideburns, he alleged that this violated his rights. The judge acknowledged that he personally regarded "dress and hair style as matters of relatively trivial importance on any scale of values in appraising the qualifications of a teacher." He noted that, logically, appearance should not be significant and that "a teacher should be able to explain the pythagorean theorem as well in a T-shirt as in a three-piece suit." But the court doubted whether grooming choices are protected by the Constitution and indicated that school officials may consider an individual's appearance as one of the factors affecting his suitability. Therefore the court concluded that if a school board decided a "teacher's style of dress or plumage" had an adverse educational impact, there was "no doubt that the interest of the teacher is subordinate to the public interest." But this court went even further and ruled that a school could restrict a teacher's grooming even if it did *not* interfere with the educational process. Why? Because the court concluded that allowing local boards "the freedom to make diverse choices" and the "latitude to discharge their responsibilities"—and inevitably "to make mistakes from time to time"—outweighs the teachers' interests in grooming cases.

In a related case upholding a school's antibeard policy for teachers, the Tennessee Supreme Court wrote: "The grooming of one person is of concern not only to himself but to all others with whom he comes in contact; we have to look at each other whether we like it or not. It is for this reason that society sets certain limits upon the freedom of individuals to choose his own grooming."[5] Commenting on the notion that the teacher's beard was an "unjustified diversion to the class," a concurring judge felt that honesty required him to observe that "without his beard," the teacher might "furnish an even more detrimental diversion of attention. Who knows?"

Is grooming a constitutional right if it reflects a teacher's racial or ethnic values and beliefs?

Yes, ruled a federal court in the case of Booker Peek, a black teacher from Florida, who wore a goatee as a matter of racial pride. Although Peek was a superior high school French teacher, he was not rehired because he refused repeated requests to remove his goatee. The principal said the denial of reappointment was based on his discretionary power to ensure appropriate dress and discipline. Peek called the action unconstitutional, and the court agreed.[6] According to the court, when a goatee is worn by a black man as an expression of his heritage, culture, and racial pride, its wearer "enjoys the protection of First Amendment rights." Furthermore, there was no evidence that the goatee disrupted school discipline. Thus it appeared that the decision not to recommend reappointment was racially motivated and tainted with "institutional racism," the effects of which were manifested in "an intolerance of ethnic diversity and racial pride."

TEACHERS' CLOTHING

Do teachers have a right to dress as they wish? Is this right protected by the Constitution?

Not usually. First, courts that do not protect a teacher's grooming choice will not protect clothing choice. Second, even courts that recognize grooming as constitutionally protected may not rule the same way in matters of dress because judges feel that school regulations concerning dress are not as personal and that their impact is not as great as grooming restrictions. Unlike beards or hair length, clothing can easily be changed after school hours. Therefore most teachers who challenge clothing regulations do not argue that they have a right to dress any way they wish; rather, they contend that the dress code is arbitrary, unreasonable, or discriminatory. This was the argument used by Edward Blanchet after he was suspended for violating a Louisiana school board dress policy requiring that male teachers wear neckties.

The state appeals court wrote positively about Blanchet's sincerity, convictions, and character and described him as "a dedicated and effective teacher, an assistant principal at his school, [and] a sober church-going family man." Nevertheless, the court ruled against him.[7] The judge wrote that the court could not overturn school policy and substitute its judgment for that of the board unless the board's action was clearly unreasonable and arbitrary. Since the purpose of the board's rule was to enhance the professional image of its teachers in the eyes of students and parents, and since there was some evidence supporting the rule, the court concluded that it could not find the necktie policy arbitrary or unreasonable.

In a related case, a twenty-five-year-old high school French teacher was not rehired because she insisted on wearing short skirts in the youthful style of the late 1960s. Observed a federal appeals court, the teacher was terminated because her "image" was "overexposed." Although the court had recognized grooming as a constitutional right, it refused to extend constitutional protection to clothing regulations, which the court felt involve less personal matters and only affect teachers during school hours.[8]

Could a teacher's refusal to conform to a school dress code be protected as a form of symbolic expression?

Not usually. This was the argument used by Richard Brimley, an English teacher from East Hartford, Connecticut. Since Brimley wanted to present himself to his students as a person not tied to "establishment conformity," he refused to comply with his school's dress code, which required a coat and tie for male teachers. Brimley argued that an individual's appearance was protected by the First Amendment as a form of symbolic expression and academic freedom, which should give teachers wide discretion over teaching methods and style of clothing—especially when they are sincere, neat, and reasonable. Moreover, he argued that a tie was no longer mandatory nor even typical among other young professionals and that the requirement did not promote discipline, respect, or good grooming among students.

Two judges of a federal appeals court were persuaded by these arguments, but the majority was not.[9] On behalf of the majority, Judge Meskill wrote that federal courts should not even overturn school rules that "appear foolish or unwise" unless they directly involve "basic constitutional values." If courts decided a dress code controversy (on the theory that it involved an "expressive activity"), then they could be asked to rule on every insubstantial school policy. Therefore, wrote Judge Meskill, "we are unwilling to expand the First Amendment protection to include a teacher's sartorial choice." If we bring "trivial activities" under constitutional protection, "we trivialize the Constitution." The court concluded that "we must be careful not to 'cry wolf' at every minor restraint on a citizen's liberty."

STUDENTS' GROOMING: A CONSTITUTIONAL RIGHT?

Are students free to wear their hair as they wish?

About half of the U.S. circuit courts of appeals answer yes to this question. A typical case arose in Indiana's Wawasee High School where a committee of students, teachers, and administrators developed a dress code "to insure the best possible overall appearance" of the student body. The code was adopted by a vote of students, and they and their parents were notified of its provisions before the beginning of the school year. Nevertheless, when school opened, Greg Carpenter, with his parents' consent, chose to violate the code's "long hair provision" and was punished. As a result Greg's father sued on his behalf to prohibit enforcement of the code's hair length regulations.*

The school board argued that because the code was adopted by a majority of the students, it was not an unreasonable interference with Greg Carpenter's constitutional rights. But the Seventh U.S Circuit Court of Appeals disagreed.[10] It held that "the right to wear one's hair at any length or in any desired manner is an ingredient of personal freedom protected by the United States Constitution." To limit that right, a school would have to bear a "substantial burden of justification." Here the board did not meet that burden. It presented no evidence that Greg's hair disrupted classroom decorum or interfered with other students, or that the hair provision was related to safety or health. The school showed no reasonable relationship between the code and a significant educational purpose. Therefore the court concluded that the democratic process by which the code was adopted did not justify the denial of Greg's constitutional right to wear his hair as he chose. The U.S. Constitution, said the court, cannot be amended by majority vote of any school or community.

What other arguments support student grooming rights?

Judges have used a variety of legal, educational, and philosophic arguments to uphold grooming as a constitutional right. Here are a few:

A personal liberty protected by the Fourteenth Amendment. In holding unconstitutional a Marlboro, Massachusetts, school policy forbidding "unusually long hair," the First Circuit Court of Appeals noted that the case involved the constitutional protection of certain "uniquely personal aspects of one's life."[11] The court ruled that grooming was protected by the Due Process Clause of the Fourteenth Amendment, which "establishes a sphere of personal liberty for every individual," subject to restriction only if the exercise of that liberty interferes with the rights of others. The court saw "no inherent reason why decency, decorum, or good conduct" requires a boy to wear his hair short. Nor, it concluded, does "compelled conformity to conventional standards of appearance seem a justifiable part of the educational process."

Symbolic speech protected by the First Amendment. Some courts argue that long hair is a form of symbolic speech by which the wearer conveys his individuality or rejection of conventional values and that it should therefore be protected under the First Amendment. According to one judge, "A person shorn of the freedom to vary the length and style of his hair is forced against his

---

* The code contained a consent provision that allowed noncompliance if at the beginning of each semester a parent appeared before the principal and gave written consent for the exception of his child. Greg's father decided not to seek an exception but to challenge the constitutionality of the code.

will to hold himself out symbolically as a person holding ideas contrary, perhaps, to ideas he holds most dear. Forced dress, including forced hair style, humiliates the unwilling complier, forces him to submerge his individuality in the 'undistracting' mass, and in general, smacks of the exaltation of organization over member, unit over component, and state over individual."*[12]

A denial of equal protection. In an Indiana case, a high school principal said his grooming regulations were required for health and safety reasons and testified that long hair could cause problems in the gym, swimming pool, and laboratories. But the Seventh Circuit Court of Appeals observed that girls engaged in similar activities, yet only boys were required to wear short hair. Since the principal offered no reason why health and safety regulations were not equally applicable to girls, the court concluded that the rules constituted "a denial of equal protection to male students" in violation of the Fourteenth Amendment.[14] The court noted that legitimate health and safety objectives could be achieved simply through rules aimed directly at the problems caused by long hair—for example, by requiring swimming caps in pools and hairnets around machinery or Bunsen burners.

A right to govern one's personal appearance. In striking down a St. Charles, Missouri, dress code that prohibited long hair, the Eighth Circuit Court of Appeals wrote that each student possesses "a constitutionally protected right to govern his personal appearance while attending public high school."[15] Although there is some disagreement about the source of this right, the judge wrote that "the common theme underlying decisions striking down hair style regulations is that the Constitution guarantees rights other than those specifically enumerated, and that the right to govern one's personal appearance is one of those guaranteed rights."

In a concurring opinion, one of the judges rejected the arguments given by school officials to defend their grooming regulations in these words:

> The gamut of rationalizations for justifying this restriction fails in light of reasoned analysis. When school authorities complain variously that such hair styles are inspired by a communist conspiracy, that they make boys look like girls, that they promote confusion as to the use of restrooms, and that they destroy the students' moral fiber, then it is little wonder even moderate students complain of "getting up-tight." In final analysis, I am satisfied a comprehensive school restriction on male student hair styles accomplishes little more than to project the prejudices and personal distastes of certain adults in authority on to the impressionable young student.

---

* In a related North Carolina case a judge wrote that long hair is simply "a harkening back to the fashion of earlier years. For example, many of the founding fathers, as well as General Grant and General Lee, wore their hair . . . in a style comparable to that adopted by the [student] plaintiffs. Although there exists no depiction of Jesus Christ, either reputedly or historically accurate, he has always been shown with hair at least the length of that of the plaintiffs." Thus the judge noted that none of these great men would have been permitted to attend high school if the disputed hair regulations were enforced.[13]

Can schools restrict student grooming?

In about half the states, they can. A case in El Paso, Texas, illustrates the views of those courts which hold that schools have the authority to restrict student hair length. In this case, the Fifth Circuit Court of Appeals considered and rejected the following arguments, which were presented by a high school junior, Chelsey Karr.[16]

Symbolic speech. Although some students wear long hair to convey a message, the court noted that many wear it simply as a matter of personal taste or as a result of peer-group influence. Karr, for example, sued not because his hair symbolized anything but "because I like my hair long." Judge Morgan felt that it would be inappropriate and unworkable to have the Constitution protect students who intend to convey a message by wearing long hair but not other students.

A protected liberty. The court pointed out that individual liberties may be "ranked in a spectrum of importance." At one end are the "great liberties" such as speech and religion specifically guaranteed in the Bill of Rights. At the other end are the "lesser liberties" that may be curtailed if the restrictions are related to a proper state activity. The court concluded that hair regulations are reasonably related to schooling, that they do not restrict any fundamental constitutional liberty, and that their interference is a "temporary and relatively inconsequential one." Judge Morgan observed that administrators "must daily make innumerable decisions which restrict student liberty" including the regulation of student parking, eating, and attendance. Students should not be able to force administrators to defend such restrictions in court when fundamental rights are not involved.

Confusion and burden. The appeals court was disturbed that different trial courts in the circuit reached opposite results based on similar facts. Some held grooming regulations reasonable; others struck them down as arbitrary. The court was even more disturbed by "the burden which has been placed on the federal courts by suits of this nature" by the number of days spent on trials and appeals. Judge Morgan noted that it was impossible for the courts to protect every citizen against every minor restriction on his liberty. Because of this burden and because these cases do not raise issues of "fundamental" importance, the court ruled that henceforth all such regulations would be presumed valid.

Can extremes be distracting?

A federal appeals court upheld a California grooming regulation, although there was no evidence that students who broke the rule caused disruption.[17] A lack of disturbance, ruled the court, "does not establish that long-haired males cannot be a distracting influence which would interfere with the educative process the same way as any extreme in appearance, dress, or deportment." The court emphasized that "this is not a question of preference for or against certain male hair styles . . . the court could not care less." It is a question of the right of school authorities to develop a dress code in accord with their responsibilities.

What cases support administrative discretion?

In a 1975 Pennsylvania case, the Third Circuit Court declined to overturn school grooming regulations because it did not believe federal courts are the place to interpret "the conflicting ideals of student liberty and school regulation in the context of students' hair."[18] On the contrary, the court wrote that in these matters "the wisdom and experience of school authorities must be deemed superior and preferable" to the court's. Because our system of public education relies on the discretion and judgment of school administrators, federal courts should not attempt to correct errors in the exercise of that discretion unless basic constitutional rights are violated.

Why doesn't the Supreme Court resolve the grooming conflict?

When federal appeals courts differ in their interpretation of the Constitution, the U.S. Supreme Court usually reviews the question, renders a decision, and thus establishes a "uniform law of the land." But despite the sharp differences of opinion among federal courts concerning student grooming, the Supreme Court has on at least nine occasions declined to review the decisions on this issue. This is because most justices of the Court apparently do not believe the cases raise important constitutional questions of national significance. In rejecting an urgent appeal to the Supreme Court in one grooming case, Justice Black wrote: "The only thing about it that borders on the serious to me is the idea that anyone should think the Federal Constitution imposes on the United States courts the burden of supervising the length of hair that public school students should wear."[19] As long as the Supreme Court refuses to hear these cases, the law will continue to vary throughout the United States.

Can I know how the various federal courts are likely to rule on grooming cases?

Yes. Despite the many conflicts over grooming regulations, the law on this subject has become relatively clear, as Figure 1 indicates. During the 1970s, most U.S. circuit courts of appeals ruled on this issue directly, and the others have indicated how they would probably rule.

What is the law in my state?

The federal appeals courts have decided that grooming is a constitutional right in the First Circuit (Maine, Massachusetts, New Hampshire, Rhode Island), the Fourth Circuit (Maryland, North Carolina, South Carolina, Virginia, West Virginia), the Seventh Circuit (Illinois, Indiana, Wisconsin), the

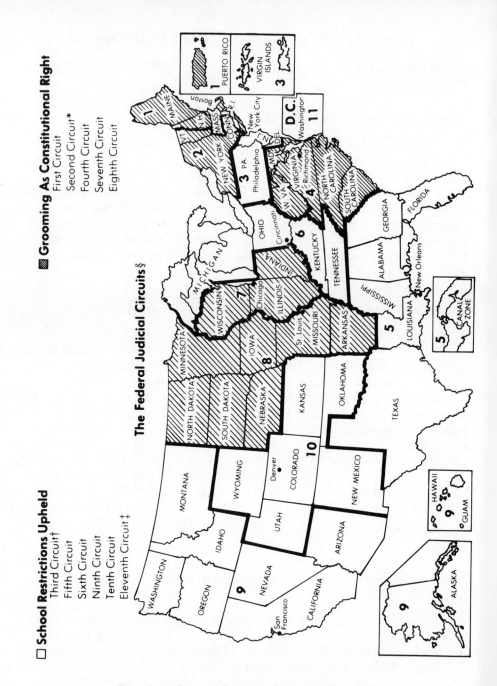

Figure 1. Circuit Court Rulings on Grooming

* Probable. See first note page 185.

† Probable. See second note page 185.

‡ Probable. See third note page 185.

§ A new federal circuit court has been added, effective October 1, 1981. See map on page 308.

Eighth Circuit (Arkansas, Iowa, Minnesota, Missouri, Nebraska, North Dakota, South Dakota), and probably the Second Circuit (Connecticut, New
York, Vermont).* In these states, courts will hold grooming regulations unconstitutional unless school officials present convincing evidence that they
are fair, reasonable, and necessary to carry out a legitimate educational purpose.

The law is different in the Fifth Circuit (Alabama, Florida, Georgia, Louisiana, Mississippi, Texas), the Sixth Circuit (Kentucky, Michigan, Ohio, Tennessee), the Ninth Circuit (Alaska, Arizona, California, Hawaiian Islands,
Idaho, Montana, Nevada, Oregon, Washington), the Tenth Circuit (Colorado, Kansas, Oklahoma, New Mexico, Utah, Wyoming), and probably in
the Third Circuit (Delaware, New Jersey, Pennsylvania)† and the Eleventh
Circuit (the District of Columbia).‡ In these states, the circuit courts have
decided that grooming is not a significant constitutional issue and that federal courts should not judge the wisdom of codes regulating hair length or
style. This does not necessarily mean that there is no legal remedy if a student is disciplined for violating school grooming regulations. It only means
that federal courts will generally not consider these cases. Such grooming restrictions may still be challenged in state courts.

SCHOOL DRESS CODES

May school codes regulate student clothing?

Yes. All courts recognize that schools have authority to regulate student
clothing. But not all dress codes are constitutional. In New Hampshire, for
example, a federal court held that a rule prohibiting the wearing of blue jeans
or dungarees was unconstitutional.[25] The court rejected the argument that
wearing jeans "detracts from discipline and a proper educational climate"
because the school presented no evidence supporting this position.

Can students wear anything they wish to school?

No. In the New Hampshire case, the judge wrote that a school "can and must
. . . exclude persons who are unsanitary, obscenely or scantily clad." Good
hygiene may require that dirty clothing be prohibited. And a school may

* In 1973, the Second Circuit clearly ruled that hair-length regulations raised "a substantial
constitutional issue."[20] Although the U.S. Supreme Court overruled that decision as it applied
to policemen,[21] the Second Circuit would probably reaffirm its decision as applied to students
because of the important differences between regulating the appearance of students and policemen and the refusal of the Supreme Court to rule on student hair cases.

† Although the Third Circuit held that civilian employees of the National Guard could challenge the Guard's hair-length regulations,[22] this court clearly ruled in 1975 that "the federal
courts should not intrude" in the area of school regulation of student hair length and that it
would no longer consider school grooming cases.[23]

‡ The D.C. Court of Appeals has not ruled directly on the issue of school grooming regulations,
but in a related case it indicated that it agreed with the U.S. Supreme Court and "sees no federal question in this area."[24]

prohibit scantily clad students "because it is obvious that the lack of proper covering, particularly with female students, might tend to distract other students" and disrupt the educational process. However, a no-jeans rule that is not clearly related to the educational process and intrudes on a student's personal liberty, "small as that intrusion may be," is unconstitutional.[26]

Can girls be prohibited from wearing slacks?

No. A state court annulled such a prohibition in a New York school district's dress code for secondary schools.[27] School boards have the authority to regulate dress for reasons of safety, order, and discipline, but they have no authority to enforce regulations not related to those factors. According to Judge Meyer, the fact that the no-slacks rule "applies only to female students" and applies to every kind of slacks "makes it evident that what is being enforced is style or taste and not safety, order, or discipline."

What kind of clothing regulations would probably be upheld by the courts?

In the New York "slacks" case, Judge Meyer gave several examples. In the interest of safety, a school board can probably prohibit "the wearing of bell-bottomed slacks by students . . . who ride bikes to school." In the interest of discipline, a regulation against slacks that are "so skintight and, therefore, revealing as to provoke or distract students of the opposite sex" might be valid. And in the interest of order, a rule against slacks "to the bottom of which small bells have been attached" would be upheld. According to the judge, such regulations would be valid because they clearly relate to the school's "authorized concerns"; a flat prohibition against all slacks is invalid "precisely because it does not."[28] Similarly an Arkansas judge indicated that the following dress code provisions would be held valid: prohibitions against girls wearing "excessively tight skirts or pants or dresses more than six inches above the knee" (to prevent immodest clothing), prohibitions against boys wearing shirttails outside their pants in "shop" (for safety reasons), or any student wearing clothing displaying obscene pictures.[29]

Will courts rule the same way in clothing cases as in hair controversies?

Sometimes. Courts that do not protect a student's choice of hairstyle will probably not protect his choice of clothing. But courts that *do* protect hairstyle may or may not protect student freedom in matters of dress. Some courts hold that the constitutional liberty that protects a student's grooming choice also protects his clothing choice. Other courts distinguish hair from clothing on the grounds that hair restrictions are more serious invasions of personal freedom. For example, a federal judge in Vermont held a school grooming code unconstitutional but noted that "the cut of one's hair style is more fundamental to personal appearance than the type of clothing he wears."[30] Clothing, wrote the judge, "can be changed at will, whereas hair, once it is cut, has to remain constant for substantial periods of time." Similarly, a Minnesota judge wrote: "Were a school to prohibit a boy attending school with no shirt," he could take off his shirt as he leaves the school grounds. But a hair regulation "invades private life beyond the school jurisdiction."[31]

Thus, some courts distinguish clothing from grooming on the following grounds: (1) hairstyle is more fundamental to personal appearance; (2) hair restrictions have a long-term effect; and (3) hairstyles today usually do not involve issues of morality and distraction, as do some clothing styles. For these reasons, some courts that recognize choice of hairstyle as a constitutional right do not protect a student choice of clothing. And even courts that protect both clothing and grooming give schools much wider discretion to regulate clothing in the interests of health, safety, order, or discipline.

SUMMARY

In the late 1960s and early '70s, several courts indicated that teacher grooming was a form of symbolic expression entitled to the protection of the First Amendment. Schools could not restrict a teacher's beard, mustache, or long hair unless they showed that it interfered with classroom effectiveness. But the trend of decision seems to have shifted. Most recent cases have indicated (1) that teachers do not have a constitutional right concerning their "style of plumage"; or (2) if they do, it deserves less protection than does the freedom of school boards to establish reasonable grooming codes for teachers.

Administrative discretion is even greater regarding teacher attire. Most courts have ruled that teachers do not have a constitutional right to dress as they please. Judges have even upheld the authority of administrators to discipline teachers for violating dress requirements the judges thought unwise or insignificant because it is assumed that all employers can establish some clothing regulations and because such restrictions on teacher freedom are relatively minor. Courts might protect certain nonconforming clothing under special circumstance—for example, a black teacher of African studies who wears a dashiki as a matter of academic freedom or racial pride. But it is doubtful that any court would protect a teacher who insisted on going to class in frayed jeans, sandals, and a T-shirt in violation of school policy.

As far as students are concerned, eight of the eleven U.S. circuit courts of appeals have clearly ruled on the constitutional right of students to choose the length of their hair.* Some circuits hold that grooming is a constitutional right, and others do not. The arguments used on each side are varied and vigorous, and no final decision establishing a uniform law has been reached be-

---

* The other three circuits have not ruled directly on this issue, but they have indicated how they probably would vote. See page 185.

cause the Supreme Court has refused to rule on the issue. Courts that support a student's right to wear his hair as he wishes argue that hairstyle is part of the personal liberty assured to citizens by the Due Process Clause of the Fourteenth Amendment; the "freedom to govern one's personal appearance" is retained by individual citizens under the Ninth Amendment, and it is part of the freedom of expression protected by the First Amendment. In addition, judges have argued that hair regulations are not related to a legitimate educational objective; they teach conformity for its own sake, and they are not necessary for health or safety. Their enforcement projects the prejudices of certain adults in authority and causes more disruption than does the presence of long-haired students. Courts that uphold school grooming regulations argue that the Constitution does not protect grooming, but even if it does, it is one of the "lesser liberties" and not a fundamental right. In addition, judges upholding school regulations note that their purpose is to eliminate distracting extremes in hairstyle, to avoid possible conflicts, and to eliminate potential health and safety hazards. Even if some codes restrict student freedom, their effect is temporary and still leave students a wide range of choice in grooming.

Most courts hold that student clothing styles are not protected by the Constitution. Moreover, some courts that protect student hair length reject students' claims to wear the clothing of their choice. Some courts justify the distinction on the grounds that restrictions on hairstyle are more serious invasions of individual freedom; clothing can be easily changed after school, but if haircuts are required, the effect is more lasting.

Compared to the "great grooming controversy," there are relatively few reported cases concerning student clothing. As one federal judge observed, this may indicate that students, teachers, and administrators do not look on clothes with the same emotion with which they regard hair length or more probably that most schools are no longer concerned with what a student wears "as long as it is clean and covers adequately those parts of the body that, by tradition, are usually kept from public view."

NOTES

1. Dale Goddy, RIGHTS AND FREEDOM OF PUBLIC SCHOOL STUDENTS (Topeka: National Organization on Legal Problems in Education, 1971), p. 25.

2. *Lucia* v. *Duggan*, 303 F.Supp. 112 (D. Mass, 1969).

3. *Finot* v. *Pasadena City Board of Education*, 58 Cal. Rptr. 520 (1967).

4. *Miller* v. *School District No. 167, Cook County, Illinois*, 495 F.2d. 658 (7th Cir. 1974).

5. *Morrison* v. *Hamilton Board of Education*, 494 S.W.2d 770 (Tenn. 1973).

6. *Braxton* v. *Board of Public Instruction of Duval County, Florida*, 303 F.Supp. 958 (M.D. Fla. 1969).

7. *Blanchet* v. *Vermilion Parish School Board*, 220 So.2d 534 (La. 1969).

8. *Tardif* v. *Quinn*, 545 F.2d. 761 (1st Cir. 1976).

9. *East Hartford Education Association* v. *Board of Education of the Town of East Hartford*, 562 F.2d. 838 (2d Cir. 1977).

10. *Arnold* v. *Carpenter*, 459 F.2d. 939 (7th Cir. 1972).
11. *Richards* v. *Thurston*, 424 F.2d. 1281 (1st Cir. 1970).
12. Judge Wisdom (dissenting), in *Karr* v. *Schmidt*, 460 F.2d. 609 (5th Cir. 1972).
13. *Massie* v. *Henry*, 455 F.2d 779 (4th Cir. 1972).
14. *Crews* v. *Cloncs*, 432 F.2d. 1259 (7th Cir. 1970).
15. *Bishop* v. *Colaw*, 450 F.2d. 1069 (8th Cir. 1971).
16. Karr v. *Schmidt*, 460 F.2d. 609 (5th Cir. 1972).
17. *King* v. *Saddleback*, 445 F.2d. 932 (9th Cir. 1971).
18. *Zeller* v. *Donegal School District Board of Education*, 517 F.2d. 600 (3rd Cir. 1975).
19. *Karr* v. *Schmidt*, 401 U.S. 1201 (1971).
20. *Dwen* v. *Barry*, 483 F.2d. 1126 (2d Cir. 1973).
21. *Kelley* v. *Johnson*, 425 U.S. 238 (1976).
22. *Syrek* v. *Pennsylvania Air National Guard*, 537 F.2d. 66 (3d Cir. 1976).
23. *Zeller* v. *Donegal*, 517 F.2d. 600 (3d Cir. 1975).
24. *Fagan* v. *National Cash Register Co.*, 481 F.2d. 1115 (D.C. Cir. 1973).
25. *Bannister* v. *Paradis*, 316 F.Supp. 185 (D. N.H. 1970).
26. *Id.*
27. *Scott* v. *Board of Education, Hicksville*, 305 N.Y. S.2d 601 (1969).
28. *Id.*
29. *Wallace* v. *Ford*, 346 F.Supp. 156 (E.D. Ark. 1972).
30. *Dunham* v. *Pulsifer*, 312 F.Supp. 411 (D. Vt. 1970).
31. *Westley* v. *Rossi*, 305 F.Supp. 706 (D. Minn. 1969).

12

What are my rights
under due process?

OVERVIEW

It is commonly accepted among lawyers that a right without adequate procedures to protect and enforce it is no right at all. This was recognized by the framers of the Constitution when they inserted the right to due process of law in both the Fifth and Fourteenth amendments. Attention in this chapter focuses on the Fourteenth Amendment, for public schools are agencies of the state, and the amendment provides that no "State deprive any person of life, liberty, or property, without due process of law." Courts have held that actions of school officials and board members are state actions; therefore, the Fourteenth Amendment applies to them.

Due process may be thought of in ordinary language as "fair process," an attempt to secure fairness in official actions. Most people gain their impressions of due process from television's presentation of criminal cases. This chapter focuses on civil cases, where individuals find themselves in conflict with school officials concerning their jobs or concerning some restrictions related to their work. In these matters, due process requires that governmental action not be arbitrary, unreasonable, or discriminatory and that fair procedures be followed by officials before depriving anyone of "life, liberty, or property."

DUE PROCESS FOR TEACHERS

When is official action arbitrary or unreasonable?

Like many other concepts used to govern human affairs, terms such as "arbitrary," "discriminatory," or "unreasonable" are not easily and simply defined. Their legal meanings become somewhat clear as we look at the ways courts have used and interpreted them. Various cases have held, for example, that it is arbitrary to dismiss teachers for membership in a controversial or even subversive organization. Since many members of such organizations are innocent of any wrongdoing and may not even be aware of the organization's purposes and activities, it is arbitrary to classify such members with those who knowingly partake of illegal activities.[1] Thus some classifications are arbitrary, while others are reasonable. It is reasonable to classify people according to age for purposes such as voting, driving a car, and running for the Senate; but it is unreasonable to use age classification for access to food or medical care. It has been held reasonable to classify males and females separately for military services but arbitary to classify them separately for purposes of voting or holding administrative positions in school.

Furthermore, as we have seen in earlier chapters, some courts consider it arbitrary to regulate teachers' or students' hair length, while others consider such policies reasonable. We must recognize that what is arbitrary or discriminatory is not always clear or simple. Courts tend to apply a three-step test to determine whether a law or policy is arbitrary: (1) they ask whether there is a legitimate social goal or objective to be attained by the law or policy; (2) they seek a rational connection between the objective and the means created to achieve it; and (3) they look for alternative and less restrictive ways of achieving the desired goal.

A further concern of courts when examining laws and policies under the Due Process Clause is vagueness. If a law or policy is so vague that a reasonable person of ordinary intelligence cannot be guided by it, it is said to violate due process. Such policies often occur in schools that attempt to control the grooming of teachers and students and are not sufficiently specific in their stated policies or rules. For example, a requirement that "teachers must dress in good taste" would be void because it is too vague. To say that the principal will be the judge of what is in good taste does not cure the defect, for it gives arbitrary power to the principal and thus violates due process.

Many lawsuits filed under other provisions of the Constitution also allege a violation of the Due Process Clause because policies or laws that involve racial, sexual, or other discrimination, or that abridge one's liberty, are also often unreasonable, arbitrary, or vague and therefore violate due process.* We now turn to questions related to fair procedures, questions that most educators think about when the right to due process is mentioned.

---

* Courts and lawyers often distinguish *substantive* and *procedural* due process. Actions that are arbitrary, unreasonable, discriminatory, or based on vague rules are said to violate substantive due process; unfair procedures violate procedural due process. For most educators, such distinctions become needlessly technical.

May local communities attach any condition they wish to the privilege of teaching?

No, they may not. Moreover, teaching can no longer be thought of as merely a privilege. Historically, the question of whether teaching was a right or a privilege was important because various conditions could be attached to the granting of a privilege, but rights could not be so restricted. Today it is clear that while no one has a right to public employment, unconstitutional conditions may not be attached to a public job. For example, as a condition for teaching in its schools, a community may not require that teachers be members of a certain religion or that they vote for candidates of a specified political party. As the Supreme Court has said. "We need not pause to consider whether an abstract right to public employment exists. It is sufficient to say that constitutional protection does extend to the public servant whose exclusion pursuant to a statute is patently arbitrary or discriminatory."[2]

Is there a distinction between tenured and probationary teachers in the right to due process?

Yes. This distinction was established and explained in chapter 3 (see pages 29–44). Since the Fourteenth Amendment applies only if one is being deprived of "life, liberty, or property," the teacher who claims a denial of due process because job security is threatened must show a deprivation of one of these rights.

A tenured teacher has a reasonable expectancy that his or her position will be continuous. Such expectation of a "continuous contract" is the meaning of tenure, and courts have held that this is a sufficient "property" right to bring on the protection of the Due Process Clause. Tenured teachers receive the full protection of due process. Probationary teachers have no continuous contract and therefore cannot make a claim to a property right on that basis. Other grounds may permit them to claim the protection of the Due Process Clause.

The *Roth* Case

When David Roth, a non-tenured assistant professor at a public institution, was informed that he would not be rehired for the upcoming academic year, he went to court.* He claimed that he was never given a notice or a hearing regarding any reasons for the non-renewal of his contract. This, he alleged, violated his constitutional rights by depriving him of his "liberty" and "property" without due process of law.

The Supreme Court disagreed with Roth.[3] The Court distinguished a probationary teacher from one on tenure and held that only the tenured teacher had a reasonable expectancy of continuous employment, which created a "property" interest meriting due process protection. The probationary

---

* Although Roth was a college professor, the legal principles of this case apply equally to public elementary and secondary schools.

teacher has a property interest only for the duration of the contract. Thus, if the probationer is dismissed *during* the year of the contract, notice, a hearing, and reasons are required. There is an important difference, however, between a dismissal during the term of the contract and a mere nonrenewal. Since the teacher does not have a right to a renewal of the contract, its nonrenewal violates no rights. That is the very meaning of the probationary period.

The Court then turned to the claim that the teacher's "liberty" interest was dimininshed. There are conceivable circumstances, reasoned the Court, where even a probationary teacher would have a right to a hearing. This would be the case if the employing school or its officials made statements against the teacher that were stigmatizing and thus seriously damaged possibilities for future employment. According to the Court, if in connection with the nonrenewal, the school damaged the teacher's "good name, reputation, honor or integrity . . . a notice and an opportunity to be heard are essential."

Unless local law requires it, schools are under no legal obligation to give reasons for not renewing the contract of a probationary teacher. If they give such reasons and allege incompetence, racism, sexism, mental or moral unfitness, fraud, or other damaging reasons, the teacher has a right to notice and a hearing where the validity of these charges are examined and refuted.[4]

In sum, the Supreme Court has ruled that important distinctions exist between tenured and probationary teachers related to the right to due process. In the ordinary case of the nonrenewal of a contract of a probationary teacher, there is no constitutional right to due process, for no property right is being violated. Under special circumstances, where the teacher's reputation is stigmatized by charges made by school officials, the teacher's "liberty" interest is implicated, and proper procedures must be followed to provide an opportunity for the teacher to clear up those charges.

While the foregoing states the constitutional law related to due process for probationary teachers, some states or local school districts expand these rights. They provide for minimal due process even for probationary teachers, though typically nothing more than a right to a statement of the reasons for nonrenewal is required.

May schools refuse to rehire probationary teachers for any reason whatever?

No. School officials do not have unlimited discretion not to renew the contract of probationary teachers. The Supreme Court in *Roth* said that only in the ordinary case of nonrenewal of a probationary teacher's contract is there no constitutional right to due process. Stigmatizing reasons for nonrenewal give rise to sufficient due process rights to enable teachers to clear their names.

Due process rights also arise if the probationary teacher's nonrenewal relates to some constitutionally protected activity (e.g., exercise of the right to free speech or union organizing activity). This principle was applied in the case of two teachers in the Miami–Dade County, Florida, Junior College. When the Board of Public Instruction of Dade County denied them tenure by refusing to hire them for a fourth year, the teachers claimed that the board's action was in retaliation for their organizing activities and also because one of them supported in her classroom some "new demands for campus freedom."

The district court upheld the board's right not to renew the probationary teachers' contract, but the circuit court of appeals reversed this ruling in a strongly worded opinion.[5] The court was not impressed by the argument that there is no right to public employment and that therefore the board may deny renewal of the contract at will. The chief judge wrote: "Equally unpersuasive is the argument that since there is no constitutional right to public employment, school officials only allowed these teacher contracts to expire. . . . The right sought to be vindicated is *not* a contractual one, nor could it be since no right to reemployment existed. What is at stake is the vindication of constitutional rights—the right not to be punished by the state or to suffer retaliation at its hand because a public employee persists in the exercise of First Amendment rights."

The judge quoted from leading Supreme Court cases to support his position: "To state that a person does not have a constitutional right to government employment is only to say that he must comply with reasonable, lawful, and nondiscriminatory terms laid down by the proper authorities. . . ."[6] Furthermore, ". . . constitutional protection does extend to the public servant whose exclusion pursuant to a statue is patently arbitrary or discriminatory."[7] Recent cases have reaffirmed these principles. For example, three Missouri teachers found their jobs in jeopardy in 1978 because they had been active in the Missouri branch of the National Education Association and had spoken out against the school board at public meetings concerned with salary increases. The courts ordered their reinstatement because it found that their terminations were motivated by their exercise of First Amendment rights.[8] In West Virginia, the court reinstated three teachers and awarded them back pay when it found that their transfers or dismissals were in retaliation for political activities on behalf of a school board candidate.[9] The West Virginia court said that "the law, applicable to the merits of this case is clear: A non-policy making, non-confidential government employee may not be discharged from a job that he or she is satisfactorily performing upon the sole ground of his political beliefs or activities."

Thus, even probationary teachers may exercise their constitutional rights. If a probationer presents evidence to indicate that nonrenewal is retaliation for the exercise of such rights, due process must be available to determine whether or not the nonrenewal is so motivated. If the facts indicate that the sole motivation for nonrenewal was constitutionally protected activity, the termination will not stand. If there are mixed reasons for nonrenewal, the outcome may be different.

The *Mt. Healthy Case*

Mr. Doyle, a public school teacher in Ohio, went to court to challenge the action of the school board not to reappoint him. Doyle was very active in the Teacher's Association, in fact, he had served as its president. During his presidency, but not directly connected with his role in the association, he had gotten into an argument and even an altercation with another teacher, which led to a one-day suspension for both teachers. He had also gotten into arguments with cafeteria employees over the amount of spaghetti served him, had referred to students as "sons of bitches," and had made obscene gestures at two girls in the cafeteria who disobeyed him. In his capacity as president of the Teachers' Association, he had called the local radio station and conveyed critical remarks to them about his principal's memorandum concerning a dress code for teachers and how such a code might influence public support of a bond issue.

Doyle contended that he had a constitutional right to communicate with the radio station and that his exercise of such a right played a "substantial" part in the board's decision not to renew his contract. The district court agreed with Doyle and ordered his reinstatement with back pay. After the court of appeals affirmed this decision, the case went to the Supreme Court.

The Supreme Court, upholding the constitutional rights of probationary teachers, said that "Doyle's claims under the First and Fourth Amendments are not defeated by the fact that he did not have tenure."[10] He might establish a claim to reinstatement if the decision not to rehire him was based on his exercise of a constitutional right. Nevertheless, the Court asked whether other legitimate grounds, independent of any First Amendment rights, were involved in not extending tenure to Doyle. If there were other professional grounds not to renew a contract, the fact that the school board included some impermissible grounds in its decision would not save the teacher's job.

The Court tried to balance the rights of the individual probationary teacher with the important social interest in conducting effective and efficient public schools. If the individual can show that the protected activity was a "substantial factor" or a "motivating factor" in the board's decision not to renew the contract, the board may still show by a preponderance of evidence that the teacher would not have been reemployed even in the absence of the protected conduct. Thus the Supreme Court sent the case back to the lower courts to determine the case in the light of these principles.

Various lower courts have followed these principles and applied the *Mt. Healthy* test to their respective cases. For example, a Louisiana teacher challenged the nonrenewal of his contract and claimed that his freedom of expression was violated by the action of the school board. Although the teacher could show that "his constitutionally protected conduct was a motivating factor in the board's decision," the court ruled that the principal's negative evaluations were sufficient for the board to reach the same conclusion.[11] By contrast, a Texas court ruled on behalf of teachers who showed that the only credible explanation for the nonrenewal of their contracts was their political activities on behalf of opponents of three recently elected board members.[12] (A related question appears on page 165.)

What is procedural due process?

In the final analysis, the legal concept of procedural due process refers to fair procedures. There is no single, technical definition for this concept; its basic elements are flexible and must be applied and interpreted in the light of the unique facts and circumstances of each case. As a general rule, fairness would require that before a teacher is deprived of any substantial "liberty" or "property" interest, there ought to be an adequate notice and a hearing before an impartial tribunal where the teacher's side of the conflict is presented. A sense of fairness also includes the right to be represented by a lawyer or a friend, to present evidence and cross-examine witnesses, to receive a written copy of the findings and conclusions, and to have an opportunity to appeal.

In addition to the constitutional right to due process, most states also have statutes that establish procedures for the termination of teachers. When such laws exist, they are strictly enforced by courts, and boards of education must follow them meticulously.

Is a school board a fair tribunal for the hearing?

Yes, according to various court decisions. Although it would seem that the board represents the administration and the community in conflict with the individual teacher being nonrenewed or dismissed, the Supreme Court ruled that this fact alone does not disqualify the board as a decision maker if the hearing is otherwise fair.[13] At a typical school board hearing, strict legal procedures need not be used, for these are administrative hearings and not court proceedings. Technical rules of evidence do not apply, but the proceedings must be orderly.[14]

Must state laws be strictly followed?

Yes, they must be, in states that have enacted statutes to govern nonrenewals or dismissals. For example, a probationary teacher in Ohio claimed that her notice of nonrenewal was late and that therefore she was entitled to reemployment for the ensuing year. The facts showed that she was aware of the actions of the board in not renewing her contract and that she was not available to receive the notice when attempts were made to deliver it at her home. Nevertheless, the Ohio Supreme Court ruled in her favor because she did not purposely avoid receiving the notice, and the school board had not exerted the necessary efforts to comply with the requirements of the statute.[15]

Questions also arise concerning the adequacy of the substance of the notice. For example, Alabama law requires adequate notice that specifies the grounds for the administrative action. When one principal wrote a letter to a teacher stating: "You have not done well enough for me to recommend that you come back next year," the state's supreme court ruled that the state statute was not satisfied by this letter.[16] Some states require two notices, one that specifies the deficiencies at a specified time prior to the later notice of dismissal charges. The purpose of the earlier notice is to provide time to overcome the specified deficiencies. When a dismissed tenured teacher in Missouri challenged the adequacy of both notices, the court ruled for the school board.[17] The court recognized the dilemma of the board as follows: "If the board sets forth the charges . . . at length and in detail including a recital of incidents to support the charges, it is contended that new and different charges have been made. If it states them in a cryptic way, it is contended that they are not set forth with particularity."

DUE PROCESS FOR STUDENTS

With the increasing application of constitutional rights to life in school, many of the oppressive features of schooling have been challenged and to some extent changed. One area of dramatic change, mandated by important decisions of the Supreme Court and further implemented by various decisions of lower courts, is the right of students to due process of law in school-related controversies. This section also explores other aspects of discpline including controversies related to "search and seizure" in schools.

What is the current status of the doctrine of in loco parentis?

In loco parentis is not as strong as it once was, but it is still often invoked by the courts. It means "in place of the parents," and has been used historically to justify the power and authority of school officials over students at school or while traveling to and from school. Although the doctrine gave substantial authority to school officials in years past, many courts and legislatures have limited its applicability. It is odd, for example, when parents notify schools not to use corporal punishment on their children, to justify such punishment with an appeal to *in loco parentis.* As more and more courts have recognized that constitutional rights apply to students and schools, the *in loco parentis* doctrine has been weakened, though not completely.

Must schools follow due process in cases of short suspension?

Yes. However, the legal requirements are not onerous or unduly demanding if the disciplinary violation is a minor one. The Supreme Court addressed this issue in *Goss* v. *Lopez.*[18] Dwight Lopez and several other students were suspended from school in Columbus, Ohio, during the 1970–71 academic year without receiving a hearing. Some of the students were suspended for documented acts of violence, but others, Lopez among them, were suspended even though they claimed to be innocent bystanders of demonstrations or disturbances. Moreover, they were never informed of what they were accused of doing. The students, who were suspended for up to ten days without a hearing, went to court and claimed that their right to due process was violated. When the federal district court agreed with them, the administrators appealed to the U.S. Supreme Court. In a 5–4 opinion, the Court ruled in favor of the students and discussed several issues of importance to students, teachers, and administrators.

The Court reiterated the key principle of the *Tinker* case, that "young people do not 'shed their constitutional rights' at the schoolhouse door." Justice White, writing for the majority, indicated that the Constitution does not require states to establish schools, but once they do, students have a "property" right in them, which may not be withdrawn without "fundamentally fair procedures." Clearly, said the Court, the Constitution protects students in cases of expulsion from the public schools. Furthermore, some degree of due process is required even in cases of short-term suspension.

A suspension for up to ten days is not so minor a punishment that it may be imposed "in complete disregard of the Due Process Clause," wrote Justice White. Such exclusion from school is a serious event in the life of the child, and it becomes even more serious if the misconduct is recorded in the student's file. Such a record is likely to damage the student's standing with teachers and "interfere with later opportunities for higher education and employment." Thus it is clear that the law requires schools to respect students' constitutional right to due process in both serious and minor disciplinary matters that might lead to either expulsion or suspension from school.

What process is due in minor disciplinary cases?

The seriousness of the possible penalty influences the extent and thoroughness of the due process requirement. Since due process is a flexible concept and not a fixed or rigid set of requirements, some minimal but fair procedures will satisfy the courts in cases that might lead to short-term suspension. As a minimum, students facing suspension "must be given some kind of notice and afforded some kind of hearing."

Notice of the charges may be oral or written, and a student who denies the charges must be given "an explanation of the evidence the authorities have and an opportunity to present his side of the story." The central concern of the Court is that there be at least "rudimentary precautions against unfair or mistaken findings of misconduct and arbitrary expulsion from school." Thus, the Court does not turn schools into courtrooms and does not place unreasonable burdens on educators faced with disciplinary problems. Most schools had followed such fair procedures long before the *Goss* case arose.

What process is due in serious cases?

Serious disciplinary cases, by contrast, may require extensive and thorough procedures. By "serious cases" is meant those that might lead to long-term suspension or expulsion. Since such actions are likely to have important consequences on students' educational and even occupational life, their "property" interests are in serious jeopardy, and meticulous procedures are required.

Cases involving serious disciplinary violations call for a written notice of the charges, the time and place of the hearing, and a description of procedures to be followed at the hearing. Students should know what evidence will be used against them, the names of witnesses who will testify, and the substance of witnesses' testimony. Students should have the right to cross-examine witnesses, as well as to present witnesses and evidence on their own behalf. A written or taped record of the proceeding should be available to students, together with the findings and recommendation of the group conducting the hearing (usually the school board). The right of appeal should also be clearly stated.[19] Although the *Dixon* case, from which these requirements were taken, involved college students, courts, including the Supreme Court, have referred to *Dixon* with approval in various cases involving high school students.

Do courts always allow the cross-examination of witnesses?

There are conflicting cases on the right to confront and cross-examine accusing witnesses. Even the Supreme Court said that a "full-dress judicial hearing, with the right to cross-examine witnesses" may not always be required. A Connecticut case ruled that confrontation and cross-examination may be dispensed with if extenuating circumstances or persuasive evidence reveals that the accusing witnesses will be inhibited to a significant degree or fearful for their personal safety due to probable revenge or retaliation.[20] A Kansas court ruled similarly.[21] But in an expulsion case, a New Jersey court required that the accusing witnesses be available for cross-examination.[22] The witnesses' fear of physical reprisal was no justification for depriving the accused of the right to confront and examine witnesses. It is a community obligation, ruled the court, to protect such witnesses against retaliation.

Do students have a right to have lawyers represent them?

There is no generally applicable answer to this question. Clearly there is no right to representation in connection with short-term suspensions. According to the Court in *Goss*, "further formalizing the suspension process and escalating its formality and adversary nature may not only make it too costly as a regular disciplinary tool but also destroy its effectiveness as part of the teaching process." On the other hand, cases have held that lawyers might attend serious disciplinary hearings to observe the procedures and give assistance to the student. This happened, for example, when a senior in a New York high school was accused of cheating on a state Regents Examination. Since this is an important exam in New York, and since a charge of cheating could lead to very serious consequences, the state court upheld the student's right to be assisted by counsel.[23] A case involving a college student came to the same conclusion.[24]

Are there disciplinary situations where due process is not a prerequisite?

Yes. In two situations teachers or school administrators may proceed without first observing any formalities of due process. The first involves the myriad of trivial disciplinary matters routinely experienced in schools. In situations involving minor infractions of rules or nonperformance of required tasks, students are given a variety of "punishments" ranging from brief detentions to extra work, verbal chastisement, being sent to the principal's office, and so forth. The legal maxim *de minimus non curat lex* (the law does not deal with trifles) is applicable to these situations, and schools ought to rely on their knowledge of pedagogical principles to deal with such matters.

The second exception involves emergencies in which educators must act quickly to preserve the safety of persons or property. The Supreme Court recognized in *Goss* that emergencies occur in school that would make notice and hearing prior to action impracticable because the situation presents danger to persons or property. In such situations, the only legal requirement is that fair procedures be followed "as soon as practicable after removal of the danger or disruption."

Is there a due process requirement for guidance conferences?

No. Under ordinary circumstances, a guidance conference is not considered to be a disciplinary proceeding. For example, guidance conferences related to the appropriate placement of a student or concerning progress in scheduled courses are not disciplinary matters. Absent special circumstances, the student is not being deprived of "liberty" or "property"; therefore there is no constitutional right to due process. In special circumstances, such right is granted by statute (e.g., in the case of exceptional students or bilingual students). By state statute or local policy it is always possible to expand the due process rights of students beyond those granted by the Constitution. Our discussion has focused on the interpretation of the constitutional provisions that apply to all public schools. Nevertheless, as in all other controversies, the importance of state law and local policy must not be underestimated.

May schools create general rules to govern student behavior?

Yes, they may, as long as such rules are sufficiently clear to guide student behavior. For example, a rule requiring students to be in their assigned homerooms and in their seats at the time the school bell signals at 8:30 A.M. is a legally valid general rule. It is clear and unambiguous. By contrast, consider a rule that required students "to dress in good taste" and avoid "extremes in style." Under this rule a student in Arcata, California, was suspended because he had long hair. The student and his parents went to court seeking reinstatement and claimed that the rule was so vague that it violated his right to due process. The California Supreme Court agreed with the student and found that the rule was void because it was too vague.[25] The court said that "a law violates due process if it is so vague and standardless that it leaves the public uncertain as to the conduct it prohibits or leaves judges or jurors free to decide, without any legally fixed standards, what is prohibited and what is not in each case."

Similarly, a school rule that is too broad will not stand up in court. The written regulations of a school in Texas gave the principal power to make rules "in the best interest of the school." When the principal acted under this regulation and expelled two students for publishing an underground newspaper, the students went to court, claiming the rule to be vague and overly broad. The court agreed with the students and said that "school rules probably need not be as narrow as criminal statutes, but if school officials contemplate severe punishment they must do so on the basis of a rule which is drawn so as to reasonably inform the student what specific conduct is proscribed."[26]

When a principal has the power to do anything "in the best interest of the school," there are no clear or objective standards by which students can guide their behavior. The rule may even cover under its broad scope constitutionally protected activities such as free speech and press. Therefore the rule is unconstitutional.

Have due process requirements turned classroooms and schools into courtrooms?

No. When the Supreme Court ruled in *Goss* that even short-term suspensions require some modicum of due process, a hue and cry arose across the land. School administrators, parents, and teachers were upset and feared that the decision would force school officials to consult lawyers before they could take any disciplinary measures in schools. These fears were ill based. Careful reading of *Goss* and other cases indicates that the legal requirements are not at all excessive and that there is no need for lawyers to be at the side of administrators or teachers. Experience shows that conscientious educators used fair procedures long before these cases ever went to court, and their procedures amply satisfy the law.

On the other hand, oppressive, authoritarian procedures that do not respect students' rights to know why they are being disciplined and do not provide opportunities for students to present their defense in a fair way are crumbling as a result of the application of the Constitution to the schools. In sum, one may think of the right to due process as applying to student disciplinary matters on a continuum represented on the following diagram:

May act without due process	*Some modicum of due process is necessary*	*Extensive, careful due process is required*
Trivial or very minor matters, or emergencies. The latter must be followed by due process as soon as posssible.	Disciplinary matters that may lead to short-term suspensions or entry on the students' record.	Disciplinary matters that may result in long-term suspension or expulsion, or in a significant penalty such as a short suspension during final exams.

CORPORAL PUNISHMENT

Is corporal punishment unconstitutional?

No. The Constitution is silent on this manner, as it is silent on education in general. Thus courts have held that education is a function of state governments (under the reserved powers of Article X of the Constitution) and that states may further delegate power over schooling to local governments. Today only two states, Massachusetts and New Jersey, clearly outlaw corporal punishment, although there is some question about its legality in Hawaii and Vermont. In most states it is still legal to use physical force to punish students in schools. Some local committees have also outlawed the practice in states where state law does not forbid it. For example, New York State allows corporal punishment, at the date of this writing, but the City of New York does not. Some school districts that allow corporal punishment restrict its administration in various ways, in which case the restrictions must be followed. The most common restriction is that an administrator is the only person authorized to spank students and then only in the presence of an adult witness. In any event, it is clear that ordinary corporal punishment does not violate the Constitution.

Is excessive corporal punishment cruel and unusual punishment?

No, it is not, ruled the Supreme Court in 1977.[27] In Dade County, Florida, James Ingraham and Roosevelt Andrews, junior high school students, were severely paddled during the 1970–71 school year. In fact, Ingraham was so harshly beaten that the resulting hematoma required medical attention, and he missed eleven days of school. The paddling Andrews received included being struck on his arms, depriving him the use of an arm for a week.

At the time of the paddling, Dade County schools used corporal punishment as one means of maintaining discipline. Simultaneously, a Florida law forbade punishment that was "degrading or unduly severe" or that took place prior to consultation with the principal or the teacher in charge of the school. The students filed suit against several school administrators and claimed that the severe beating they received constituted cruel and unusual punishment. The district court, the court of appeals, and finally the Supreme Court all ruled that the beating, although excessive and unreasonable, did not violate the Eighth Amendment, which prohibits cruel and unusual punishment.

Does that mean that the Court recommends physical punishment of students or condones excessive punishment? Not at all. Whether schoolchildren and youth ought to be physically punished is not a legal matter. It is a policy question for educators to decide with appropriate consideration of psychological, developmental, and other factors. Even when such punishment is allowed, it must remain within reasonable limits. To be "reasonable," punishment must relate to an educational purpose and not be merely an expression of teacher anger, frustration, or malice. The severity of the punishment should relate to the gravity of the offense and should consider the ability of the student to bear it. Therefore the size, age, sex, and physical and emotional condition of the child must be considered. Excessive punishment is unreasonable, and the law has always provided ways for legal redress against it. Students may sue the perpetrators for money damages for the suffering endured as well as seek an indictment for assault and battery. The Supreme Court has ruled that these traditional remedies are sufficient to deter educators and minimize abuse. The Court examined the history of the Eighth Amendment and concluded that it was never intended to apply to schools but was created to control the punishment of criminals, who are incarcerated in closed institutions. The very "openness of the public school and its supervision by the community afford significant safeguards against the kind of abuse from which the Eighth Amendment protects the prisoner."

Must due process be used before administering corporal punishment?

The Court ruled that existing remedies would suffice and the addition of procedural safeguards while protecting student rights "would entail a significant intrusion into an area of primary educational responsibility." Thus the question of whether to have corporal punishment is for legislatures and local school boards to decide. Courts will intrude only when the punishment is excessive and unreasonable.

A different issue was raised and decided in 1980 by the Court of Appeals for the Fourth Circuit. It ruled that excessive corporal punishment in a public school might be a violation of "constitutional rights given protection under the rubric of substantive due process."[28] The court spoke of "the right to be free of state intrusions into realms of personal privacy and bodily security through means so brutal, demeaning, and harmful as literally to shock the conscience of a court. The existence of this right to ultimate bodily security—the most fundamental aspect of personal privacy—is unmistakably established in our constitutional decisions as an attribute of the ordered liberty that is the concern of substantive due process."

In this case it was alleged that a young girl was so severely paddled in school that she was badly bruised and required ten days' hospitalization and treatment "of traumatic injury to the soft tissue of the left hip and thigh, and trauma to the soft tissue with ecchymosis of the left buttock," with possible injuries to her lower back and spine. The court held that the student's substantive due process rights were violated if the evidence showed that "the force applied caused injury so severe, was so disproportionate to the need presented and was so inspired by malice or sadism rather than a merely careless or unwise excess of zeal that it amounted to a brutal and inhumane abuse of official power literally shocking to the conscience."

Thus, while corporal punishment does not necessarily require prior procedural due process, and while it does not violate the Eighth Amendment prohibition against cruel and unusual punishment, excessive punishment might violate the substantive due process rights embodied in the Fourteenth Amendment.

May parents forbid the use of corporal punishment?

In general, they may not. If a state allows corporal punishment, parental objection to the practice will not necessarily prevail. The Supreme Court so ruled in a North Carolina case in which a sixth-grade boy was spanked for violating a school rule against throwing balls at certain specified times.[29] Mrs. Virginia Baker had requested that her son not be spanked or paddled, for she opposed such practices in principle. While the law of North Carolina allowed the use of force reasonably necessary "to restrain or correct pupils and to maintain order," Mrs. Baker claimed the law was unconstitutional because it allowed such punishment over parental objections. Though recognizing the parents' basic right to supervise the upbringing of children, the Court also considered the "legitimate and substantial interest" of the state "in maintaining order and discipline in the public schools." In the final analysis, since both professional and popular opinion are split on the question of the use of corporal punishment, the Court refused to allow "the wishes of a parent to restrict school officials' discretion in deciding the methods to be used in . . . maintaining discipline."

Some states, California for example, have passed laws that provide for prior written parental approval before a student may be spanked. At times, local school districts create their own policies regulating this matter. In the absence of state legislation or local regulation, it is clear that schools do not have to get parental approval to use corporal punishment, and, in fact, may use it over the objections of parents. As a general rule, school discipline is a local matter, and school boards may adopt reasonable rules and regulations to conduct their schools efficiently. The authority of school personnel, in the conduct of the ordinary affairs of the school, derives in part from the doctrine of *in loco parentis* introduced earlier in this chapter.

May students be disciplined for conduct outside of school?

Yes, they may, if the rule they violate is reasonably connected to the operation of the school. A Texas court so ruled, upholding the suspension of a student for drinking vodka on school grounds, violating a known school rule.[30] If the alleged wrong took place away from the school and the school grounds, school officials should allow the civil authorities to handle the matter.[31] However, when a student's conduct gets him or her in trouble with the civil authorities, that does not preclude the schools from applying appropriate disciplinary measures if the behavior is connected to the school. Punishment by both school and outside authorities does not constitute double jeopardy, which is a technical legal concept that applies to criminal proceedings. School disciplinary matters are not criminal proceedings.

May schools lower grades or withhold diplomas as disciplinary measures?

No. In the past, schools often withheld diplomas as punishment and teachers often lowered student's grades for misbehaving in class. The trend among educators is to assign separate grades for academic work and for behavior, or "citizenship." As a general rule, the law does not intrude into disputes over grading policies or practices. These are matters for educators to decide. Nevertheless, if a student can show that a grade was lowered for disciplinary reasons or that the teacher acted out of prejudice or malice, the courts will listen and help. The burden of proof is on the student to establish that the reasons for the low grade were illegitimate and not related to the quality of the work. This is a difficult burden of proof, and there are no cases reported wherein a student below the college level has succeeded in such a suit.

Diplomas should not be withheld as punishment for an alleged violation of a school rule. The reason for this principle is that the diploma is a symbol and recognition of academic accomplishment and not a reward for good behavior. Misbehavior should be faced directly through disciplinary procedures, not indirectly through the withholding of a symbol of academic accomplishment.

SCHOOL SEARCHES

May school officials search student lockers?

Yes, they may, if they have reasonable grounds to suspect that something illegal or dangerous is hidden in the locker. In recent years, students have objected to locker searches on the grounds that since they were unauthorized, a search without a warrant violates the Fourth Amendment right against illegal search and seizure.

The *Overton* Case

In a high school in New York, police showed the vice-principal a search warrant and with his help searched the lockers of two students. They found four marijuana cigarettes in Carlos Overton's locker. When the search warrant turned out to be defective, the student claimed that the entire search was illegal and therefore the evidence obtained could not be used in court. The police and the school claimed that the vice-principal gave consent for the search; therefore, since no unauthorized search took place, the evidence found could be used. The court ruled against the student and upheld the validity of the search and the use of the evidence.[32] The court held that students had exclusive use of the lockers vis-à-vis other students but not in relation to school authorities. School officials have the locker combinations, and if they have reason to suspect that something illegal or dangerous is hidden in a locker, they have a right to inspect it. In fact, the New York court went further and said that "not only have the school authorities the right to inspect but the right becomes a duty when suspicion arises that something of an illegal nature may be secreted there."

In typical situations away from school, law enforcement officials need "probable cause" to secure a search warrant to search one's home, a rented locker, or even a telephone booth one occupies. Schools, however, are special environments where school officials have the duty and responsibility for the safety, health, and learning of children. Therefore, less demanding standards are applied by courts to searches conducted by school personnel than by law enforcement officials.

May school officials search students' clothing?

Yes. However, there are important differences between searching lockers, which are school property, and searching students' clothes, which are not. Because clothing or body searches entail a great danger of invasion of privacy, courts have imposed high standards of protection against such searches. For example, a seventeen-year-old student was subjected to a body search when he was observed entering a bathroom with a fellow student twice within the same hour, and leaving within a few seconds. For months he had been suspected of dealing in drugs. The search revealed illegal drugs, yet the Court of Appeals of New York excluded the evidence and ruled the search unconstitutional.[33] Though the court recognized the widespread use of drugs and the need to protect the school environment, it held that even these considerations did "not permit random, causeless searches" that might result in "psychological damage to sensitive children" and expose them to serious consequences, such as possible criminal convictions.

An extreme example is that of a school that conducted a strip-search of an entire fifth-grade class over a report of $3 missing from a student's coat pocket. The search, which was conducted by separating boys and girls, was fruitless. The court considered the school's action to be excessive and thus illegal.[34]

As when other student rights are violated, courts may award money damages for illegal and unauthorized searches. For example, $7,500 in damages was awarded to a student in connection with a strip-search a federal court found to be illegal.[35] The Second Circuit Court of Appeals indicated that "reasonable suspicion" might suffice to search students' lockers, but for highly invasive searches, such as body or strip-searches, a higher standard is required (i.e., "probable cause"). The distinction between these two standards is not crystal clear, but in law they are significantly different. "Probable cause" is also the standard used by law enforcement officials when they request a search warrant from a court.

May the police search school lockers or students without search warrants?

No. In general, the same legal principles apply to police behavior in and out of schools. Nevertheless, school officials often cooperate with the police in warrantless searches. The question becomes whether evidence so gathered may be used in criminal proceedings against students.

The Supreme Court developed the "exclusionary rule" whereby illegally obtained evidence may not be used in court. Cases have raised the question whether evidence obtained in locker searches through the cooperation of police and school officials falls within the "exclusionary rule." So far, courts are divided on this question with some courts excluding such evidence and others allowing it if school officials had at least "reasonable suspicion" concerning the particular student's locker.

An unusual case arose when police and school officials, with the aid of specially trained dogs, planned and conducted a search in the junior and senior high schools of Highland, Indiana. On a predetermined day, students were kept in their first-period classes for two and a half hours while a team of handlers led the dogs on a room-to-room inspection tour. Particular students singled out by the dogs were asked to empty their pockets and purses, and some of them were strip-searched in the nurse's office. With this dragnet, seventeen students were caught with illegal drugs. Of these, twelve withdrew from school voluntarily, two were suspended, and three were expelled. Five sets of parents whose children were strip-searched went to court, though four of them withdrew before trial.

In the final analysis, the U.S. District Court ruled that the strip-searches were illegal in that they violated the Fourth Amendment right against unreasonable search and seizure.[36] The court did not consider a dog alert to be a "reasonable suspicion" sufficient to warrant a strip-search. On the other hand, it saw nothing wrong with the use of dogs and with asking suspected students to empty their pockets or purses. The court ruled on the *in loco parentis* doctrine to uphold the action of the administrators and the school board to use the canine units to search students in every classroom if the school officials felt they had reasonable suspicion of drug violations. (The American Civil Liberties Union plans to appeal this decision, for it believes the school can deal with the drug problem in ways less destructive of students' rights.) One important aspect of this case was a prior agreement between school officials and the police that illegal materials discovered during the search would not be used in any criminal investigations or proceedings.

SUMMARY

This chapter presented the major dimensions of due process rights of teachers and students. It is clear that laws or policies that are arbitrary, capricious, unreasonable, or overly vague violate the Due Process Clause of the Fourteenth Amendment. Lawyers and courts refer to these as "violations of substantive due process." There are also "procedural due process" rights based on the same amendment, where it prohibits states from depriving anyone of "life, liberty or property" without fair procedures.

Tenured teachers have a "property" interest in their continuing contract, and any attempts to suspend or dismiss them must be carried out with full observance of fair procedures. Statutes usually specify the steps that are part of such procedures, and these must be meticulously followed. Although all teachers have a right to due process if they are dismissed *during* the term of their contract, probationary teachers do not have a "property" right in continuous employment; therefore, if their employment is not renewed, they may not claim the constitutional right to due process. Nevertheless, if the announced grounds for the nonrenewal are stigmatizing, if their reputation is damaged and thus their opportunities for further employment are diminished, due process must be observed so that the stigmatizing charges can be challenged. Probationary teachers also have a right to due process if the grounds for nonrenewal were constitutionally protected activities (e.g., controversial speech or unionizing activity).

If a teacher has a constitutional right to due process, the administrative hearing before the board must be orderly and fair but it need not be formal and technical. Elements of a fair procedure include a written notice of the charges; a hearing before an impartial tribunal; an opportunity to present evidence and cross-examine witnesses; a right to representation; a written statement of the findings, conclusions, and recommendations; and the right to appeal. In addition to the constitutional right to due process, many states provide some due process by state law. Such laws must be meticulously followed by school boards, and courts will enforce them strictly.

Historically, schools all too often have used arbitrary and authoritarian disciplinary methods to control student behavior. These practices have been altered in some places by more enlightened educational theories and in others by legal challenges that claimed the Due Process Clause of the Constitution applies to the schools. Students and their parents have challenged administrative authority to suspend and expel students without open and fair procedures, the use of corporal punishment in schools, and the practice of searching students and their lockers.

The U.S. Supreme Court has ruled that the right to due process applies to the schools, for a suspension or expulsion affects the "property" or "liberty" interests of students, protected by the Fourteenth Amendment. Such interests may not be diminished without due process of law. The Court has ruled that even a short suspension requires some modicum of due process. But the courts do not want to turn schools into courtrooms and recognize the need for administrative authority and discretion. Therefore, a brief, informal process usually satisfies the law in cases where the punishment might be a short suspension. More serious infractions, ones that are likely to lead to long-term suspensions, entries in school records, or expulsions, require more meticulous due process. While no fixed formula for such process exists, it should include a written notice specifying the charges; a hearing at which the student should have an opportunity to respond to the charges, present evidence, cross-examine witnesses, and be represented by his parents or by counsel; a fair tribunal; a written statement of the findings and conclusions; and the right to appeal. A student who constitutes a danger to people or property may be removed from school immediately as long as due process follows such removal as soon as practicable.

As a general rule, school discipline is a matter within the discretion of school authorities and local school boards. Challenges have arisen to the practice of corporal punishment in public schools. Only two states (New Jersey and Massachusetts) clearly prohibit corporal punishment, though California requires parental consent. In addition, some school districts prohibit it through local policy. Where challenged, courts have upheld the legality of *reasonable* use of corporal punishment. Excessive brutal punishment is nowhere sanctioned by the law; if used, educators may be sued for money damages as well as prosecuted for assault and battery. But even excessive punishment does not constitute "cruel and unusual punishment" under the Constitution, for the Supreme Court has ruled that the Eighth Amendment was intended to apply to "closed" institutions, like prisons, and not to schools. One appeals court ruled, however, that excessive corporal punishment may be a violation of substantive due process protected by the Fourteenth Amendment.

School lockers may be searched by appropriate school officials if they have reasonable suspicion that unlawful or dangerous materials are hidden there. The search of one's clothing or body merits greater protection. School officials must have a "probable cause" to conduct such searches, which means that they must have evidence from highly reliable sources that a particular student is hiding illegal or dangerous materials. Mass searches or arbitrary ones (e.g., search every seventh locker on alternate Tuesdays) are frowned upon by courts and violate the Constitution. As a general rule, the police need a search warrant before they conduct locker searches in schools. Evidence gathered in warrantless searches, or without the student's consent, is excluded by some courts but allowed in by others on the theory that school administrators may consent on behalf of the students. Many courts are concerned that such collaboration between administrators and the police undermines the relationship between administrators and students.

NOTES

1. *Wieman* v. *Updegraff*, 344 U.S. 183 (1952).

2. *Id.*

3. *Board of Regents* v. *Roth*, 408 U.S 564 (1972).

4. *Lombard* v. *Board of Education of City of New York*, 502 F.2d. 631 (2d Cir. 1974); *Huntley* v. *North Carolina State Board of Education*, 493 F.2d. 1016 (4th Cir. 1974); *McGhee* v. *Draper*, 564 F.2d. 903 (10th Cir. 1977); *Perry* v. *Sindermann*, 408 U.S. 593 (1972).

5. *Pred* v. *Board of Public Instruction*, 415 F.2d 851 (5th Cir. 1969).

6. *Slochower* v. *Board of Higher Education*, 350 U.S. 551 (1965).

7. *Wieman* v. *Updegraff*, 344 U.S. 183 (1952).

8. *Greminger* v. *Seaborne*, 584 F.2d. 275 (8th Cir. 1978).

9. *Miller* v. *Board of Education of the County of Lincoln*, 450 F.Supp. 106 (S.D. W.Va. 1978).

10. *Mt. Healthy City School District Board of Education* v. *Doyle*, 429 U.S. 274 (1977).

11. *Foreman* v. *Vermillion Parish School Board*, 353 So.2d 471 (La. App. 1978).

12. *Guerra* v. *Roma Independent School District*, 444 F.Supp. 812 (S.D. Tex. 1977).

13. *Hortonville District* v. *Hortonville Education Association*, 426 U.S. 482 (1976).

14. *Adams* v. *Professional Practices Commission*, 524 P.2d 932 (Okla. 1974).

15. *State ex rel. Curry* v. *Grand Valley Local Schools Board of Education*, 375 N.E.2d 48 (Ohio 1978).

16. *Johnson* v. *Selma Board of Education*, 356 So.2d 649 (Ala. 1978).

17. *Rafael* v. *Meramac Valley R-111 Board of Education*, 591 S.W.2d 309 (Mo. App. 1978).

18. *Goss* v. *Lopez*, 419 U.S. 565 (1975).

19. *Dixon* v. *Alabama State Board of Education*, 294 F.2d. 150 (5th Cir. 1961).

20. *De Jesus* v. *Penberthy*, 344 F.Supp. 70 (D. Conn. 1971).

21. *Smith* v. *Miller*, 514 P.2d 377 (Kan. 1973).

22. *Tibbs* v. *Board of Education of Township of Franklin*, 584 A.2d 179 (N.J. 1971).

23. *Goldwyn* v. *Allen*, 281 N.Y.S.2d 899 (Sup. Ct. N.Y. 1967).

24. *Gabrilowitz* v. *Newman*, 582 F.2d. 100 (1st Cir. 1978).

25. *Meyers* v. *Arcata Union High School District*, 75 Cal. Rptr. 68 (Cal 1969).

26. *Sullivan* v. *Houston Independent School District*, 333 F.Supp. 1149 (S.D. Tex. 1971).

27. *Ingraham* v. *Wright*, 420 U.S. 651 (1977).

28. *Faye Elizabeth Hall et al.* v. *G. Garrison Tawney et al.*, 621 F.2d 607 (4th Cir. 1980).

29. *Baker* v. *Owens*, 395 F.Supp. 294 (M.D. N.C. 1975), *aff'd.* 423 U.S. 907 (1975).

30. *Wingfield* v. *Fort Bend Independent School District,* (D.C. S.D. Texas No. 72–H–232 1973).

31. *Howard* v. *Clark,* 299 N.Y.S.2d 65 (1969).

32. *People* v. *Overton,* 249 N.E.2d 366 (N.Y. 1969).

33. *New York* v. *Scott,* 358 N.Y.S.2d 403 (1974).

34. *Bellnier* v. *Lund,* 438 F.Supp. 47 (N.D. N.Y. 1977).

35. *M. M.* v. *Anker,* 607 F.2d. 588 (2d Cir. 1979).

36. *Doe* v. *Renfrow, Superintendent of Highland Town District,* 475 F.Supp. 1012 (N.D. Ind. 1979).

13

How free is my personal life?

OVERVIEW

In past generations, teachers who violated their community's moral standards either resigned or were quickly dismissed. Few educators doubted that teachers could be fired for adultery, drunkenness, homosexual conduct, using illegal drugs, committing a felony, or becoming pregnant while single, but community consensus about what constitutes immoral conduct has broken down in recent years. The concept of morality seems to vary according to time and place. As the California Supreme Court observed: "Today's morals may be tomorrow's ancient and absurd customs." Moreover, many educators believe that their personal behavior away from school is their own business. Yet many administrators argue that educators teach by example, that they should be adult models for their students, and that they should conform to the moral standards of the community. This chapter examines how courts have resolved this conflict between teacher freedom and community control. It focuses on three questions: What constitutes immoral conduct for teachers? When can teachers be punished for such behavior? And can schools consider other aspects of a teacher's personal life, such as age, weight, or citizenship?

IMMORAL CONDUCT

The *Morrison* Case[1]

In 1969 the California Supreme Court rejected the notion that teachers can automatically be dismissed for immoral behavior. The case involved Marc Morrison, who engaged in a brief homosexual relationship with another teacher. About a year later, the other teacher reported the incident to Morrison's superintendent. This led the board of education to revoke Morrison's teaching credentials on the grounds of immoral and unprofessional conduct. The board defended its action by saying that teachers take the place of parents during school hours and should be models of good conduct, that state law requires teachers to impress on their pupils "principles of morality," that homosexual behavior is contrary to the moral standards of the people of California, and that the board of education is required to revoke a teacher's credentials for immoral conduct.

Despite these arguments, the California court ruled in favor of Morrison. The court explained that it was dangerous to allow the terms "immoral" and "unprofessional" to be interpreted broadly. To many people, "immoral conduct" includes laziness, gluttony, selfishness, and cowardice. To others, "unprofessional conduct" for teachers includes signing petitions, opposing majority opinions, and drinking alcoholic beverages. Therefore, unless these terms are defined carefully and narrowly, they could be applied to most teachers in the state. Furthermore, the court ruled that the board should not be able to dismiss an educator because it disapproved of his personal, private conduct unless the conduct is clearly related to his professional work. According to the court, when a teacher's job is not affected, his private behavior is his own business and should not be a basis for discipline.

But how can a board determine whether a teacher's behavior affects his job and indicates that he is unfit to teach? In making this decision, the court suggested that the board consider all the circumstances. Here there was no evidence that Morrison's conduct affected his teaching. There was no evidence that he "even considered any improper relationship with any student," that he "failed to teach the principles of morality," or that the single homosexual incident "affected his relationship with his co-workers." Therefore the court ruled against the board because it failed to present evidence that Morrison's retention in the profession would be harmful. In the words of the court: "An individual can be removed from the teaching profession only upon a showing that his retention in the profession poses a significant danger of harm to either students, school employees, or others who might be affected by his actions as a teacher."

Morrison marked a change in the way many courts considered questions of teachers' immoral conduct. In the past, the fact that a teacher engaged in behavior a community considered immoral would have been enough to support his dismissal. After *Morrison*, other courts began to rule that teachers could not be dismissed simply because of such conduct unless there was evidence that it was clearly related to teacher effectiveness.

When can a teacher be dismissed for homosexual behavior?

As *Morrison* indicated, this depends on the circumstance. In California, for example, the board of education revoked the teaching credentials of Thomas Sarac after he was arrested and convicted for making a "homosexual advance" to a plainclothes policeman at a public beach; and the court ruled in favor of the board.[2] The California Supreme Court distinguished the *Sarac* ruling from the *Morrison* decision on the grounds that the circumstances were different. Unlike Morrison, Sarac admitted a recent history of homosexual activity and pleaded guilty to a criminal charge arising from a public homosexual advance.[3]

In addition to the facts of a case, decisions about teacher homosexuality may differ according to state law and judicial opinion. For example, a federal judge in Oregon ruled in favor of teacher Peggy Burton, who acknowledged that she was a "practicing homosexual" and was dismissed for immoral conduct.[4] Judge Solomon held that the state statute empowering school boards to dismiss teachers for immorality was unconstitutionally vague because it did not define "immorality," which means different things to different people and allows board members to be "the arbiters of morality for the entire community." The judge concluded that the statute was unconstitutional because (1) it fails to give warning of what conduct is prohibited, (2) it permits erratic and prejudicial exercise of authority, and (3) it does not require a connection between the alleged conduct and teaching.

In contrast, the Supreme Court of Washington in 1977 upheld the dismissal of James Gaylord, an excellent high school teacher, after he admitted to his vice-principal that he was a homosexual.[5] The Washington court pointed out that a teacher's efficiency is determined by his relations with students and their parents, fellow teachers, and school administrators. The judge noted that "at least one student plus several administrators, teachers, and parents publicly objected to Gaylord remaining on the teaching staff" and testified that his continued presence "would create problems." According to the court, this evidence supported the school's concern that the continued presence of Gaylord after he voluntarily became known as a homosexual would result in confusion, fear, and parental concern, which would impair his efficiency as a teacher.

Gaylord argued that he should not have been dismissed because it was the school officials who publicized his homosexual status. The court disagreed, noting that "it was the vice-principal's duty to report the information to his superior because it involved the performance capabilities of Gaylord." The court concluded that to say school officials must wait for prior specific overt expression of homosexual conduct before they act to prevent harm is to ask them "to take an unacceptable risk" in discharging their responsibilities.

Can teachers be dismissed for being unwed mothers?

Again, this depends on the circumstance. A school might be able to terminate a single teacher who became visibly pregnant during the school year but might not be able to dismiss a teacher because she had a child in the past.

In 1976, a federal judge in Nebraska upheld the action of Omaha officials who terminated a junior high school teacher "because of her being pregnant and unwed."[6] The court noted that a teacher who develops a good relationship with her students "is likely to be a model to those students in wide-ranging respects, including personal values." This teacher had developed such a relationship with her students, who knew that she was unmarried and pregnant. Therefore the court said that it was reasonable for the school board to believe that permitting the teacher to remain in the classroom would be viewed by the students as condoning pregnancy out of wedlock. The court concluded that "there is a rational connection between the plaintiff's pregnancy out of wedlock and the school board's interest in conserving marital values, when acts probably destructive of those values are revealed, verbally or non-verbally, in the classroom."*

On the other hand, a federal appeals court voided a Mississippi rule that automatically disqualified school employees who were parents of illegitimate children.[7] The policy led administrators to investigate and reject several present and prospective employees. Officials offered these reasons for the rule: unwed parenthood is proof of immoral conduct, unwed parents are improper role models for students, and such teachers contribute to the problem of student pregnancy.

In rejecting these reasons, the judge explained that "present immorality" does not necessarily follow from unwed parenthood. Under the school rule, a teacher "could live an impeccable life yet be barred as unfit for employment for an event . . . occurring at any time in the past." This policy, wrote the court, "equates the single fact of the illegitimate birth with irredeemable moral disease. Such a presumption is not only patently absurd, it is mischievous and prejudicial, requiring those who administer the policy to investigate the parental status of school employees and prospective applicants. Where no stigma may have existed before, such inquisitions by over-zealous officialdom can rapidly create it."

The court also did not agree that unwed parents would be improper models. The judge doubted that students would seek information on the private family life of teachers and then try to emmulate them. Moreover, the school district offered no evidence, beyond speculation, that the presence of unwed parents in school contributed to student pregnancy. Finally, the court noted that "unwed mothers only, not unwed fathers" were penalized by the policy. For these reasons, the court ruled that the policy violated the constitutional right to equal protection and due process.

Can teachers be dismissed for immoral conduct with students?

Yes. Although many courts will not allow teachers to be dismissed for immorality with other adults unless there is clear evidence that such conduct will negatively affect their teaching, judges rule differently concerning immoral

---

* This decision was later reversed on procedural grounds by a divided appeals court. *Brown* v. *Bathke*, 566 F.2d 588 (8th Cir. 1977).

behavior with students. In these cases courts are generally quite strict and require less evidence to uphold teacher dismissals. This is especially true in the area of sexual relations with students.

Joseph Stubblefield was a teacher in a California junior college. After teaching one night, he drove one of his female students to a deserted side street and parked. Later a deputy sheriff stopped to investigate and discovered Stubblefield and the student involved in a sexual relationship. After recognizing the deputy, Stubblefield knocked him down and drove away at speeds of 80 to 100 miles per hour before he finally pulled over. Because of these events, the teacher was dismissed for immoral conduct.

Stubblefield argued that the evidence against him concerned only his out-of-school conduct, not his teaching. But a California appeals court supported his dismissal.[8] The court noted that "there are certain professions which impose upon persons attracted to them, responsibilities and limitations on freedom of action which do not exist in regard to other callings. Public officials such as . . . school teachers fall into such a category." Therefore, "as a minimum, responsible conduct on the part of a teacher, even at the college level, excludes meretricious relationships with his students." According to the court, Stubblefield's assault on the police officer, his misconduct with his student, and the notoriety of his behavior were evidence of his unfitness to teach. In conclusion the court wrote: "The integrity of the educational system under which teachers wield considerable power in the grading of students and the granting or withholding of certificates and diplomas is clearly threatened when teachers become involved in relationships with students such as is indicated by the conduct here."

Similarly, an Illinois court upheld the dismissal of a Peoria teacher because he was discovered partially undressed playing strip poker in his automobile with a female high school student.[9] In a related Washington case, teacher Gary Denton was discharged after a high school student he had dated became pregnant. Denton admitted being the prospective father. But he claimed his discharge was improper since his girl friend was not a student at his school, and there was no evidence that their relationship had a negative impact on his teaching. The court ruled that no direct evidence is needed when the sexual misconduct involves "a teacher and a minor student."[10] The court held that in such a situation a school board may properly conclude that "the conduct is inherently harmful to the teacher-student relation, and thus to the school district."

Can a teacher be dismissed for sexual advances toward students?

Yes. Cases indicate that courts tend to be quite strict in this area. In 1978, for example, a Pennsylvania court upheld the dismissal of a teacher because of two incidents involving his proposal to "spank" two of his female high school students, which each perceived as a sexual advance.[11] Although the teacher admitted he had sexual fantasies about spanking the girls, he denied that his *conduct* was immoral. The court acknowledged that a teacher "cannot be found guilty of immorality based solely on his admitted fantasies." But when teachers discuss sex with students, this is often a serious problem "because of the significant influence teachers exert." According to the court, when such a discussion is not related to the curriculum, a school board can conclude that the conduct is improper. Such a conclusion, wrote the judge, is an adequate basis to dismiss a teacher "on the grounds that his conduct offended the moral standards of the community and set a bad example to the youth under his charge."

In a related Alabama case, Montgomery teacher Howard Kilpatrick was discharged for immoral conduct because he made "sexual advances towards female students." The teacher claimed that the term "immoral conduct" was unconstitutionally vague and could include innocuous activity. Although the judge acknowledged that the "ultimate reach" of the term immorality was not clear, he did not feel there was any problem about vagueness in this case. According to the judge, any teacher can be expected to know that sexual advances toward students "cannot be condoned in the classroom setting."[12] Similarly, a state court upheld the firing of a Colorado high school teacher because of his "horseplay" with several female students on a field trip.[13] This consisted of tickling them all over their bodies and carrying on a vulgar and sexually suggestive dialogue. The teacher viewed his behavior as an attempt to act his "natural self to gain rapport" with his students. But the court viewed his conduct as "sordid," ruled that it had "no legitimate professional purpose," and upheld his dismissal.

Can teachers be punished for talking to their students about sex?

Sometimes. Talking about sex may subject a teacher to disciplinary action, especially when such talk is not related to the curriculum. A high school band instructor in Florida was dismissed for making remarks in a coed class relating to virginity and premarital sex relations. A state court sustained his discharge for immorality because of his "unbecoming and unnecessary risque remarks."[14] The judge concluded that "instructors in our schools should not be permitted to so risquely discuss sex problems in our teenage mixed classes as to cause embarrassment to the children or to involve in them other feelings not incident to the course of study being pursued."

In a similar Wisconsin case, a state court upheld the dismissal of a Milwaukee teacher because of a series of discussions about sex in his twelfth-grade speech classes.[15] Specifically, he explained the operation of houses of prostitution and indicated which students were old enough to be admitted; he told stories about intercourse with a cow and about the size of a penis; and he discussed premarital sex in an approving way. The teacher argued that the speech curriculum was broad enough to include sex education, which was never specifically prohibited. But the court concluded that the teacher's discussions transcended the bounds "of propriety of the contemporary community" and constituted immoral conduct.

On the other hand, a Mississippi teacher who merely answered a student's question about sex on one occasion was held not guilty of immoral behavior.[16] After several boys in an eighth-grade spelling class asked "What is a queer?" she briefly discussed homosexuality. Although some parents objected, a federal court ruled that this single incident was not enough to disqualify the teacher. While the judge questioned the judgment of a woman teacher discussing such a subject with young boys, he concluded that such a discussion was "certainly not an act 'repulsive to the minimum standards of decency' required of public school teachers." In other cases where teachers have been dismissed for using objectionable language in the classroom, courts have sometimes ruled that their actions are protected by their right to freedom of speech under the First and Fourteenth amendments. (For a detailed discussion of this issue, see chapter 8.)

Can teachers be dismissed because of rumors of immoral conduct?

No. If teachers are terminated for immoral conduct, such action should be based on fact, not rumor. This was the ruling in the 1979 case of Annabel Stoddard, a divorced mother who taught in a small, religiously oriented Wyoming community.[17] Stoddard was a competent teacher, but her contract was not renewed. Despite the official written reasons given for her nonrenewal, the evidence indicated that the real reasons were because of "rumors that she was having an affair" and because she was unattractive and did not attend church regularly. As a result of this evidence, a federal court ruled that the school officials were "motivated by constitutionally impermissible reasons" in not renewing her contract, and she was awarded $33,000 in "compensatory damages."

Moreover, an Iowa court ruled that even an admission of adultery does not make a person automatically unfit to teach.[18] The case involved an excellent teacher whose certification was revoked after he was discovered committing adultery. The court ruled that this "isolated incident" was not grounds for revocation when there was no evidence to indicate it would adversely affect his teaching.

Are there other reasons why teachers have been dismissed on grounds of immoral or unprofessional conduct?

Yes. Here are a few. A tenured California elementary teacher was dismissed after she was arrested by an undercover policeman for openly engaging in sexual activity with three different men at a swingers' club party in Los Angeles. A state court upheld her dismissal because her conduct at the semipublic party reflected "a total lack of concern for privacy, decorum or preservation of her dignity and reputation" and indicated "a serious defect of moral character, normal prudence, and good common sense."[19]

In Maryland, a federal court upheld the dismissal of a teacher for misrepresentation because he intentionally failed to state on his job application that he had been a member of the Homophiles.[20] The court acknowledged that the teacher had a constitutional right to join the Homophiles and promote public acceptance of homosexuality. He also had a right to challenge some of the questions on the school application. But the court said he had no right to certify that the application was accurate "when he knew that it contained a significant omission." The court concluded that when a teacher purposely misleads school officials by making false statements, he cannot then defend his actions by arguing that the questions were unconstitutional.

In another federal case, the University of Minnesota refused to hire a librarian after he applied to marry a homosexual friend.[21] Although the event was widely publicized in several newspaper articles (e.g., *Prospective Newlyweds Really in a Gay Mood*), the librarian charged that the decision not to hire him was unconstitutional. But an appeals court ruled against the librarian. "This," wrote the judge, "is not a case in which an applicant is excluded from employment becuse of a desire to clandestinely pursue homosexual conduct." Instead it is a case in which a prospective employee demands the right "to foist tacit approval" of homosexuality upon his employer. "We know of no constitutional fiat," concluded the court, "which requires an employer to accede to such extravagant demands."

Finally a New Jersey court upheld the dismissal of a male tenured music teacher, Paul Monroe Grossman, after he underwent "sex-reassignment" surgery.[22] The operation changed his external anatomy to that of a female, Paula Miriam Grossman, who began to live and dress as a woman. While there was conflicting testimony about Ms. Grossman's probable future effectiveness, the court supported her termination because of "potential psychological harm to students" if she were retained.

Can a teacher be dismissed for excessive drinking?

Yes. California teacher Joseph Watson was denied a secondary teaching credential on grounds of immorality because of six convictions involving the use of alcohol. Although there was no proof that his convictions affected his teaching, the court ruled that the evidence amply demonstrated his unfitness to teach.[23] First, Watson's use of alcohol had gotten out of control and indicated that he did not have the proper attitude necessary for successfully counseling students away from the harmful effects of alcohol, as state law requires. Second, being arrested as a "public drunk" and for driving under the influence of alcohol was a poor example for high school students. Through his behavior, Watson had repeatedly violated important community values and jeopardized the welfare of his students and the public. Finally, the judge wrote: "I don't know what better evidence there could be of immorality than a series of criminal convictions."

In a related Wyoming case, a state court upheld the dismissal of a teacher who was found drunk in school in front of his students and had to be removed from class by other teachers.[24] Similarly, an Arizona court ruled that a teacher could be dismissed after pleading guilty to fighting and "disturbing the peace by being under the influence of intoxicants."[25] On the other hand, the Supreme Court of Montana ruled that convictions for driving while intoxicated were not enough to discharge a teacher for immorality.[26] In this 1973 case, a teacher was arrested and pleaded guilty of "driving under the influence" for the third time. Based on this "conviction," he was dismissed. In overruling the school authorities, the Montana court held that "violations for driving under the influence of intoxicating liquor" are not in themselves "tantamount to immorality." To sustain the dismissal of such a teacher, the court indicated that school officials would have to present evidence indicating that the convictions would affect the teacher's professional performance.

CRIMINAL CONDUCT

Is conviction of a crime grounds for dismissal?

Usually, a teacher who is convicted of a serious crime (e.g., a felony) can be dismissed. This was the ruling of a Delaware court in the case of Leon Skripchuk, an outstanding industrial arts teacher.[27] After Skripchuk pleaded guilty to charges of theft and aggravated assault with a gun, he was dismissed for immorality. This was the only blemish in his long teaching career, and experts testified that it was "most unlikely" that he would ever again be involved in similar criminal conduct. But school officials testified that his conviction, which received widespread publicity, would make parents fearful and would impair his teaching effectiveness. In view of the seriousness of this crime, the court ruled that the teacher's actions were "unquestionably immoral," and his termination was reasonable.

In a similar Florida case, a state court upheld a dismissal of a teacher who pleaded guilty to manslaughter after killing her husband with a shotgun.[28] The court held that under the circumstances, her guilty plea was sufficient evidence of immorality. On the other hand, a California court pointed out that not all felonies involve immoral behavior or crimes of such seriousness that by themselves they would be sufficient to justify dismissing a teacher.[29]

Should conviction for a serious crime preclude future employment as a teacher?

Not necessarily. According to some courts, commission of a crime is not always sufficient to permanently bar a person from teaching. In considering this issue, the liberal California Supreme Court wrote that dismissal for illegal conduct is reasonable only under two conditions: (1) the teacher's conduct must be "sufficiently notorious" that students know or are likely to learn of it, and (2) "the teacher must continue to model his past conduct." According to the court: "The teacher who committed an indiscretion, paid the penalty, and now seeks to discourage his students from committing similar acts may well be a more effective supporter of legal and moral standards than the one who has never been found to violate those standards. Since these conditions will vary from case to case, proof that one has at some past time committed a crime should not in itself suffice to demonstrate that he is not now and never will be a suitable behavior model for his students."[30]

Can a teacher be punished for considering a crime?

No. David Bogart, a Kansas teacher, was charged with possession of marijuana because of drugs his son kept in his room. Although Bogart was cleared of the charge, he was dismissed by the school committee for "conduct unbecoming an instructor." Before the committee, Bogart admitted that he considered trying to protect his son and taking the blame himself, though he did neither. But a federal court held that this was not a lawful basis for dismissal.[31] "It is fortunate," wrote the court, "the state is not allowed to penalize its citizens for their thoughts, for it would be the rare and either mindless, supine, or super-saintly citizen who has not at some time contemplated and then rejected the illegal."

Can a teacher be dismissed for the use or possession of illegal drugs?

It depends on the circumstances. Courts, for example, might not support the firing of a teacher solely because he once was indicted for possessing a small amount of marijuana. But they would probably support a dismissal based on evidence of a widely publicized conviction combined with testimony indicating how the teacher's criminal behavior would undermine his effectiveness. California courts have decided four relevant cases on this question.

Arthur Comings' teacher certification was revoked for immoral and unprofessional conduct based on evidence that he had been convicted for possession of marijuana. But at Comings' hearing no evidence was presented indicating whether his conduct adversely affected students or fellow teachers, the likelihood of its recurrence, the teacher's motives, or any other evidence concerning his unfitness to teach. Under these circumstances, the court held that there was not sufficient evidence to revoke Comings' certification.[32] The court said it was not ruling that marijuana offenders must be permitted to teach, only that they cannot be dismissed without adequate evidence of their unfitness.

In a later case, a liberal California appeals court ruled that teacher Theodor Judge could not be discharged after being convicted for cultivating a marijuana plant.[33] Although school authorities testified that there would be an "adverse reaction" if Judge were to continue to teach after his felony conviction, the court nevertheless ruled that "the evidence was insufficient" to establish he was unfit to teach. The ruling was based on substantial testimony indicating there was little likelihood that Judge would repeat his crime, that his return to teaching would not have a negative effect on the school, and that firing him for possessing a single marijuana plant (that he found while taking a walk) would be an "excessive reaction." Moreover, the court wrote that in this case, "a felony conviction, standing by itself is not a ground for discipline in the absence of moral turpitude," and "marijuana related offenses need not necessarily always be crimes of moral turpidude . . . measured by the morals of our day."

Barnet Brennan was the teaching principal of a California school when she wrote an affidavit in support of a friend who had been convicted of possessing marijuana. In the sworn statement, she said: "Marijuana is not harmful to my knowledge, because I have been using it since 1949 almost daily, with only beneficial results." Brennan urged the court "to set aside these unconstitutional laws" depicting marijuana as addictive and harmful and providing "harsh and cruel penalties for its possession, sale, and use." Because Brennan's statement attracted wide publicity and her students learned of its content, she was dismissed and went to court.

Brennan argued that she should not be penalized when there was no evidence that her statement had a negative effect on students. The court responded that the school acted so promptly after learning of the affidavit that there was little time for such evidence to develop. Here, said the court, there was "competent evidence" on the "likely" effect of Brennan's conduct on students. As one witness testified: "I would be inclined to believe that the pupil would be thinking, 'If my teacher can gain her ends by breaking the law, then I, too, can gain my ends by breaking the law!'" The court concluded that her affidavit did not simply advocate a change in state law; it indicated that she had defied the law for many years and believed such violations were appropriate.[34]

In a related case, art teacher Selwyn Jones was fined for possessing marijuana while on a trip to Hawaii. His conduct was reported in the *San Francisco Chronicle* and reached the attention of Daly City school officials, who dismissed him. At a hearing the vice-principal testified that Jones' return to the school would adversely affect its art department, faculty, student body, and parents because many of these persons had expressed "disapproval" or "concern" at reinstating a teacher convicted of using marijuana. According to the vice-principal, Jones' return "would be an example in opposition to the instructions we are giving to the students" concerning drug use; in fact, his return would "work against the total goals of our school." Based on this "substantial evidence" concerning Jones' fitness to teach, the court upheld his dismissal.[35]

LIFE STYLE

Can a teacher be fired for using vulgar or "obscene" language?

Perhaps. It depends on where and with whom the language is used. Vulgar language that may be protected when used with adults may be grounds for dismissal if used with students. Thus a foreign-language teacher was discharged for immoral conduct after he called a fourteen-year-old student a "slut" and implied that she was a prostitute. In this 1977 case, a Pennsylvania court upheld the dismissal.[36] It explained that school officials must be able to protect students from abusive language by teachers. The court concluded that in the context of the teacher-student relationship, this teacher's language was "totally inappropriate" and indicated that he did not have the proper "moral character" to teach in the public schools.

On the other hand, an Ohio court reached a different conclusion in a case involving two offensive letters written by a high school teacher named Jarvella.[37] The letters were sent to a former student who had just graduated; they were found by the student's mother, who was shocked by their language and gave them to the police. As a result, local newspapers wrote several stories about the letters. The prosecuting attorney said that they contained hard-core obscenity and that "a person who would write letters of this kind is not fit to be a school teacher." Subsequently the school board terminated Jarvella's contract on grounds of immorality, but a state court ruled in his favor.

The letters, wrote the court, contain language that many adults would find "gross, vulgar, and offensive" and that some eighteen-year-old males would find "unsurprising and fairly routine." Moreover, there was no evidence that these letters adversely affected the schools—except after public disclosure. And this, wrote the judge, "was the result not of any misconduct on [Jarvella's] part, but of misconduct on the part of others." The court concluded that a teacher's private conduct is a proper concern of his employer only when it affects him as a teacher; "his private acts are his own business and may not be the basis of discipline" as long as his professional achievement is not affected.

Does the right to privacy protect teachers' personal lives?

Probably not. The right to privacy is a relatively new and evolving constitutional freedom that has not yet been adequately clarified by the courts to provide much protection for teachers' personal lives. This was the opinion of a federal appeals court in the case of Kathleen Sullivan, an elementary teacher who began living with a male friend in a small, rural South Dakota town. When parents, students, and administrators learned that the couple was not married, Sullivan's principal asked her to change her living arrangement. Sullivan replied that who she lived with was her business, not a school matter. As a result, Sullivan was fired because she violated local mores, was a "bad example" for her students, and would not get parental cooperation due to her improper conduct. Sullivan claimed that her dismissal violated her right to privacy.

Although the court acknowledged that this case posed "very difficult constitutional issues," it ruled in favor of the school board.[38] First, it wrote that the scope and limits of the "newly evolving constitutional right to privacy" are not clear. Judges have not yet decided whether "the right of a couple to live together without benefit of matrimony" falls within the scope of this right. Second, even if courts rule that the Constitution does protect a teacher's personal life style, this would not necessarily resolve a case such as this. A court would still have to balance the privacy interest of the teacher against the legitimate interest of the board in promoting the education of its students.

AGE, CITIZENSHIP, PHYSICAL FITNESS

May teachers be fired because of age?

Yes and no. On January 1, 1979, the Age Discrimination in Employment Act Amendment of 1978 became effective. This statute abolished mandatory retirement at age sixty-five for teachers. But it still permits forced retirement at seventy.* The cases that follow reflect the arguments and law on both sides of this issue.

The *Palmer* Case[40]

When New York kindergarten teacher Lois Palmer was told that she had to retire because she had reached the age of seventy, she sued. She was willing and able to continue teaching and claimed that compulsory retirement at age seventy violated the Equal Protection Clause of the Constitution by unfairly creating "an irrebuttable presumption of incompetency based on age." But a federal appeals court disagreed.

In an earlier case, the U.S. Supreme Court had ruled that compulsory retirement statutes could be upheld if there was a reasonable connection between the law and a legitimate state interest. According to the appeals court, states might require mandatory retirement for teachers to open up employment for younger teachers, to open up more places for minorities, to bring new people with fresh ideas in contact with students, or to assure predictability in administering pension plans. "A compulsory retirement system," wrote the court, "is rationally related to the fulfillment of any or all of these legitimate state objectives."

The court acknowledged the "debilitating effects" that compulsory retirement has on many able people. But these considerations "must be weighed against the social goals that compulsory retirement furthers." The court concluded that the resolution of these competing social goals is best left to the legislative process. Thus courts generally have found a "rational basis" for supporting compulsory retirement at seventy.

The *Kuhar* Case[41]

When Raymond Kuhar argued that he should not be required to retire at sixty-five, his Pennsylvania school district defended mandatory retirement with the same rational arguments used by the court to justify its decision in

* The act broadly prohibits age discrimination in employment and the 1978 amendments apply "to individuals who are at least 40 years of age but less than 70."[39]

Palmer. But another federal court ruled in Kuhar's favor. Why? Because Kuhar's case was tried in 1978 after the President signed the Age Discrimination in Employment Act Amendments, which raised the age of mandatory retirement from sixty-five to seventy. Even though the amendments did not become effective until January 1979, the court felt that the principles of the statute should apply in Kuhar's case. Congressional policy underlying the act indicated that

—Mandatory retirement based solely on age is arbitrary, and age alone is a poor indicator of ability.

—There is evidence that mandatory retirement decreases life expectancy and that the right to work as long as one can is basic to the right to survive.

—Mandatory retirement will have little effect on recruiting younger people or preventing job opportunities for minorities and women, and it is a poor method for eliminating incompetent or unproductive people.

—Research indicates that older workers are as good or better than younger co-workers "with regard to dependability, judgment, work quality, work volume, human relations, [and] absenteeism."

The school district presented evidence to indicate that Kuhar's job involved considerable pressure, that a younger person should be favored, and that its mandatory retirement policy was therefore reasonable. But the court labeled such arguments "speculative and conjectural." It concluded that the new national policy "to the effect that 70 years is the earliest time for mandatory retirement" of state employees should apply to Kuhar. In short, under current federal law, mandatory retirement for teachers is illegal at sixty-five but permissible at seventy.

Can teachers be fired because of obesity?

Probably not. Although weight may be a relevant factor in considering whether teachers can perform their jobs effectively, cases indicate that teachers cannot be fired solely because of obesity. Elizabeth Blodgett, a forty-two-year-old physical education teacher from California, was not rehired because her overweight condition allegedly rendered her "unfit for service." Blodgett was 5 feet 7 inches tall and weighed about 225 pounds. Although she was following a medical diet, her principal recommended she not be rehired because she was unable "to serve as a model of health and vigor" and was "restricted in her ability to perform or teach aspects of the physical education program [such as] modern dance, trampoline, gymnastics, track and field."

Blodgett argued that obesity may justify discharging a teacher only when her weight "has impaired her ability to function effectively." Since the evidence in this case indicated she had been a successful teacher and coach, Blodgett felt that the school acted arbitrarily in refusing to rehire her. The court agreed.[42] As to her inability to serve as a "model of health," the court wrote: "Any requirement that the teachers embody all the qualities which they hope to instill in their students will be utterly impossible of fulfillment." As for the contention that the teacher set a bad example, which her students might imitate, the court observed that "obesity, by its very nature, does not inspire emulation." Furthermore, there was extensive testimony that physical education teachers "need not excel at demonstration in order to perform their instructional duties competently and well." Since there was no evidence that Blodgett's weight had a negative effect on her teaching, the court concluded that her termination was arbitrary and ruled in her favor.

In a related New York case, Nancy Parolisi was denied a teaching license solely because she was overweight. Although she had established an excellent record during three terms of teaching, a Board of Examiner's physical fitness policy excluded candidates who were "extremely overweight or underweight." While Parolisi was admittedly overweight, the court ruled that "obesity, standing alone, is not reasonably related to the ability to teach or to maintain discipline."[43]

Can teachers be denied certification because they are not citizens?

Yes. Although several federal laws prohibit discrimination based on "national origin," the U.S. Supreme Court recently ruled that a state could prohibit individuals from becoming certified as public school teachers if they were not citizens or applying for citizenship.[44]

The case involved two qualified New York teachers who applied for elementary certification but were turned down because they were not American citizens. In a 5–4 decision, Justice Powell noted that the distinction between alien and citizen is ordinarily irrelevant to private activity. But it is fundamental to certain state functions, especially teaching, which "goes to the heart of representative government." The court emphasized that teachers "play a crucial part in developing students' attitude toward government and understanding of the role of citizens in our society." Moreover, a teacher "serves as a role model for his students, exerting a subtle but important influence over their perceptions and values." According to Justice Powell, all public school teachers, not just those who teach government or civics, may influence student attitudes toward the political process and a citizen's responsibilities. And schools "may regard all teachers as having an obligation to promote civic virtues" in their classes. Therefore, the court ruled that the state's citizenship requirement for teachers was rationally related "to a legitimate state interest."

Can teachers be denied jobs because they are handicapped?

No, not merely because of their handicap. In 1973 Congress passed a law which stated that "no otherwise qualified individual . . . shall, solely by reason of his handicap, be excluded from participation in . . . or be subjected to discrimination under any program" receiving federal funds.[45]

In many school situations, the question arises concerning what the statute means by an "otherwise qualified individual." In one case, a federal court explained that the term does not mean that a handicapped individual must be hired despite his handicap. Rather it prohibits the nonhiring of a handicapped individual when the disability does not prevent that individual from performing the job.[46]

SUMMARY

An increasing number of courts now hold that teachers cannot be dismissed for personal conduct simply because it is contrary to the mores of a community. Thus the fact that a teacher has done something most people regard as immoral (e.g., smoking marijuana, committing adultery, engaging in homosexual activity, or using vulgar language) is not by itself sufficient grounds for dismissal. To dismiss such a teacher there must be substantial evidence that the immorality is likely to have a negative effect on his or her teaching. As long as competence as a teacher is unaffected, most courts hold that private behavior is a teacher's own business.

On the other hand, courts usually uphold the dismissal of teachers if their immoral conduct becomes known through the teacher's fault and has a negative impact on their effectiveness. In cases of notoriously illegal or immoral behavior, some courts allow teachers to be fired even without evidence that the conduct impaired their teaching. For example, in cases involving repeated convictions for drunk driving, armed assault, or using illegal drugs, judges may say that the negative impact of such behavior is obvious. Whether being known as a homosexual, being an unwed mother, or committing a simple felony could result in dismissal probably would depend on the circumstances. Courts might consider the size, sophistication, and values of the community; the notoriety of the activity; when it took place; and whether it occurred in the community where the teacher is employed.

In cases of immoral conduct with students, courts tend to be strict. Evidence of a single homosexual relationship between a teacher and a student would probably be enough to sustain a teacher's dismissal even if the relationship occurred years before and even if no other students, teachers, or parents knew about it. Similarly, a teacher who made sexual advances toward students or who smoked marijuana, drank excessively, or used obscene language with them would probably receive no protection from the courts. In some situations, however, the age and maturity of the students might make a difference.

In addition to immoral behavior, schools also consider other aspects of teachers' personal life, such as age, weight, handicap, and citizenship, when deciding whether to employ or rehire them. Under current federal law, it is illegal to discriminate against a teacher solely because of a handicap or to compel a teacher to retire before age seventy. In addition, cases indicate that a teacher cannot be fired merely because of obesity. On the other hand, a state may refuse to certify teachers if they are not U.S. citizens or applying for citizenship.

As the cases in this chapter have indicated, the law concerning the removal of teachers for immoral conduct is not always precise. There are no recent Supreme Court opinions on the topic, and decisions in different states sometimes appear inconsistent. Much depends on the circumstances of the case. Nevertheless, most courts recognize that teachers should not be penalized for their private behavior unless it has a clear impact on their effectiveness as eduators.

NOTES

1. *Morrison* v. *State Board of Education*, 461 P.2d 375 (Cal. 1969).
2. *Sarac* v. *State Board of Education*, 57 Cal. Rptr. 69 (1967).
3. *Id.*
4. *Burton* v. *Cascade School District Union High School No. 5*, 353 F.Supp. 254 (D. Ore. 1973).
5. *Gaylord* v. *Tacoma School District No. 10*, 559 P.2d 1340 (Wash. 1977).
6. *Brown* v. *Bathke*, 416 F.Supp. 1194 (D. Neb. 1976).
7. *Andrews* v. *Drew Municipal Separate School District*, 507 F.2d 611 (5th Cir. 1975).
8. *Board of Trustees of Compton Junior College District* v. *Stubblefield*, 94 Cal. Rptr. 318 (1971).
9. *Yang* v. *Special Charter School District No. 150, Peoria County*, 296 N.E.2d 74 (Ill. 1973).
10. *Denton* v. *South Kitsap School District No. 402*, 516 P.2d 1080 (Wash. 1973).
11. *Penn-Delco School District* v. *Urso*, 382 A.2d 162 (Pa. 1978).
12. *Kilpatrick* v. *Wright*, 437 F.Supp. 397 (Ala. 1977).
13. *Weissman* v. *Board of Education of Jefferson County School District No. R-1*, 547 P.2d 1267 (Colo. 1976).
14. *Pyle* v. *Washington County School Board*, 238 So.2d 121 (Fla. 1970).
15. *State* v. *Board of School Directors of Milwaukee*, 111 N.W.2d 198 (Wis. 1961).
16. *United States* v. *Coffeeville Consolidated School District*, 365 F.Supp. 990 (N.D. Miss. 1973).
17. *Stoddard* v. *School District No. 1, Lincoln County, Wyoming*, 590 F.2d 829 (10th Cir. 1979).
18. *Erb* v. *Iowa State Board of Instruction*, 216 N.W.2d 339 (Iowa 1974).
19. *Pettit* v. *State Board of Education*, 513 P.2d 889 (Cal. 1973).
20. *Acanfora* v. *Board of Education of Montgomery County*, 491 F.2d 498 (4th Cir. 1974).
21. *McConnell* v. *Anderson*, 451 F.2d 193 (8th Cir. 1971).
22. *In re Grossman*, 316 A.2d 39 (N.J. 1974).
23. *Watson* v. *State Board of Education*, 99 Cal. Rptr. 468 (Cal. App. 1971).

24. *Tracy* v. *School District No. 22, Sheridan County, Wyoming*, 243 P.2d 932 (Wyo. 1952).

25. *Williams* v. *School District No. 40 of Gila County*, 417 P.2d 376 (Ariz. 1966).

26. *Lindgren* v. *Board of Trustees, High School District No. 1*, 558 P.2d 468 (Mont. 1976).

27. *Skripchuk* v. *Austin*, 379 A.2d 1142 (Del. 1977).

28. *Kiner* v. *State Board of Education*, 344 So.2d 657 (Fla. 1977).

29. *Board of Trustees of Santa Maria Joint High School District* v. *Judge*, 123 Cal. Rptr. 830 (1975).

30. *Board of Education of Long Beach Unified School District* v. *Jack M.*, 139 Cal. Rptr. 700 (1977).

31. *Bogart* v. *Unified School District No. 298 of Lincoln County Kansas*, 432 F.Supp. 895 (D. Kan. 1977).

32. *Comings* v. *State Board of Education*, 100 Cal. Rptr. 73 (1972).

33. *Board of Trustees of Santa Maria Joint Union High School District* v. *Judge*, 123 Cal. Rptr. 830 (1975).

34. *Governing Board* v. *Brennan*, 95 Cal. Rptr. 712 (Cal. App. 1971).

35. *Jefferson Union High School District* v. *Jones*, 100 Cal. Rptr. 73 (1972). Jones was decided together with *Comings, supra.*

36. *Bovino* v. *Board of School Directors of the Indiana Area School District*, 377 A.2d 1284 (Penn. 1977).

37. *Jarvella* v. *Willoughby-East Lake City School District*, 233 N.E.2d 143 (Ohio 1967).

38. *Sullivan* v. *Meade Independent School District, No. 101*, 530 F.2d 799 (8th Cir. 1976).

39. U.S.C.A. chap. 14 §621–23, 631 (1980).

40. *Palmer* v. *Ticcione*, 576 F.2d 459 (2d. Cir. 1978).

41. *Kuhar* v. *Greersburg-Salem School District*, 466 F.Supp. 806 (W.D. Pa. 1979).

42. *Blodgett* v. *Board of Trustees, Tamalpais Union High School District*, 97 Cal. Rptr. 406 (1971).

43. *Parolisi* v. *Board of Examiners of City of New York*, 285 N.Y.S.2d 936 (1967).

44. *Ambach* v. *Norwick*, 99 S.Ct. 1589 (1979).

45. 29 U.S.C.A. §794 (1980 Supplement).

46. *Carmi* v. *Metropolitan St. Louis Sewer District*, 471 F.Supp. 119 (E.D. Mo. 1979).

14

Am I protected against racial discrimination?

OVERVIEW

Many scholarly studies have established that American culture, throughout its history, has been fraught with racism. There have been regional differences in the openness and intensity of racial discrimination, but rare indeed is the community that can claim to have been completely free from it. Even at the beginning of the twentieth century, blacks were "considered by many whites, North and South, to be depraved, comic, childlike, or debased persons."[1]

Schools, like other institutions in American culture, have reflected this widespread prejudice against blacks, Native Americans, Orientals, and Latins. Many social forces have interacted to influence the schools, including the courts and the law. While no claim is made here that law is the most important force influencing attitudes toward different racial groups, it is recognized as one important influence on people in general and public schools in particular.

This chapter examines the impact of the courts and the law on racial discrimination against students and school personnel in the light of the Supreme Court ruling that segregation in schools is unconstitutional.

SCHOOL DESEGREGATION

Why is racial segregation in schools unconstitutional?

The Equal Protection Clause of the Fourteenth Amendment has been the major legal vehicle used to challenge various aspects of racial discrimination in public life. Section I specifies that "no State shall . . . deny to any person within its jurisdiction the equal protection of the laws." Early in the history of the amendment, it was determined that since public schools are state institutions, actions by public school officials and employees are *state* actions. However, the famous case of *Plessy* v. *Ferguson*[2] established the principle that separate but equal facilities satisfy the Equal Protection Clause of the amendment. Though *Plessy* involved public transportation facilities, the Supreme Court followed it as precedent in a public school conflict in 1927.[3] A successful challenge to the "separate but equal" doctrine did not arise until 1954, in the landmark case of *Brown* v. *Board of Education.* This is not to say that segregated education went unchallenged until the *Brown* case. Between *Plessy* in 1896 and *Brown* in 1954, many lawsuits challenged the separate but equal doctrine, particularly in graduate and professional schools. Several such suits succeeded because it was not possible for the southern states engaged in segregated schooling to provide law schools or medical schools of equal quality in separate facilities for blacks and whites. These suits ultimately prepared the way for Linda Brown's successful legal action.

The *Brown* Case[4]

Linda Brown, an elementary school student in Topeka, Kansas, filed suit challenging a Kansas law that sanctioned the racially separate schools she was attending. The district court found "that segregation in public education has a detrimental effect upon Negro children" but upheld the arrangement since schools for white children and black children "were substantially equal with respect to buildings, transportation, curricula, and educational qualifications of teachers." When Brown appealed to the Supreme Court, school officials argued that the Fourteenth Amendment was never meant to apply to the schools and that in any event, the *Plessy* principle of "separate but equal" should be followed and the Kansas law upheld.

Was the Fourteenth Amendment meant to apply to public schools? Chief Justice Earl Warren, writing for a unanimous Court, answered in the affirmative. He wrote that the amendment must be considered in the light of current facts and conditions and not those of 1868 when the amendment was adopted. Only by considering the importance of public schools in the middle of the twentieth century could it be determined whether segregated schooling deprives students of equal protection of the law. Other judges and scholars have voiced the same conviction by asserting that the Constitution and its amendments stay alive by constant application to new conditions, lest they become mere "parchment under glass."

Should the Court follow the precedent set by *Plessy?* Courts do not follow precedents blindly. Changing conditions, as well as new knowledge generated by the sciences, may lead to the overruling of a precedent. This is precisely what happened in the *Brown* case.

The Court recognized that education has become "perhaps the most important function of state and local governments. . . . It is the very foundation of good citizenship. Today it is a principal instrument in awakening the child to cultural values, in preparing him for later professional training, and in helping him to adjust normally to his environment. In these days, it is doubtful that any child may reasonably be expected to succeed in life if he is denied the opportunity of an education. Such an opportunity, where the state has undertaken to provide it, is a right which must be available to all on equal terms."

The Court then considered evidence offered by social scientists concerning the impact of segregation on school children and concluded that "segregation . . . has a detrimental effect upon the colored children. The impact is greater when it has the sanction of the law; for the policy of separating the races is usually interpreted as denoting the inferiority of the Negro group. A sense of inferiority affects the motivation of the child to learn. Segregation with the sanction of law, therefore, has a tendency to retard the educational and mental development of Negro children and to deprive them of some of the benefits they would receive in a racially integrated school system." Thus, in rejecting *Plessy* v. *Ferguson* the Court concluded that ". . . in the field of public education the doctrine of 'separate but equal' has no place. Separate educational facilities are inherently unequal."

How soon must schools desegregate?

Each community had its unique history of segregation, its unique traffic and residential pattern, and its own educational system, so the Court considered it unwise to pronounce one formula or timetable for desegregation applicable to all throughout the country. Instead, after hearing arguments on behalf of various possible remedies, the Court ordered that schools must desegregate "with all deliberate speed." Local school districts were to create desegregation plans, under the supervision of federal district courts, which are the courts closest to each locality. Thus, school authorities were given the primary responsibility to solve local educational problems, but local courts were to decide whether the school officials acted in "good faith implementation of the governing constitutional principles."[5]

Are parents free to choose which schools their children will attend?

No, they are not, if their choices will perpetuate segregated schooling. This question arose after *Brown,* when various arrangements were created to delay and even avoid the mandate of the Court. Some localities even closed their public schools and then used public funds to support segregated private schools. Such subterfuge was ruled unconstitutional.[6]

The "freedom-of-choice" plan appealed to many parents and politicians. The plan gave individual families the choice of where to send their children to school, and it was quickly adopted in many communities and legislatures. One such plan was challenged in New Kent County, Virginia, where segregated schools existed under a law enacted in 1902. In three years of operation of the "freedom-of-choice" plan, not a single white child chose to attend what had historically been the black school, and 85 percent of the black children continued to attend the all-black school. The dual system of schooling had not been eliminated eleven years after *Brown I* and ten years after *Brown II.*

The Supreme Court struck down the "freedom-of-choice" plan in this community as ineffective. In the words of the Court: " 'Freedom-of-Choice' is not a Sacred Talisman; it is only a means to a constitutionally required end—the abolition of the system of segregation and its effects. If the means prove effective, it is acceptable, but if it fails to undo segregation, other means must be used to achieve this end. The school officials have the continuing duty to take whatever action may be necessary to create a 'unitary, nonracial system.' " A lower court gave a simple, pragmatic test for similar cases: "The only school desegregation plan that meets constitutional standards is one that works."[7]

Must all one-race schools be eliminated?

Not necessarily. Geographic factors, population concentrations, location of schools, traffic patterns, and good-faith attempts to create a unitary school system must all be taken into consideration. The Supreme Court addressed this question in the *Swann* case.[8] The North Carolina schools in this case in 1965 had adopted a desegregation plan that was being challenged during the 1968–69 school year as inadequate. Chief Justice Burger, in writing for a unanimous Court, recognized that in large cities minority groups are often concentrated in one part of the city. In some situations, certain schools remain all or largely of one race until new schools can be built or the neighborhood changes. Thus the mere existence of such schools is not in itself proof of unconstitutional segregation. Nevertheless, the courts will carefully scrutinize such arrangements, and the presumption is against such schools. District officials have the burden of showing that single-race schools are genuinely nondiscriminatory.

May racial quotas be used in attempts to desegregate schools?

It depends on how such quotas are used. The Supreme Court ruled in *Swann* that "the constitutional command to desegregate schools does not mean that every school in every community must always reflect the racial composition of the school system as a whole." Thus, if a mathematical quota were used, requiring a particular percentage of racial mixing, the Court would disapprove. On the other hand, it is legitimate to use mathematical ratios as starting points or as general goals in efforts to achieve racial balance in a previously segregated school system.

Are there limits to using buses for desegregation?

Yes, in a general sense. Courts have recognized that "bus transportation has been an integral part of the public school system for years, and was perhaps the single most important factor in the transition from the one-room schoolhouse to the consolidated school." During the year that the *Swann* case went to court, 18 million public school children, or about 39 percent of the nation's enrollment, were bused to school. The Supreme Court has accepted bus transportation as an important tool of desegregation. Its use may be limited "when the time or distance of travel is so great as to either risk the health of the children or significantly impinge on the educational process." Furthermore, "it hardly needs stating that the limits on time of travel will vary with many factors, but probably with none more than the age of the students."

May an ethnic group be exempt from desegregation?

No. This was illustrated in San Francisco when Chinese parents brought suit to exclude their children from a citywide desegregation plan. The children attended neighborhood elementary schools that enrolled mostly Chinese-American students. Parents valued this enrollment pattern, for it helped them maintain and perpetuate their subculture and the Chinese language. They expressed fear that a dispersal of Chinese-American students, as part of an overall plan to achieve racial balance, would destroy their subculture and make it more difficult to teach their children the Chinese language. They also argued that San Francisco never had a dual school system so it need not create a unitary one. Moreover, claimed the parents, San Francisco had no rules or regulations segregating the races; district officials merely drew attendance lines to determine who goes to which school.

The district court ruled that if school officials draw attendance lines knowing that the lines maintain or heighten racial imbalance, their actions constitute officially imposed segregation and are therefore unconstitutional. The fact that San Francisco never had an official dual system is irrelevant. It developed such a system partly by the location of different racial groups and partly by the actions of school officials in arranging and rearranging attendance lines.

While sympathetic to the concern of parents, the court ruled that the Chinese-American students must participate in the overall desegregation of the schools. Nevertheless, the court also supported efforts to develop bilingual classes for Chinese-speaking children, as well as courses that taught the "cultural background and heritages of various racial and ethnic groups."[8a]

Is unintentional segregation against the law?

No. Since the Fourteenth Amendment forbids the state from denying anyone the equal protection of the law, some state action or actions by state officials must be identified as discriminatory action. In the early years of school desegregation, attention focused on southern states because they typically had laws that explicitly mandated or permitted segregated schooling. Such laws led courts to distinguish *de jure* and *de facto* segregation. *De jure* meant "by law"; *de facto* meant "as a matter of fact." The former was a violation of the Constitution; the latter was not.

As more and more cases were brought to court, in northern as well as southern communities, it became clear that segregation often occurs without explicit laws yet with the help of state, municipal, and school officials. Are such actions *de jure?* Yes, said the courts, for any action by governmental officials in the course of their duties is action "under color of the law." Examples of such official actions are the drawing of school district lines and attendance zones, zoning ordinances, creating housing and other residential restrictions, governmental support or insurance of home loans, and governmental enforcement of restrictive covenants in deeds to private property. All these practices have been used to create residential segregation and hence segregated schools. When the Supreme Court established these legal principles, it became clear that *de jure* segregation has occurred in virtually every city in the nation. School boards often contributed to such segregation without malice or bad faith but simply by being unaware of the consequences of their actions. Nonetheless, *their actions were intentional* in establishing district lines, attendance zones, location of new schools, hiring policies, and so forth.

In 1979, the Supreme Court ruled once again, in cases involving Columbus and Dayton, Ohio, that intentional acts by school or other governmental officials were required for *de jure* segregation to be established.[9] If such acts occurred, the school district had the affirmative duty to eliminate all vestiges of segregation, even if the acts occurred years ago. In Dayton, for example, the segregative acts occurred twenty years previously, but the city never completely overcame the effects of past segregation; therefore, said the Court, the duty to do so was never completely satisfied.

If part of a school district is segregated, must the entire district undergo desegregation?

That depends on what portion of the school district is unconstitutionally segregated. The Court ruled in a case involving Denver, Colorado, that if a substantial portion of the district is unlawfully segregated, the entire district must be involved in the remedy. How much is a "substantial portion"? That depends on the circumstances; the district court closest to the facts is in the best position to determine whether the segregation is substantial enough to have an impact on the student composition in the entire district.[10]

What if a desegregated district becomes resegregated?

A community may desegregate its schools, yet, as a result of population shifts and without any official action, resegregation may occur. Is there a duty to desegregate all over again? No, ruled the Supreme Court in Pasadena, California.[11] Once the school district creates a "racially neutral system of student assignment" it does not have to readjust attendance zones when population shifts occur because no official action caused the new imbalance. The new segregation is *de facto* and thus not unconstitutional.

May desegregation plans cross district lines to include suburbs with the city in the same plan?

Yes and no. This question has arisen in metropolitan areas where the core city, made up predominantly of racial minorities, is surrounded by suburbs that are predominantly white. In Detroit, for example, the city population (64 percent black, 36 percent white) made it impossible to achieve substantial desegregation within the city. Yet people living in Detroit's suburbs (81 percent white, 19 percent black) objected to a metropolitan area desegregation plan that would have included busing students across district lines.

Proponents of the "metropolitan plan" (also known as "cross-district plan") argued that since education is a state function and the state only delegates its responsibility to local districts, Michigan had the obligation to desegregate Detroit's schools. Since many other governmental functions are performed on a regional basis rather than a citywide basis, there is no compelling reason why school desegregation should not be regionalized. District and appeals courts agreed, but the Supreme Court rejected this line of argument. In a close decision (5-4), the Court ruled that desegregation must take place within the city of Detroit because that is where the constitutional violation occurred: ". . . the scope of the remedy is determined by the nature and extent of the constitutional violation."[12]

Chief Justice Burger noted, however, that "an interdistrict remedy might be in order where the racially discriminatory acts of one or more districts caused racial segregation in an adjacent district, or where district lines have been deliberately drawn on the basis of race." A case in Wilmington, Delaware, involved just such facts. When the evidence showed cross-district collaboration through official policies that created segregated schooling, and when it was clear that an interdistrict remedy was feasible, the court ordered such a remedy. The Supreme Court affirmed this decision.[13]

Do state constitutions and laws relate to desegregation?

Yes. Since the Constitution is the basic law of the land, no federal law, state constitution, or law may contradict it. State constitutions, laws, and policies may go further than the federal Constitution, as long as they are not inconsistent with it. For example, several states have erased the *de jure–de facto* distinction by state law or by policies of state boards of education, and made them both illegal. Examples of such states are Connecticut, Illinois, New Jersey, and New York. Similarly, California eliminated the distinction by its state constitution.[14]

May private schools exclude black students?

No. Many private schools genuinely welcome students from all racial, ethnic, and religious groups, but some schools accept applications only from Caucasians or certain religious denominations. The First Amendment of the Constitution protects freedom of religion and thus the creation and maintenance of separate, private religious schools. No such protection is extended to racial prejudice. When black parents brought suit against a private school that denied admission to their children, the Supreme Court ruled in favor of the parents.[15]

Since no state action is involved when a private school denies admission, why did the Court rule for the parents? A federal law protects the equal right to enter into contracts.[16] The Court ruled that this law prohibits private, commercially operated nonsectarian schools from denying admission to an applicant simply on the basis of race. Even private schools must submit to reasonable government regulation.

RACIAL DISCRIMINATION AGAINST TEACHERS AND STAFF

Does the Brown case apply to teachers and staff?

Yes. While *Brown I* dealt with the general constitutional principles related to desegregation, the Court addressed the question of judicial remedy a year later in *Brown II*. Considering the appropriate remedies, the Court was mindful that the wide variety of local conditions would make a single monolithic order inappropriate. Therefore it generated several guiding principles. First, it required that school districts "make a prompt and reasonable start toward full compliance" with the ruling in *Brown I* and proceed "with all deliberate speed." Second, it gave supervisory responsibility to the district courts to oversee school officials as they proceeded with good-faith implementation to desegregate the schools. The courts were to be "guided by equitable principles," which has traditionally meant "a practical flexibility in shaping remedies and by a facility for adjusting and reconciling public and private needs." Third, courts may consider "the physical condition of the school plant, the school transportation system, personnel," and other factors in supervising good-faith compliance.[17] Courts have relied heavily on *Brown II* in the breadth of their discretionary powers and in considering the role of teachers, administrators, and staff in efforts to desegregate schools.

May schools still delay desegregation?

No. Massive resistance met the Supreme Court's ruling in the *Brown* case. The resistance took many forms, some blatant and some subtle, but schools were not desegregating. Therefore, fifteen years later, the Court declared that the doctrine of desegregating "with all deliberate speed" had run its course. It was time to direct schools that they may no longer operate a dual school system based on race or color but must "begin immediately to operate as unitary systems within which no person is to be effectively excluded from any school because of race or color."[18]

How quickly must faculty and staff be desegregated?

That depends on the local situation, including the racial composition of the teaching force and the staff, as well as the overall plan to desegregate in good faith. For example, in Montgomery County, Alabama, the district court required the immediate desegregation of "the substitute teachers, the student teachers, [and] the night faculties," since this could be accomplished without any administrative problems. The desegregation of the regular faculties was ordered on a slower, more gradual basis. The Supreme Court approved the actions of the district court, saying that it has repeatedly recognized faculty and staff desegregation "to be an important aspect of the basic task of achieving a public school system wholly free from racial discrimination."[19]

May minorities be dismissed when reductions occur as a result of desegregation?

Yes, but only if objective criteria are used to make the reduction decisions. This question arose in many school districts that maintained a dual system, one for black students and the other for whites. There were many underenrolled classes and small schools with administrators in charge of each school. When unitary school districts were being formed as a result of court-ordered desegregation it became clear that many communities had been supporting a surplus of teachers and administrators as a price of segregation. What happened to the teachers, administrators, and staff no longer needed when schools were consolidated? More often than not, black educators lost their jobs. When some black educators in Mississippi challenged such practices, the courts generated some guiding principles.

In Jackson, Mississippi, the U.S. Court of Appeals, in connection with a suit to desegregate the schools, ordered that principals, teachers, teacher aides, and staff who work with children be so assigned within the district that "in no case will the racial composition of a staff indicate that a school is intended for Negro students or white students." Subsequent hiring should be conducted so that the racial composition of teachers and staff within each school will reflect the racial composition in the entire school system.[20] Moreover, if there is to be any reduction in the number of administrators, faculty, or staff, or if there are any demotions, members to be demoted or dismissed "must be selected on the basis of objective and reasonable and nondiscriminatory standards from among all the staff of the school district." If demotions or dismissals occur, no replacements may be made by hiring or promoting a person of a different race or national origin from that of the dismissed or demoted individual until each displaced staff member who is qualified has had an opportunity to fill the vacancy. This is the *Singleton* principle.

Where do we get the objective criteria for use in dismissals or demotions?

Criteria must be developed by the school district for use in connection with demotions or dismissals. Such nonracial objective criteria must be available for public inspection.

Do faculty and staff members have access to the evaluations?

Yes. This was a requirement in the *Singleton* case and many subsequent courts, including the Supreme Court, have referred to the *Singleton* principles with approval.

What is a demotion?

Singleton held that a demotion is any reassignment that (1) leads to less pay or less responsibility, (2) requires less skill than the previous assignment, or (3) requires a teacher to teach a subject or grade other than one for which he or she is certified or for which he or she has had substantial experience within the past five years.

Must objective criteria always be used before a black teacher can be dismissed?

No, not always, only when faculty reduction accompanies school desegregation. This question arose concerning Mrs. Watts, a black teacher who taught for 25 years in the Tuscaloosa County school system in Alabama, 24 of those years in all-black schools. When the schools were desegregated pursuant to a court order in 1970, she was transferred to a predominantly white school. According to the testimony presented at the trial, Mrs. Watts had severe discipline problems, which she could not master. The school board suspended her a year later and held hearings with respect to her competence. She called no witnesses on her own behalf, nor did she cross-examine those who testified about her lack of competence.

When the hearings resulted in her dismissal for incompetence, she appealed to a state administrative commission, and when that agency upheld the decision of the school board, she went to court. The court held that the *Singleton* principles that require the application of objective criteria before a teacher can be dismissed govern only reductions resulting from court-ordered conversion to a unitary system. In Mrs. Watts' case, there was no faculty or staff reduction immediately before or following desegregation. Courts will be reluctant "to intrude upon the internal affairs of local school authorities in such matters as teacher competency." Thus, if there is substantial evidence to support the board's finding of incompetence, courts will not substitute their judgment for that of the board. The appeals court upheld the dismissal of Mrs. Watts.[21]

May school boards hire by race to fill vacancies?

Yes and no. In a school district undergoing court-ordered desegregation to overcome the results of past unconstitutional actions, the district court may order school officials to take race into account when filling vacancies. This happened in Boston where the district court, as part of an overall plan of desegregation, ordered (1) the hiring of black and white teachers on a one-to-one basis until the percentage of black faculty reaches 20 percent, (2) the creation of an affirmative action program to recruit black faculty until their proportion reaches 25 percent of the faculty, (3) a coordinator of minority recruitment and a recruiting budget for 1975–76 of no less than $120,000, and (4) periodic reports to the court on recruiting and hiring.[22]

The same question arose in Alabama when a school board practice of filling "white vacancies" and "black vacancies" was challenged. The court ruled that if a school district is not involved in a desegregation process, if there are no reductions, dismissals, or hirings in connection with such desegregation, then boards must seek the most qualified applicants, regardless of race.[23]

Must principals be selected on a nondiscriminatory basis?

Yes, the selection of principals must be based on professional qualifications. If a school district is reducing the number of its administrators or is hiring but not in connection with desegregation, it is not required that objective criteria be used to select new administrators. If a black teacher claims non-promotion to a principalship because of race, the burden of proof is on the teacher to support such a claim. Cases have held that this could be established by showing a large reduction in the number of black administrators in a district that had no reduction in the percentage of white administrators. The burden of proof then falls on the school board to show that there were nondiscriminatory reasons for its actions.[24]

May a minority counselor be demoted?

Yes, if there are adequate nonracial reasons for the demotion. In El Paso, Texas, Eduardo Molina, a Mexican-American high school teacher, was appointed school counselor. After serving in that capacity for three years at two different schools, he was demoted to classroom teaching. Molina claimed that his demotion reflected his ethnic status and his involvement in Mexican-American affairs. The school district claimed that the demotion was based on his unsatisfactory performance as a counselor and his inability to get along with students, faculty, and other counselors.

The court was satisfied with the evidence establishing Molina's unsatisfactory performance as a counselor. Even though there was also evidence of discrimination in the school system at large, in the opinion of the court there were sufficient nondiscriminatory reasons for demoting this particular individual.[25]

May objective tests be used to screen applicants for jobs even if more blacks than whites fail the test?

Yes, if the tests are reasonable and relevant to the job for which people are being screened. The Supreme Court, in a case involving the recruiting of police officers, said that it has "not embraced the proposition that a law or other official act, without regard to whether it reflects a racially discriminatory purpose, is unconstitutional solely because it has a racially disproportionate impact."[26] This became a very important case because, earlier, some courts have ruled that a law or official act was unconstitutional if it had a discriminatory intent, purpose, or impact. Thus today the Court would require the intent to discriminate to declare such tests unconstitutional.

May objective tests be used for certification or pay if they disproportionately fail more blacks than whites?

Yes, if the tests are valid and reliable and are not used with the purpose and intent of discriminating against any race. In South Carolina, they used the National Teacher Examination (NTE) to screen people for certification. Candidates had to achieve a minimum score to be certified to teach in the state, and their pay levels were also determined by their scores. The use of the test was challenged because more blacks than whites failed to acquire the minimum score, and this allegedly created a racial classification in violation of the Fourteenth Amendment as well as Title VII of the Civil Rights Act of 1964.

The district court, after examining the NTE used to screen candidates for certification, concluded that the test was a well developed instrument reasonably calculated to assess the presence or absence of knowledge. It also found that the test was not created or used with the intent to discriminate, therefore its use was proper and legal.[27]

In the same case, the court held that using the NTE to determine the level of teachers' pay was reasonable and rationally connected to a legitimate state interest. A unitary pay system had been introduced in South Carolina together with the new bases for certification. The court found that the reason for the new arrangement was the state's desire to use its limited resources to improve the quality of the teaching force "and to put whatever monetary incentives were available in the salary schedule to that task." Thus, finding no discriminatory intent in the use of the NTE for salary purposes, the court upheld the state policy.

How do courts determine employment discrimination—by the racial composition of the schools or of the larger area?

The latter, according to the Supreme Court. In a case in St. Louis County, Missouri, the school district suggested that the comparison be made between the teacher work force and the student population. The Court rejected this position and held that ". . . a proper comparison was between the racial composition of [the] teaching staff and the racial composition of the qualified public school teacher population in the relevant labor market."[28]

SUMMARY

Schools are at the center of the storm as various interest groups attempt to put their ideas into practice and use the schools to attain their social goals. The meaning of the Equal Protection Clause is generally agreed upon in bold outlines by the courts, even though many details and "legal wrinkles" remain to be ironed out. The major remaining tasks are those of implementation, to carry out the Supreme Court's clear pronouncement in the landmark *Brown* case that "in the field of public education the doctrine of 'separate but equal' has no place."

Brown I declared that segregated public schools are unconstitutional; *Brown II* ordered schools to desegregate "with all deliberate speed." Most communities resisted the Court's mandate. As legal challenges were mounted against the different forms of resistance to desegregation, courts tended to respect various plans to overcome historic patterns of racial separation as long as the plans were advanced in good faith and were likely to work.

Busing is a legitimate means by which schools may desegregate. Factors such as time and distance to be traveled must be considered in any plan for busing children, and the age of the children is a vital factor. Quotas may not be used as fixed requirements in attempts to achieve racially balanced schools, but they may be used as general goals in a previously segregated school system. In a school district undergoing desegregation all racial groups must participate; no group may be exempt.

The Fourteenth Amendment prohibition against segregated schooling applies to the entire country and to all situations where official acts were involved in the creation or perpetuation of segregated schooling. Any intentional act that has a segregative impact is unconstitutional, however indirect or hidden the act may be. Not only the laws of the state and the formal policies of a school district must be examined to determine whether *de jure* segregation exists, but other official actions as well. These include the drawing of school attendance zones, zoning ordinances, residential restrictions, government support for housing and insurance, and all other actions used to create residential and therefore school segregation.

The Supreme Court has ruled that if a substantial portion of a city has been unlawfully segregated, the entire school district must be involved in the remedy. On the other hand, once a school district has undergone legitimate desegregation and through ordinary events, without any official action, some desegregation occurs, the U.S. Constitution does not require a new effort to desegregate. Such a situation would be a *de facto* segregation and thus not unconstitutional.

Efforts to create metropolitan area desegregation plans have met with mixed results in the courts. If there is evidence to prove that officials of a city and its surrounding suburbs collaborated in the creation of a city heavily populated by racial minorities with suburbs largely populated by whites, a plan for interdistrict desegregation will be ordered. In the absence of such cooperation (or collusion), the district lines will be respected by the courts and the remedy will have to be restricted to the area wherein the constitutional violation occurred.

In any effort to achieve desegregation, both federal and state laws must be consulted. All public schools must meet the minimum requirements of the national Constitution and the federal laws; state laws and constitutions may provide some remedies that go beyond the federal law. Private schools may not exclude students on the grounds of race. The Supreme Court ruled that federal law protects the equal right to enter into contracts, thus a private nonsectarian school may not deny admission to an otherwise qualified applicant simply on the basis of race.

The general principles pronounced by the Court in *Brown* apply to all aspects of schooling including teachers and staff. Racial segregation is unconstitutional, and racial discrimination in all forms is illegal. This does not mean that race cannot be taken into account when teachers and staff are assigned. *Swann* makes a strong argument for the assignment of teachers and staff to enhance faculty desegregation and specifically rejects the notion that teachers must always be assigned on a "color blind" basis. The implementation of desegregation is a complex and demanding task. As the Supreme Court said, "There is no universal answer to complex problems of desegregation; there is obviously no one plan that will do the job in every case. The matter must be assessed in light of the circumstances present and the options available in each instance. It is incumbent upon the school board to establish that its proposed plan promises meaningful and immediate progress toward disestablishing state imposed segregation. It is incumbent upon the district court to weigh that claim in light of the facts at hand and in light of any alternatives which may be shown as feasible and more promising in their effectiveness."[29]

Desegregation with "all deliberate speed" has run its course, and schools must begin to desegregate immediately. Nevertheless, courts still allow individual school districts reasonable time to achieve desegregation as long as they are proceeding in good faith. If in the process of desegregation a surplus of teachers, administrators, or staff appears, individuals to be dismissed or demoted must be selected on the basis of objective, reasonable, and nondiscriminatory criteria. In ordinary cases of reduction in force, or in dismissals based on incompetence, in the absence of desegregation, courts will allow school districts to follow their usual procedures.

Objective tests may be used by public schools and state agencies in the process of certification, as well as in deciding where to place teachers on a salary scale, if the objective tests are reasonable, relevant to the ocupational tasks, and were not created with the intent to discriminate. The fact that the tests have a disproportionate negative impact on a racial or ethnic minority does not invalidate an otherwise acceptable test.

In sum, the courts continue their efforts to apply the Equal Protection Clause of the Fourteenth Amendment to the functioning of all school personnel. The problems change with changing times and conditions, but the powerful principles of the *Brown* case are still alive and controlling in all situations related to racial integration of schools and school personnel.

NOTES

1. J. W. Peltason, 58 LONELY MEN: SOUTHERN FEDERAL JUDGES AND SCHOOL DESEGREGATION (Urbana: University of Illinois Press, 1971).

2. 163 U.S. 537 (1896).

3. *Gong Lum* v. *Rice*, 275 U.S. 78 (1927).

4. 347 U.S. 483 (1954).

5. This decision is known as *Brown II*, *Brown* v. *Board of Education*, 349 U.S. 294 (1955).

6. *Griffin* v. *Prince Edward County*, 377 U.S. 218 (1964).

7. *U.S.* v. *Jefferson*, 372 F.2d 836 (5th Cir. 1966).

8. *Swann* v. *Charlotte-Mecklenburg Board of Education*, 402 U.S. 1 (1971).

8a. *Lee* v. *Johnson*, 404 U.S. 1215 (1971).

9. *Columbus Board of Education* v. *Penick; Dayton Board of Education* v. *Brinkman*, 443 U.S. 449 and 526 (1979).

10. *Keyes* v. *School District No. 1, Denver Colo.*, 413 U.S 189 (1974).

11. *Pasadena City Board of Education* v. *Spangler*, 427 U.S. 424 (1976).

12. *Bradley* v. *Milliken*, 418 U.S. 717 (1974).

13. *Evans* v. *Buchanan*, 393 F.Supp. 428 (D. Del. 1975).

14. *Crawford* v. *Board of Education in City of Los Angeles*, 551 P.2d 28 (Cal. 1976).

15. *Runyon* v. *McCrary*, 427 U.S. 160 (1976).

16. 42 U.S.C. §1981.

17. *Brown* v. *Board of Education, supra*.

18. *Alexander* v. *Holmes County Board of Education*, 396 U.S. 19 (1969).

19. *U.S.* v. *Montgomery Board of Education*, 395 U.S. 225 (1969).

20. *Singleton* v. *Jackson Municipal Separate School District*, 419 F.2d 1211 (5th Cir. 1970).

21. *Lee* v. *Tuscaloosa County Board of Education*, 591 F.2d 324 (5th Cir. 1978).

22. *Morgan* v. *Kerrigan*, 509 F.2d 580 (2d Cir. 1974).

23. *Lee* v. *Conecuh County Board of Education*, 464 F.Supp. 333 (S.D. Ala. 1979).

24. *Id.*

25. *Molina* v. *El Paso Independent School District*, 583 F.2d 213 (5th Cir. 1978).

26. *Washington* v. *Davis*, 426 U.S. 229 (1976).

27. *United States of America* v. *State of South Carolina*, 434 U.S. 1026 (1978).

28. *Hazelwood* v. *United States*, 433 U.S. 299 (1977).

29. *Green* v. *County School Board*, 391 U.S. 430 (1968).

15

Am I protected against sexual discrimination?

OVERVIEW

The history of sexual discrimination among teachers is well documented. In recent years we have seen a variety of challenges to such discrimination, and many school policies have been revised in the light of court cases, legislation, and a new public concern for equal treatment of men and women. This chapter examines questions concerning equal pay, promotions, marriage, and pregnancy as they affect teachers.

Both the culture at large and our schools functioned as if there were significant differences between boys and girls that should be reflected in their schooling. Though some of these "differences" persist, many of them have faced legal challenges. This chapter summarizes these challenges by examining questions regarding students on equal access to school sports, curricular exclusions, separate schools, and married or pregnant students.

EQUAL PAY

May schools pay men more than women?

No, not for the same work, provided that the men and women have the same qualifications in preparation and experience. When a Texas court found in 1977 that males were paid $300 per year more than females for doing identical work, it ordered a stop to such practices. This action was based not on the Constitution but on the federal Fair Labor Standards Act.[1]

When may schools pay some teachers more than others?

Schools' salaries may be based on formal preparation and experience, and thus teachers may be placed on different steps of a schedule based on those factors. Given objectively equal preparation and experience, may some teachers be paid more than others? Yes, if such additional pay is based on merit, additional duties, or head-of-household status. These, however, must apply equally to men and women. (Biology is not merit!)

May coaches receive extra pay?

Yes. Schools may create policies to pay for extra duties, whether these duties involve coaching, drama, outing club, or others.

May male coaches receive more pay than female coaches?

The principle of equal pay for equivalent work has been difficult to apply in the area of coaching. Historically, significant disparities existed in favor of male coaches. While Title IX has equalized some aspects of the funding of athletics, it has not been applied to coaching because Congress intended this particular law to apply to students and not to coaches.

The federal Equal Pay Act of 1963 and similar state laws have been used to challenge unequal pay. For example, in Ohio a female junior high physical education teacher, Ms. Harrington, sued and claimed discrimination by school administrators. The facts showed that the athletic facilities, equipment, and program provided for the girls were substantially inferior to those provided for the boys. Furthermore, the working conditions provided Ms. Harrington were inferior to those of her male counterparts. Therefore the court ruled in her favor and awarded her $6,000 money damages and $2,000 for attorney fees. Currently, efforts are afoot to enact an equal pay policy related to coaching. The Department of Labor claims that regardless of the sport in question, coaches perform substantially similar duties. If this proposed policy becomes law, pay differentials among different kinds of coaches and between male and female coaches will disappear. In the meantime, some discrepancies continue, based on the differences in assigned duties.

May schools prefer males over females in administrative positions?

No. In matters of promotion and in the selection of administrators, sex is not a relevant factor. It would be a violation of the Equal Protection Clause of the Fourteenth Amendment to give preference to either sex over the other in the selection of school administrators. Such preference would be arbitrary because there is no rational connection between sex and administrative competence in public schools. An exception to this general principle might be the selection of a Dean of Girls or Dean of Boys in schools where the job descriptions specify some duties that are particularly sensitive and where being a male or female would be a job-related qualification.

MARRIAGE AND PREGNANCY

May teachers be dismissed for getting married?

Not public school teachers. Whatever rules of celibacy private schools may wish to impose on their teachers, public schools can no longer fire teachers for entering wedlock. This is not to say that teachers always had such a freedom. Historically many communities had contractual provisions forbidding marriage or did so by rule of the school board. Economic and/or moral justifications were offered for such rules. Today, courts would strike down such rules as being arbitrary, against public policy, and a violation of the "liberty" provision of the Fourteenth Amendment.

Must pregnant teachers take specified pregnancy leaves?

Until recently, most school systems required that teachers who became pregnant take a leave of absence without pay at the fourth or fifth month of their pregnancy. Furthermore, they usually specified that the teacher could not return to work for a certain period of time after having the baby. Many schools required the new mother to stay home for at least six months; some school specified even longer leaves. In recent years, women have gone to court to challenge such school policies; they claimed that such policies were arbitrary as they violated due process. School boards claimed that such policies were legitimate, for they were reasonably related to the maintenance of an orderly efficient school system. These and related issues have been argued in court and were faced recently by the U.S. Supreme Court.

The *LaFleur* and *Cohen* Cases[2]

The Cleveland Board of Education adopted a rule in 1952 that required pregnant schoolteachers to take a leave of absence without pay beginning five months before the expected birth of the child. A teacher on a maternity leave is not allowed to return to work until the beginning of the next semester that follows the date when her child attains the age of three months. A doctor's health certificate is required as a prerequisite for return. Moreover, the teacher on maternity leave is not guaranteed reemployment but is merely given priority for a position for which she is qualified. Failure to comply with the mandatory leave provision is grounds for dismissal.

The Ohio rule was in effect in 1971 when Jo Carol LaFleur, a junior high school teacher, became pregnant. She did not wish to take an unpaid leave but wanted to teach until the end of the school year. Her child was expected late in July. By the school district requirement, she had to commence her leave in March 1971. Mrs. LaFleur filed suit in a U.S. district court challenging the constitutionality of the maternity leave rule. She lost, but on appeal the Court of Appeals for the Sixth Circuit ruled in her favor.

At the same time, a similar case was working its way through the courts in Virginia. Susan Cohen challenged a school board maternity leave regulation requiring pregnant teachers to take unpaid leaves of absence at least four months before delivery. In this case the district court ruled in her favor, but the Court of Appeals of the Fourth Circuit upheld the constitutionality of the regulation.

Since two courts of appeal reached contradictory conclusions on essentially the same facts, the U.S. Supreme Court agreed to decide the constitutionality of the school board's rules. The Court has often recognized that freedom of personal choice in matters of marriage and family life is one of the liberties protected under the Due Process Clause of the Fourteenth Amendment. Among other things, this means that there can be no unreasonable or arbitrary governmental regulation of one's freedom "to bear or beget a child."

The school boards argued that their regulations were not unreasonable but in fact were necessary for the efficient operation of the schools. They gave two reasons for the rules: (1) such rules maintain continuity of classroom instruction, since advance knowledge of when a pregnant teacher will begin her leave makes it possible to arrange for a qualified substitute; and (2) some pregnant teachers became physically incapable of performing their duties, and thus the leave policy protects the health of the teacher and her unborn child at the same time that it ensures the presence in the classroom of a physically capable teacher.

The Court recognized continuity of instruction as a significant and legitimate concern of school boards. Advance notice of pregnancy leaves undoubtedly facilitates administrative planning for continuity. Nevertheless, the absolute requirement of taking a leave at the fourth or fifth month of pregnancy is arbitrary and does not necessarily help continuity in instruction. Teachers become pregnant at different times, and thus their leaves must begin at different times. Therefore the Court held that "the arbitrary cutoff dates embodied in the mandatory leave rules before us have no rational relationship to the valid state interest of preserving continuity of instruction."

On the second argument of the school boards, the physical incapacities of pregnant teachers, the court also thought it desirable to keep physically unfit teachers out of the classroom. Furthermore, it accepted the fact that *some* teachers are unable to perform their duties during the late months of pregnancy. Is that sufficient to uphold the rule mandating *all* pregnant teachers to take a leave? No, it is not, ruled the Court, for such a regulation sweeps too broadly. It presumes that all pregnant teachers become physically incapacitated after a certain time, and there is no individual determination of abilities. A rule that contains a conclusive presumption that is neither necessarily nor universally true is overly broad and thus violates the Due Process Clause of the Fourteenth Amendment.

What about rules that limit the teacher's eligibility to return to work after giving birth? The Cleveland rule made the teacher ineligible to return until the beginning of the semester following the child's age of three months. The Virginia rule allowed the return at any time upon submission of a satisfactory medical certificate. Once again, the school boards offered continuity of instruction and physical competence as reasons for the rules.

The Court ruled that the three-month age provision of the Cleveland rule was wholly arbitrary and irrational: "The age limitation serves no legitimate state interest, and unnecessarily penalizes the female teacher for asserting her right to bear children." Since each child will reach the age of three months at a different time, the purpose of continuity is not served by the rule. Thus the Cleveland rule was struck down as a violation of the Due Process Clause of the Fourteenth Amendment, while the Virginia rule was upheld.

In sum, a school policy that requires all pregnant teachers to begin leaves at the fourth or fifth month of pregnancy may be administratively convenient, but it conclusively presumes such women to be unfit to teach past those dates. Such presumption is overly broad and unduly penalizes female teachers who bear children; therefore the policy is unconstitutional. A "return policy" that specifies any number of months or years after childbirth before the teacher may return to work fails because it is arbitrary.

What are reasonable requirements in a pregnancy-leave policy?

School officials may require a written notice of intention to begin a pregnancy leave as well as a notice of intention of the date of return. They may also require a medical certificate attesting to the medical competence of the teacher to continue or resume her work. This would amount to a complete individualization of pregnancy-leave practices.

On the other hand, if the school district wanted to provide continuity of instruction, it could create a policy requiring teachers to commence their pregnancy leaves at the beginning of the semester during which they expect to deliver. The policy could also require that they not return until the beginning of the semester following delivery.

May teachers be dismissed because of pregnancy?

Absurd as it may seem today, some cases have held, as recently as 1945, that pregnancy can constitute "neglect of duty" or "incompetency" and be a ground for dismissal since it renders a teacher unable to carry out her job. More recently, the law has recognized the right "to bear and beget a child" as one of the liberties protected by the Due Process Clause of the Fourteenth Amendment. Married pregnant teachers would undoubtedly be protected in their right to bear children. (Questions concerning the pregnancy of unmarried teachers are discussed in chapter 13.)

Do teachers on maternity leave have a right to sick-leave pay?

As of 1979, yes. Earlier, the Supreme Court ruled that states or municipalities could exclude normal pregnancies from disability insurance coverage programs. When asked whether that violates the Equal Protection Clause, the Court ruled that when a state attempts to take care of a problem by legislation, it does not have to tackle every aspect of that problem. When other efforts also failed to secure sick-leave benefits for pregnant women, Congress in 1979 passed the Pregnancy Disability Bill. The law now provides that pregnancy-related disabilities receive the same insurance coverage and sick-leave benefits as other disabilities. This law is an amendment to Title VII of the Civil Rights Act of 1964.

SCHOOL SPORTS

Must girls and boys have equal access to school sports?

This area of schooling has turned out to both complex and controversial. Because no simple answer is appropriate to this question, a variety of subquestions must be explored. They follow below.

May girls try out for the boys' team in tennis, golf, and swimming?

This question was raised in 1972 when Peggy Brenden was the top-ranked eighteen-year-old woman tennis player in her area of Minnesota. Because there was little interest in tennis among the girls at St. Cloud Technical High School, where Brenden was a senior, she wanted to play on the boys' team. The boys' team had a coach and a full schedule of interscholastic matches, neither of which was available for girls. Peggy was told that she could not try out for the boys' team because the Minnesota State High School League rules forbade girls' participation on boys' teams, and vice versa.

Brenden went to court, claiming that her right to equal protection and due process were violated. She requested an injunction against the enforcement of the rules that prevented her from interscholastic athletic participation.[3] The school claimed that the rule was reasonable and that its aim was to achieve fair competition among all student athletes. They claimed that they separated boys and girls in sport activities because significant physiological differences exist between boys and girls and because the growth patterns of the two sexes are so different.

Was the separation of girls and boys in athletic activities arbitrary and therefore a violation of the girls' constitutional rights? The federal district court was guided by legal principles set fourth by the U.S. Supreme Court: "A classification must be reasonable and not arbitrary, and must rest upon some ground of difference having a fair and substantial relation to the object of the legislation, so that all persons similarly circumstanced shall be treated alike."[4]

The Court recognized substantial physiological differences between boys and girls in muscle mass, size of the heart, and construction of the pelvic area, which "may, on the average, prevent the great majority of women from competing on an equal level with the great majority of males." Thus, these differences may form the basis for classifying by sex in athletic competition and thus separating boys and girls. Nevertheless, the statistical picture, though accurate for large populations, does not accurately portray all individuals. Peggy Brenden did not fit the statistical abstraction and had reached a high level of performance in her chosen sport. There was no evidence that she would in any way be damaged by competing in the boys' league, nor did any evidence suggest that boys would be harmed by her participation. (The school officials had also argued that separate sports programs were desirable to encourage more participation by all boys and girls.)

In sum, the court ruled that Peggy was prevented from playing interscholastic tennis "on the basis of the fact of sex and sex alone." The school offered no competitive athletic programs for girls. Therefore the court held that the rules as applied to Peggy were unreasonable, discriminatory, and thus unconstitutional and that she must be allowed to try out for the boys' team.

Consistently with this case, other courts have also ruled that in noncontact sports such as golf, swimming, or cross-country skiing, where no teams exist for girls, they may compete for positions on boys' teams. Where competitive teams are available for both boys and girls, most courts will be satisfied with the provision of separate teams, even though the quality of competition tends to be higher for the boys.[5]

How has Title IX affected school sports?

Congress made a significant impact on sex discrimination in schools by enacting Title IX of the Education Amendments of 1972.[6] The law provides that "no person in the United States shall on the basis of sex be excluded from participation, be denied the benefits of, or be subjected to discrimination under any education program or act or activity receiving Federal financial assistance." Title IX is relied upon in many situations to strike down discrimination against students based on sex because it is specifically aimed at such discrimination, whereas the clauses of the Fourteenth Amendment are much more general and abstract.

The regulations interpreting and implementing Title IX specifically allow separate teams for boys and girls in contact sports. Thus, schools may provide separate teams in football, wrestling, and other contact sports if the demand warranted. Where demand does not warrant separate teams, the occasional girl who desires to try out for the school team in a contact sport has a right to try out on a basis equal with tryouts for boys.

Some students choose to sue under the Constitution despite the availability of Title IX. Such was the case in Colorado, where the state athletic association forbade coeducational interscholastic contact sports. Ms. Hoover, a high school student, went to court when she was prevented from playing on the boys' soccer team.[7] The athletic association argued that the aim of the rule was physical safety: to prevent girls from being harmed. The court rejected this position as "patronizing protection to females" and said that "the failure to establish any physical criteria to protect small or weak males destroys the credibility of the reasoning urged in support of the sex classification. . . ." The court held that the rule was in violation of the Equal Protection Clause in that it arbitrarily separated girls and boys by sex without regard to the wide range of individual variations within each group. Similarly, a Wisconsin state association rule that broadly forbade girls and boys from competing against one another in all interscholastic sports fell in a Fourteenth Amendment challenge.[8]

Cases have even held that portions of Title IX are unconstitutional. For example, a district court ruled in an Ohio case that the Title IX regulations that allow for the separation of boys and girls in contact sports are unconstitutional. According to the court, governmental policies based on a presumption that girls are uniformly physically weaker or inferior to boys are arbitrary and thus violate due process.[9] This case seems to go further than others, for it strikes down distinctions between contact and noncontact sports.[10]

What effect do state Equal Rights Amendments have?

Although many states have added Equal Rights Amendments (ERAs) to their constitutions, the legal meaning of such amendments is not yet clearly established. There is no uniformity among the states on just what the amendments mean for coeducational athletic competition, and it is probable that variations will persist from state to state because such state constitutional provisions are interpreted by the courts of the respective states and not by the U.S. Supreme Court.

Under a state ERA, a Washington case ruled that girls are allowed to try out for the football team on an equal basis with boys. A Pennsylvania case similarly ruled that under its state's ERA, boys and girls may try out for all school teams, including those in contact sports. Massachusetts also has an ERA. Consequently, when the Massachusetts legislature was considering enacting a law prohibiting girls from participating with boys in contact sports, the advice of the state supreme court was sought.[11] The Justices advised that such a law would be inconsistent with the state's ERA. However, they specifically declined to render an opinion whether such a law would be valid "if equal facilities were available for men and women in a particular sport which was available separately for each sex."

What options are available to victims of sex discrimination?

Students who believe that they are victims of sex discrimination may sue under the U.S. Constitution, Title IX, state ERAs, and other state laws. As a general rule, schools are under no obligation to provide interscholastic athletics. If they have such a program, however, it should be available on an equal basis for boys and girls. Some courts are satisfied with separate teams as long as similar coaching, support, and a competitive schedule is available for each sex. Others have ruled that all sports, even contact sports, must be equally available for boys and girls. Because state laws vary and state ERAs have been variously interpreted, when controversies arise, it is very important to check the applicable state law as well as the prior opinion of federal courts for the area.

Must schools provide equal funds for girls' and boys' sports?

Schools must fund sports for both sexes equitably, though no mathematical equality is necessary. Title IX forbids discrimination in financial support for sports in equipment and coaching. Fairness and equity are the guiding principles, for each sport activity has its unique needs and costs. If the sports are comparable, such as tennis teams for girls and boys, or swimming or golf teams for each sex, substantial equality is easier to determine. In dealing with high-cost and high-revenue sports, such as football or basketball, questions of equity and comparability become much more complex. Title IX regulations to implement the law in these areas are still in the process of formulation. These regulations do require that if a school offers athletic scholarships for boys, scholarships must also be available for girls' sports on an equal basis.

May some courses in the curriculum be restricted to boys only or to girls only?

In general, no. Girls and boys must have access to the full curriculum on an equal basis without an imposition of stereotypic views of what girls and boys ought to be. The historic exclusion of girls from shop courses and boys from cooking or home economics is no longer legal. Title IX, state laws, and local political pressures have erased any legal bases of such exclusions, though in some schools they are perpetuated through custom and informal pressures. Guidance counselors, teachers, parents, and others who advise students have important roles to play here, together with peer pressures that tend to be so important in secondary schools. While the law is clear in forbidding such restrictions, ingrained attitudes often perpetuate practices that force students into believing that some courses are for boys only and some for girls only. Nothing in the law, however, prevents schools from separating boys and girls for instruction in highly sensitive areas, such as sex education.

SEPARATE SCHOOLS AND SEPARATE STANDARDS

May public schools provide separate schools for boys and girls?

The answer depends on the facts of the particular situation. In Philadelphia, for example, the school system maintained separate high schools for academically talented boys and girls. When evidence showed that the separate schools were genuinely equal in terms of size, prestige, and academic quality, a federal court upheld the arrangement. School officials argued that there were educational merits of such separation during the years of early adolescence, and the court was reluctant to substitute its judgment of what is educationally sound for the judgment of educators. Applying the "rational basis" test, the court concluded that such an arrangement is reasonable.[12]

Could schools compel students to attend sex-segregated schools?

Probably not. The foregoing cases involved voluntary attendance to boys' and girls' schools and only by those who qualified on the basis of academic examination. In Hinds County, Mississippi, an entire school district was sex-segregated as part of a racial desegregation plan. A circuit court struck down this arrangement as a violation of the Equal Educational Opportunities Act of 1974.[13] Thus it seems that a limited, *voluntary* plan of sex-segregated schooling is acceptable whereas a *compulsory* one is not, particularly if it might be construed to be a vestige of historic patterns of racial segregation.

May schools set different admission standards for boys and girls?

No. Such practices violate the Equal Protection Clause of the Fourteenth Amendment. A case arose in Boston where girls had to score 133 or above on a standardized test to gain entrance into Girls Latin School, compared with a score of 120 or above for boys who wanted to enter Boys Latin School. Although the different scores were based on different capacities in the two school buildings, the court struck down the arrangement as discriminatory.[14]

May school districts provide alternative separate schools for pregnant students?

Yes, they may, as long as the alternative is a genuine option that students may choose. Several cities have provided such alternatives where the curriculum also reflects the special needs of the pregnant students.

May married students be required to attend adult school instead of regular day school?

No, they may not. Many school districts used to force married and/or pregnant students out of school by requiring them to choose between no schooling or adult or correspondence courses. The school districts stated their reasons as (1) the presence of pregnant students encourages immoral behavior among students, (2) their presence encourages early marriages, (3) their presence encourages "sex talk" in schools, and (4) pregnant students suffer psychological harm in school. In spite of these reasons, the courts protected the right of these students to continue attending regular schools.

Courts have not been impressed with the reasons stated above because no reliable evidence has been found to support such reasons. In fact, psychological evidence shows that pregnant students suffer more by exclusion than from attendance in regular day school. Moreover, the courts have pointed out that where state laws make public education available up to a certain age, students have a right to attend even if they are married and/or pregnant.[15]

May married students be excluded from extracurricular activities?

While earlier cases upheld such exclusions, the current trend of legal decisions is against them. Why did earlier cases uphold such restrictions against married students? The *Kissick* case gives the typical reasons used by schools and courts to reach such conclusions.

The *Kissick* Case[16]

The Garland Public School in Texas had a policy that barred "married students or previously married students . . . from participating in athletic or other exhibitions" and from holding "class offices or other positions of honor." When 16-year-old Jerry Kissick, Jr., a letterman in football, married a 15-year-old-girl, he received notice from the school barring him from further athletic participation, based on the school policy. Kissick, who planned to earn a college scholarship with his football prowess, filed suit claiming that the school policy was unreasonable and discriminatory and that it violated his Fourteenth Amendment rights to due process and equal protection. School officials argued that the policy was adopted in order to discourage "teen-age" marriages, which often lead to dropping out of school. They also indicated that Kissick's right to continue his academic work was untouched and that only his participation in football, an extracurricular activity, was denied.

The evidence showed overwhelming parental support for the school policy. There was a high rate of juvenile marriage at Garland School; many of the married students dropped out of school, and of those who remained, a high proportion experienced a drop in grades. A psychologist also testified in favor of the policy.

The court upheld the school policy and recognized the earlier dominant view that "Boards of Education, rather than Courts, are charged with the important and difficult duty of operating the public schools.... The Court's duty, regardless of its personal views, is to uphold the Board's regulation unless it is generally viewed as being arbitrary and unreasonable." In effect, the court accepted the distinction between academic and extracurricular activities and upheld the right of school officials to control access to the latter.

The trend of recent decisions is more accurately reflected in the *Davis* case in Ohio.[17] This case involved a similar policy: excluding married students from school-sponsored athletic and other extracurricular activities. When Davis challenged the policy in court, the policy was struck down. The court acknowledged the importance of extracurricular activities and considered exclusion from them to be a significant deprivation. The *Tinker* case was used by the judge to examine whether the school rule was necessary to maintain appropriate discipline or whether it was part of an "enclave of totalitarianism." Since Davis's marriage did not lead to any "material or substantial" interference with school discipline, the court ruled in his favor.

In sum, the current legal trend is to protect students' rights to participate in both curricular and extracurricular activities, whether the students remain single, get married, or become pregnant. Health and safety considerations may be used by school officials in making individual decisions, and officials may also act to prevent significant disruption of the processes of schooling.

SUMMARY

Recent changes in public attitudes, together with important court rulings and new legislation, have led to significant reductions in sex discrimination in public schools. It is no longer legal to pay men more than women for the same work, though differences in pay are still acceptable if based on material differences in work load. Merit pay is proper if based on meritorious work but not if it is based on sexual differences.

Males may no longer be given preference over females in administrative positions or in other job assignments. Sex may still be considered a relevant factor in assignments where some duties call for particular sensitivities concerning boys or girls.

Courts have rejected the time-honored policies of schools that mandated maternity leave at the fifth month of pregnancy and did not allow the teacher to return to work for three months after delivery. Such policies were arbitrary and therefore violated the Fourteenth Amendment. Current school policies must allow the teacher and her physician to decide when to take the leave and when to return, or the policies must be based on the schools' needs for continuity of instruction. Arbitrary cutoff dates are illegal. Teachers may not be dismissed for getting married or for becoming pregnant; and for purposes of sick-leave pay, pregnancy leaves must be treated the same as disability leaves.

Sex discrimination and stereotyping in the school life of students have also been challenged in recent years. It is no longer legally acceptable to exclude girls or boys from parts of the curriculum, though in practice cultural pressures remain influential. Preferential treatment of boys in school athletics has spawned many lawsuits as well as new legislation. As a result, girls and boys must have equal access to noncontact sports, on separate teams if the schools provide them, and on integrated teams if only one team is available in the particular sport. Schedules, coaching, equipment, and other support must be comparable for girls' and boy's teams. Title IX and its regulations are the most important laws to achieve equal treatment of the sexes in public schools.

Several states have enacted Equal Rights Amendments, which also must be considered in sex-related controversies in those particular states. There is no uniform interpretation of such amendments in the area of school sports. Some courts, for example, interpret state ERAs as mandating equal access even in contact sports, while courts in other states allow the separation of the sexes in such athletic activities.

Different admission standards for girls and boys to selective public schools are unconstitutional, but separate facilities are currently acceptable if they are genuinely equal. Married and/or pregnant students may not be excluded from school nor compelled to attend separate classes, separate schools, or evening classes. Similarly, courts now tend to protect the rights of such students to participate in extracurricular activities, though health and safety considerations may always be used to exclude an individual from a particular activity.

In general, though some vestiges of inequality and stereotyping remain as a function of tradition and habit, significant strides have been made in recent years toward the eradication of sex discrimination in the public schools.

NOTES

1. 20 U.S.C. §206(d).

2. *Cleveland Board of Education* v. *LaFleur; Cohen* v. *Chesterfield County School Board*, 414 U.S. 632 (1974).

3. *Brenden* v. *Independent School District 742*, 342 F.Supp. 1224 (D. Minn. 1972), *aff'd.* 477 F.2d 1292 (8th Cir. 1973).

4. *Reed* v. *Reed*, 404, U.S. 71 (1971).

5. See, for example, *Bucha* v. *Illinois High School Association*, 351 F.Supp. 69 (N.D. Ill. 1972).

6. 20 U.S.C. §1681.

7. *Hoover* v. *Meiklejohn*, 430 F.Supp. 164 (D. Colo. 1977).

8. *Leffel* v. *Wisconsin Interscholastic Athletic Association*, 444 F.Supp. 1117 (E.D. Wis. 1978).

9. *Yellow Springs Exempted Village School District Board of Education* v. *Ohio High School Athletic Association*, 443 F.Supp. 753 (S.D. Ohio 1978).

10. *Id.*

11. *Opinion of the Justices Re House Bill No. 6723,* Mass. Adv. Sh. 2728, Massachusetts Supreme Judicial Court (12/22/77).

12. *Vorchheimer* v. *School District,* 532 F.2d 880 (3d Cir. 1976), *aff'd.* 430 U.S. 703 (1977).

13. *U.S.* v. *Hinds County,* 560 F.2d 619 (5th Cir. 1977).

14. *Bray* v. *Lee,* 377 F.Supp. 934 (D. Mass. 1972).

15. *Alvin Independent School District* v. *Cooper,* 404 S.W.2d 76 (Tex. 1966).

16. *Kissick* v. *Garland Independent School District,* 330 S.W.2d 708 (Tex. 1959).

17. *Davis* v. *Meek,* 344 F.Supp. 298 (N.D. Ohio 1972).

16

Are there special rights for handicapped and non-English-speaking students?

OVERVIEW

In recent years, much public attention has focused on exceptional children and on children with limited English-speaking ability. Perceived inequalities in their education have been challenged in courts and debated by legislative bodies. As a result of court cases, legislation, and political activism, significant gains have been registered by these groups toward the achievement of equal educational opportunities. This chapter examines the major developments in each of these areas, first as they relate to students with special needs and then the emerging law related to bilingual-bicultural education.

Until recently, the compulsory education laws of most states made exceptions for children who were retarded, emotionally disturbed, deaf, blind, or otherwise handicapped. For various reasons, most of them based on ignorance, prejudice, or finance, many parents kept these children out of school with the consent of local school officials and the sanction of state laws. When handicapped children attended school, it was all too often in an aura of charity for which they and their parents were to be grateful.

Recent developments have brought substantial changes in attitudes toward the handicapped and in laws related to their schooling. These changes are based in part on scientific evidence that has reliably established that all humans can learn and benefit from appropriate education and training. The changes are also based in part on the civil rights movements of the 1950s and '60s, which reverberated throughout the American culture and stimulated the handicapped to make their claims on the basis of right and not of charity.

Historically, the language in all public schools has been English. Children who spoke little or no English had no choice in the language of instruction and, typically, no special help to acquire the language. It was generally assumed that such children would pick up English through their daily interaction in and out of school, as well as through the efforts of kind-hearted teachers. Americanization, as expressed in the "melting pot" ideal, relied on English as the common language necessary for survival and success in school and in the worlds of commerce and industry.

Indeed, for millions of children, sons and daughters of immigrants and first-generation Americans, schools became important places for language acquisition and an important step up the mythical ladder of success in the new world. For countless others, however, schools were unfriendly places conducted in a strange tongue where too many teachers had little sympathy for non-English-speaking students. These students left school early and, by and large, became industrial workers and unskilled laborers in various segments of our economy. As immigration continued and "the melting pot refused to melt," serious questions began to surface about the rights of minorities whose mother tongue was other than English. They too had their consciousness raised by the civil rights movements in the latter half of the century, and they began to organize and assert their rights and those of their school-age children.

EDUCATING THE HANDICAPPED

Are the rights of handicapped children based on the Constitution, federal legislation, or both?

On both. Earlier challenges to excluding and misclassifying handicapped children were based on the Constitution. These challenges (discussed below) helped raise public consciousness about the issue to the point where state and federal laws were enacted to ensure the schooling rights of *all* children. It is interesting to realize that a landmark case in school desegregation, the *Brown* case, was heavily relied upon to establish the right to education of all children and bring the federal government into an important role in public education. A key paragraph of *Brown*, often used by advocates of the rights of handicapped children, recognizes the pervasive influence and importance of education in contemporary American life.

> Today, education is perhaps the most important function of state and local governments. Compulsory school attendance laws and the great expenditures for education both demonstrate our recognition of the importance of education to our democratic society. It is required in the performance of our most basic public responsibilities, even service in the armed forces. It is the very foundation of good citzenship. Today it is a principal instrument in awakening the child to cultural values, in preparing him for later professional training, and in helping him to adjust normally to his environment. In these days, it is doubtful that any child may reasonably be expected to succeed in life if he is denied the opportunity of an education. Such an opportunity, where the state has under-

taken to provide it, is a right which must be made available to all on equal terms.[1]

What key constitutional provisions are related to the rights of handicapped children?

Historically, two kinds of practices worked to the educational disadvantage of handicapped children: exclusion from school and misclassification. *Exclusion* occurs when a school-age child is denied access to schooling or is provided grossly inappropriate education. The phrase "functional exclusion" is also used to describe grossly inappropriate placement, as exemplified by the placement of retarded children into regular classes with no special assistance for the children or the teacher, or the placement of non-English-speaking children into an English-speaking school program without special assistance. *Misclassification* occurs when a child is erroneously placed or tracked in a school program. Both exclusion and misclassification have been attacked on constitutional grounds.

The *PARC* Case[2]

In 1971 the laws of Pennsylvania, like those of many other states, kept children out of public schools if they were certified by psychologists as "uneducable and untrainable." In that year a lawsuit was filed on behalf of seventeen children by their parents and by the Pennsylvania Association for Retarded Children (PARC), requesting that the state law and practices based on it be declared violations of the Equal Protection and Due Process clauses of the Constitution. They claimed that the laws (1) violated due process by not giving parents a notice and a hearing; (2) denied equal protection by assuming certain children to be uneducable without a rational basis in fact, and (3) because the state constitution guaranteed education for all children, but arbitrarily and capriciously excluded retarded children.

When the federal district court ruled that retarded children may not be excluded from public schools, the contending parties worked out an agreement. The Consent Agreement, approved by the court, acquired the force of law, binding on both parties. The decision became a landmark (together with the *Mills* case, which follows), for it gave retarded children in the state access to public schools as well as tuition and maintenance costs at qualified institutions (or home instruction where that was appropriate). In addition, careful and elaborate due process is provided before any child may be placed in special classes or before any change in such placement may be made.

PARC incorporated into the law the conviction of knowledgeable professionals regarding the educability of retarded children. Expert testimony indicated that all mentally retarded persons are capable of benefiting from a program of education and training; that the greatest number of retarded persons, given such education and training, are capable of achieving self-sufficiency, and the remaining few, with education and training, are capable of achieving some degree of self-care; that the earlier education and training begins, the more thoroughly and the more efficiently a mentally retarded person can benefit.

The court recognized the danger of misclassification and mislabeling, for labeling a child "retarded" and placing him in a class for the retarded creates a handicap and a stigma. The parties to the suit agreed that mild cases of retardation can be integrated with normal children, or "mainstreamed," but that most retarded students need special classes taught by qualified teachers. It was also agreed that homebound instruction was the least desirable alternative; when it was used as a last resort, qualified teachers must be involved. Such arrangements must be reevaluated every three months, with proper notice to the parent or guardian, who may request a hearing on the case.

The *Mills* Case[3]

Mills was filed in Washington, D.C., and challenged exclusion and misclassification practices related not only to retarded children but to all handicapped children. This case also challenged the practice of suspending and expelling from school those children the schools did not want to serve.

The court found that of the approximately 22,000 handicapped children in the D.C. school district, close to 18,000 were "not being furnished with programs of specialized education." They were either excluded completely, or inappropriately placed. In the words of the court:

> The defendants' conduct here, denying plaintiffs and their class not just an equal publicly supported education but all publicly supported education while providing such education to other children, is a violation of the Due Process Clause.
>
> Not only are plaintiffs and their class denied the publicly supported education, to which they are entitled, many are suspended or expelled from regular schooling or specialized instruction or reassigned without any prior hearing and are given no periodic review thereafter. Due process of law requires a hearing prior to exclusion.

School officials argued that not enough funds were available for the appropriate schooling of all children and that handicapped children were particularly expensive to educate. The court did not accept their argument. If funds are inadequate, ruled the court, they must nevertheless be used equally for all children and in particular, no child should be completely excluded. As the court said: "The inadequacies of the District of Columbia Public School System, whether occasioned by insufficient funding or administrative inefficiency, certainly cannot be permitted to bear more heavily on the 'exceptional' or handicapped child than on the normal child."

The *PARC* and *Mills* cases established the constitutional basis to attack the exclusion from schooling and misclassification of handicapped children. They paved the way for the conviction that the Equal Protection and Due Process clauses protect the right of such children to access to public schools and free and appropriate education. They also paved the way for major federal legislation, setting nationwide standards for the education of handicapped children.

What major federal laws establish the rights of handicapped children?

The most important federal laws related to the rights of handicapped students are Public Law 94-142, the Education of All Handicapped Children Act, enacted in 1975;[4] and Section 504, the Rehabilitation Act of 1973.[5] These two federal laws overshadow all other federal legislation related to educating the handicapped. P.L. 94-142 makes certain federal funds available to schools that comply with its requirements. Section 504 would cut off *any and all* federal funds from schools that discriminate against the handicapped. Thus, the two laws have the same objectives, but Section 504 applies a broader sanction, namely the cutting off of funds, whereas 94-142 would only withhold funds under its allocation formula.

Public Law 94-142

When Congress enacted the Education of All Handicapped Children Act in 1975, it found that there were more than 8 million handicapped children in the country and that over half of them were not receiving an appropriate education. Furthermore, approximately 1 million were completely excluded from the public schools. In the preamble, in addition to recognizing these disturbing facts, Congress stated that the main purpose of the act was to assure that states provide all handicapped children with "a free appropriate public education and related services designed to meet their unique needs." While Congress recognized that education remains a state responsibility, it also acknowledged that federal assistance was necessary "to assure equal protection of the law."

The law specified that all handicapped children between the ages of 3 and 18 must have "free appropriate public education" by September 1, 1978; all such children between the ages of 3 and 21 must be accommodated by September 1, 1980. Since schooling is basically a state responsibility, however, P.L. 94-142 applies only to the ages covered by state laws. For example, if state law exempts children from 3 to 5 or from 18 to 21, the federal law cannot extend to those age groups.

Who are the handicapped?

Federal regulations define "handicapped children" to include those who are mentally retarded, hard of hearing, deaf, speech impaired, visually handicapped, seriously emotionally disturbed, orthopedically impaired, other health impaired, deaf-blind, multihandicapped, or with specific learning disabilities and who, because of those impairments, need special education and related services. Regulations published in 1977 further define each of these terms (see Appendix C).

May schools require parents to pay for the cost of educating handicapped children?

No. The law specifies that such education must be free. Since special education in public or private schools is often expensive, school officials have tried various ways to shift all or part of the cost on to the parents. Courts, however, have consistently held that public schools have the obligation to provide appropriate education, including testing, guidance, and other special and support services, at no cost to the parents. This principle holds whether the schooling is provided in public or private facilities. The only exception occurs when appropriate free public facilities are available for a particular child, but the parents chose a private facility instead. In that case, they must bear the cost of the private education.

What is the legal meaning of "appropriate" education?

P.L. 94-142 and its regulations conceive of an "appropriate" education as one designed specifically to meet the unique needs of the particular handicapped child. Thus an individual educational program or plan (an IEP) must be drawn up for each child under the law, and such plan is to be carried out in an appropriate educational setting.

It is not enough to provide "equal" access, in the sense of identical schooling for handicapped and nonhandicapped children. Without special provisions and support services, handicapped students might not gain anything from instruction, even though they are physically exposed to the same experiences as the other children. Such treatment is referred to as "functional exclusion" by courts and lawyers. One important case considered functional exclusion as similar to the placement of non-English-speaking students in ordinary classrooms without support services. They "are certain to find their classroom experiences wholly incomprehensible and in no way meaningful."[6] In *Fialkowski*, children with the mental abilities of preschoolers were placed in a program that emphasized reading and writing skills way beyond their abilities. This was held to be inappropriate placement and does not satisfy the law.

The requirements of appropriateness and the IEP are best considered as complementary notions. The IEP is a tailor-made plan that follows careful assessment and evaluation of a particular student's abilities and disabilities. Curricular plans and instructional approaches are based on such evaluation, and periodic assessments follow to ascertain progress and the continuing appropriateness of the plan. The education provided must be comparable to that offered the nonhandicapped, and procedural safeguards are provided in order to keep parents informed and solicit their participation in the appropriate placement of their children.

What are the due process rights of parents and children under P.L. 94-142?

It was clear to Congress that in the past, parents were all too often left out of educational decisions that were crucial in the lives of their handicapped children. The current law has changed that and requires at least the following:

1. Prior written notice must be given a reasonable time before any proposed change in the child's educational program, together with a written explanation of the procedures to be followed in effecting the change.
2. All notices must be written in "language understandable to the general public" and in the primary language of the parents. If the parents cannot read, the notices must be interpreted to them orally or by other means.
3. The testing of children must be nondiscriminatory in language, race, or culture.
4. There is a right to independent testing and evaluation, free or at low cost.
5. Parents must have access to the records relevant to the case and the right to have the records explained; to make copies; to amend records parents consider to be inaccurate, misleading, or invade privacy; or the right to a hearing on the issue if the school refuses to amend the records.
6. Opportunity for a fair and impartial hearing must be conducted by the State Educational Agency (SEA) or local school district, *not* by the employee "involved in the education or care of the child." At any hearing, parents have the right to be represented by a lawyer or an individual trained in the problems of handicapped children; the right to present evidence and to subpoena, confront, and cross-examine witnesses; and the right to obtain a transcript of the hearing and a written decision by the hearing officer. Parents may appeal the decision to the SEA and, if they are still not satisfied, may appeal the SEA ruling in court.
7. The student has a right to remain in current placement until the due process proceedings are completed. A child who is just beginning school may be enrolled until the proceedings determining proper placement are completed.
8. A "surrogate parent" will be appointed for children who are wards of the state or whose parents or guardians are unknown or unavailable.
9. The child's records are confidential. Parents and the student may restrict access to the records; they have a right to be informed before any information in the file is destroyed and a right to be told to whom information has been disclosed.

While further details are given in regulations interpreting the law, the foregoing list presents the main procedural safeguards.

A case involving a high school student in Danbury, Connecticut, illustrates the powerful due process protection afforded special-needs students by P.L. 94-142. School records indicated that Kathy Stuart had a variety of academic deficiencies as a consequence of a combination of learning disabilities and limited intelligence. When, as punishment for disruptive behavior, the school wanted to expel her, she went to court. The federal district court believed that she was exactly the type of student intended to be protected by the federal law. While it interpreted the law and its regulations to allow short-term suspensions or new placements of disruptive handicapped students, after following due process, it prohibited their expulsion. As the court stated: "The expulsion of handicapped children not only jeopardizes their right to an education in the least restrictive environment, but is inconsistent with the procedures established by the Handicapped Act for changing the placement of disruptive children."[7]

What is the least restrictive educational alternative?

Historically, handicapped children tended to be segregated from the non-handicapped. Various reasons were advanced for such isolation, but these reasons have been challenged and in most instances rejected in recent years. Current law requires that handicapped students be educated in "the least restrictive alternative" program. In brief, this means that the handicapped child should be educated in a setting that deviates least from the regular nonhandicapped program yet is appropriate for the particular child.

Courts have recognized that various educational arrangements, or "treatments," have been "restrictive" in the legal sense. For example, segregation of the handicapped that further handicaps or stigmatizes them is restrictive in the eyes of the law. So is the use of medication for many children. If a child is enabled to learn through medication, that use might be justifiable; if the chemical treatment merely restrains a child for the convenience of the staff, that use is "restrictive."

Mattie T. v. Holladay capsulizes the provisions of the federal law regarding "the least restrictive alternative" educational placement of a child: "The Bureau of Education for the Handicapped Guidelines establish, inter alia, two important steps to be taken by school districts . . . (1) 'a variety of program alternatives (e.g., continuum of education services) must be available in every L.E.A. [local educational agency] to meet the varying needs of handicapped children' and (2) an individual determination of the appropriate program alternatives must be made for each child in conformance with the procedures for nondiscriminatory evaluations."[8]

The principle of least restrictive alternative educational placement is what is popularly referred to as "mainstreaming." The law does not require that each child be mainstreamed, that is, fully integrated with nonhandicapped students. Such placement is appropriate for some children; others might benefit more by spending part of the day mainstreamed and part of the day in special classes with specially prepared teachers. Students who cannot handle either arrangement may have to be in special classes all day, which is preferable to separate special schools. Finally, such schools are preferable to home schooling, although home schooling is better than no schooling at all.

Is private schooling an alternative available under the law?

Yes, it is, if no appropriate public facilities are available that can effectively meet the needs of the particular student. Public funds must be used to pay for the child's education including room and board and transportation, where necessary, and there should be no extra costs to the parents.

What if the parents and the school disagree concerning the placement of the child?

The law is clear that such disagreements must be resolved through a fair procedure: "Disagreements between a parent and a public agency regarding the availability of a program appropriate for the child, and the question of financial responsibility, are subject to the due process procedure."[9] Under federal law, local schools also have the obligation to locate all children who might fit the criteria, specified by law, to receive services provided the handicapped. Though some schools have urged that this obligation is properly placed on parents, courts have rejected this view. Courts have held that parents are not in the best position always to recognize that their children are not functioning well academically or that special support services are available to help with a particular handicap. Parents may or may not be aware of due process provisions provided by law, nor have the expert advice available to schools. Therefore, particularly with respect to children already in school, the duty rests with the provider of services to identify children in need of special services. Efforts are underway in several states to extend to regular students similar rights to "appropriate educational programs" currently available to the handicapped. For example, the Wisconsin legislature enacted laws in 1980 which give students and their parents a wide range of choices if they are dissatisfied with their assignment in public schools. (Reported in NOLPE Notes, Oct. 1980, pp. 3–4).

May handicapped children ever be excluded from a school activity?

Yes, they may, if the school has substantial justification for the exclusion. Cases have arisen when students who were wholly or partially blind in one eye were not allowed to participate in contact sports. The schools excluded them from participation because of the risk of injury to their sighted eye. Courts would not overturn the educators' decision because school officials had a reasonable basis to act as they did. To win such a case, students would either have to show that school officials had no reasonable grounds for their action or that the students would suffer irreparable harm by not having an opportunity to participate in the contact sport.[10]

Similarly, the U.S. Supreme Court upheld the exclusion of a severely hearing impaired student from a nursing program to which she applied. The student sued under Section 504, which prohibits discrimination against "otherwise qualified handicapped" individuals. The Court found that the student was not "otherwise qualified" for "otherwise qualified [means] otherwise able to function sufficiently in the position sought in spite of the handicap, if proper training and facilities are suitable and available." However, the Court said that Section 504 does not "compel the college to undertake affirmative action that would dispense with the need for effective oral communication in the college's nursing program."[11]

Thus it is clear that the handicapped can be excluded from some school activities or programs, but only if sound educational grounds exist for such exclusion. Such grounds might relate to health and safety considerations or to requirements inherent in the program that the handicapped person cannot meet without support services.

What does the law require for program "accessibility"?

For some years now, concerns have been expressed about difficulties that certain handicapped persons have experienced in gaining physical access to buildings. The Architectural Barriers Act, which became law in 1968, addressed some of these issues and incorporated certain standards to be applied in buildings "designed, constructed, or altered" after the effective date of the law. A 1976 amendment to this act extended its application, but the most fundamental regulation of program accessibility is derived from Section 504, which provides that no qualified handicapped person, "because facilities are inaccessible to or unusable by handicapped persons," shall be denied benefits, be excluded from participation, or otherwise be subjected to discrimination.

Under this law, schools and all other programs receiving federal assistance must make facilities and programs accessible through the use of ramps, sufficiently wide doors, elevators, accessible lavatory facilities, interpreters, support services, and other modifications of existing facilities and programs that might be necessary. This does not mean that every *building* on a campus must be modified, but that each *program* must be accessible. In their efforts to make programs accessible to the handicapped, schools must take care that they do not segregate or isolate them from nonhandicapped students. Much of this can be achieved through careful scheduling, relocating offices, making services available at alternate accessible sites, new construction, and the remodeling of existing facilities.

In addition to the federal law, many states have enacted laws against architectural barriers and on behalf of accessibility by the handicapped. State laws cover public places that do not necessarily receive federal support and are thus beyond the reach of Section 504, such as local parks, public toilets, elevators, stairs, doors, ramps, and sidewalks.

BILINGUAL-BICULTURAL EDUCATION

Are there federal laws that apply to the schooling of non-English-speaking children?

Yes, there are, the most important among them being Title VI of the Civil Rights Act of 1964[12] and the Bilingual Education Act of 1974.[13] The most important case in this area is *Lau* v. *Nichols*.

The *Lau* Case[14]

Among the thousands of Chinese-American students attending public schools in San Francisco, approximately 3,000 spoke little or no English, and of these, close to 1,800 received no special services designed to meet their linguistic needs. In 1970 these students and their parents filed suit in a federal district court and claimed that their right to equal protection under the Fourteenth Amendment of the Constitution, as well as their rights under Title VI of the Civil Rights Act of 1964, were being denied by the public schools. The main issue was whether non-English-speaking students are denied an equal educational opportunity when taught in a language they cannot understand. Title VI provides that "no person in the United States shall, on the ground of race, color or national origin, be excluded from participation in, be denied the benefit of, or be subjected to discrimination under any program or activity receiving Federal financial assistance."

The district court considered Title VI and the Fourteenth Amendment together and concluded that the non-English-speaking children did not have any of their rights violated when "the same education [was] made available on the same terms and conditions to the other tens of thousands of students in the San Francisco Unified School District" as to these students. When the Ninth Circuit affirmed this ruling, the case was appealed to the U.S. Supreme Court. The Court ruled in favor of the students and their parents, basing its decision on Title VI and deliberately not ruling on constitutional grounds. (The Court will, as a general policy, avoid ruling on a constitutional issue if it can dispose of the case on statutory grounds.)

While the lower courts were satisfied that the provision of identical educational services to all students would satisfy the law, the Supreme Court disagreed. It held that students who understand little or no English are denied equal opportunities when English is the sole medium of instruction and when there are no systematic efforts to teach that language to non-English-speaking students. "Under these state-imposed standards there is no equal treatment merely by providing students with the same facilities, textbooks, teachers, and curriculum; for students who do not understand English are effectively foreclosed from any meaningful education."

The Court did not specify what schools should do for these students, for remedies are usually left to educators under the supervision of district court judges closer to the local conditions. Various educational arrangements might satisfy the courts, including ESL (English as a second language), bilingual education, or some combination of either approach. In fact, disagreements over appropriate remedies have spawned further lawsuits as well as governmental regulations to guide school districts. The most important feature of any plan is its effectiveness with students.

Since *Lau*, several other cases based on Title VI have resulted in court orders requiring bilingual programs in schools.[15] These cases, however, require such instruction only if children have limited English-speaking abilities. For example, when a group of Chicano school children claimed that their school programs were inappropriate because they were "oriented for middle-class, Anglo children . . . staffed with non-Chicano personnel who do not understand and cannot relate with Chicano students who are linguistically and culturally different," the courts rejected their claims.[16] The court found that the plaintiffs did not prove the necessary facts to show violation of either Title VI or the Fourteenth Amendment.

Similarly, children of Mexican-American and Yaqui Indian origin went to court to compel the schools to provide bilingual-bicultural education. They wanted not only bilingual education for students deficient in English but continuous instruction in English and in the child's native language, Spanish or Yaqui, from kindergarten through high school. The district court ruled against them, and the court of appeals agreed.[17] The court held that education, though important, is not a fundamental right under the Constitution. "Differences in the treatment of students in the educational process, which in themselves do not violate specific constitutional provisions, do not violate the . . . Equal Protection Clause if such differences are rationally related to legitimate state interests."

What are the rights of parents in these issues?

The first bilingual education act became law in 1968; following *Lau*, Congress passed a second act in 1974, which is commonly referred to as the Bilingual Education Act. Among its various provisions the law specifies that programs "of bilingual education shall be developed in consultation with parents of children of limited English-speaking ability, teachers, and, where applicable, secondary school students. . . ." It is clear that the law intends to integrate these students, whenever practicable, with English-speaking students and separate them for special instruction only when necessary. For example, they should attend regular classes in art, music, physical education, and other courses where language skills are not of central importance to instruction.

Are there state laws that provide special instruction for non-English-speaking students?

Yes, in some states. Massachusetts, Texas, California, Illinois, and Connecticut have laws related to bilingual education that predate the *Lau* decision and federal legislation. The federal law, of course, applies to all public schools, but state laws may go further than the federal law and provide more extensive education for non-English-speaking students.

It must be recognized that the federal law provides only transitional bilingual education and only for students of no or limited English ability. Thus, schools are not required to provide any special instruction for students who benefit from instruction in English. Most state laws similarly provide only for transitional bilingual education, but states or local schools may, at their discretion, provide further instruction in the students' native language.

Do federal laws apply to students who speak "black English"?

Yes, ruled a district court in Michigan. Suit was filed by black students living in a low-income housing project located in an affluent section of Ann Arbor, near the University of Michigan. They claimed that their language, black English, was a distinct language that was different from standard English. They further claimed that they were denied equal educational opportunities because their language constituted a barrier to their learning and using the written materials of the school, which were in standard English. The students alleged that section 1703(f) of Title 20 of the U.S. Code was violated by the school. This statute provides: "No state shall deny equal educational opportunity to an individual on account of his or her race, color, sex, or national origin, by (f) the failure by an educational agency to take appropriate action to overcome language barriers that impede equal participation by its students in its instructional program."

Evidence showed that the school provided various services to students including speech and language specialists, school psychologists, individualized instruction, and tutoring. Nevertheless, the court found that the teachers' lack of awareness and knowledge of black English, the home language of the children, was in part the reason for their not learning. Thus the school board was ordered to develop a plan whereby teachers would become aware of the language usage in students' homes and in the community so that they might identify children who use the dialect and in turn use that knowledge to instruct them more effectively in standard English. The court did not require the creation of a bilingual program, nor did it require the teaching of black English. It did find that the teachers' lack of knowledge in their area denied students equal educational opportunities.[18]

SUMMARY

Until very recently, handicapped children were by and large excluded from schooling and misclassified and improperly placed in educational programs. Case law as well as legislative enactments have changed this dramatically. While significant developments have occurred in some states through state legislation, the most powerful developments are embodied in Public Law 94-142, the Education for All Handicapped Children Act of 1975, and in Section

504 of the Rehabilitation Act of 1973. Taken together, these laws mandate that free and appropriate education, with all necessary support services, be available to all handicapped children and youth in America. In fact, while P.L. 94-142 applies to ages 3 to 21, Section 504 has no age limit and forbids discrimination against the handicapped in any program or activity receiving federal support. To qualify for federal funds under P.L. 94-142, states must comply with standards set forth by law, which include individual education plans, appropriate placement of children in the least restrictive educational alternative, periodic reevaluation, and full due process rights for parents as well as students.

When no appropriate public school placement is available for a particular child, he or she may be placed in a private school at no extra cost to the parents. Thus it is clear that major strides have been made toward extending equal protection of the law and due process to all school-aged handicapped children. This is not to say that all their educational and social problems have been resolved. Important obstacles still prevent their full functioning in our society. Some of these obstacles relate to social prejudices and others to the lack of professional knowledge and even trained personnel. Nevertheless, the legal standards and tools are substantially in place to help the handicapped achieve their full human potential.

Significant strides have also been made to provide equal educational opportunities for children of limited English-speaking ability. These developments contrast dramatically with our historic attitude of "swim or sink" toward such students. Attempts to use the Fourteenth Amendment's Equal Protection Clause on behalf of such students have not been successful. Title VI of the Civil Rights Act of 1964 was relied on by the Supreme Court in the landmark case of *Lau* v. *Nichols* to require transitional bilingual education for children who cannot benefit from instruction in English. *Lau* was followed by the Bilingual Education Act of 1974, which similarly mandates bilingual education for children of limited English. The law provides for parental participation in program planning, personnel preparation, and other support services. Several states have laws that further provide for bilingual education, some of which go beyond transitional, bilingual education and provide for maintenance instruction to help perpetuate the students' second language.

Thus it is clear that in recent years both the Constitution and legislation have been used to gain a significant degree of equality in education for handicapped and for limited-English-ability students.

NOTES

1. *Brown* v. *Board of Education*, 347 U.S. 483 (1954).

2. *Pennsylvania Association for Retarded Children* v. *Commonwealth of Pennsylvania*, 343 F.Supp. 279 (E.D. Pa. 1972).

3. *Mills* v. *Board of Education of the District of Columbia*, 348 F.Supp. 866 (D. D.C. 1972).

4. 20 U.S.C. §1401, 1402, 1411–20.

5. 29 U.S.C. §794. Final regulations published at 42 *Fed. Reg.* 22676 (May 4, 1977), codified as 45CFR84. Section 504 is brief and to the point: "No otherwise qualified handicapped individual in the United States, as defined in section 7(6), shall, solely by reason of his handicap, be excluded from the participation in, be denied the benefits of, or be subjected to discrimination under any program or activity receiving Federal financial assistance."

6. *Fialkowski v. Shapp,* 405 F.Supp. 946 (E.D. Pa. 1975).

7. *Stuart v. Nappi,* 443 F.Supp. 1235 (D. Conn. 1978).

8. *Mattie T. v. Holladay,* C.A. 75–31–5 (N.D. Miss. 28 July 1977).

9. 45 CFR 121 *a.* 403(b).

10. *Kampmeier v. Nyquist,* 553 F.2d 296 (2d Cir. 1977).

11. *Southeastern Community College v. Davis,* 442 U.S. 397 (1979).

12. 42 U.S.C. §2000d (1970).

13. 20 U.S.C. §800b.

14. *Lau v. Nichols,* 414 U.S. 563 (1974).

15. *Serna v. Portales Municipal Schools,* 499 F.2d 1147 (10th Cir. 1974); *Aspira v. Board of Education of City of New York,* 423 F.Supp. 647 (S.D. N.Y. 1976); and *Rios v. Read,* 73 C. 296 (E.D. N.Y. 14 January 1977) (memorandum of decision and order).

16. *Otero v. Mesa County Valley School District No. 51,* 408 F.Supp. 162 (D. Colo., 1975).

17. *Guadalupe Organization, Incorporated v. Temple Elementary School District No. 3,* 557 F.2d 1022 (9th Cir. 1978).

18. *Martin Luther King, Jr., El'y. Sch. Children v. Michigan Bd. of Education,* 473 F.Supp. 1371 (E.D. Mich. 1979).

17

Who controls
student records?

OVERVIEW

In 1974 Congress passed the Family Educational Rights and Privacy Act (also known as the Buckley Amendment) to define who may and may not see student records. The law guarantees that parents have access to their children's school records; it also prohibits release of the records without parental permission, except to those who have a legitimate "right to know." Many administrators, teachers, and guidance counselors felt the act would cause more harm than good. Some teachers decided to put nothing critical in student records, fearing that any negative information could become the basis for a possible libel suit. Counselors were concerned that able students would be handicapped by a law that required nonconfidential recommendations, since all such recommendations would tend to sound the same and simply consist of positive platitudes. And many administrators saw this as another intervention in the field of education, creating additional unnecessary procedures and paperwork and threatening to cut off federal funds for noncompliance. In view of these concerns, this chapter examines the reasons for the act, what the act does and does not require, and some of its consequences and controversies.

THE BUCKLEY AMENDMENT

Why did Congress pass the Buckley Amendment?

Congress acted because of problems and abuses in the use of student records, especially the way schools tended to provide access to outsiders but deny access to students and their parents. The establishment of health, guidance, and psychological records on students was originally seen as a progressive development. It enabled teachers, counselors, and administrators to have access to information about the "whole child," not just about grades and subjects studied. In subsequent years, many schools developed extensive records on each student. In New York City, for example, student records typically included a guidance record of the counselor's evaluations of aptitude; behavior and personality characteristics; disciplinary referral cards; recommendations for tracking; a teacher's anecdotal file on student behavior; and cards containing standardized test results, grades, and health information. These records were open to government inspectors, employers, and other nonschool personnel. But they were not open to parents.[1]

As the quantity of information grew, so did the abuses. One mother was told she had no right to see records that resulted in her son's being transferred to a class for the mentally retarded. A father, attending a routine parent-teacher conference, discovered in teachers' comments in his son's record that he was "strangely introspective" in the third grade, "unnaturally interested in girls" in the fifth grade, and had developed "peculiar political ideas" by the time he was twelve.[2] Edward Van Allen, who was told by teachers that his son needed psychological treatment, had to get a judicial order to see all of the school's records on the boy.[3] During the 1960s, researchers found that the CIA and the FBI had complete access to student files in more than 60 percent of school districts, while parents had access in only about 15 percent.[4]

A few years before the Buckley Amendment was passed, a group of prominent educators and lawyers, convened by the Russell Sage Foundation, reported these problems in school recordkeeping:

—Information about pupils and their parents is often collected without informed consent.

—Pupils and their parents typically have little knowledge of what information about them is contained in school records or of how it is used.

—Policies for regulating access to records by nonschool personnel do not exist in most school systems.

—The secrecy with which school records are usually maintained makes it difficult for parents to assess their accuracy, and formal procedures for challenging erroneous information generally do not exist.[5]

The report concluded that these deficiencies "constitute a serious threat to individual privacy in the United States." Although many state and local regulations to control misuse of student records were developed during the 1960s, they were neither uniform nor comprehensive. Because of all these problems, Congress passed the Family Educational Rights and Privacy Act, which will be referred to in this chapter as the Buckley Amendment.

What are the main features of the act?

The Buckley Amendment contains several important features. It requires school districts to develop a policy on how parents can inspect their child's records and to inform parents of where they can see the policy and what rights they have under the act. It protects the confidentiality of student records by requiring parental permission before sharing their child's records with outsiders. And it establishes procedures through which parents can challenge questionable information in student records. The act applies to all schools receiving federal education funds. Parents may assert their children's rights of access and consent until they become eighteen or begin attending a postsecondary institution; after this, these rights will "only be accorded to . . . the student."[6]

RIGHT OF ACCESS

How does the act guarantee access to parents and students?

The Buckley Amendment states that no federal funds will be made available to any school that prevents parents from exercising "the right to inspect and review the education records of their children." This includes the right (1) to be informed about the kinds and location of education records maintained by the school and the officials responsible for them, (2) to obtain copies of records where necessary, and (3) to receive an explanation or interpretation of the records if requested. Officials must comply with a parental request to inspect "within a reasonable time, but in no case more than 45 days after the request." Either parent has the right to inspect, unless prohibited by court order. Although a school may not deny parental access to student records, it may for a legitimate reason deny a request for a copy of such records.

In a court case on this point, former students sued their college for not sending out certified copies of their transcripts because they failed to repay their student loans. The students claimed that the Buckley Amendment required the college to send out their records when they requested them. A federal court disagreed.[7] It ruled that the amendment was "for the inspection of records by students and their parents, not for the release of records to outside parties."

Does a parent have the right to see teachers' personal notes about their students?

No. The Buckley Amendment does not give parents the right to review the educational records of teachers and administrators. These records are in their "sole possession" and are not revealed to any other individual except a substitute teacher.

What other records are not accessible?

Parents do not have the right to see records of a physician, psychologist, or other recognized professional used *only* in connection with the treatment of the student; records of a law enforcement unit of the school maintained *solely* for law enforcement purposes; or job-related records of students who are employees of the school.

May students waive their right of access?

Yes. Individuals who are applicants for admission to postsecondary institutions may waive their right to inspect confidential letters of recommendation. Although institutions may not require such waivers "as a condition of admission," they may "request" them. These waivers must be signed by individual students, regardless of age, rather than by their parents. Just as a college is not required to permit students to see these confidential recommendations, so it may also prohibit students from inspecting the financial statements of their parents.

How does the Buckley Amendment restrict access to outsiders?

The act requires that a school obtain "the written consent of the parent . . . before disclosing personally identifiable information from the education records of a student." The consent must be signed and dated and include the specific records to be disclosed and the purpose and the individual or group to whom the disclosure may be made. Schools must keep a file of all requests for access to a student's record; the file must indicate who made the request and the legitimate interests in seeking the information.

Are there exceptions to the consent requirement?

Yes, there are several. For example, prior consent is not required when education records are shared with (1) teachers or administrators of the same school who have "legitimate educational interests," (2) officials of another school in which the student seeks to enroll (provided the parents are notified), (3) persons for whom the information is necessary "to protect the health or safety of the student or other individuals," and (4) in connection with financial aid for which a student has applied.

May a former student block disclosure of his or her records to a grand jury?

No. In a recent New York case, Benjamin Ostrer was unsuccessful in trying to prohibit his law school from disclosing his records to a grand jury that was investigating him. The court noted that the Buckley Amendment required the school to try to notify Ostrer of the jury's subpoena of his records. While it allowed him to object to their disclosure, the act also allowed the school to comply with a judicial order or subpoena. Therefore the court ruled that it would uphold the subpoena unless Ostrer was able to show the "documents can have no conceivable relevance to any legitimate object of investigation by the grand jury." This Ostrer was unable to do.[8]

Does the Buckley Amendment require schools to restrict distribution of personal student information in school newspapers?

It depends upon the source of the information. In defending their seizure of a school newspaper that contained personal information about a student's sus- pension, school officials argued that the Buckley Amendment prevented schools from disclosing such information about their students. However, the court ruled that the act could not justify the seizure. Although some of the information in the newspaper would fall within the act's protection "if the source of that information had been school records," the court wrote that "the Amendment cannot be deemed to extend to information which is derived from a source independent of school records."[9]

In a related case, the University of North Carolina Law School argued that its official faculty meetings could not be open to the public because the meetings might concern the personally identifiable educational records of students, and this would be inconsistent with the Buckley Amendment. The court ruled that the amendment does not prohibit open faculty meetings that might discuss student records, although it might penalize schools that have a regular practice of releasing such information.[10]

May courts require schools to disclose personal information about students without their parents' permission?

Yes, under certain conditions. A case occurred in New York when a group of parents claimed that the schools failed to provide their children with ade- quate bilingual education. As part of their suit, the parents asked a federal court to order the schools to provide the names, test results, class schedules, and other information about bilingual students who had English deficiencies. The school refused, claiming that the Buckley Amendment prohibited them from disclosing this information without parental consent. The court ruled that the school may disclose such "personally identifiable information" if it does so in compliance with a judicial order and if those seeking the order "demonstrate a genuine need for the information that outweighs the privacy interest of the student." Since this information was essential to determine whether the suit was justified, the court ruled that a genuine need was shown.[11]

The school also expressed concern about violating the act's requirement that they notify all parents of students concerned before disclosure. Since several hundred students were potentially involved, the judge said that the school could meet this requirement by making "a reasonable effort" to notify the parents by publishing a notice in Spanish and English in the local newspapers. The court explained that the act did not establish a school-student privilege analogous to an attorney-client privilege, but merely sought to deter schools from releasing personal student information unless there were appropriate educational, medical, or legal reasons. The act, concluded the court, was certainly not intended "as a cloak" for allegedly discriminatory practices.

What information about students may be shared without consent?

A school may disclose "directory information" from the education records of a student without requiring prior parental consent. Directory information includes such facts as a student's name, address, phone number, date and place of birth, field of study, sports activities, dates of attendance, awards received, and similar information. Before freely releasing such information, a school must try to notify parents of current students about what facts it regards as directory information and of the parents' right to refuse to permit the release of such information. It is the parent's obligation to notify the school in writing if they refuse. A school may release directory information about former students without first trying to notify them, however.

OTHER RIGHTS

May schools destroy student records?

Yes. If state law does not determine how long student records must be kept, schools may destroy some or all of a student's educational records at any time, except where there is an outstanding request to inspect them.

Must parents be informed of their rights under the Buckley Amendment?

Yes. Every school must give parents of all current students "annual notice" of their rights under the act, where they can obtain copies of the school's policy for implementing and protecting these rights, and their "right to file complaints" for the school's failure to comply with the act. In addition, the act requires that elementary and secondary schools find a way to "effectively notify parents" of students whose primary language is not English.

Do parents have a right to challenge their children's records?

Yes. If the parents of a student believe that a school record is "inaccurate or misleading or violates the privacy or other rights of the student," they may request that the school amend it. If the school refuses, it must so inform the parents and advise them of their rights to a hearing. The hearing may be conducted by anyone "who does not have a direct interest" in its outcome. Parents must be given "a full and fair opportunity" to present their evidence and may be represented by counsel, at their own expense, if they wish. The school must make its decision in writing "based solely on the evidence presented at the hearing" which must include the reasons and evidence to support its decision.

If, as a result of the hearing, the school decides the record was inaccurate or misleading, it must amend the record accordingly. But if the school decides that the information was correct, it must inform the parents of "the right to place in the education records of the student a statement commenting upon the information . . . and/or setting forth any reasons for disagreeing with the decision" of the school. Such explanation must be maintained by the school as part of the student's record; if the contested portion of the record is disclosed to anyone, the explanation must also be disclosed.

LEGAL ENFORCEMENT

Are there any procedures to enforce the Buckley Amendment?

Yes. There are detailed federal regulations concerning enforcement. The Family Educational Rights and Privacy Act Office of the Department of Education has been established to "investigate, process, and review violations and complaints." After receiving written complaints regarding alleged violations, the office will notify the school involved and provide an opportunity to respond. After its investigation, the office will send its findings to the complainant and the school. If there has been a violation, the office will indicate the specific steps the school must take to be in compliance. If the school does not comply, a review board hearing will be held. If the review board determines "that compliance cannot be secured by voluntary means," federal education funds will be terminated.

Thousands of complaints have been received by the Privacy Act Office, and over 90 percent of them have been resolved informally through phone calls to the school districts involved. As of June, 1980, there have been only 160 formal investigations. No cases have yet been referred to the review board; thus federal funds have never been terminated for noncompliance.[12]

In addition to enforcing the act, the Family Educational Rights and Privacy Act Office tries to help educators understand it. Its staff will consult with teachers and administrators by letter or phone and will answer questions concerning the act, its regulations, and their interpretation and application in specific school districts.[13]

What have been the results of the act?

Initially schools were slow to comply with the statute. Federal regulations for implementation were not published until a year and a half after the act became law in 1974. Even in 1977, an article published by the U.S. Office of

Education said: "Many school administrators, from superintendents to assistant principals, are not aware of the law's requirements. A large majority of parents do not know of their legal rights, and many teachers do not know that most of the written comments they make [about students] must now be shown at a parent's request."[14] But as hundreds of complaints have been filed with the Washington enforcement office each year, information about the act has increased, and compliance has become more widespread.

According to some observers, two notable results of the Buckley Amendment have been the destruction of old records and the improvement of new ones. Afer the law was passed, many schools across the country conducted "massive housecleanings" of records. Emptying school files of "undesirable material," wrote Lucy Knight, "remains the single most effective way for a school to attempt compliance with the Buckley Amendment."[15] Second, the quality of student records and the caliber of recommendations "has improved substantially," according to Chester Nolte. This, wrote Professor Nolte, reflects the fact that under the act teachers, principals, and counselors "must adhere to absolute truth, rather than opinion, when writing reports on individual students."[16]

Fears that teachers would be sued for libel if they wrote anything negative in student records have been greatly exaggerated. There is little chance of students winning libel suits against teachers whose comments are based on firsthand observations, are accurate, and are educationally relevant. (For more on libel, see chapter 6.)

Two other areas of misunderstanding have regularly occurred concerning the act. First, many educators are still unaware that access applies to all student records, not just to the cumulative file. Second, many parents believe the act gives them the right to challenge the fairness of a student grade. But the Privacy Act Office has repeatedly ruled that neither students nor parents may challenge an academic grade under the statute.[17]

SUMMARY

Abuses in the use of student records led Congress to pass the Family Educational Rights and Privacy Act (the Buckley Amendment) in 1974. The act has several important features. First, it guarantees parents the right to inspect and review the educational records of their children, but this does not include teachers' personal notes about students. Second, it limits access to student records by providing that such records cannot be released to outsiders without a parent's written consent. However, such consent is not required when the records are shared with teachers in the school, who have a "legitimate educational interest" in the student, or when they are released pursuant to a court order. Third, the act gives parents the right to challenge recorded information that is "inaccurate, misleading, or otherwise in violation of privacy or other rights of students." It also gives parents the right to place an explanation in the record of any information with which they disagree. Students who apply to college may waive their right to inspect confidential letters of recommendation. And when students become eighteen or begin attending a postsecondary institution, they take over their parents' rights under the act. Although the act initially imposed additional administrative responsibilities on the schools, it has generally led to an improvement in the quality and accuracy of student records.

NOTES

1. Diane Divoky, "Cumulative Records: Assault on Privacy," *Learning Magazine*, September 1973, p. 9.

2. *Id.*

3. *Van Allen* v. *McCleary*, 211 N.Y.S.2d 501 (1961).

4. Michael Stone, "Off the Record: The Emerging Right to Control One's School Files," 5 *N.Y.U. Review of Law and Social Change*, 39, 42 (1975).

5. Divoky, *supra*, p. 10.

6. The text of the act is contained in the UNITED STATES CODE Title 20 §1232g. Regulations for implementing the act can be found in the CODE OF FEDERAL REGULATIONS, Title 45, Part 99 (1979). Quotations about the act in this chapter are from the *Code* or *Regulations*, unless otherwise indicated.

7. *Girardier* v. *Webster College*, 421 F.Supp. 45 (E.D. Mo. 1976), 563 F.2d 1267 (8th Cir. 1977).

8. *In re Grand Jury Subpoena Served Upon New York Law School*, 448 F.Supp. 822 (S.D. N.Y. 1978).

9. *Frasca* v. *Andrews*, 463 F.Supp. 1043 (E.D. N.Y. 1979).

10. *Student Bar Association Board of Governors* v. *Byrd*, 239 S.E.2d 415 (N.C. 1977).

11. *Rios* v. *Read*, 73 F.R.D. 589 (E.D. N.Y. 1977).

12. Telephone interview with William Riley, director, Family Educational Rights and Privacy Act Office, 2 June 1980.

13. For copies of the regulations or a Model Policy Document for elementary and secondary schools, teachers can contact the Family Educational Rights and Privacy Act Office, U.S. Department of Education, Room 4511, Switzer Building, FOB6, Washington, D.C. 20202, or phone (202) 245-0233.

14. Lucy Knight, "Facts About Mr. Buckley's Amendment," *American Education*, June 1977, p. 6.

15. *Id.*, p. 7.

16. M. Chester Nolte, *American School Board Journal*, April 1977, p. 38.

17. Telephone Interview with William Riley.

18

Must all children go to school?

OVERVIEW

Universal, publicly supported education is a uniquely American idea, one that has been borrowed from us by many other nations. Based on the conviction that an enlightened citizenry can best serve the needs of society, the states provide free schools for children and youth, and most states require them to attend. Thus, since every state provides schools at public expense, schooling is a *right* provided not by the U.S. Constitution but by each state. Furthermore, where attendance is compulsory, children and youth have a *duty* to attend school. At this writing, every state except Mississippi and New Mexico have compulsory attendance laws. The age of mandatory school attendance varies, beginning at ages 6, 7, or 8 and extending through ages 15 to 18, depending on the wording of the specific state statute.

With the rise of compulsory schooling came disagreements concerning the constitutionality of such compulsion and proposals for alternatives to the public schools. Laws requiring that children attend school have been uniformly sustained, and it is clear today that there is no constitutional provision violated by such a mandate.[1] Nevertheless, specific questions continue to arise regarding such matters as conflicts between parents' rights and compulsory schooling, educational choice, home schooling, and parental objection to teaching materials or to the curriculum.

COMPULSORY SCHOOLING AND PARENTS' RIGHTS

Must all children attend public schools?

In 1922, Oregon passed a law, effective September 1, 1926, requiring every parent or guardian of a child between the ages of eight and sixteen to send such child "to a public school for the period of time a public school shall be held during the current year." Failure to comply with the law was a misdemeanor. The Society of Sisters, a religious organization that maintained various schools in Oregon, challenged the state law claiming it to be unconstitutional in that it took away property rights arbitrarily, in violation of the Due Process Clause of the Fourteenth Amendment.

No questions were raised about the right of the state to require school attendance or regulate all schools; what was questioned was the requirement that all children attend *public* schools. To this challenge, the Supreme Court, recognizing the basic right of parents and guardians "to direct the upbringing and education of children under their control," said: "The fundamental theory of liberty upon which all governments in this Union repose excludes any general power of the state to standardize its children by forcing them to accept instruction from public teachers only. The child is not the mere creature of the state; those who nurture him and direct his destiny have the right, coupled with the high duty, to recognize and prepare him for additional obligations."[2]

Since this *Pierce* case, courts have uniformly held that a state's requirement that children attend school can be met either through public or private schools; furthermore, if the school is private, it may be either religious or secular.

If parents have religious objections to schooling, may they avoid sending their children to school?

No, not in states that have compulsory education laws. Nevertheless, a variation on this question led to a partial exemption from schooling for children of the Amish religion. Several Amish parents in Wisconsin decided not to send their fourteen- and fifteen-year-old children to school beyond the eighth grade, in violation of the state's compulsory attendance law. The parents claimed that high school attendance would be destructive of the children's religious beliefs and, ultimately, of the Amish way of life. The Amish way rejects material success, competition, intellectual and scientific accomplishment, self-distinction, and other values central to the high school curriculum and the social climate in high schools. The parents further claimed that competition in classwork, sports, and peer pressure would alienate Amish children from their families and from their close-knit, cooperative, agrarian, religion-based lives.

The Amish did not object to elementary schooling, for they believed in the necessity of the three Rs to read the Bible, to be good farmers and citizens, and to be able to interact occasionally with non-Amish people. The Supreme Court, after considering the conflicting interests of the State of Wisconsin and the Amish, exempted the students from schooling beyond the eighth grade. The Court based its decision on the religious freedom clause of the First Amendment and in effect considered the Amish way of life as an acceptable alternative to formal secondary education. Protecting the Amish, the Court wrote that "there can be no assumption that today's majority is 'right' and the Amish and others like them are 'wrong.' A way of life that is odd or even erratic but interferes with no rights or interest of others is not to be condemned because it is different."[3]

A related question appears in chapter 9.

May other parents, individually or in groups, avoid the requirements of compulsory schooling?

No. The Amish case cannot be used as legal precedent for those who simply disagree with today's schools or who even form "religious" groups to gain exemption from schooling. As Justice Burger wrote: "A way of life, however virtuous and admirable, may not be interposed as a barrier to reasonable state regulation of education if it is based on purely secular considerations. . . . It cannot be overemphasized that we are not dealing with a way of life and mode of education by a group claiming to have recently discovered some 'progressive' or more enlighted [sic] process for rearing children for modern life."

Thus, parental rights to guide the upbringing of their children are respected by allowing parents to choose among existing schools or even set up new schools. At the same time, the compulsory laws of the states are upheld, mandating that all children go to some school.

HOME SCHOOLING

May parents educate their children at home?

State laws that mandate school attendance for children usually provide for alternative ways of satisfying the legal requirement. The most common equivalent is private schooling that meets certain minimum state requirements related to health and safety, curriculum, and teacher qualification. Some states allow for alternatives to public schools as long as such alternatives are "equivalent" in scope and quality. Still others provide that alternatives to public schooling must meet the approval of the local superintendent of schools and/or the school board. In considering whether parents have the choice of educating their school-age children at home, in general the answer is yes, but only if the requirements of their particular state statute are satisfied. State laws vary in their wording, and state courts have interpreted these laws differently, so one must look carefully at the law of the particular state where the question of home teaching arises.

A typical state law requires that the alternative to public schooling include teaching "the branches of education taught to children of corresponding age and grade in public schools," that the education be "equivalent," and that some systematic reporting be made to the local school superintendent to enable the state to supervise the alternative schooling. Disagreements often arise concerning the meaning of "equivalent" education as well as the qualification of the parents to teach their children. Roughly speaking, courts can be characterized as bringing a liberal or a strict interpretation to such state statutes.

All courts are more concerned with the requirement that the child be educated than with the specific form or place of that education. Some courts place the burden on the parent to prove that the home teaching is adequate and equivalent to the public schools, while others place the burden of proof on the state or school officials to show that the particular home schooling is not adequate. Where the burden of proof is placed is very important in a lawsuit, for the party that has the burden of proof must present the initial evidence to establish the claim it is making. If the initial evidence is insufficient, the case is dismissed; if it is sufficient, the other side must refute it in order to prevail. Which side has the burden of proof is usually indicated by the relevant state statute under which the suit is brought.

The liberal interpretation can be exemplified by an Illinois case where parents were accused of violating the state compulsory education law by teaching their seven-year-old daughter at home. At the trial, evidence proved that her mother, "who had two years of college and some training in pedagogy and educational psychology," taught her at home for five hours each day and that the child could perform comparably with average third-grade students. Nevertheless, the laws of Illinois made no specific provision for home teaching, only for "private or parochial school where children were taught the branches of education, taught to children of corresponding age and grade in public schools." The parents claimed that their daughter was attending a "private school" within the meaning of the state law, since she was receiving instruction comparable to that of the public school.

The Supreme Court of Illinois agreed with the parents, noting that the purpose of the law "is that all children shall be educated, not that they shall be educated in a particular manner or place."[4] The court was satisfied that the intent of the law in specifying "private school" as an alternative included the "place and nature of instruction" provided in this case. While wanting to protect children against educational deprivation, the law did not intend to punish conscientious parents. In the words of the Illinois court: "The law is not made to punish those who provide their children with instruction equal or superior to that obtainable in the public schools. It is made for the parent who fails or refuses to properly educate his child."

State courts using a strict interpretation of the law tend to emphasize that the requirement of equivalent instruction includes qualified and even certified teachers. Some states specify that certification is the evidence necessary to prove qualification for home teaching. California is one of these states, and the court of appeals there ruled that children enrolled in a correspondence course were not receiving equivalent instruction.[5]

What about the social development of children schooled at home?

A New Jersey case ruled that "equivalent" instruction requires that standard, approved teaching materials be used, that the parent doing the teaching have the necessary qualifications, and that the children have the full advantages supplied by the public schools including free association with other children.[6] In this case, the home instruction was found not to be "equivalent" because the mother, though certified to teach in secondary schools, had not kept up with educational developments for the past twenty years. Furthermore, the children's home school did not include opportunities for social interaction with others of their age.

The requirement that there be opportunities for social development is a difficult one for home schools to meet. And, in fact, most courts do not impose this requirement, for it effectively eliminates the alternative of home schooling. Courts have said that the inclusion of social development in deciding whether or not home schooling is "equivalent" would in effect eliminate "instruction elsewhere than at school." Group interaction and instruction in groups would constitute a *de facto* school, and if that is what the legislature intended, it should so specify. With this line of reasoning, most courts do not impose social interaction as a requirement for home schooling, and even a later case in New Jersey refused to follow the requirement imposed by the earlier decision in the state.[7]

What constitutional and statutory grounds are there for home schooling?

A trial court in Massachusetts faced the home schooling issue in 1978 in the light of a state statute on compulsory attendance that exempted children who are "being otherwise instructed in a manner approved in advance by the superintendent or the school committee." The court found both constitutional and statutory grounds to protect the right to home education. The constitutional grounds are derived from the right to privacy, which, though nowhere mentioned explicitly in the Constitution, is nonetheless an important right recognized by various decisions of the Supreme Court.

The Massachusetts court relied on the words of Justice Douglas, who expressed the following as a source of parents' rights: "The Ninth Amendment obviously does not create federally enforceable rights. It merely says, 'the enumeration in the Constitution of certain rights shall not be construed to deny or disparage others retained by the people.' But a catalogue of these rights includes customary, traditional and time honored rights, amenities and privileges. . . . Many of them, in my view, come within the meaning of the term 'liberty' as used in the Fourteenth Amendment . . . [one] is *freedom of choice in the basic decisions of one's life* respecting marriage, divorce, contraception, *and the education and upbringing of children. . . .*"[8]

In addition to the constitutional source of parents' rights, the court also noted that when the Massachusetts legislature revised its compulsory attendance law, it chose to retain the phrase "otherwise instructed." From this, the inference can be drawn that home education was intended to be maintained as an alternative available to the parents of the state. The court nonetheless recognized the interest of the state in an educated citizenry and thus wanted to preserve reasonable regulatory powers in the hands of school officials. In search of an appropriate balance between the rights of parents and the interests of the state, the judge ordered the School Committee to consider the following in determining the adequacy of home instruction:

1. The competency of the teachers ("and though certification would not be required, the presence or absence of the requirements that would lead to certification may be considered")
2. The teaching of subjects required by law or regulation
3. The "manner in which the subjects are taught so as to impart comparable knowledge as given in the local schools"
4. The "number of hours and days devoted to teaching"
5. The "adequacy of the texts, materials, methods, and programs being used"
6. The "availability of periodic tests and measurements of the child's educational growth"

School officials were *not* to consider the following factors in judging the adequacy of the home educational plan:

1. The parents' reasons for wanting to educate their child at home
2. The lack of a curriculum identical to that of the school
3. The lack of group experience
4. The possibility that this exemption may become a precedent for other cases[9]

In sum, whether a particular home teaching arrangement satisfies the law depends on court interpretation of "equivalence" and tends to turn on whether the parent is qualified to teach, whether systematic instruction is given, how well the children are progressing in comparison with their age mates in public schools, and the adequacy of a reporting system supervised by a responsible school official.

OBJECTIONS TO THE CURRICULUM

May parents object to certain courses or materials?

The answer depends on the grounds of the parental objection, the nature of the course or material to which the parent is objecting, and relevant state and constitutional laws. At the base of all parental objections to curriculum and instruction lie two conflicting propositions. The first asserts that parents have the basic right to guide the upbringing of their children. The second proclaims that states and boards of education have the power to make and enforce reasonable regulations for the efficient and effective conduct of schools.

Every state has some laws prescribing portions of the curriculum, and it is clear that legislatures can require children to study subjects that are "essential to good citizenship." Although what this phrase covers is often controversial, there have not been a large number of cases concerning this question. The most common objections to curriculum and instruction have had a religious basis. Perhaps the best-known issue is parental objection, on religious grounds, to the inclusion of theories of natural evolution in the school curriculum. When the Arkansas legislature forbade the teaching of evolution in the public schools of that state, the Supreme Court declared the state law unconstitutional, as a violation of the Establishment Clause of the First Amendment.[10]

May children be exempt from portions of the curriculum to which their parents object on religious grounds?

Yes, they may, if their parents have bona fide religious or moral objections. A California court so ruled in 1921, when parents objected, on religious grounds, to their children's participation in dancing, which was part of the school's physical education program. The court, ruling in favor of the parents, noted that beyond religious objections, parents may also have moral objections "which may concern the conscience of those who are not affiliated with any particular religious sect."[11]

In recent years, objections have arisen concerning a variety of sex education classes. For example, some New Jersey parents raised objections, on grounds of religion, to their children being required to take a course entitled "Human Sexuality." School board surveys indicated widespread citizen support for the program (70 percent approval), but the court indicated that issues such as this are not decided by majority vote.[12] "If majority vote were to govern in matters of religion and conscience, there would be no need for the First Amendment," wrote the judge. That amendment was adopted precisely to protect the small minority "who is sincere in a conscientious religious conviction." The Supreme Court of Hawaii and a U.S. Court of Appeals also ruled that parents' rights in general, or their religious freedom, are not violated simply by the inclusion in the curriculum of family life or sex education, as long as children of objecting parents may be excused from the instruction.[13]

May parents have their children excused from parts of the curriculum for reasons other than religious or moral objections?

Yes, they may, as long as the studies to be missed are not "essential for citizenship." The leading case on this issue arose in Nebraska in 1891 and involved a father's objection to his daughter's studying rhetoric and his desire that she study grammar instead. After his wish was granted, he changed his mind and ordered her not to study grammar. When the school board expelled her, the Supreme Court of Nebraska ordered a reinstatement without the requirement that she study grammar.[14] The court protected the parents' preference because the study of neither grammar nor rhetoric was considered to be essential for citizenship.

Similarly, in recent years, the deputy attorney general of California supported the "good citizenship" standard under which "elementary mathematics could be required, although calculus could not; handwriting could be required, creative writing could not." He further wrote that "when the state chooses to override a parent's wish, the burden is on the state to establish that in order to function effectively as a citizen, one must be versed in the subject to which the parents object."[15] Thus parents could withdraw their children from a music class and have them take private music lessons instead. Local schools could not object to such parental decision unless the state law required instruction in the particular subject.

May schools require certain courses as prerequisites for graduation?

Yes they may, as long as their requirements are reasonable. Students who meet such requirements are entitled to their diplomas even if they may violate some school rule, such as the requirement that they wear a cap and gown and attend graduation ceremonies. At least one court ruled that a student has a right to the diploma, but the school may exclude the student from participating in the graduating exercises.[16]

Can parents require a local school system to offer certain courses of instruction, use particular books or materials, or exclude books or materials?

No, they may not. Local school boards must offer courses of study required by state law, and they may not violate state and federal constitutional provisions. Within the boundaries of such laws, however, school boards have discretion to determine what courses will be taught, books and materials used, personnel selected, and even methods of instruction employed. Although the states have basic authority over the provision of public education, significant authority and responsibility have been delegated, in almost all states, to local school districts. Courts are reluctant to interfere with the discretion of local boards in the operation of public schools and will do so only in clear cases of arbitrary and unreasonable exercises of authority or violation of constitutional rights. In a celebrated case in West Virginia, for example, courts upheld the discretion of a local board in its choice of books, since parents chould not show that such books were "subversive" or "maliciously written."[17]

SUMMARY

Although the national Constitution and federal laws neither mandate nor provide public schools, each of the fifty states make publicly supported schools available for all children. State laws provide such schools, although the age of compulsory attendance varies somewhat from state to state.

State compulsory education laws generally have been upheld by the courts because important social interests are served by a well-educated citizenry. The state requirement that children attend school can be satisfied by attending public or private schools, and if private, religious or secular schools. Generally speaking, states have the authority to supervise the quality of schooling in both public and private institutions, but states vary in the provision and rigor of such supervision.

State laws that require children to attend school usually provide for alternative ways of meeting such requirements if the alternatives are "equivalent" to public schools. Home schooling has been ruled to satisfy such "equivalencies" as long as the parents or tutors are qualified, the time spent on instruction is comparable to time spent in schools, and the subjects taught cover the "common branches of knowledge" taught in public schools. In one case involving a traditional Amish religious group, the courts exempted children from attendance beyond the eighth grade when evidence indicated that such attendance would be destructive to their religious beliefs and way of life. This kind of exemption would be very difficult for others to achieve.

Where state laws prescribe part of the curriculum, local school systems must follow such prescriptions. Beyond that, local boards have wide discretion over curriculum and instruction as well as book and material selection, personnel, and other aspects of schooling. Parents may exempt their children from parts of the curriculum that clearly conflict with their religious or moral values. They may also exempt their children from elective studies in order to substitute other, out-of-school experiences. Courses of study considered "essential for citizenship" may not be avoided by children, even if their parents object to them. Finally, local school officials may specify requirements for graduation as long as such requirements are reasonable and not arbitrary. Thus courts and the law attempt to maintain an appropriate balance between the needs of society and the rights of parents to guide the upbringing of their children.

NOTES

1. *Concerned Citizens for Neighborhood Schools Inc.* v. *Board of Educ. of Chattanooga,* 379 F.Supp. 1233 (E.D. Tenn. 1974).

2. *Pierce* v. *Society of Sisters,* 268 U.S. 510 (1925).

3. *Wisconsin* v. *Yoder*, 406 U.S. 205 (1972).

4. *People* v. *Levisen*, 90 N.E.2d 213 (Ill. 1950).

5. *In re Shinn*, 195 Cal.App.2d 683 (1961).

6. *Knox* v. *O'Brien*, 72 A.2d 389 (N.J. 1950).

7. *State* v. *Massa*, 231 A.2d 252 (N.J. 1967).

8. *Roe* v. *Wade*, 410 U.S. 113 (1973). Emphasis added.

9. *Perchemlides* v. *Frizzle*, No. 16641 (Mass. Super. 13 November 1978).

10. *Epperson* v. *State of Arkansas*, 393 U.S. 97 (1968).

11. *Hardwick* v. *Board of Trustees*, 205 P.49 (Cal. 1921).

12. *Valent* v. *New Jersey State Board of Education*, 274 A.2d 832 (N.J. 1971).

13. *Medeiros* v. *Kiyosaki*, 478 P.2d 314 (Hawaii, 1970); *Cornwell* v. *State Board of Education*, 428 F.2d 471 (4 Cir. 1970), *cert. den.* 400 U.S. 942 (1970).

14. *State ex rel. Sheibley* v. *School Dist. No. 1*, 48 N.W. 393 (Neb. 1891).

15. Joel S. Moskowitz, "Parental Rights and Responsibilities," 50 *Washington Law Review* 623 (1975).

16. *Valentine* v. *Independent School Dist.*, 183 N.W. 434 (Iowa 1921).

17. *Williams* v. *Board of Education of County of Kanawha*, 388 F.Supp. 93 (S.D. W.Va. 1975).

APPENDIXES

Appendix A

Selected Provisions of the U.S. Constitution

ARTICLE I

* * *

Section 8. [1] The Congress shall have Power To lay and collect Taxes, Duties, Imposts and Excises, to pay the Debts and provide for the common Defence and general Welfare of the United States; . . .

ARTICLE III

Section 1. The judicial Power of the United States, shall be vested in one supreme Court, and in such inferior Courts as the Congress may from time to time ordain and establish. The Judges, both of the supreme and inferior Courts, shall hold their Offices during good Behaviour, and shall, at stated Times, receive for their Services a Compensation, which shall not be diminished during their Continuance in Office. . . .

Section 2. [1] The judicial Power shall extend to all Cases, in Law and Equity, arising under this Constitution, the Laws of the United States and Treaties made, or which shall be made, under their Authority; . . . to Controversies to which the United States shall be a Party;—to Controversies between two or more States;—between a State and Citizens of another State;—between Citizens of different States;—between Citizens of the same State claiming Lands under the Grants of different States, and between a State, or the Citizens thereof, and foreign States, Citizens or Subjects. . . .

ARTICLE VI

[2] This Constitution, and the Laws of the United States which shall be made in Pursuance thereof; and all Treaties made, or which shall be made, under the Authority of the United States, shall be the supreme Law of the Land; and the Judges in every State shall be bound thereby, any Thing in the Constitution or Laws of any State to the Contrary notwithstanding.

* * *

AMENDMENT I [1791]

Congress shall make no law respecting an establishment of religion, or prohibiting the free exercise thereof; or abridging the freedom of speech, or of the press; or the right of the people peaceably to assemble, and to petition the Government for a redress of grievances.

* * *

AMENDMENT IV [1791]

The right of the people to be secure in their persons, houses, papers, and effects, against unreasonable searches and seizures, shall not be violated, and no Warrants shall issue, but upon probable cause, supported by Oath or affirmation, and particularly describing the place to be searched, and the persons or things to be seized.

AMENDMENT V [1791]

No person shall be ... compelled in any criminal case to be a witness against himself, nor be deprived of life, liberty, or property, without due process of law; nor shall private property be taken for public use, without just compensation.

*   *   *

AMENDMENT VIII [1791]

Excessive bail shall not be required, nor excessive fines imposed, nor cruel and unusual punishments inflicted.

AMENDMENT IX [1791]

The enumeration in the Constitution, of certain rights, shall not be construed to deny or disparage others retained by the people.

AMENDMENT X [1791]

The powers not delegated to the United States by the Constitution, nor prohibited by it to the States, are reserved to the States respectively, or to the people.

*   *   *

AMENDMENT XIV [1868]

Section 1. All persons born or naturalized in the United States, and subject to the jurisdiction thereof, are citizens of the United States and of the State wherein they reside. No State shall make or enforce any law which shall abridge the privileges or immunities of citizens of the United States; nor shall any State deprive any person of life, liberty, or property, without due process of law; nor deny to any person within its jurisdiction the equal protection of the laws.

*   *   *

AMENDMENT XXVII [Proposed]

Section 1. Equality of rights under the law shall not be denied or abridged by the United States or by any State on account of sex.

Section 2. The Congress shall have the power to enforce, by appropriate legislation, the provisions of this article.

Section 3. This amendment shall take effect two years after the date of ratification.

Appendix B

Education and the American Legal System

In this appendix we look first at the role of state governments in education. Then we present the organization of U.S. court systems and indicate the way they relate to educational controversies. In reality the United States has fifty-one court systems; each of the fifty states has its own system, and there is one federal system. However, there are sufficient similarities in the state systems that a general model can represent them all, and similarly, a general model of the federal system, [without all details,] will suffice for our purposes.

EDUCATION IS CONTROLLED BY STATE GOVERNMENTS

Unlike most countries, the United States has no national system of education. In fact, the national Constitution is silent on the matter; however, under its Tenth Amendment, education is considered to be among the powers reserved to the states. Courts have accepted this interpretation of the Constitution, and the Supreme Court has repeatedly stated that federal courts may interfere with the actions of state and local school officials only when such actions somehow threaten a personal liberty or property right protected by the Constitution or violate federal law.

All fifty states provide for public education in their constitutions. With America's historic commitment to decentralized government and local control, states have delegated much power and responsibility over schooling to local governments. Such delegation is a choice made by the people of a state, who could, like the state of Hawaii, choose to have one statewide school district instead. In spite of the existence of local school districts, legally schools remain a responsibility of the state government; school officials, teachers and staff, are agents of the state when performing their official duties. This is a significant principle; because the Constitution only protects individuals against actions by the government. The first ten amendments to the Constitution (more commonly, the Bill of Rights) prohibit certain actions on the part of the federal government. The Fourteenth Amendment applies to actions by the states. Since all actions of school officials and school boards are "state actions," the Fourteenth Amendment prohibits certain arbitrary and discriminatory practices. What makes this all the more important is the historic development whereby all the guarantees of the First Amendment, and many other provisions of the Bill of Rights, have been incorporated into the "liberty clause" of the Fourteenth and thus made applicable to all the states. While there is a complex and controversial legal history to this incorporation, for our purposes it will suffice to understand that all civil rights protections of the First Amendment, and most civil rights protections of the other Bill of Rights provisions, apply to the actions of public school officials just as much as those of the Fourteenth Amendment.

Thus, while states have the primary power and responsibility for public schools, their power must be exercised at all times consistently with the rights guaranteed in the national Constitution.

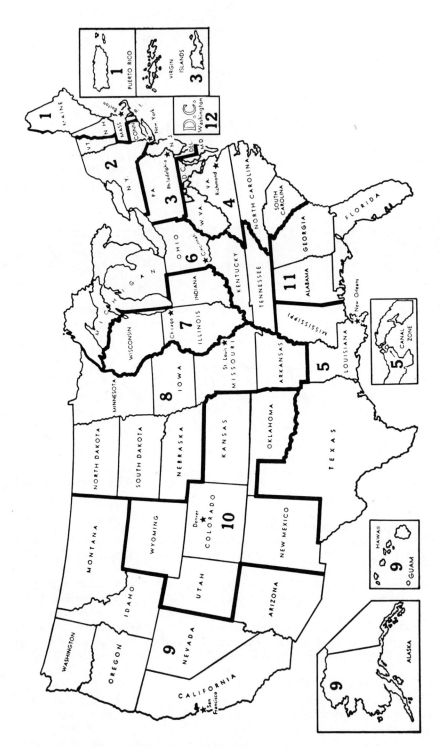

Figure 2.   The Twelve Federal Judicial Circuits

Figure 3.   The Federal Court System

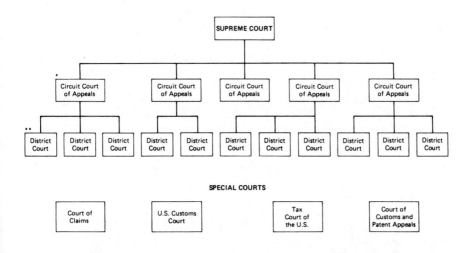

* There are currently 12 Circuit Courts of Appeals, including one in the District of Columbia. Several judges may serve on any of these courts, on District Courts as well as other courts.
** There are currently 96 District Courts, including one in the District of Columbia.

THE FEDERAL COURT SYSTEM

The U.S. Supreme Court is the only court specifically created by the Constitution (Article III, Section 2); all other federal courts were established by Congress. Below the Supreme Court are twelve circuit courts of appeal (see figure 2), and within each circuit there are trial courts called district courts. Currently, there are about 96 district courts, at least one in each state, though their numbers may change from time to time. Except for special courts, such as the court of claims, tax court, or court of customs and patent appeals, we have a three-tiered hierarchy of federal courts. School-related cases involving federal issues may be brought to trial in a district court; from this court an appeal may be taken to a circuit court of appeals and eventually to the Supreme Court (see figure 3).

The Constitution specifies what cases the Supreme Court will consider (Article III, Section 2, Clause 1). For all other federal courts, Congress determines which cases will be tried where, the route appeals will take, and the relationship of courts to the many administrative agencies of government. In general, federal courts take only two kinds of cases: (1) those that present substantial questions under federal laws and the Constitution, and (2) those involving a diversity of jurisdiction (i.e., where suits involve different states or citizens of different states). Many cases present questions involving both federal and state laws and may initially be tried in either federal or state courts. If such a case is brought to trial in a federal court, however, it must decide questions of state law according to the laws of the affected state. Conversely, if the case was initially filed in a state court, it must follow the federal law governing that area.

While decisions of the Supreme Court are applicable to the entire nation, the decisions of circuit courts are binding only within their territories; thus different rules may apply in different regions of the country until the Supreme Court decides the issue. This resolution was illustrated several years ago by a Supreme Court ruling on teacher pregnancy-leave policies, and the unresolved conflict is illustrated by conflicts in holdings in personal appearance cases in different circuits.

Except for the cases specified by the Constitution, the Supreme Court has great discretion over which cases to accept for review. Literally thousands of petitions are submitted yearly to the Court, urging it to consider particular cases. In these petitions (known as a "petition for *certiorari*") the parties attempt to convince the Court of the significance of the particular issue. Approximately 3,000 such petitions are submitted each year, but only a small number is granted by the Court. (The November 1979 issue of the *Harvard Law Review* presents a statistical summary and analysis of the annual work of the Court.)

THE STATE COURT SYSTEM

Most school-related cases are litigated in state courts. Since these courts are created by state constitutions and legislatures, however, they vary considerably in titles, procedures, and jurisdiction. A general pattern among the states is a three-tiered system, excluding the lower courts of special jurisdiction (see figure 4).

At the foundation of the state court system, we find the trial courts, often organized along county lines. From these, appeals go to intermediate appeals courts and finally to the highest court of the state, variously named in different states. For example, the highest state court is named the Supreme Judicial Court in Massachusetts, the Court of Appeals in Kentucky, the Supreme Court of Errors in Connecticut, and the Supreme Court in California.

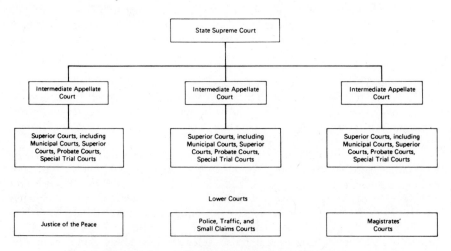

Figure 4.   A Typical State Court System

THE FUNCTIONS OF TRIAL AND APPEALS COURTS

A school-related controversy that cannot be resolved without a lawsuit first goes to a trial court. Here the facts are established and the relevant legal principles applied to the facts. If the case is appealed, the appellate court will not retry the case; it will usually accept the facts as established by the trial court unless it is very clear that evidence to support such facts was inadequate. The main concern of appeals courts is whether correct legal principles were applied to the facts determined by the court below.

For example, a school may want to terminate Teacher X for insubordination. Teacher X would typically fight such a case in a state court unless the claim could be reasonably made that a constitutionally protected activity (e.g., free speech) formed the basis of the dismissal. The trial court would hear evidence from both sides in order to establish whether the alleged behaviors occurred and whether they constituted insubordination. Once the facts were established, the trial court would apply the relevant law and arrive at a decision on the case. The judge would consider all laws, state and federal, applicable to the case, for Article IV of the Constitution provides that the Constitution and the "Laws of the United States" and "Treaties . . . shall be the Supreme Law of the Land" and that "Judges in any state shall be bound thereby." If the case were appealed, the appeals court would consider whether or not the principles of law were properly applied by the trial court.

The highest state court will be the final authority on legal questions related to the law of that state unless there is federal law on the same matter. The U.S. Supreme Court is the final authority on matters arising out of the Constitution, treaties, federal laws, or conflicts among state laws. In matters that involve only state laws, the state courts have the authoritative voice.

ADMINISTRATIVE BODIES

It is generally recognized today that the courts are overburdened and their calendars overcrowded. It is all too true that "justice delayed is justice denied," yet in many cities it takes over a year for a criminal case to come to trial and several years for a civil suit to be tried. This situation would be worse if we did not have administrative agencies acting in quasi-judicial capacities. Without a doubt, the largest and most detailed body of law is created by administrative rules and regulations, by agencies created by statutes to regulate public affairs. Administrative law functions at both federal and state levels, and the lives of educators are heavily influenced by them. (See, for example, Title IX regulations, Special Education regulations, Department of Education regulations, and others.)

HOW TO FIND REPORTS OF COURT CASES

Every county has a courthouse that contains a law library. Every law school has such a library, and most universities and colleges have legal collections. In each of these places a librarian can help one find cases of interest. The following brief comments constitute an introduction to legal research.

Appellate courts almost always publish their decisions. The decisions of the highest appellate court, the U.S. Supreme Court, can be found in the *United States Reports.* For example, the citation *Brown* v. *Board of Education of Topeka, Kansas,* 349 U.S. 294 (1955), indicates that the case, decided in 1955, is reported in volume 349 of the *United States Reports* at page 294. Since Supreme Court cases are reported in several publications, the same case may be followed by the notations 75 S.Ct. 753, 99 L.Ed. 1083. This means that the same case also appears in volume 75 of the *Supreme Court Reporter* at page 753 and in volume 99 of the *Lawyers Edition* at page 1083. The most recent cases decided by the Supreme Court appear in a looseleaf volume called

United States Law Week, cited, for example, as *Givhan* v. *Western Line Consolidated School District,* 47 *Law Week* 4102 (Jan. 9, 1979).

Cases decided by the U.S. Courts of Appeals are reported in the *Federal Reporter, Second Series.* For example, *Clark* v. *Whiting,* 607 F.2d 634 (4th Cir. 1979) would indicate that this case can be found in volume 607 of the *Federal Reporter, Second Series* at page 634 and that the case was decided by the Fourth Circuit Court of Appeals in 1979. Decisions of the Federal District Courts are reported in the *Federal Supplement* and are similarly cited. For example, *Valencia* v. *Blue Hen Conference,* 476 F.Supp. 809 (D. Del. 1979), indicates that this case was decided by a district court in Delaware in 1979 and is reported in volume 476 of the *Federal Supplement* at page 809.

The best-known set of publications in this field is the National Reporter System of the West Publishing Company, which covers both federal and state courts and has separate series for states and for regions. For example, cases decided by the appellate courts of California are reported both in a California series and in a regional report called *The Pacific Reporter;* thus, *Morse* v. *San Diego High,* 34 Cal. App. 134, 166 P. 839 (1917), is reported both in volume 34 of the *California Appellate Reporter* at page 134 and in volume 166 of *The Pacific Reporter* at page 839. When a series becomes too long and thus the volume numbers too large, a second series is begun and cited, for example, as "P.2d" rather than as "P."

In addition to reading cases, teachers interested in a particular topic might go to one of the standard legal encyclopedias to gain an overview of the topic. The best known of these encylopedias are *Corpus Juris Secundum* (cited as "C.J.S.") and *American Jurisprudence* (cited as "Am. Jur.").

The foregoing should suffice as an introduction to legal research for teachers. Anyone interested in a more thorough understanding of the field should consult with a law librarian and read one of the standard guides on the subject.

Appendix C

Major Civil Rights Laws Affecting Schools

EARLY POST-CIVIL WAR STATUTES

Acts of 1866, 1870, 42 U.S.C., sec. 1981 (the right to make contracts regardless of race).

Acts of 1871, 42 U.S.C., sec. 1983 (protects against deprivation of any constitutional right by officials or anyone acting under color of law).

Acts of 1871, 42 U.S.C., sec. 1956 and 1986 (protects against conspiracy to deprive people of their constitutional rights).

MODERN STATUTES AND EXECUTIVE ORDERS

Equal Pay Act of 1963, 29 U.S.C. 206 (d) (sex discrimination in pay).

Civil Rights Act of 1964, 42 U.S.C., sec. 2000. Title VI (general prohibition—sec. 2000 (d); Title VII (employment discrimination—sec. 2000 (e)).

Education Amendments of 1972 (Title IX), 20 U.S.C., sec. 1681 (discrimination in education programs).

Age Discrimination in Employment Act of 1967, as amended 1978 (92 Stat. 189), 29 U.S.C., sec. 621.

Equal Employment Opportunity Act of 1972, as amending Title VII (*supra*), 42 U.S.C., sec. 2000 (e).

Equal Educational Opportunities Act of 1974, 20 U.S.C., sec. 1701.

Rehabilitation Acts of 1973, 29 U.S.C., sec. 794 (see particularly sec. 504 prohibiting discrimination against the handicapped).

Education for All Handicapped Children Act of 1975, 20 U.S.C., sec. 1401 (federal funds to provide educational opportunities for handicapped).

Education of Gifted and Talented Children, Education Amendments of 1974, 20 U.S.C., sec. 1863.

Bilingual Education Act of 1974, 20 U.S.C., sec. 880 (b).

State and Local Assistance Act, 31 U.S.C., sec. 1242 (antidiscrimination conditions in federal revenue sharing).

Presidential Executive Orders (barring discrimination by all federal contractors on same grounds as Civil Rights Act of 1964, as amended): 10925 (1961); 11246 (1965); 11375 (1967).

Family Educational Rights and Privacy Act of 1974, 20 U.S.C., sec. 1232 (confidentiality of school records and access to them).

42 U.S.C. § 1981—CIVIL RIGHTS ACTS OF 1866, 1870*

Section 1981: "All persons within the jurisdiction of the United States shall have the same right . . . to make and enforce contracts, to sue, be parties, give evidence, and to the full and equal benefit of all laws and proceedings for the security of per-

---

* 42 U.S.C. § 1981 refers to Volume 42 of United States Codes of section 1981. "Civil Rights Act of 1866, 1870" is the popular name of the law. The same pattern is followed throughout.

sons and property as is enjoyed by white citizens, and shall be subject to like punishments, pains, penalties, taxes, licenses, and exactions of every kind, and to no other."

42 U.S.C. § 1983—THE CIVIL RIGHTS ACT OF 1871

Section 1983: "Every person who, under color of any statute, ordinance, regulation, custom or usage, of any State or Territory, subjects, or causes to be subjected, any citizen of the United States or other person within the jurisdiction thereof to the deprivation of any rights, privileges or immunities secured by the Constitution and laws, shall be liable to the party injured in an action at law, suit in equity, or other proper proceeding for redress."

42 U.S.C. §§ 1985 AND 1986—THE CIVIL RIGHTS ACT OF 1871

Section 1985(3): "If two or more persons in any State or Territory conspire or go in disguise on the highway or on the premises of another, for the purpose of depriving, either directly or indirectly, any person or class of persons of the equal protection of the laws, or of equal privileges and immunities under the laws: or for the purpose of preventing or hindering the constituted authorities of any State or Territory from giving or securing to all persons within such State or Territory the equal protection of the laws . . . : in any case of conspiracy set forth in this section, if one or more persons engaged therein do, or cause to be done, any act in furtherance of the object of such conspiracy, whereby another is injured in his person or property, or deprived of having and exercising any right or privilege of a citizen of the United States, the party so injured or deprived may have an action for the recovery of damages, occasioned by such injury or deprivation, against any one or more of the conspirators."

Section 1986: "Every person who, having knowledge that any of the wrongs conspired to be done, and mentioned in Section 1985 of this title, are about to be committed, and having the power to prevent or aid in preventing the commission of the same, neglects or refuses so to do, if such wrongful act be committed, shall be liable to the party injured, or his legal representatives, for all damages caused by such wrongful act, which such person by reasonable diligence could have prevented; and such damages may be recovered in an action on the case; and any number of persons guilty of such wrongful neglect or refusal may be joined as defendants in the action. . . ."

42 U.S.C. § 1988—CIVIL RIGHTS ACTS OF 1866, 1870

As amended 1976, § 1988 provides:
Proceedings in vindication of civil rights. The jurisdiction in civil and criminal matters conferred on the district courts by the provisions of this chapter and Title 18, for the protection of all persons in the United States in their civil rights, and for their vindication, shall be exercised and enforced in conformity with the laws of the United States, so far as such laws are suitable to carry the same into effect; but in all cases where they are not adapted to the object, or are deficient in the provisions necessary to furnish suitable remedies and punish offenses against law, the common law, as modified and changed by the constitution and statues of the State wherein the

court having jurisdiction of such civil or criminal cause is held, so far as the same is not inconsistent with the Constitution and laws of the United States, shall be extended to and govern the said courts in the trial and disposition of the cause, and, if it is of a criminal nature, in the infliction of punishment on the party found guilty. In any action or proceeding to enforce a provision of sections 1981, 1982, 1983, 1985, and 1986 of this title, title IX of Public Law 92-318, or in any civil action or proceeding, by or on behalf of the United States of America, to enforce, or charging a violation of, a provision of the United States Internal Revenue Code, or title VI of the Civil Rights Act of 1964, the court, in its discretion, may allow the prevailing party, other than the United States, a reasonable attorney's fee as part of the costs.

As amended Pub.L. 94-559, § 2, Oct. 19, 1976.

42 U.S.C. § 2000(D)—CIVIL RIGHTS ACT OF 1964, TITLE VI

Section 601 of Title VI: "No person in the United States shall, on the ground of race, color, or national origin, be excluded from participation in, be denied the benefits of, or be subjected to discrimination under any program or activity receiving Federal financial assistance."

42 U.S.C. § 2000(E)—CIVIL RIGHTS ACT OF 1964, TITLE VII

Section 702 of Title VII: "This title shall not apply to . . . a religious corporation, association, educational institution, or society with respect to the employment of individuals of a particular religion to perform work connected with the carrying on by such corporation, association, educational institution, or society of its activities."

Section 703(a): "It shall be an unlawful employment practice for an employer—(1) . . . to discriminate against any individual with respect to his compensation, terms, conditions, or privileges of employment, because of such individual's race, color, religion, sex, or national origin; or (2) to limit, segregate, or classify his employees . . . in any way which would deprive or tend to deprive any individual of employment opportunities or otherwise adversely affect his status as an employee, because of such individual's race, color, religion, sex, or national origin."

Section 703(e): "Notwithstanding any other provision of this [title], (1) it shall not be an unlawful employment practice for an employer to hire and employ employees, for an employment agency to classify or refer for employment any individual, for a labor organization to classify its membership or to classify or refer for employment any individual, or for an employer, labor organization, or joint labor-management committee controlling apprenticeship or other training or retraining programs to admit or employ any individual in any such program, on the basis of his religion, sex, or national origin in those certain instances where religion, sex, or national origin is a bona fide occupational qualification reasonably necessary to the normal operation of that particular business or enterprise. . . ."

Section 703(h): "Notwithstanding any other provision of this title, it shall not be an unlawful employment practice for an employer to apply different standards of compensation, or different terms, conditions, or privileges of employment pursuant to a bona fide seniority or merit system, . . . provided that such differences are not the result of an intention to discriminate because of race, color, religion, sex, or national origin. . . ."

20 U.S.C. § 1681—EDUCATION AMENDMENTS OF 1972, TITLE IX

Section 901 of Title IX:

SEC. 901. (A) No person in the United States shall, on the basis of sex, be excluded from participation in, be denied the benefits of, or be subjected to discrimination under any education program or activity receiving Federal financial assistance, except that:

(1) in regard to admissions to educational institutions, this section shall apply only to institutions of vocational education, professional education, and graduate higher education, and to public institutions of undergraduate higher education. . . .

(3) this section shall not apply to an educational institution which is controlled by a religious organization if the application of this subsection would not be consistent with the religious tenets of such organization. . . .

(5) in regard to admissions this section shall not apply to any public institution of undergraduate higher education which is an institution that traditionally and continually from its establishment has had a policy of admitting only students of one sex.

29 U.S.C. § 206(D)—EQUAL PAY ACT

Section 206: "No employer having employees subject to [the minimum wage provisions of the FLSA] shall discriminate, within any establishment . . . , between employees on the basis of sex by paying wages to employees in such establishment at a rate less than the rate at which he pays wages to employees of the opposite sex in such establishment for equal work on jobs the performance of which requires equal skill, effort, and responsibility, and which are performed under similar working conditions. . . ."

The Act nevertheless permits differences in wages if paid pursuant to: "(i) a seniority system; (ii) a merit system; (iii) a system which measures earnings by quantity or quality of production; or (iv) a differential based on any factor other than sex. . . ."

29 U.S.C. § 621—AGE DISCRIMINATION ACT

Section 623:

(a) It shall be unlawful for an employer—

(1) to fail or refuse to hire or to discharge any individual or otherwise discriminate against any individual with respect to his compensation, terms, conditions, or privileges of employment, because of such individual's age. . . .

(c) It shall be unlawful for a labor organization—

(1) to exclude or to expel from its membership, or otherwise to discriminate against, any individual because of his age. . . .

(3) to cause or attempt to cause an employer to discriminate against an individual in violation of this section. . . .

(f) It shall not be unlawful for an employer, employment agency, or labor organization—

(1) to take any action otherwise prohibited under subsections (a), (b), (c), or (e) of this section where age is a bona fide occupational qualification reasonably necessary to the normal operation of the particular business, or where the differentiation is based on reasonable factors other than age. . . .

(3) to discharge or otherwise discipline an individual for good cause. . . .

20 U.S.C. § 1703—EQUAL EDUCATION OPPORTUNITIES ACT

Section 1703: No State shall deny equal educational opportunity to an individual on account of his or her race, color, sex, or national origin, by—

(a) the deliberate segregation by an educational agency of students on the basis of race, color, or national origin among or within schools. . . .

(c) the assignment by an educational agency of a student to a school, other than the one closest to his or her place of residence within the school district in which he or she resides, if the assignment results in a greater degree of segregation of students on the basis of race, color, sex, or national origin. . . .

(d) discrimination by an educational agency on the basis of race, color, or national origin in the employment, employment conditions, or assignment to schools of its faculty or staff, except to fulfill the purposes of subsection (f) below. . . .

(e) the transfer by an educational agency, whether voluntary or otherwise, of a student from one school to another if the purpose and effect of such transfer is to increase segregation of students on the basis of race, color, or national origin among the schools of such agency; or

(f) the failure by an educational agency to take appropriate action to overcome language barriers that impede equal participation by its students in its instructional programs.

29 U.S.C. § 794—REHABILITATION ACT OF 1973

Section 504: "No otherwise qualified handicapped individual . . . shall, solely by reason of his handicap, be excluded from the participation in, be denied the benefits of, or be subjected to discrimination under any program or activity receiving Federal financial assistance."

20 U.S.C. § 1232—FAMILY EDUCATIONAL RIGHTS AND PRIVACY ACT OF 1974

The following is a "Fact Sheet" issued by the Department of Health, Education, and Welfare, interpreting the above law:

This law was passed by Congress in 1974 to protect the privacy of student education records, and applies to all schools that receive money from the U.S. Office of Education.

The Act gives certain rights to parents regarding their child's education records. These rights transfer to the student or former student who has reached the age of 18 or is attending any school beyond the high school level. Students and former students to whom the rights have transferred are called eligible students.

—*A school must allow parents or eligible students to inspect and review all of the student's education records maintained by the school.* However, this does not include the review of personal notes of teachers, or, at the college level, medical or law enforcement records. Schools are not required to provide copies of material in education records unless, for reasons such as illness or great distance, it is impossible to inspect the records personally. The school may charge a fee for copies.

—*Parents and eligible students may request that a school correct records believed to be inaccurate or misleading.* If the school refuses to change the records, the parent or eligible student then has the right to a formal hearing. After the hearing, if the school still refuses the correction, the parent or eligible student has the right to put a note in the record explaining his or her concerns.

—*Generally, the school must have written permission from the parent or eligible student before releasing any information from a student's record.* In an effort to permit the school to continue its normal business and activities, the law allows a school to set its own rules about who among the following people may see records without the required consent:

- School employees who have a need-to-know;
- Other schools to which a student is transferring;
- Parents when a student over 18 is still a dependent;
- Certain government officials who need-to-know to carry out lawful functions;
- Sponsors of financial aid to a student;
- Organizations doing certain studies for the school;
- Individuals who have obtained court orders or subpoenas;
- Persons who need to know in cases of health and safety emergencies.

Also, "directory" type information such as one's name, address, telephone number, date and place of birth, honors and awards, and activities, may be released to anyone without first getting permission. However, the school must tell parents and students the type of information that is classified as directory information and provide a reasonable amount of time to allow the parent or eligible student to tell the school not to reveal directory information about them.

—The school must notify parents and eligible students of their rights under this law. The actual means of notification (special letter, inclusion in a PTA bulletin or student handbook, or newspaper article) is left to each school.

If you wish to see your child's education record, or if you are over 18 or are attending college and would like to see your records, you should contact the school to find out the procedure to follow.

If there are any questions the school cannot answer, or, if you have problems in securing your rights under this Act, you may call (202) 245-7488, or write to: FERPA Office, Room 526F, Humphrey Building, 200 Independence Avenue, S.W., Washington, D.C. 20202.

20 U.S.C., § 1401—EDUCATION FOR ALL HANDICAPPED CHILDREN ACT OF 1975 (PUBLIC LAW 94-142)

(b) The Congress finds that—

(1) there are more than eight million handicapped children in the United States today;

(2) the special educational needs of such children are not being fully met;

(3) more than half of the handicapped children in the United States do not receive appropriate educational services which would enable them to have full equality of opportunity;

(4) one million of the handicapped children in the United States are excluded entirely from the public school system and will not go through the educational process with their peers;

(5) there are many handicapped children throughout the United States participating in regular school programs whose handicaps prevent them from having a successful educational experience because their handicaps are undetected;

(6) because of the lack of adequate services within the public school system, families are often forced to find services outside the public school system, often at great distance from their residence and at their own expense;

(7) developments in the training of teachers and in diagnostic and instructional procedures and methods have advanced to the point that, given appropriate funding, State and local educational agencies can and will provide effective special education and related services to meet the needs of handicapped children;

(8) State and local educational agencies have a responsibility to provide education for all handicapped children, but present financial resources are inadequate to meet the special educational needs of handicapped children; and

(9) it is in the national interest that the Federal Government assist State and local efforts to provide programs to meet the educational needs of handicapped children in order to assure equal protection of the law.

(c) It is the purpose of this Act to assure that all handicapped children have available to them, within the time periods specified in section 612(2) (B), a free appropriate public education which emphasizes special education and related services designed to meet their unique needs, to assure that the rights of handicapped children and their parents or guardians are protected, to assist States and localities to provide for the education of all handicapped children, and to assess and assure the effectiveness of efforts to educate handicapped children.

EXCERPTS FROM REGULATIONS UNDER PUBLIC LAW 94-142

§ *121a.5 Handicapped children*

(a) As used in this part, the term "handicapped children" means those children evaluated in accordance with §§ 121a.530–121a.534 as being mentally retarded, hard of hearing, deaf, speech impaired, visually handicapped, seriously emotionally disturbed, orthopedically impaired, other health impaired, deaf-blind, multi-handicapped, or as having specific learning disabilities, who because of those impairments need special education and related services.

(b) The terms used in this definition are defined as follows:

(1) "Deaf" means a hearing impairment which is so severe that the child is impaired in processing linguistic information through hearing, with or without amplification, which adversely affects educational performance.

(2) "Deaf-blind" means concomitant hearing and visual impairments, the combination of which causes such severe communication and other developmental and educational problems that they cannot be accommodated in special education programs solely for deaf or blind children.

(3) "Hard of hearing" means a hearing impairment, whether permanent or fluctuating, which adversely affects a child's educational performance but which is not included under the definition of "deaf" in this section.

(4) "Mentally retarded" means significantly subaverage general intellectual functioning existing concurrently with deficits in adaptive behavior and manifested during the developmental period, which adversely affects a child's educational performance.

(5) "Multihandicapped" means concomitant impairments (such as mentally retarded-blind, mentally retarded-orthopedically impaired, etc.), the combination of which causes such severe educational problems that they cannot be accommodated in special education programs solely for one of the impairments. The term does not include deaf-blind children.

(6) "Orthopedically impaired" means a severe orthopedic impairment which adversely affects a child's educational performance. The term includes impairments caused by congenital anomaly (e.g., clubfoot, absence of some member, etc.), impairments caused by disease (e.g., poliomyelitis, bone tuberculosis, etc.), and impairments from other causes (e.g., cerebral palsy, amputations, and fractures or burns which cause contractures).

(7) "Other health impaired" means limited strength, vitality or alertness, due to chronic or acute health problems such as a heart condition, tuberculosis, rheumatic fever, nephritis, asthma, sickle cell anemia, hemophilia, epilepsy, lead poisoning, leukemia, or diabetes, which adversely affects a child's educational performance.

(8) "Seriously emotionally disturbed" is defined as follows:

(i) The term means a condition exhibiting one or more of the following characteristics over a long period of time and to a marked degree, which adversely affects educational performance:

(A) An inability to learn which cannot be explained by intellectual, sensory, or health factors;

(B) An inability to build or maintain satisfactory interpersonal relationships with peers and teachers;

(C) Inappropriate types of behavior or feelings under normal circumstances;

(D) A general pervasive mood of unhappiness or depression; or

(E) A tendency to develop physical symptoms or fears associated with personal or school problems.

(ii) The term includes children who are schizophrenic or autistic. The term does not include children who are socially maladjusted, unless it is determined that they are seriously emotionally disturbed.

(9) "Specific learning disability" means a disorder in one or more of the basic psychological processes involved in understanding or in using language, spoken or written, which may manifest itself in an imperfect ability to listen, think, speak, read, write, spell, or to do mathematical calculations. The term includes such conditions as perceptual handicaps, brain injury, minimal brain dysfunction, dyslexia, and developmental aphasia. The term does not include children who have learning problems which are primarily the result of visual, hearing, or motor handicaps, of mental retardation, or of environmental, cultural, or economic disadvantage.

(10) "Speech impaired" means a communication disorder, such as stuttering, impaired articulation, a language impairment, or a voice impairment, which adversely affects a child's educational performance.

(11) "Visually handicapped" means a visual impairment which, even with correction, adversely affects a child's educational performance. The term includes both partially seeing and blind children.

SELECTIONS FROM THE BILINGUAL EDUCATION ACT OF 1978

Section 701: This title may be cited as the "Bilingual Education Act."

Policy; appropriations

Section 702: (a) Recognizing—

(1) that there are large numbers of children of limited English proficiency;

(2) that many of such children have a cultural heritage which differs from that of English-speaking persons;

(3) that a primary means by which a child learns is through the use of such child's language and cultural heritage;

(4) that, therefore, large numbers of children of limited English proficiency have educational needs which can be met by the use of bilingual educational methods and techniques;

(5) that, in addition, children of limited English proficiency and children whose primary language is English benefit through the fullest utilization of multiple language and cultural resources;

(6) children of limited English proficiency have a high dropout rate and low median years of education; and

(7) research and evaluation capabilities in the field of bilingual education need to be strengthened.

The Congress declares it to be the policy of the United States, in order to establish equal educational opportunity for all children (A) to encourage the establishment and operation, where appropriate, of educational programs using bilingual educational practices, techniques, and methods, and (B) for that purpose, to provide financial assistance to local educational agencies, and to State educational agencies for certain purposes, in order to enable such local educational agencies to develop and carry out such programs in elementary and secondary schools, including activities at the preschool level, which are designed to meet the educational needs of such children, with particular attention to children having the greatest need for such programs; and to demonstrate effective ways of providing, for children of limited English proficiency, instruction designed to enable them, while using their native language, to achieve competence in the English language.

(b) (1) For the purpose of carrying out the provisions of this title, there are authorized to be appropriated $200,000,000 for fiscal year 1979; $250,000,000 for fiscal year 1980; $300,000,000 for fiscal year 1981; $350,000,000 for fiscal year 1982; and $400,-000,000 for the fiscal year 1983.

(2) There are further authorized to be appropriated to carry out the provisions of section 721 (b) (5) $12,000,000 for fiscal year 1979; $14,000,000 for fiscal year 1980; $16,000,000 for fiscal year 1981; and such sums as may be necessary for each of the two succeeding fiscal years.

(3) From the sums appropriated under paragraph (1) for any fiscal year, the Commissioner shall reserve $16,000,000 of that part thereof that does not exceed $70,000,-000 for training activities carried out under section 721(a)(3), and shall reserve for those activities not less than 20 per centum of that part thereof which is in excess of $70,000,000.

(4) The Commissioner shall reserve from the amount not reserved pursuant to paragraph (3) of this subsection such amount as may be necessary, but not in excess of 1 per centum thereof, for the purposes of section 732.

Definitions; Regulations

Section 703: (a) The following definitions shall apply to the terms used in this title:

(1) The term 'limited English proficiency' when used with reference to individuals means—

(A) individuals who were not born in the United States or whose native language is a language other than English,

(B) individuals who come from environments where a language other than English is dominant, as further defined by the Commissioner by regulation, and

(C) individuals who are American Indian and Alaskan Native students and who come from environments where a language other than English has had a significant

impact on their level of English language proficiency, subject to such regulations as the Commissioner determines to be necessary;
and by reason thereof, have sufficient difficulty speaking, reading, writing, or understanding the English language to deny such individuals the opportunity to learn successfully in classrooms where the language of instruction is English.

(2) The term 'native language,' when used with reference to an individual of limited English proficiency, means the language normally used by such individuals, or in the case of a child, the language normally used by the parents of the child.

(3) The term 'low-income' when used with respect to a family means an annual income for such a family which does not exceed the poverty level determined pursuant to section 111(c)(2) of title I of the Elementary and Secondary Education Act of 1965.

(4)(A) The term 'program of bilingual education' means a program of instruction, designed for children of limited English proficiency in elementary or secondary schools, in which, with respect to the years of study to which such program is applicable—

(i) there is instruction given in, and study of, English and, to the extent necessary to allow a child to achieve competence in the English language, the native language of the children of limited English proficiency, and such instruction is given with appreciation for the cultural heritage of such children, and of other children in American society, and, with respect to elementary and secondary school instruction, such instruction shall, to the extent necessary, be in all courses or subjects of study which will allow a child to progress effectively through the educational system; and

(ii) the requirements in subparagraphs (B) through (F) of this paragraph and established pursuant to subsection (b) of this section are met.

(B) In order to prevent the segregation of children on the basis of national origin in programs assisted under this title, and in order to broaden the understanding of children about languages and cultural heritages other than their own, a program of bilingual instruction may include the participation of children whose language is English, but in no event shall the percentage of such children exceed 40 per centum. The objective of the program shall be to assist children of limited English proficiency to improve their English language skills, and the participation of other children in the program must be for the principal purpose of contributing to the achievement of that objective. The program may provide for centralization of teacher training and curriculum development, but it shall serve such children in the schools which they normally attend.

(C) In such courses or subjects of study as art, music, and physical education, a program of bilingual education shall make provision for the participation of children of limited English proficiency in regular classes.

(D) Children enrolled in a program of bilingual education shall, if graded classes are used, be placed, to the extent practicable, in classes with children of approximately the same age and level of educational attainment. If children of significantly varying ages or levels of educational attainment are placed in the same class, the program of bilingual education shall seek to insure that each child is provided with instruction which is appropriate for his level of educational attainment.

(E) An application for a program of bilingual education shall—

(i) be developed in consultation with an advisory council, of which a majority shall be parents and other representatives of children of limited English proficiency, in accordance with criteria prescribed by the Commissioner;

(ii) be accompanied by documentation of such consultation and by the comments which the Council makes on the application; and

(iii) contain assurances that, after the application has been approved, the applicant will provide for the continuing consultation with, and participation by, the committee of parents, teachers, and other interested individuals (of which a majority shall be parents of children of limited English proficiency) which shall be selected by and predominantly composed of parents of children participating in the program, and in the case of programs carried out in secondary schools, representatives of the secondary students to be served.

(F) Parents of children participating in a program of bilingual education shall be informed of the instructional goals of the program and the progress of their children in such program.

(5) The term 'Office' means the Office of Bilingual Education.

(6) The term 'Director' means the Director of the Office of Bilingual Education.

(7) The term 'Council' means the National Advisory Council on Bilingual Education.

(8) The term 'other programs for persons of limited English proficiency' when used in sections 731 and 732 means any programs within the Office of Education directly involving bilingual education activities serving persons of limited English proficiency, such as the program authorized by section 708(c) of the Emergency School Aid Act, as in effect for fiscal year 1979, section 608(a)(4) of this Act for subsequent fiscal years, and the programs carried out in coordination with the provisions of this title pursuant to section 122(a)(4)(C) and part J of the Vocational Education Act of 1963, and section 306(a)(11) of the Adult Education Act, and programs and projects serving areas with high concentrations of persons of limited English proficiency pursuant to sections 6(b)(4) of the Library Services and Construction Act.

(b) The Commissioner, after receiving recommendations from State and local educational agencies and groups and organizations involved in bilingual education, shall establish, publish, and distribute, with respect to programs of bilingual education, suggested models with respect to pupil-teacher ratios, teacher qualifications, and other factors affecting the quality of instruction offered in such programs.

(c) In prescribing regulations under this section, the Commissioner shall consult with State and local educational agencies, appropriate organizations representing parents and children of limited English proficiency, and appropriate groups and organizations representing teachers and educators involved in bilingual education.

TABLE C.1. Overview of Major Federal Civil Rights Statutes Related to Elementary and Secondary Schools

Statute	Groups Protected	Interests Protected	Schools Covered	Schools Exempted
Sec. 1981, 1982; acts of 1866, 1870	Race	Right to make contracts	Public and private if they solicit clients	Not settled
Sec. 1983; act of 1871	All groups; general civil rights	Constitutional rights	Public and private if operates "under color of law"	Schools not acting "under color of law"
Sec. 1985 (3) (Conspiracy)	All groups; general civil rights	Equal protection of law	Any conspiracy by any persons	Not applicable
Sec. 1988; acts of 1866, as amended	All groups	Federal court proceedings if civil rights are violated	According to the law violated	Not applicable
Equal Pay Act	Sex	Salaries and wages	All who are subject to the Fair Labor Standards Act	← See
Civil Rights Act of 1964, Title VI	Race, color, or national origin	All benefits under federally aided programs	All, in federally supported activities	← See
Civil Rights Act of 1964, Title VII	Race, color, national origin, religion, sex	Employment benefits	All with 15 or more employees	Religious schools for religion-related sex preference

Education Amendments of 1972, Title IX	Sex	Educational benefits that are federally supported	All, in federally supported activities	Religious schools for religion-related sex preference
Family Rights and Privacy Act of 1974	All students	Access to records & confidentiality of records	All, in federally supported activities	← See
Rehabilitation Act of 1963 (Sec. 504)	All handicapped persons	All benefits under federally aided programs	All, in federally supported activities	None
Education of all Handicapped Children Act of 1975	All handicapped children	Educational benefits under federally aided programs	All, in federally supported activities	None
Bilingual Education Act of 1978, Title VII	All children of limited-English-speaking ability	Educational benefits under federally supported programs	All, in federally supported activities	None

Appendix D

Charts Related to State Standards for Public Education*

ATTENDANCE REQUIREMENTS

Description of Column Headings for Chart on Attendance Requirements

Compulsory Attendance: During these years (inclusive) a child must attend school.

Attendance Permitted: During these years (inclusive) a child may attend school on a tuition-free basis.

Basis for Exemption:

(1) *Employment at Age:* A child is exempt from attendance requirements if she/he is legally employed at a certain age.

(2) *Grade Completed:* If she/he has completed a certain grade, a child can be exempt.

(3) *Local Decision:* A mark in this column indicates that the district board or other local authority has some discretionary latitude in choosing to exempt certain pupils who might not be exempt under state guidelines.

(A, B) *Mental Condition, Handicapped:* These columns indicate exemptions for those children whose mental or physical condition prevents their being placed in regular or special education programs. It is customary that this exemption be granted only after a licensed physician or qualified psychologist has certified that the child would not benefit from any education program the state offers.

(C) *Court Decision:* A decision by a juvenile court can exempt a child.

(D) *Academic Equivalency Test:* A child is exempt if she/he achieves a certain score on a standard test.

(E) *Alternate Equivalent Education:* This column covers education in private or parochial schools or by a private tutor.

(F) *Chronic Ill Health:* Ill health could exempt a child from meeting the minimum annual attendance requirements, or it could exempt her/him from attendance altogether.

(G) *Great Distance:* If a child must walk a great distance to the nearest school or bus route and no other transportation is available, then the child is exempt. The distance can be as short as a mile and a half. In some states this exemption applies only to children in elementary school.

(H) *Parental Objection:* If approved by the district board of superintendent, a parent's objection can exempt a child.

(I) Other: This column covers other general exemptions.

* All charts in Appendix D are from *State Legal Standards for the Provision of Public Education* (Washington, D.C.: HEW, The National Institute of Education, 1978).

CHART D.1. Attendance Requirements

States	Compulsory Attendance	Attendance Permitted	Employment At age	Basis for Exemption — Grade Completed	Local Decision	A	B	C	D	E	F	G	H	I	Fines for Violation — Jail (Days)	1st Offense	2nd Offense
Alabama	7–16					x	x	x						x	x	1–90	$1–100	
Alaska	7–16					x	x	x	x								$50–200	
Arizona	8–16	6–21				x	x	x			x				x	1–90	$5–300	
Arkansas	7–15	6–21				x	x	x							x		$10	
California	6–16		14				x	x		x	x				x	1–5	$1–25	$25–250
Colorado	7–16	6–21					x	x							x			
Connecticut	7–16	5–21										x						
Delaware	6–16	6–21					x	x			x				x	2–5	$5–21	$25–50
Florida	7–16		14										x					
Georgia	7–16					x	x	x	x		x				x			
Hawaii	6–18		15				x	x			x				x	1–60	$5–50	
Idaho	7–16	5–21					x	x							x			
Illinois	7–16						x	x			x				x	1–5	$5–20	$10–50
Indiana	7–16						x	x			x				x	1–180	$1–150	
Iowa	7–16	5–21	14	8			x	x	x		x				x		$5–20	
Kansas	7–16	5–21					x	x			x	x						
Kentucky	7–16						x	x			x				x			
Louisiana	7–15		15				x	x							x	1–10	$10	
Maine	7–17	5–20	15									x				1–30	$1–25	

State												
Maryland	6–16	5–20		x	x				x		x	$1–50
Massachusetts		14	6	x	x				x		x	$1–20
Michigan	6–16	5–20						x	x	2–90	x	$5–50
Minnesota	7–16	5–21	10	x	x			x	x			
Mississippi				x	x							
Missouri	7–16	5–20	14	x	x	x		x	x	2–10		$10–25
Montana	7–16	6–21	8	x	x	x		x	x	10–30	x	$5–20
Nebraska	7–16		14	8	x	x		x	x	1–90		$5–100
Nevada	7–17	6–17	8	x	x	x		x	x			
New Hampshire	6–16		14	x	x				x			$5–25
New Jersey	6–16	5–20	14	x	x							
New Mexico	8–17		14	10	x	x		x	x			
New York	6–16	5–21	15	x	x		x	x	x	1–10	$1–10	$1–50
North Carolina	7–16				x	x				1–30		$1–50
North Dakota	7–16	6–21	14	x	x			x	x		$1–100	$1–200
Ohio	6–18	14			x	x		x	x	10–30		
Oklahoma	7–18	5–21		x	x			x	x	1–10		$1–50
Oregon	7–18	6–21	16	x	x		x	x	x			
Pennsylvania	8–17	6–18	14	x	x			x	x	1–5	$1–2	$1–5
Rhode Island	7–16				x	x			x			$20
South Carolina	7–16	6–21	8	x	x	x		x	x	1–30		$1–50

CHART D.1. Attendance Requirements (continued)

States	Compulsory Attendance	Attendance Permitted	Employment At age	Basis for Exemption												Fines for Violation		
				Grade Completed	Local Decision	A	B	C	D	E	F	G	H	I	Jail (Days)	1st Offense	2nd Offense
South Dakota	7–16	5–21		8	x	x	x	x	x					x		$10–50	$25–100
Tennessee	7–16	6–21				x	x				x			x		$2–5	
Texas	7–17	5–21	17	9	x	x	x	x	x					x		$5–25	$10–50
Utah	6–18		16		x	x	x	x	x		x			x			
Vermont	7–16			10	x	x	x	x	x					x		$5–50	
Virginia	6–17	5–20				x	x	x		x		x	x	x			
Washington	8–18	6–21	15	9		x	x		x					x			
West Virginia	7–16		15			x	x		x		x	x					
Wisconsin	7–16	6–20			x	x	x	x	x					x	90	$5–50	
Wyoming	7–16	6–21		8		x	x		x					x	10	$5–25	
Dist. of Col.	7–16		14	8		x	x		x					x	5	$10	

CURRICULUM

In all states the local school district must offer a curriculum precribed by the state. The degree of control exercised by the education agency differs from state to state. In most states a local district must offer the curriculum devised by the state. In those states where districts retain some discretion, course offerings must still be chosen within state guidelines. Oftentimes the guideline is a specific legal requirement that the district must observe; for example, all schools must offer courses in American history and government. The statutes of nearly all states contain such requirements. In states where the choice of course offerings is left to the district, it is often limited by state board guidelines regulating the number, content, or quality of the courses.

Some states provide that a district must offer a specified number of courses. These directives of the state education agency are usually requirements for accreditation. Sanctions for noncompliance could include nonrecognition of the district or school and/or loss of state aid.

Description of Headings for Chart on Curriculum

Local Selection of Curriculum: The local district selects its curriculum offerings on the basis of the extent of authority delegated by the state.

(1) *Determined by State:* The state decides the requirements for curriculum in the public schools. It acts through its legally constituted executive authority (usually the State Board of Education) or through an independent committee established to make decisions on curriculum.
(2) *Within State Guidelines:* The state promulgates guidelines which the district must follow when it selects its curriculum.

Program Specifications:

(1) *Minimum Number of Required Courses:* The school must offer the stated number of required courses to comply with the standard.
(2) *Minimum Number of Electives:* The school must offer the stated number of elective courses to comply with the standard.
(3) *Requirement for Accreditation:* A school must offer the required number and subject matter of courses in order to receive or maintain its accreditation status.
(4) *Bilingual Education:* The school program makes provision for bilingual education. Such programs are either mandatory (M) or discretionary (D).

Sanctions for Noncompliance: The local district faces loss of aid or accreditation status if it fails to comply with state standards or devise satisfactory course offerings of its own.

CHART D.2 Curriculum

States	Local Selection of Curriculum — Determined by State: Executive Agency	Local Selection of Curriculum — Determined by State: Independent	Within State Guidelines	Secondary Schools: Program Specifications — Minimum No. of Req'd. Courses	Maximum No. of Electives	Req'mnt. for Accredit	Bilingual Educ.	Sanctions for Non-compliance
Alabama		x						
Alaska	x						M	
Arizona	x						M	
Arkansas	x							
California			x				M	
Colorado			x				M	
Connecticut	x						D	
Delaware	x							
Florida	x		x					
Georgia	x							
Hawaii	x		x					
Idaho			x					
Illinois			x					
Indiana			x				M	
Iowa			x	26				
Kansas	x						D	
Kentucky	x		x					
Louisiana	x		x					

State						
Maine	x					
Maryland	x					
Massachusetts	x	(a)				x
Michigan	x	(b)				
Minnesota	(c)	D	1950 hrs.	1200 hrs.		x
Mississippi	x		x		12	
Missouri	x					
Montana	x					
Nebraska	x		x		18	
Nevada	x		x			
New Hampshire	x					
New Jersey	x					
New Mexico	x	D			30	
New York	x	D	x			x
North Carolina	x		x			
North Dakota	x		x			
Ohio	x					
Oklahoma	x				36	
Oregon	x		x			x
Pennsylvania	x	M				
Rhode Island	x	(d)				
South Carolina	x				40	
South Dakota	x					

CHART D.2 Curriculum (continued)

| States | Local Selection of Curriculum | | | Secondary Schools: Program Specifications | | | | |
| | Determined by State | | Within State Guidelines | Minimum No. of Req'd. Courses | Maximum No. of Electives | Req'mnt. for Accredit | Bilingual Educ. | Sanctions for Non-compliance |
	Executive Agency	Independent						
Tennessee			x					
Texas			x					
Utah	x		x					
Vermont	x		x					
Virginia			x					
Washington	x		x					
West Virginia			x					
Wisconsin	x		x					
Wyoming	x		x					
Dist. of Col.	(e)		x				M	

M-Mandatory   D-Discretionary

(a) Massachusetts: on request of parent or guardian.
(b) Michigan: if guidelines for implementation are met.
(c) Minnesota: school submits detailed outlines for which curriculum guides are not available to commissioner.
(d) Rhode Island: mandatory if 20 or more pupils register for it.
(e) District of Columbia: Superintendent of Schools.

EXTRACURRICULAR ACTIVITIES

Extracurricular activities cover a wide range of nonacademic pursuits including such items as school organizations and athletic contests. In some states school districts are required to offer a program of extracurricular activities in elementary and/or secondary schools. This requirement is often one of the prerequisites to accreditation. A state education agency's requirements for extracurricular activities usually contain a general statement encouraging the school district to ensure broad student participation by providing a balanced program of activities.

Only a few states provide detailed regulations concerning minimum program specifications. Two states, Iowa and Kansas, require that each district submit its plan for extracurricular activities to the state education agency for approval. The activity most commonly subject to state regulations is participation in athletic events. In addition, many state legislatures have prohibited schools from allowing any secret societies or organizations.

Description of Headings for Chart on Extracurricular Activities

District Must Provide: The state requires that each district or school provide a program of extracurricular activities for elementary (E) or secondary (S) schools.

Detailed State Regulations: The state sets forth detailed requirements for a district or school's extracurricular activities.

State Approval Required: The state assumes a supervisory role for each district or school's extracurricular activities. The state may require that each activity be registered or its program content be approved.

Regulations for Athletic Competition: The state establishes certain guidelines for interscholastic contests. These guidelines might include requirements for game scheduling, transportation, insurance for players, etc.

Secret Societies Prohibited: The state prohibits any school from setting up any secret society or organization.

District Must Provide Facilities for Public Purposes: The state requires that the district allow school facilities to be used at the request of the community.

No Provision: The state has established no requirements for extracurricular activities.

CHART D.3. Extracurricular Activities

States	District Must Provide	Program Specifications					
		No Provisions	Detailed State Regulations	State Approval Required	Regulations for Athletic Competition	Secret Societies Prohibited	District Must Provide Facilities for Public Use
Alabama					x		
Alaska		x					
Arizona		x					
Arkansas		x					
California	ES						
Colorado					x	x	
Connecticut		x					
Delaware		x					
Florida						x	
Georgia		x					
Hawaii		x					
Idaho		x					
Illinois	ES					x	
Indiana	ES						
Iowa	S		x	x			
Kansas	E			x	x		
Kentucky		x					
Louisiana	ES				x	x	

State				
Maine				x
Maryland			x	x
Massachusetts			x	x
Michigan		x	x	x
Minnesota	S			x
Mississippi				x
Missouri	ES			x
Montana				x
Nebraska	ES		x	x
Nevada		x		
New Hampshire		x		
New Jersey	ES		x	x
New Mexico			x	
New York		(a)		(b)
North Carolina			x	
North Dakota	ES		x	
Ohio			x	
Oklahoma		x	x	
Oregon		x	x	x
Pennsylvania		x	x	
Rhode Island			x	
South Carolina		(c)	x	
South Dakota		x		

CHART D.3. Extracurricular Activities (continued)

States	District Must Provide	Program Specifications					
		No Provisions	Detailed State Regulations	State Approval Required	Regulations for Athletic Competition	Secret Societies Prohibited	District Must Provide Facilities for Public Use
Tennessee					x		
Texas						x	
Utah							x
Vermont		x					
Virginia							x
Washington						x	
West Virginia		x					
Wisconsin		x					
Wyoming		x					
Dist. of Col.		x					

E-Elementary   S-Secondary

(a) New York: the Board of Education of each school district having a population of less than one million as well as an educational program beyond the sixth grade level shall make such regulations.

(b) New York: district board may prohibit.

(c) South Carolina: regulations for transportation to extracurricular activities.

INDIVIDUAL PUPIL RECORDS

Description of Headings for Charts on Individual Pupil Records

Statute and/or Regulation: The state requires that the school keep individual pupil records by statute and/or regulation.

Contents of Records:

(1) Biographical: This category includes basic biographical information such as age, address, etc.
(2) *Attendance:* This category includes a record of each pupil's attendance.
(3) *Testing:* Testing information includes records of scores on intelligence and aptitude tests.
(4) *Health:* Health records include information on school-conducted examinations, immunizations, infirmary visits, etc.
(5) *Local Discretion:* The state explicitly grants the district the discretion to keep additional information.

Custodian of Records: The state requires that the district office and/or each school shall keep copies of each pupil's record.

Access to Records: These columns indicate both who has access to records and who controls access to records.

(1) *Discretion of: Local School:* The local school determines who can see a pupil's record. Parent or Student: An X indicates that a parent or pupil has discretion over who sees the records.
(2) *All Interested Persons:* All interested persons have access to a pupil's records.
(3) *Professional Staff:* The professional staff (teachers and administrators) has access to a pupil's records.
(4) *Law Enforcement Agency:* The state requires that the school release records to a law enforcement agency.
(5) *Confidentiality Provisions:* The state either requires that certain information remain confidential or requires that the district board develop regulations concerning confidentiality.

Permanence of Records:

(1) *Mandatory Updating:* A school or district must update all pupil information.
(2) *Provisions for Correction:* Some mechanism is provided whereby a pupil's records can be corrected if they contain errors.
(3) *Copy of Records Transferred:* If a pupil transfers to another school, district, or state, the school must forward copies of her/his records.
(4) *Files Destroyed:* The state requires that a pupil's records be destroyed a certain number of years after a pupil's graduation or transfer to another school.
(5) *Kept Indefinitely:* The state requires that pupil records be kept indefinitely.

CHART D.4.a. Individual Pupil Records

States	Statute	Regulation	Biographical	Attendance	Testing	Health	Local Discretion	District Officer	Local School
			Contents of Records					**Custodian of Records**	
Alabama	S						x		x
Alaska	S	R	x		x	x	x		x
Arizona	S	R			x	x		x	x
Arkansas	S			x				x	x
California	S	R	x	x	x	x		x	
Colorado	S	R		x	x	x			x
Connecticut	S	R				x			x
Delaware	S		x	x	x	x			x
Florida	S	R	x	x	x	x			x
Georgia	S	R		x		x			x
Hawaii		R		x	x				
Idaho		R			x				x
Illinois	S	R	x	x	x				x
Indiana	S			x		x			x
Iowa	S	R		x	x	x			x
Kansas	S		x	x	x	x			x
Kentucky	S	R	x	x	x	x		x	x
Louisiana	S	R	x	x	x	x		x	x

State	S	R							
Maine	S	R	x	x					x
Maryland	S	(a)	x			x			x
Massachusetts	S		x	x				x	x
Michigan	S	R	x	x		x		x	x
Minnesota	S	R	x	x		x		x	x
Mississippi	S	R	x	x		x			x
Missouri	S	R	x	x		x			x
Montana		R	x	x	x			x	x
Nebraska	S	R	x	x	x				x
Nevada	S		x	x	x				x
New Hampshire	S	R	x	x		x		x	x
New Jersey	S	R	x			x	x	x	x
New Mexico	S	R	x	x		x	x	x	x
New York	S	R	x	x		x			x
North Carolina	S	R	x	x			x		x
North Dakota		R	x	x		x	x		x
Ohio	S	R	x	x		x		x	x
Oklahoma	S	R	x	x		x			x
Oregon	S	R	x	x		x			x
Pennsylvania	S	R	x	x		x		x	x
Rhode Island	S	R	x	x		x			x
South Carolina	S	R	x	x					
South Dakota	S	R	x	x		x			

CHART D.4.a. Individual Pupil Records (continued)

States	Statute	Regulation	Contents of Records					Custodian of Records	
			Biographical	Attendance	Testing	Health	Local Discretion	District Officer	Local School
Tennessee	S	R	x	x					
Texas	S		x	x					
Utah	S	R		x		x			
Vermont	S	R	x	x	x	x			
Virginia	S	R	x	x		x			
Washington	S			x		x			x
West Virginia	S			x				x	
Wisconsin	S		x	x					x
Wyoming	S	R	x	x	x	x			x
Dist. of Col.	S	R	x	x	x				x

(a) Maryland: further pupil record information contained in *Maryland Pupil Data System—Manual for Instruction*, not received before publication of this Study.

CHART D.4.b. Individual Pupil Records

States	Access to Records							Mandatory Up Dating	Provisions for Correction	Permanence of Records		
	Discretion of:			All Interested Persons	Profes- sional Staff	Law Enforce- ment Agency	Confiden- tiality Provision			Copy of Record Trans- fered	Files De- stroyed	Kept Indefi- nitely
	Local School	Parent	Student									
Alabama										x		x
Alaska	x				x					x		x
Arizona		x			x	x			x			
Arkansas												
California		x	x		x		x		x	x		x
Colorado	x											
Connecticut	x											
Delaware		x	(b)		x	(c)				x		
Florida		x			x			x		x		
Georgia		x	(d)		x					x		(e)
Hawaii		x	x		x	x	x			x		
Idaho					x							
Illinois		x	x		x		x					
Indiana	x											
Iowa	x			x						x		x
Kansas												
Kentucky					x			x		x		

343

CHART D.4.b. Individual Pupil Records (continued)

States	Access to Records								Permanence of Records			
	Discretion of:			All Interested Persons	Professional Staff	Law Enforcement Agency	Confidentiality Provision	Mandatory Up Dating	Provisions for Correction	Copy of Record Transfered	Files Destroyed	Kept Indefinitely
	Local School	Parent	Student									
Louisiana	x				x				x	x		
Maine	x				x			x				
Maryland	x				x		x			x		x
Massachusetts	x											
Michigan												
Minnesota				x				x	x			x
Mississippi					x		x			x		x
Missouri							x			x		
Montana												
Nebraska		x								x		
Nevada												
New Hampshire												
New Jersey	x				x	x	x					
New Mexico	x		x		x	x	x					
New York	x				x							
North Carolina	x											
North Dakota							x					

State									
Ohio	x	x							
Oklahoma	x			x		x			
Oregon	x	x	x	x		x	x		
Pennsylvania	x	x		x		x	x		
Rhode Island				x		x			
South Carolina				x		x			
South Dakota									
Tennessee	x			x				x	
Texas	x	x	x	x					
Utah									
Vermont									
Virginia	x	x	x	x	x	x	x	x	
Washington	x		x	x					
West Virginia	x		x	x					
Wisconsin			x	x					
Wyoming	x	x	x	x		x		x	x
Dist. of Col.	x	x	x	x		x			

(b) Delaware: if the student is 14 years old or older.

(c) Delaware: duly authorized agent of the federal government.

(d) Georgia: all rights to records accorded to parents shall be accorded to pupils at age 18.

(e) Georgia: student academic redords are to be kept for a period of at least 70 years.

345

CHART D.4.c. Individual Pupil Records Citations

State	Statutes	Regulations
Alabama	§§16-8-31; 16-4-15; 16-9-29; 16-11-10; 16-12-13; 16-28-7; 16-28-9	
Alaska	§14.48.060	Administrative Manual #2.3
Arizona	§§15-151–15-154	R7-2-301(G)(2)
Arkansas	§80-1215	
California	§§46000; 49061; 49069; 49076; 49068; 49067; 49073; 49076	R400–R450
Colorado	§22-1-116	2202-R-12.04
Connecticut	§§10-206; 10-15b	R10-212a-2
Delaware	§4111	
Florida	§§232.021; 232.023; 232.03; 232.031	RGA-1.955
Georgia	§32-1020	R40-2110; 40-200; 40-4300
Hawaii		R-31.0; 50.1–50.14
Idaho		Guidelines and Procedures for Junior High/Middle Schools, p. 36
Illinois	§§24-18, 22-14	Rules and Regulations to Govern Student Records
Indiana	§§20-8.1-7-9; 20-8.1-3-22	
Iowa	§299.7	R670-3.3(10); 570-3.3(11)
Kansas	§§72-5203; 72-5213–72-1111	
Kentucky	§159.160–159.170	704 KAR 4:020 (sec.3)
Louisiana	§§17:229; 17-2112	Bulletin 741, p. 1, 2, 4, 74, 93, 99
Maine	§961	
Maryland	Art. 77§94	R13.07.05.01

Massachusetts	Art. 72§2
Michigan	§§380.1177; 380.1571; 380.1576–380.1578
Minnesota	§121.11
Mississippi	§§37-15-1; 37-15-3
Missouri	§§167.081; 171.151
Montana	R48-2.6(2)-S6030
Nebraska	§79-207
Nevada	R14-(13)
New Hampshire	§§132:16; 189:38
New Jersey	§18A:36-19
New Mexico	§12-3-4.4
New York	§§905; 3211; 3222
North Carolina	§§115-165; 115-166
North Dakota	
Ohio	§§33.01; 25.06; 37.03; 3317.021
Oklahoma	§10-103
Oregon	§§336.185-136.215
Pennsylvania	§§15-1531; 15-1532; 15-1533; 13-1332
Rhode Island	§16-12-4
South Carolina	§21-764

	R325.352
	EDU 7, EDU 140C
	Bulletin 171, p. 7
	5 CSR 50-340(2)(j)
	R2C.0203(g)
	Pupil Accounting Manual (1973) p. 6, 7
	R6:27-1.10; 6:29-3.1; 6:29-4.4
	R72-6; 70–20
	CH II Sec. 104
	R2C.0203(g)
	Administrative Manual (1973), p. 58–62
	R3301-37-03(c); 3301-37-03(d)
	Annual Bulletin for Elementary and Secondary Schools (1976), p. 15
	R581-22-258
	R12.12; 12.31
	Educational Program Development, p. 4–42 *Educational Program for Very Young Children* p. 6
	R43-273; 43-277

CHART D.4.c. Individual Pupil Records Citations (continued)

State	Statutes	Regulations
South Dakota	§13-27-15	R24:03:04:10; 24:03:08:01
Tennessee	§§49-1717; 49-1307(3)	Rules, Regulations and Minimum Standards—1976–77, p. 75, 80
Texas	§21.251	
Utah	§53-6-12	R16-1422
Vermont	§14-1422	Reference Manual for State Board of Education in Vermont, p. 7
Virginia	§§22-275.8; 22-248; 22-275.26	Regulations for State Board of Education of Virginia, p. 75, 85
Washington	§§28A-27.040; 28A-31.040	
West Virginia	§18-8-6	
Wisconsin	§§118.18;115.30	
Wyoming	§21.1-52	CHX Sec. 11; CHXV Sec. 1; CHXVI Sec. 1; CHXVII Sec. 1; CHXVIII Sec. 1; CH 1 Sec. 2; Appendix C Sec. 9-692.3(d)(8)
Dist. of Col.	§31-205	R402.7; 440.1–440.9; 703.8; 703.2; 443.1

INSERVICE TRAINING

In most of the states that have inservice training programs, the training takes place at the district level. Most of the states have developed statutes and/or regulations dealing with training programs. However, this figure is deceptive since many of these district programs apply to teachers in certain subject areas only. The net result is that very few states have a broad and well-developed program of inservice training.

Although some states have a defined training program, only a few discuss teachers' attendance requirements at these programs. In only a very few states are there regulations requiring all teachers to attend training sessions. In two states the district board selects the teachers who must attend a training session.

Description of Headings for Chart on Inservice Training

Statutory Requirements for Inservice Training: The legislature requires that the state education agency or the district provide inservice training.

Annual District Conference: The state requires that each district sponsor an annual training conference which is customarily held at the beginning of each school year.

District Must Provide Training: Besides the annual conference, the state requires that the district provide other in-service training.

District Selects Teachers for Training: When a district sets up a training program, the district also selects those teachers who must participate in the training.

All Teachers Must Attend Training: When a district sets up a training program, all teachers must attend.

CHART D.5. Inservice Training

States	Statutory Requirements for Inservice Training	Annual District Conference	District Must Provide Training	District Selects Teachers for Training	All Teachers Must Attend Training	No Provisions
Alabama		M	x		x	
Alaska	x					
Arizona	(a)					
Arkansas	(b)					
California	x		x			
Colorado	x		x		x	
Connecticut	(c)					
Delaware						x
Florida	x	D				
Georgia					x	
Hawaii						x
Idaho	(d)					
Illinois	x				x	
Indiana	x			x		
Iowa	(e)					
Kansas	x					x
Kentucky	x	D				
Louisiana	(b)					
Maine	x					

State					
Maryland					x
Massachusetts	x				
Michigan			x		x
Minnesota					x
Mississippi			(f)		
Missouri			x		x
Montana					x
Nebraska			x		x
Nevada			x	M	
New Hampshire	x				x
New Jersey			x	D	x
New Mexico		(h)	(g)	D	
New York			x	M	x
North Carolina		x			x
North Dakota				(i)	x
Ohio		x			x
Oklahoma	x				
Oregon					(j)
Pennsylvania				D	(k)
Rhode Island	x				
South Carolina				M	
South Dakota			x		
Tennessee			x	M	

CHART D.5. Inservice Training (continued)

States	Statutory Requirements for Inservice Training	Annual District Conference	District Must Provide Training	District Selects Teachers for Training	All Teachers Must Attend Training	No Provisions
Texas						x
Utah						x
Vermont						x
Virginia	x	D	D			
Washington	x					
West Virginia	x					
Wisconsin						x
Wyoming	(b)					
Dist. of Col.						x

M-Mandatory   D-Discretionary

(a) Arizona: state board of education provides training at the request of the school district.

(b) Arkansas, Louisiana, Wyoming: inservice training for special education programs.

(c) Connecticut: inservice training for alcohol and drug education program.

(d) Idaho: district school board may establish requirements.

(e) Iowa: determined by the education agency administration.

(f) Mississippi: school district shall have a policy which ensures continuous professional growth for all teachers.

(g) New Mexico: provided by district with state approval.

(h) New Mexico: degree credit allowable to teachers that participate.

(i) North Dakota: teachers must earn a minimum of two semester hours at the graduate level or attend four approved conferences or workshops.

(j) Oregon: training for accident prevention.

(k) Pennsylvania: for vocational education personnel.

PERSONNEL POLICIES

Description of Headings for Charts on Teacher Personnel Policies/Employment Practices

Salary: The amount that the teacher earns is subject to state statute, rules, or regulations or to local determination. When the state determines the salary requirements, it is usually to set a minimum salary requirement which district boards may supplement.

Probationary Period: This period of employment occurs before the teacher has achieved professional or career status.

(1) *Length:* The duration of the probationary period indicates how long a teacher must be employed before she/he is eligible for career status.
(2) *Termination of Employment:* A teacher may be dismissed from employment if the contracting party complies with the stated statutory procedures: adequate notice to the teacher of the board's decision not to renew the contract; the right to a fact-finding hearing with attendant procedural safeguards; and the right of the aggrieved teacher to appeal.

Teacher's File: The contracting party invariably maintains a record for personnel purposes containing information about the teacher's performance. The two categories indicate whether there is a file which contains evaluations of the teacher's performance and whether the teacher has access to this file.

Health Standards: The state provides by statute or regulation that a teacher must be in good health prior to and during her/his work in the classroom.

(1) *Prior Certification:* the teacher must present an affidavit or certificate signed by a licensed physical as proof of her/his good health before she/he will be allowed to teach.
(2) *Periodic Reexaminations:* The teacher must periodically furnish additional proof from a physician that she/he continues to be in good health.
(3) *Suspension for Ill Health:* A teacher may be suspended from teaching for the period of time that her/his health endangers the well-being of her/his pupils and associates.

Tenured Teachers: This category deals with some of the important features of the tenured or career status of teachers.

(1) *Automatic Status:* The teacher automatically achieves professional status when she/he completes the probationary period and the board does not terminate her/his contract.
(2) *Discharge or Demotion for Cause:* The teacher must be accorded certain procedural rights before she/he can be fired or given a lower position, even if the board has a reason which is valid on its face.
(3) *Sabbatical Leave:* The contracting party allows the teacher to interrupt her/his teaching in order to study or to otherwise improve the quality of her/his services without diminution of benefits of her/his career status.

Professional Ethics: The state or local agency has established an agency whose function is to maintain the standards of the teaching profession. This agency may have only advisory powers, or it may have the authority to issue regulations and enforce them.

Mandatory Retirement Age: The statutes or regulations contain a stated age after which teachers may no longer perform their duties.

CHART D.6.a. Teacher Personnel Policies

States	Salary		Probationary Period	Termination of Employment			Teacher's File		Health Standards		
	State	Local	Length (in yrs.)	Notice	Hearing	Appeal	Personnel Evaluations	Access of Teacher	Prior Certification	Periodic Re-exams	Suspension For Ill Health
Alabama	x		3	x							
Alaska	x		2	x	x						
Arizona	x		4	x	x	x	x			x	x
Arkansas	x			x	x				x	x	
California	x			x	x	x			x	x	
Colorado		x	3	x							
Connecticut		x	3	x	x						
Delaware	x		3								
Florida	x		3				x	x			
Georgia	x		3	x	x	x					
Hawaii	x		2	x	x				x	x	
Idaho	x		3	x	x				x		x
Illinois		x	2	x					x	x	
Indiana	x		5								
Iowa	x		4	x	x				x	x	
Kansas	x		3	x			x	x	x	x	
Kentucky	x		4	x					x	(a)	
Louisiana	x		3	x							
Maine	x		2	x	x						x

354

State			No.						
Maryland	x		2	x	x				x	x
Massachusetts		x	3	x	x					x
Michigan	x		3	x	x			x	x
Minnesota	x		3	x	x				
Mississippi		x						x	x	x
Missouri	x		5	x		x		x	
Montana			4	x				x	
Nebraska	x		3					x	
Nevada	x		3	x					
New Hampshire			3	x					
New Jersey	x		3	x					
New Mexico	x		3	x				x	x
New York	x		3	x					
North Carolina	x		3	x				x	x
North Dakota	x			x	x	x	(b)		
Ohio	x		3	x	x	x			
Oklahoma		x		x		x			
Oregon	x		3	x	x	x		x	x
Pennsylvania	x		2	x					
Rhode Island	x		3	x	x	x			
South Carolina	x		1					x	x
South Dakota	x		3	x				x	x
Tennessee	x		3					x	

CHART D.6.a. Teacher Personnel Policies (continued)

States	Salary		Probationary Period	Termination of Employment			Teacher's File		Health Standards		
	State	Local	Length (in yrs.)	Notice	Hearing	Appeal	Personnel Evaluations	Access of Teacher	Prior Certification	Periodic Re-exams	Suspension For Ill Health
Texas	x		3	x	x				x	x	x
Utah	x										
Vermont	x										
Virginia	x		3	x							
Washington		x		x	x				x		
West Virginia	x		4								
Wisconsin	x		3	x					x		
Wyoming		x	3				x				
Dist. of Col.			2	x							

CHART D.6.b. Teacher Personnel Policies

States	Tenured Teachers					Professional Ethics			Mandatory Retirement Age
	Automatic Status	Discharge or Demotion for Cause			Sabbatical Leave	Name of Agency	Advisory	Regulatory	
		Notice	Hearing	Appeal					
Alabama	x	x	x						
Alaska	x	x	x	Court	x	1	x	x	65
Arizona		x	x	Court					
Arkansas		x	x						72
California		x	x		x	2		x	
Colorado	x	x	x	Court		3	x		65
Connecticut	x	x	x						70
Delaware		x	x	Court	x				
Florida		x	x	SDE	x	3	x	x	70
Georgia		x	x	SBE		3			
Hawaii	x	x	x		x				65
Idaho	x	x	x			4	x	x	
Illinois	x	x	x	Court	x				65
Indiana	x	x	x	Court					66
Iowa	x	x	x		x	1		x	
Kansas		x	x						65
Kentucky	x	x	x	Court		3	x	x	65
Louisiana		x	x	Court	x				
Maine	x	x	x						65

CHART D.6.b. Teacher Personnel Policies (continued)

States	Tenured Teachers Automatic Status	Discharge or Demotion for Cause Notice	Hearing	Appeal	Sabbatical Leave	Professional Ethics Name of Agency	Advisory	Regulatory	Mandatory Retirement Age
Maryland	x	x	x	SBE					
Massachusetts		x	x		x				
Michigan	x	x	x	Court	x				
Minnesota		x	x		x				65
Mississippi		x	x	Court					
Missouri		x	x						
Montana	x	x	x						
Nebraska	x	x	x		x	3	x	x	
Nevada	x	x	x	Court		5	x		
New Hampshire		x	x			4	x		
New Jersey	x	x	x	SBE					
New Mexico	x	x	x	SBE	x	8			
New York	x	x	x	CE	x				
North Carolina	x	x	x	Court		5			
North Dakota	x	x	x			3	x	x	
Ohio	x	x	x	Court					
Oklahoma		x	x	SBE		3	x		
Oregon		x	x	Court		7			

358

State				Agency	SPI / SDE/Court		
Pennsylvania		x	x	SPI	x		
Rhode Island	x	x	x				
South Carolina				Court			
South Dakota		x	x			3	65
Tennessee		x	x	Court			70
Texas		x	x	SBE	x	6	x
Utah							
Vermont		x	x	BSD			
Virginia	x	x	x				
Washington							
West Virginia		x	x		x		
Wisconsin	x	x	x				
Wyoming		x	x				
Dist. of Col.		x	x	SBE	x		62

SDE - State Department of Education
SBE - State Board of Education
CE - Commissioner of Education
SPI - Superintendent of Public Instruction
BSD - Board of School Directors

[1] Professional Teaching Practice Commission
[2] Teachers' Professional Standards Commission
[3] Professional Practices Commission
[4] Professional Standards Commission
[5] Professional Review Commission
[6] Teachers' Professional Practices Commission
[7] Teacher Standards and Practices Commission
[8] Professional Practices and Ethics Commission

(a) Kentucky: at the discretion of local boards of education.
(b) North Dakota: teacher preparation file not available to teacher, teacher personnel file is available.

Appendix E

State Laws Affecting Public Education

Typical State Law Outlining Procedure for Dismissing a Tenured Teacher

"No teacher who has become permanently employed under this section may be refused employment, dismissed, removed or discharged, except for inefficiency or immorality, for willful and persistent violation of reasonable regulations of the governing body of the school system or school or for other good cause, upon written charges based on fact preferred by the governing body or other proper officer of the school system or school in which the teacher is employed. Upon the teacher's written request and no less than 10 nor more than 30 days after receipt of notice by the teacher, the charges shall be heard and determined by the governing body of the school system or school by which the teacher is employed. Hearings shall be public when requested by the teacher and all proceedings thereat shall be taken by a court reporter. All parties shall be entitled to be represented by counsel at the hearing. The action of the governing body is final." WIS. STAT. ANN. §118.23 (West 1973).

Typical State Law Outlining Procedure for Dismissing a Nontenured Teacher

"Nonrenewal of limited contracts.—(1) Any teacher employed under a limited contract shall at the expiration of such limited contract be deemed reemployed for the succeeding school year at the same salary plus any increment or decrease as provided by the salary schedule, unless the superintendent of schools has recommended to the board of education that the contract of the teacher not be renewed and unless the board has voted to approve said recommendation.

(2) If the board of education approves the superintendent's recommendation, as provided in subsection (1) of this section, the board must present written notice to the teacher that the contract will not be renewed no later than April 30 of the school year during which the contract is in effect. Upon receipt of a request by the teacher, the board shall provide a written statement containing the specific, detailed and complete statement of grounds upon which the nonrenewal of contract is based.

(3) Upon failure of the employing board of education to act favorably on the recommendation of the superintendent not to renew a contract as required by subsection (1) of this section, to give written notice of said nonrenewal as required by subsection (2) of this section or to provide the written statement of grounds required by subsection (2) of this section the teacher shall receive a contract of employment for the next school year; and, if the teacher has served the number of years as required, said contract of employment shall be a continuing contract. Such teacher shall be presumed to have accepted such employment, unless he shall notify the board of education in writing to the contrary on or before the fifteenth day of June, and a

written contract for the succeeding year shall be executed accordingly." Ky. Rev. Stat. §161.750 (1978).

Typical State Law Providing for Reduction in Force

"Whenever in any school year the average daily attendance in all of the schools of a district for the first six months in which school is in session shall have declined below the corresponding period of either of the previous two school years, whenever the governing board determines that attendance in a district will decline in the following year as a result of the termination of an interdistrict tuition agreement, or whenever a particular kind of service is to be reduced or discontinued not later than the beginning of the following school year, and when in the opinion of the governing board of said district it shall have become necessary by reason of either of such conditions to decrease the number of permanent employees in said district, the said governing board may terminate the services of not more than a corresponding percentage of the certificated employees of said district, permanent as well as probationary, at the close of the school year; provided, that the services of no permanent employee may be terminated under the provisions of this section while any probationary employee, or any other employee with less seniority, is retained to render a service which said permanent employee is certificated and competent to render. As between employees who first rendered paid service to the district on the same date, the governing board shall determine the order of termination solely on the basis of needs of the district and the students thereof. Upon the request of any employee whose order of termination is so determined, the governing board shall furnish in writing no later than five days prior to the commencement of the hearing held in accordance with Section 44949, a statement of the specific criteria used in determining the order of termination and the application of the criteria in ranking each employee relative to the other employees in the group. This requirement that the governing board provide, on request, a written statement of reasons for determining the order of termination shall not be interpreted to give affected employees any legal right or interest that would not exist without such a requirement. . . ." CAL. EDUCATION CODE §44955 (West 1979).

Appendix F

Selected Supreme Court Cases

In this appendix, the *Pickering, Tinker,* and *Goss* cases have been substantially edited, with most citations deleted.

PICKERING v. BOARD OF EDUCATION

Supreme Court of the United States, 391 U.S. 563, 88 S.Ct. 1731, 20 L.Ed.2d 811 (1968).

Mr. Justice Marshall delivered the opinion of the Court.

Appellant Marvin L. Pickering, a teacher in Township High School District 205, Will County, Illinois, was dismissed from his position by the appellee Board of Education for sending a letter to a local newspaper in connection with a recently proposed tax increase that was critical of the way in which the Board and the district superintendent of schools had handled past proposals to raise new revenue for the schools. Appellant's dismissal resulted from a determination by the Board, after a full hearing, that the publication of the letter was "detrimental to the efficient operation and administration of the schools of the district" and hence, under the relevant Illinois statute . . . that "interests of the school require[d] [his dismissal]."

Appellant's claim that his writing of the letter was protected by the First and Fourteenth Amendments was rejected. . . . For the reasons detailed below we agree that appellant's rights to freedom of speech were violated and we reverse.

In February of 1961 the appellee Board of Education asked the voters of the school district to approve a bond issue to raise $4,875,000 to erect two new schools. The proposal was defeated. Then, in December of 1961, the Board submitted another bond proposal to the voters which called for the raising of $5,500,000 to build two new schools. This second proposal passed and the schools were built with the money raised by the bond sales. in May of 1964 a proposed increase in the tax rate to be used for educational purposes was submitted to the voters by the Board and was defeated. Finally, on September 19, 1964, a second proposal to increase the tax rate was submitted by the Board and was likewise defeated. It was in connection with this last proposal of the School Board that appellant wrote the letter to the editor (which we reproduce in an Appendix to this opinion) that resulted in his dismissal.

Prior to the vote on the second tax increase proposal a variety of articles attributed to the District 205 Teachers' Organization appeared in the local paper. These articles urged passage of the tax increase and stated that failure to pass the increase would result in a decline in the quality of education afforded children in the district's schools. A letter from the superintendent of schools making the same point was published in the paper two days before the election and submitted to the voters in mimeographed form the following day. It was in response to the foregoing material, together with the failure of the tax increase to pass, that appellant submitted the letter in question to the editor of the local paper.

The letter constituted, basically, an attack on the School Board's handling of the 1961 bond issue proposals and its subsequent allocation of financial resources between the schools' educational and athletic programs. It also charged the superintendent of schools with attempting to prevent teachers in the district from opposing or criticizing the proposed bond issue.

The Board dismissed Pickering for writing and publishing the letter. Pursuant to Illinois law, the Board was then required to hold a hearing on the dismissal. At the hearing the Board charged that numerous statements in the letter were false and that the publication of the statements unjustifiably impugned the "motives, honesty, integrity, truthfulness, responsibility and competence" of both the Board and the school administration. The Board also charged that the false statements damaged the professional reputations of its members and of the school administrators, would be disruptive of faculty discipline, and would tend to forment "controversy, conflict and dissension" among teachers, administrators, the Board of Education, and the residents of the district. Testimony was introduced from a variety of witnesses on the truth or falsity of the particular statements in the letter with which the Board took issue. The Board found the statements to be false as charged. No evidence was introduced at any point in the proceedings as to the effect of the publication of the letter on the community as a whole or on the administration of the school system in particular, and no specific findings along these lines were made. [The Illinois Supreme Court upheld the action of the board] . . .

To the extent that the Illinois Supreme Court's opinion may be read to suggest that teachers may constitutionally be compelled to relinquish the First Amendment rights they would otherwise enjoy as citizens to comment on matters of public interest in connection with the operation of the public schools in which they work, it proceeds on a premise that has been unequivocally rejected in numerous prior decisions of this Court. E. g., *Wieman* v. *Updegraff,* 344 U.S. 183 (1952); *Shelton* v. *Tucker,* 364 U.S. 479 (1960); *Keyishian* v. *Board of Regents,* 385 U.S. 589 (1967). "[T]he theory that public employment which may be denied altogether may be subjected to any conditions, regardless of how unreasonable, has been uniformly rejected." *Keyishian* v. *Board of Regents, supra,* at 605–606. At the same time it cannot be gainsaid that the State has interests as an employer in regulating the speech of its employees that differ significantly from those it possesses in connection with regulation of the speech of the citizenry in general. The problem in any case is to arrive at a balance between the interests of the teacher, as a citizen, in commenting upon matters of public concern and the interest of the State, as an employer, in promoting the efficiency of the public services it performs through its employees.

The Board contends that "the teacher by virtue of his public employment has a duty of loyalty to support his superiors in attaining the generally accepted goals of education and that, if he must speak out publicly, he should do so factually and accurately, commensurate with his education and experience." Appellant, on the other hand, argues that the test applicable to defamatory statements directed against public officials by persons having no occupational relationship with them, namely, that statements to be legally actionable must be made "with knowledge that [they were] . . . false or with reckless disregard of whether [they were] . . . false or not," *New York Times Co.* v. *Sullivan,* 376 U.S. 254, 280 (1964), should also be applied to public statements made by teachers. Because of the enormous variety of fact situations in which critical statements by teachers and other public employees may be thought by their superiors, against whom the statements are directed, to furnish grounds for dismissal, we do not deem it either appropriate or feasible to attempt to lay down a general standard against which all such statements may be judged. However, in the course of evaluating the conflicting claims of First Amendment protection and the need for orderly school administration in the context of this case, we shall indicate some of the general lines along which an analysis of the controlling interests should run.

An examination of the statements in appellant's letter objected to by the Board reveals that they, like the letter as a whole, consist essentially of criticism of the Board's allocation of school funds between educational and athletic programs, and of both the Board's and the superintendent's methods of informing, or preventing the informing of, the district's taxpayers of the real reasons why additional tax revenues were being sought for the schools. The statements are in no way directed towards any person with whom appellant would normally be in contact in the course of his daily work as a teacher. Thus no question of maintaining either discipline by immediate superiors or harmony among coworkers is presented here. Appellant's employment relationships with the Board and, to a somewhat lesser extent, with the superintendent are not the kind of close working relationships for which it can persuasively be claimed that personal loyalty and confidence are necessary to their proper functioning. Accordingly, to the extent that the Board's position here can be taken to suggest that even comments on matters of public concern that are substantially correct—such as statements (1)-(4) of appellant's letter, see Appendix, *infra*, may furnish ground for dismissal if they are sufficiently critical in tone, we unequivocally reject it.

We next consider the statements in appellant's letter which we agree to be false. The Board's original charges included allegations that the publication of the letter damaged the professional reputations of the Board and the superintendent and would foment controversy and conflict among the Board, teachers, administrators, and the residents of the district. However, no evidence to support these allegations was introduced at the hearing. So far as the record reveals, Pickering's letter was greeted by everyone but its main target, the Board, with massive apathy and total disbelief. The Board must, therefore, have decided, perhaps by analogy with the law of libel, that the statements were *per se* harmful to the operation of the schools.

However, the only way in which the Board could conclude, absent any evidence of the actual effect of the letter, that the statements contained therein were *per se* detrimental to the interest of the schools was to equate the Board members' own interests with that of the schools. Certainly an accusation that too much money is being spent on athletics by the administrators of the school system (which is precisely the import of that portion of appellant's letter containing the statements that we have found to be false, . . .) cannot reasonably be regarded as *per se* detrimental to the district's schools. Such an accusation reflects rather a difference of opinion between Pickering and the Board as to the preferable manner of operating the school system, a difference of opinion that clearly concerns an issue of general public interest.

In addition, the fact that particular illustrations of the Board's claimed undesirable emphasis on athletic programs are false would not normally have any necessary impact on the actual operation of the schools, beyond its tendency to anger the Board. For example, Pickering's letter was written after the defeat at the polls of the second proposed tax increase. It could, therefore, have had no effect on the ability of the school district to raise necessary revenue, since there was no showing that there was any proposal to increase taxes pending when the letter was written.

More importantly, the question whether a school system requires additional funds is a matter of legitimate public concern on which the judgment of the school administration, including the School Board, cannot, in a society that leaves such questions to popular vote, be taken as conclusive. On such a question free and open debate is vital to informed decision-making by the electorate. Teachers are, as a class, the members of a community most likely to have informed and definite opinions as to how funds allotted to the operation of the schools should be spent. Accordingly, it is essential that they be able to speak out freely on such questions without fear of retaliatory dismissal.

In addition, the amounts expended on athletics which Pickering reported erroneously were matters of public record on which his position as a teacher in the district did not qualify him to speak with any greater authority than any other taxpayer. The Board could easily have rebutted appellant's errors by publishing the accurate figures itself, either via a letter to the same newspaper or otherwise. We are thus not presented with a situation in which a teacher has carelessly made false statements about matters so closely related to the day-to-day operations of the schools that any harmful impact on the public would be difficult to counter because of the teacher's presumed greater access to the real facts. Accordingly, we have no occasion to consider at this time whether under such circumstances a school board could reasonably require that a teacher make substantial efforts to verify the accuracy of his charges before publishing them.

What we do have before us is a case in which a teacher has made erroneous public statements upon issues then currently the subject of public attention, which are critical of his ultimate employer but which are neither shown nor can be presumed to have in any way either impeded the teacher's proper performance of his daily duties in the classroom or to have interfered with the regular operation of the schools generally. In these circumstances we conclude that the interest of the school administration in limiting teachers' opportunities to contribute to public debate is not significantly greater than its interest in limiting a similar contribution by any member of the general public.

The public interest in having free and unhindered debate on matters of public importance—the core value of the Free Speech Clause of the First Amendment—is so great that it has been held that a State cannot authorize the recovery of damages by a public official for defamatory statements directed at him except when such statements are shown to have been made either with knowledge of their falsity or with reckless disregard for their truth or falsity. . . . It is therefore perfectly clear that, were appellant a member of the general public, the State's power to afford the appellee Board of Education or its members any legal right to sue him for writing the letter at issue here would be limited by the requirement that the letter be judged by the standard laid down in *New York Times.* . . .

While criminal sanctions and damage awards have a somewhat different impact on the exercise of the right to freedom of speech from dismissal from employment, it is apparent that the threat of dismissal from public employment is nonetheless a potent means of inhibiting speech. We have already noted our disinclination to make an across-the-board equation of dismissal from public employment for remarks critical of superiors with awarding damages in a libel suit by a public official for similar criticism. However, in a case such as the present one, in which the fact of employment is only tangentially and insubstantially involved in the subject matter of the public communication made by a teacher, we conclude that it is necessary to regard the teacher as the member of the general public he seeks to be.

In sum, we hold that, in a case such as this, absent proof of false statements knowingly or recklessly made by him, a teacher's exercise of his right to speak on issues of public importance may not furnish the basis for his dismissal from public employment. Since no such showing has been made in this case regarding appellant's letter . . . his dismissal for writing it cannot be upheld and the judgment of the Illinois Supreme Court must, accordingly, be reversed. . . .

Appendix to Opinion of the Court: Appellant's letter

I enjoyed reading the back issues of your paper which you loaned to me. Perhaps others would enjoy reading them in order to see just how far the two new high schools have deviated from the original promises by the Board of Education. First, let me state that I am referring to the February thru November, 1961 issues of your paper, so that it can be checked.

One statement in your paper declared that swimming pools, athletic fields, and auditoriums had been left out of the program. They may have been left out but they got put back in very quickly because Lockport West has both an auditorium and athletic field. In fact, Lockport West has a better athletic field than Lockport Central. It has a track that isn't quite regulation distance even though the board spent a few thousand dollars on it. Whose fault is that? Oh, I forgot, it wasn't supposed to be there in the first place. It must have fallen out of the sky. Such responsibility has been touched on in other letters but it seems one just can't help noticing it. I am not saying the school shouldn't have these facilities, because I think they should, but promises are promises, or are they?

Since there seems to be a problem getting all the facts to the voter on the twice defeated bond issue, many letters have been written to this paper and probably more will follow, I feel I must say something about the letters and their writers. Many of these letters did not give the whole story. Letters by your Board and Administration have stated that teachers' salaries total $1,297,746 for one year. Now that must have been the total payroll, otherwise the teachers would be getting $10,000 a year. I teach at the high school and I know this just isn't the case. However, this shows their "stop at nothing" attitude. To illustrate further, do you know that the superintendent told the teachers, and I quote, "Any teacher that opposes the referendum should be prepared for the consequences." I think this gets at the reason we have problems passing bond issues. Threats take something away; these are insults to voters in a free society. We should try to sell a program on its merits, if it has any.

Remember those letters entitled "District 205 Teachers Speak," I think the voters should know that those letters have been written and agreed to by only five or six teachers, not 98% of the teachers in the high school. In fact, many teachers didn't even know who was writing them. Did you know that those letters had to have the approval of the superintendent before they could be put in the paper? That's the kind of totalitarianism teachers live in at the high school, and your children go to school in.

In last week's paper, the letter written by a few uninformed teachers threatened to close the school cafeteria and fire its personnel. This is ridiculous and insults the intelligence of the voter because properly managed school cafeterias do not cost the school district any money. If the cafeteria is losing money, then the board should not be packing free lunches for athletes on days of athletic contests. Whatever the case, the taxpayer's child should only have to pay about 30¢ for his lunch instead of 35¢ to pay for free lunches for the athletes.

In a reply to this letter your Board of Administration will probably state that these lunches are paid for from receipts from the games. But $20,000 in receipts doesn't pay for the $200,000 a year they have been spending on varsity sports while neglecting the wants of teachers.

You see we don't need an increase in the transportation tax unless the voters want to keep paying $50,000 or more a year to transport athletes home after practice and to away games, etc. Rest of the $200,000 is made up in coaches' salaries, athletic directors' salaries, baseball pitching machines, sodded football fields, and thousands of dollars for other sports equipment.

These things are all right, provided we have enough money for them. To sod football fields on borrowed money and then not be able to pay teachers' salaries is getting the cart before the horse.

If these things aren't enough for you, look at East High. No doors on many of the classrooms, a plant room without any sunlight, no water in a first aid treatment room, are just a few of many things. The taxpayers were really taken to the cleaners. A part of the sidewalk in front of the building has already collapsed. Maybe Mr. Hess would be interested to know that we need blinds on the windows in that building also.

Once again, the board must have forgotten they were going to spend $3,200,000 on the West building and $2,300,000 on the East building.

As I see it, the bond issue is a fight between the Board of Education that is trying to push tax-supported athletics down our throats with education, and a public that has mixed emotions about both of these items because they feel they are already paying enough taxes, and simply don't know whom to trust with any more tax money.

I must sign this letter as a citizen, taxpayer and voter, not as a teacher, since that freedom has been taken from the teachers by the administration. Do you really know what goes on behind those stone walls at the high school?

Respectfully,
Marvin L. Pickering. . . .

Mr. Justice White, concurring in part and dissenting in part.

The Court holds that truthful statements by a school teacher critical of the school board are within the ambit of the First Amendment. So also are false statements innocently or negligently made. The State may not fire the teacher for making either unless, as I gather it, there are special circumstances, not present in this case, demonstrating an overriding state interest, such as the need for confidentiality or the special obligations which a teacher in a particular position may owe to his superiors. The core of today's decision is the holding that Pickering's discharge must be tested by the standard of *New York Times Co.* v. *Sullivan,* 376 U.S. 254 (1964). To this extent I am in agreement. . . .

. . . As I see it, a teacher may be fired without violation of the First Amendment for knowingly or recklessly making false statements regardless of their harmful impact on the schools. As the Court holds, however, in the absence of special circumstances he may not be fired if his statements were true or only negligently false, even if there is some harm to the school system. . . . If Pickering's false statements were either knowingly or recklessly made, injury to the school system becomes irrelevant, and the First Amendment would not prevent his discharge. . . .

Nor can I join the Court in its findings with regard to whether Pickering knowingly or recklessly published false statements. . . .

TINKER v. DES MOINES, FEB. 24, 1969

Mr. Justice Fortas delivered the opinion of the Court.

Petitioner John F. Tinker, 15 years old, and petitioner Christopher Eckhardt, 16 years old, attended high schools in Des Moines, Iowa. Petitioner Mary Beth Tinker, John's sister, was a 13-year-old student in junior high school.

In December 1965, a group of adults and students in Des Moines held a meeting at the Eckhardt home. The group determined to publicize their objections to the hostilities in Vietnam and their support for a truce by wearing black armbands during the holiday season and by fasting on December 16 and New Year's Eve. Petitioners and their parents had previously engaged in similar activities, and they decided to participate in the program.

The principals of the Des Moines schools became aware of the plan to wear armbands. On December 14, 1965, they met and adopted a policy that any student wearing an armband to school would be asked to remove it, and if he refused he would be suspended until he returned without the armband. Petitioners were aware of the regulation that the school authorities adopted.

On December 16, Mary Beth and Christopher wore black armbands to their schools. John Tinker wore his armband the next day. They were all sent home and suspended from school until they would come back without their armbands. They did not return to school until after the planned period for wearing armbands had expired—that is, until after New Year's Day. . . .

I.

As we shall discuss, the wearing of armbands in the circumstances of this case was entirely divorced from actually or potentially disruptive conduct by those participating in it. It was closely akin to "pure speech" which, we have repeatedly held, is entitled to comprehensive protection under the First Amendment.

First Amendment rights, applied in light of the special characteristics of the school environment, are available to teachers and students. It can hardly be argued that either students or teachers shed their constitutional rights to freedom of speech or expression at the schoolhouse gate. This has been the unmistakable holding of this Court for almost 50 years. . . .

In *West Virginia State Board of Education* v. *Barnette*, the Court said:

> The Fourteenth Amendment, as now applied to the States, protects the citizen against the State itself and all of its creatures—Boards of Education not excepted. These have, of course, important, delicate, and highly discretionary functions, but none that they may not perform within the limits of the Bill of Rights. That they are educating the young for citizenship is reason for scrupulous protection of Constitutional freedoms of the individual, if we are not to strangle the free mind at its source and teach youth to discount important principles of our government as mere platitudes.

On the other hand, the Court has repeatedly emphasized the need for affirming the comprehensive authority of the States and of school officials, consistent with fundamental constitutional safeguards, to prescribe and control conduct in the schools. Our problem lies in the area where students in the exercise of First Amendment rights collide with the rules of the school authorities. . . .

II.

Only a few of the 18,000 students in the school system wore the black armbands. Only five students were suspended for wearing them. There is no indication that the work of the schools or any class was disrupted. Outside the classrooms, a few students made hostile remarks to the children wearing armbands, but there were no threats or acts of violence on school premises.

The District Court concluded that the action of the school authorities was reasonable because it was based upon their fear of a disturbance from the wearing of the armbands. But, in our system, undifferentiated fear or apprehension of disturbance is not enough to overcome the right to freedom of expression. Any departure from absolute regimentation may cause trouble. Any variation from the majority's opinion may inspire fear. Any word spoken, in class, in the lunchroom, or on the campus, that deviates from the views of another person may start an argument or cause a disturbance. But our Constitution says we must take this risk, and our history says that it is this sort of hazardous freedom—this kind of openness—that is the basis of our national strength and of the independence and vigor of Americans who grow up and live in this relatively permissive, often disputatious, society.

In order for the State in the person of school officials to justify prohibition of a particular expression of opinion, it must be able to show that its action was caused by something more than a mere desire to avoid the discomfort and unpleasantness that always accompany an unpopular viewpoint. Certainly where there is no finding and no showing that engaging in the forbidden conduct would "materially and substantially interfere with the requirements of appropriate discipline in the operation of the school," the prohibition cannot be sustained. . . .

In the present case, school authorities did not purport to prohibit the wearing of all symbols of political or controversial significance. The record shows that students in some of the schools wore buttons relating to national political campaigns, and some even wore the Iron Cross, traditionally a symbol of Nazism. The order prohibiting the wearing of armbands did not extend to these. Instead, a particular symbol—black armbands worn to exhibit opposition to this Nation's involvement in Vietnam—was singled out for prohibition. Clearly, the prohibition of expression of one particular opinion, at least without evidence that it is necessary to avoid material and substantial interference with schoolwork or discipline, is not constitutionally permissible.

In our system, state-operated schools may not be enclaves of totalitarianism. School officials do not possess absolute authority over their students. Students in school as well as out of school are "persons" under our Constitution. They are possessed of fundamental rights which the State must respect, just as they themselves must respect their obligations to the State. In our system, students may not be regarded as closed-circuit recipients of only that which the State chooses to communicate. They may not be confined to the expression of those sentiments that are officially approved. In the absence of a specific showing of constitutionally valid reasons to regulate their speech, students are entitled to freedom of expression of their views. As Judge Gewin, speaking for the Fifth Circuit, said, school officials cannot suppress "expressions of feelings with which they do not wish to contend."

In *Meyer* v. *Nebraska*, Mr. Justice McReynolds expressed this Nation's repudiation of the principle that a State might so conduct its schools as to "foster a homogeneous people." He said:

> In order to submerge the individual and develop ideal citizens, Sparta assembled the males at seven into barracks and entrusted their subsequent education and training to official guardians. Although such measures have been deliberately approved by men of great genius, their ideas touching the relation between individual and State were wholly different from those upon which our institutions rest; and it hardly will be affirmed that any Legislature could impose such restrictions upon the people of a state without doing violence to both letter and spirit of the Constitution.

This principle has been repeated by this Court on numerous occasions during the intervening years. Mr. Justice Brennan, speaking for the Court, said:

> The vigilant protection of constitutional freedoms is nowhere more vital than in the community of American schools. The classroom is peculiarly the "marketplace of ideas." The Nation's future depends upon leaders trained through wide exposure to that robust exchange of ideas which discovers truth "out of a multitude of tongues," [rather] than through any kind of authoritative selection.

The principle of these cases is not confined to the supervised and ordained discussion which takes place in the classroom. The principal use to which the schools are dedicated is to accommodate students during prescribed hours for the purpose of certain types of activities. Among those activities is personal intercommunication among the students. This is not only an inevitable part of the process of attending school; it is also an important part of the educational process. A student's rights, therefore, do not embrace merely the classroom hours. When he is in the cafeteria, or on the playing field, or on the campus during the authorized hours, he may express his opinions, even on controversial subjects like the conflict in Vietnam, if he does so without "materially and substantially interfer[ing] with the requirements of appropriate discipline in the operation of the school" and without colliding with the rights of others. But conduct by the student, in class or out of it, which for any reason—whether it stems from time, place, or type of behavior—materially disrupts classwork or involves substantial disorder or invasion of the rights of others is, of course, not immunized by the constitutional guarantee of freedom of speech.

Under our Constitution, free speech is not a right that is given only to be so circumscribed that it exists in principle but not in fact. Freedom of expression would not truly exist if the right could be exercised only in an area that a benevolent government has provided as a safe haven for crackpots. The Constitution says that Congress (and the States) may not abridge the right to free speech. This provision means what it says. We properly read it to permit reasonable regulation of speech-connected activities in carefully restricted circumstances. But we do not confine the permissible exercise of First Amendment rights to a telephone booth or the four corners of a pamphlet, or to supervised and ordained discussion in a school classroom.

If a regulation were adopted by school officials forbidding discussion of the Vietnam conflict, or the expression by any student of opposition to it anywhere on school property except as part of a prescribed classroom exercise, it would be obvious that the regulation would violate the constitutional rights of students, at least if it could not be justified by a showing that the students' activities would materially and substantially disrupt the work and discipline of the school. . . .

These petitioners merely went about their ordained rounds in school. Their deviation consisted only in wearing on their sleeves a band of black cloth, not more than two inches wide. They wore it to exhibit their disapproval of the Vietnam hostilities and their advocacy of a truce, to make their views known, and, by their example, to influence others to adopt them. They neither interrupted school activities nor sought to intrude in the school affairs or the lives of others. They caused discussion outside of the classrooms, but no interference with work and no disorder. In the circumstances, our Constitution does not permit officials of the State to deny their form of expression.

We express no opinion as to the form of relief which should be granted, this being a matter for the lower courts to determine. We reverse and remand for further proceedings consistent with this opinion.

Mr. Justice Black, dissenting.

The Court's holding in this case ushers in what I deem to be an entirely new era in which the power to control pupils by the elected "officials of state supported public schools . . ." in the United States is in ultimate effect transferred to the Supreme Court. . . .

Assuming that the Court is correct in holding that the conduct of wearing armbands for the purpose of conveying political ideas is protected by the First Amendment, the crucial remaining questions are whether students and teachers may use the schools at their whim as a platform for the exercise of free speech—"symbolic" or "pure"—and whether the courts will allocate to themselves the function of deciding how the pupils' school day will be spent. . . .

While the absence of obscene remarks or boisterous and loud disorder perhaps justified the Court's statement that the few armband students did not actually "disrupt" the classwork, I think the record overwhelmingly shows that the armbands did exactly what the elected school officials and principals foresaw they would, that is, took the students' minds off their classwork and diverted them to thoughts about the highly emotional subject of the Vietnam war. [And I repeat that] if the time has come when pupils of state-supported schools, kindergartens, grammar schools, or high schools, can defy and flout orders of school officials to keep their mind on their own schoolwork, it is the beginning of a new revolutionary era of permissiveness in this country fostered by the judiciary. . . .

I deny [therefore] that it has been the "unmistakable holding of this Court for almost 50 years" that "students" and "teachers" take with them into the "schoolhouse gate" constitutional rights to "freedom of speech or expression." The truth is that a teacher of kindergarten, grammar school, or high school pupils no more carries into a school with him a complete right to freedom of speech and expression than an anti-Catholic or anti-Semite carries with him a complete freedom of speech and religion into a Catholic church or Jewish synagogue. It is a myth to say that any person has a constitutional right to say what he pleases, where he pleases, and when he pleases. Our Court has decided precisely the opposite.

In my view, teachers in state-controlled public schools are hired to teach there . . . certainly a teacher is not paid to go into school and teach subjects the State does not hire him to teach as a part of its selected curriculum. Nor are public school students sent to the schools at public expense to broadcast political or any other views to educate and inform the public. The original idea of schools, which I do not believe is yet abandoned as worthless or out of date, was that children had not yet reached the point of experience and wisdom which enabled them to teach all of their elders. It may be that the Nation has outworn the old-fashioned slogan that "children are to be seen not heard," but one may, I hope, be permitted to harbor the thought that taxpayers send children to school on the premise that at their age they need to learn, not teach. . . .

Change has been said to be truly the law of life but sometimes the old and the tried and true are worth holding. The schools of this Nation have undoubtedly contributed to giving us tranquility and to making us a more law-abiding people. Uncontrolled and uncontrollable liberty is an enemy to domestic peace. We cannot close our eyes to the fact that some of the country's greatest problems are crimes committed by the youth, too many of school age. School discipline, like parental discipline, is an integral and important part of training our children to be good citizens—to be better citizens. Here a very small number of students have crisply and summarily refused to obey a school order designed to give pupils who want to learn the opportunity to do so. One does not need to be a prophet or the son of a prophet to know that after the Court's holding today some students in Iowa schools and indeed in all schools will be ready, able, and willing to defy their teachers on practically all orders. This is the more unfortunate for the schools since groups of students all over the land are already running loose, conducting break-ins, sit-ins, lie-ins, and smash-ins. Many of these student groups, as is all too familiar to all who read the newspapers and watch the television news programs, have already engaged in rioting, property seizures, and destruction. They have picketed schools to force students not to cross their picket lines and have too often violently attacked earnest but frightened students who wanted an education that the pickets did not want them to get. Students engaged in such activites are apparently confident that they know far more about how to operate public school systems than do their parents, teachers, and elected school officials. It is no answer to say that the particular students here have not yet reached such high points in their demands to attend classes in order to exercise their political pressures. Turned loose with lawsuits for damages and injunctions against their teachers as they are here, it is nothing but wishful thinking to imagine that young, immature students will not soon believe it is their right to control the schools rather than the right of the States that collect the taxes to hire the teachers for the benefit of the pupils. This case, therefore, wholly without constitutional reasons in my judgment, subjects all the public schools in the country to the whims and caprices of their loudest-mouthed, but maybe not their brightest, students. I, for one, am not fully persuaded that school pupils are wise enough, even with this Court's expert help from Washington, to run the 23,390 public school systems in our 50 States. I wish, therefore, wholly to disclaim any purpose on my part to hold that the Federal Constitutional compels the teachers, parents, and elected school officials to surrender control of the American public school system to public school students. I dissent.

GOSS v. LOPEZ, JAN. 22, 1975

Mr. Justice White delivered the opinion of the Court.

This appeal by various administrators of the Columbus, Ohio, Public School System ("CPSS") challenges the judgment of a three-judge federal court, declaring that appellees—various high school students in the CPSS—were denied due process of law contrary to the command of the Fourteenth Amendment in that they were temporarily suspended from their high schools without a hearing either prior to suspension or within a reasonable time thereafter, and enjoining the administrators to remove all reference to such suspensions from the students' records. . . .

Two named plaintiffs, Dwight Lopez and Betty Crome, were students at the Central High School and McGuffey Junior High School, respectively. The former was suspended in connection with a disturbance in the lunchroom which involved some physical damage to school property. Lopez testified that at least 75 other students were suspended from his school on the same day. He also testified below that he was not a party to the destructive conduct but was instead an innocent bystander. Because no one from the school testified with regard to this incident, there is no evidence in the record indicating the official basis for concluding otherwise. Lopez *never had a hearing.*

Betty Crome was present at a demonstration at a high school different from the one she was attending. There she was arrested together with others, taken to the police station, and released without being formally charged. Before she went to school on the following day, she was notified that she had been suspended for a 10-day period. Because no one from the school testified with respect to this incident, the record does not disclose how the McGuffey Junior High School principal went about making the decision to suspend Betty Crome nor does it disclose on what information the decision was based. It is clear from the record that *no hearing* was ever held. . . .

II.

At the outset, appellants contend that because there is no constitutional right to an education at public expensse, the Due Process Clause does not protect against expulsions from the public school system. This position misconceives the nature of the issue and is refuted by prior decisions. The Fourteenth Amendment forbids the State to deprive any person of life, liberty or property without due process of law. Protected interests in property are normally "not created by the Constitution. Rather, they are created and their dimensions are defined" by an independent source such as state statutes or rules entitling the citizen to certain benefits. Having chosen to extend the right to an education to people of appellees' class generally, Ohio may not withdraw that right on grounds of misconduct absent fundamentally fair procedures to determine whether the misconduct has occurred. The authority possessed by the State to prescribe and enforce standards of conduct in its schools, although concededly very broad, must be exercised consistently with constitutional safeguards. Among other things, the State is constrained to recognize a student's legitimate entitlement to a public education as a property interest which is protected by the Due Process Clause and which may not be taken away for misconduct without adherence to the minimum procedures required by that clause.

The Due Process Clause also forbids arbitrary deprivations of liberty. "Where a person's good name, reputation, honor, or integrity is at stake because of what the government is doing to him," the minimal requirements of the clause must be satisfied. School authorities here suspended appellees from school for periods of up to 10 days based on charge of misconduct. If sustained and recorded, those charges could seriously damage the students' standing with their fellow pupils and their teachers as well as interfere with later opportunities for higher education and employment. It is apparent that the claimed right of the State to determine unilaterally and without process whether that misconduct has occurred immediately collides with the requirements of the Constitution.

Appellants proceed to argue that even if there is a right to a public education protected by the Due Process Clause generally, the clause comes into play only when the State subjects a student to a "severe detriment or grievous loss." The loss of 10 days, it is said, is neither severe nor grievous and the Due Process Clause is therefore of no relevance. Appellee's argument is again refuted by our prior decisions; for in determining "whether due process requirements apply in the first place, we must look not to the 'weight' but to the *nature* of the interest at stake." . . .

A short suspension is of course a far milder deprivation than expulsion. But, "education is perhaps the most important function of state and local governments." . . . and the total exclusion from the educational process for more than a trivial period, and certainly if the suspension is for 10 days, is a serious event in the life of the suspended child. Neither the property interest in educational benefits temporarily denied nor the liberty interest in reputation, which is also implicated, is so insubstantial that suspensions may constitutionally be imposed by any procedure the school chooses, no matter how arbitrary.

III.

"Once it is determined that due process applies, the question remains what process is due." At the very minimum, therefore, students facing suspension and the consequent interference with a protected property interest must be given *some* kind of notice and afforded *some* kind of hearing. "Parties whose rights are to be affected are entitled to be heard; and in order that they may enjoy that right they must first be notified."

The student's interest is to avoid unfair or mistaken exclusion from the educational process, with all of its unfortunate consequences. The Due Process Clause will not shield him from suspensions properly imposed, but it disserves both his interest and the interest of the State if his suspension is in fact unwarranted. The concern would be mostly academic if the disciplinary process were a totally accurate, unerring process, never mistaken and never unfair. Unfortunately, that is not the case, and no one suggests that it is. Disciplinarians, although proceeding in utmost good faith, frequently act on the reports and advice of others; and the controlling facts and the nature of the conduct under challenge are often disputed. The risk of error is not at all trivial, and it should be guarded against if that may be done without prohibitive cost or interference with the educational process.

The difficulty is that our schools are vast and complex. Some modicum of discipline and order is essential if the educational function is to be performed. Events calling for discipline are frequent occurrences and some times require immediate, effective action. Suspension is considered not only to be a necessary tool to maintain order but a valuable educational device. The prospect of imposing elaborate hearing requirements in every suspension case is viewed with great concern, and many school authorities may well prefer the untrammeled power to act unilaterally, unhampered by rules about notice and hearing. But it would be a strange disciplinary system in an educational institution if no communication was sought by the disciplinarian with the student in an effort to inform him of his defalcation and to let him tell his side of the story in order to make sure that an injustice is not done. . . .

We do not believe that school authorities must be totally free from notice and hearing requirements if their schools are to operate with acceptable efficiency. Students facing temporary suspension have interests qualifying for protection of the Due Process Clause, and due process requires, in connection with a suspension of 10 days or less, that the student be given oral or written notice of the charges against him and, if he denies them, an explanation of the evidence the authorities have and an opportunity to present his side of the story. The clause requires at least these rudimentary precautions against unfair or mistaken findings of misconduct and arbitrary exclusion from school.

There need be no delay between the time "notice" is given and the time of the hearing. In the great majority of cases the disciplinarian may informally discuss the alleged misconduct with the student minutes after it has occurred. We hold only that, in being given an opportunity to explain his version of the facts at this discussion, the student first be told what he is accused of doing and what the basis of the accusation is. . . .

Since the hearing may occur almost immediately following the misconduct, it follows that as a general rule notice and hearing should precede removal of the student from school. We agree with the District Court, however, that there are recurring situations in which prior notice and hearing cannot be insisted upon. Students whose presence poses a continuing danger to persons or property or an ongoing threat of disrupting the academic process may be immediately removed from school. In such cases, the necessary notice and rudimentary hearing should follow as soon as practicable, as the District Court indicated.

In holding as we do, we do not believe that we have imposed procedures on school disciplinarians which are inappropriate in a classroom setting. Instead we have imposed requirements which are, if anything, less than a fair-minded school principal would impose upon himself in order to avoid unfair suspensions. . . .

We stop short of construing the Due Process Clause to require, country-wide, that hearings in connection with short suspensions must afford the student the opportunity to secure counsel, to confront and cross-examine witnesses to verify his version of the incident. Brief disciplinary suspensions are almost countless. To impose in each such case even truncated trial type procedures might well overwhelm administrative facilities in many places and, by diverting resources, cost more than it would save in educational effectiveness. Moreover, further formalizing the suspension process and escalating its formality and adversary nature may not only make it too costly as a regular disciplinary tool but also destroy its effectiveness as part of the teaching process.

On the other hand, requiring effective notice and informal hearing permitting the student to give his version of the events will provide a meaningful hedge against erroneous action. At least the disciplinarian will be alerted to the existence of disputes about facts and arguments about cause and effect. He may then determine himself to summon the accuser, permit cross-examination and allow the student to present his own witnesses. In more difficult cases, he may permit counsel. In any event, his discretion will be more informed and we think the risk of error substantially reduced.

Requiring that there be at least an informal give-and-take between student and disciplinarian, preferably prior to the suspension, will add little to the fact-finding function where the disciplinarian has himself witnessed the conduct forming the basis for the charge. But things are not always as they seem to be, and the student will at least have the opportunity to characterize his conduct and put it in what he deems the proper context.

We should also make it clear that we have addressed ourselves solely to the short suspension, not exceeding 10 days. Longer suspensions or expulsions for the remainder of the school term, or permanently, may require more formal procedures. Nor do we put aside the possibility that in unusual situations, although involving only a short suspension, something more than the rudimentary procedures will be required.

IV.

The District Court found each of the suspensions involved here to have occurred without a hearing, either before or after the suspension, and that each suspension was therefore invalid and the statute unconstitutional insofar as it permits such suspensions without notice or hearing. Accordingly, the judgment is *Affirmed.*

Mr. Justice Powell, with whom The Chief Justice, Mr. Justice Blackmun, and Mr. Justice Rehnquist join, dissenting.

The Court today invalidates an Ohio statute that permits student suspensions from school without a hearing "for not more than ten days." The decision unnecessarily opens avenues for judicial intervention in the operation of our public schools that may affect adversely the quality of education. The Court holds for the first time that the federal courts, rather than educational officials and state legislatures, have the authority to determine the rules applicable to routine classroom discipline of children and teenagers in the public schools. It justifies this unprecedented intrusion into the process of elementary and secondary education by identifying a new constitutional right: the right of a student not to be suspended for as much as a single day without notice and a due process hearing either before or promptly following the suspension. . . .

In an age when the home and church play a diminishing role in shaping the character and value judgments of the young, a heavier responsibility falls upon the schools. When an immature student merits censure for his conduct, he is rendered a disservice if appropriate sanctions are not applied or if procedures for their application are so formalized as to invite a challenge to the teacher's authority—an invitation which rebellious or even merely spirited teenagers are likely to accept.

The lesson of discipline is not merely a matter of the student's self-interest in the shaping of his own character and personality; it provides an early understanding of the relevance to the social compact of respect for the right of others. The classroom is the laboratory in which this lesson of life is best learned.

In assessing in constitutional terms the need to protect pupils from unfair minor discipline by school authorities, the Court ignores the commonality of interest of the State and pupils in the public school system. Rather, it thinks in traditional judicial terms of an advisory situation. To be sure, there will be the occasional pupil innocent of any rule infringement who is mistakenly suspended or whose infraction is too minor to justify suspension. But, while there is no evidence indicating the frequency of unjust suspensions, common sense suggests that they will not be numerous in relation to the total number, and that mistakes or injustices will usually be righted by informal means.

One of the more disturbing aspects of today's decision is its indiscriminate reliance upon the judiciary, and the adversary process, as the means of resolving many of the most routine problems arising in the classroom. In mandating due process procedures the Court misapprehends the reality of the normal teacher-pupil relationship. There is an ongoing relationship, one in which the teacher must occupy many roles—educator, adviser, friend and, at times, parent-substitute. It is rarely adversary in nature except with respect to the chronically disruptive or unsubordinate pupil whom the teacher must be free to discipline without frustrating formalities. . . .

We have relied for generations upon the experience, good faith and dedication of those who staff our public schools, and the nonadversary means of airing grievances that always have been available to pupils and their parents. One would have thought before today's opinion that this informal method of resolving differences was more compatible with the interests of all concerned than resort to any constitutionalized procedure, however blandly it may be defined by the Court. . . .

No one can foresee the ultimate frontiers of the new "thicket" the Court now enters. Today's ruling appears to sweep within the protected interest in education a multitude of discretionary decisions in the educational process. Teachers and other school authorities are required to make many decisions that may have serious consequences for the pupil. They must decide, for example, how to grade the student's work, whether a student passes or fails a course, whether he is to be promoted, whether he is required to take certain subjects, whether he may be excluded from interscholastic athletics or other extracurricular activities, whether he may be removed from one school and sent to another, whether he may be bused long distances when available schools are nearby, and whether he should be placed in a "general," "vocational," or "college-preparatory" track.

In these and many similar situations claims of impairment of one's educational entitlement identical in principle to those before the Court today can be asserted with equal or greater justification. . . .

If, as seems apparent, the Court will now require due process procedures whenever such routine school decisions are challenged, the impact upon public education will be serious indeed. The discretion and judgment of federal courts across the land often will be substituted for that of the 50-state legislatures, the 14,000 school boards and the 2,000,000 teachers who heretofore have been responsible for the administration of the American public school system. If the Court perceives a rational and analytically sound distinction between the discretionary decision by school authorities to suspend a pupil for a brief period, and the types of discretionary school decisions described above, it would be prudent to articulate it in today's opinion. Otherwise, the federal courts should prepare themselves for a vast new role in society.

Appendix G

Other Legal Resources for Teachers

1. American Civil Liberties Union
   22 East 40th Street
   New York, New York 10016

   The ACLU has state and local affiliates accessible to teachers.

   Publications: Children's Rights Report (monthly), *First Principle* (monthly), and *Civil Liberties*, bimonthly

2. American Federation of Teachers
   11 DuPont Circle, N.W.
   Washington, D.C. 20036

   The AFT has state and local affiliates accessible to teachers.

3. National Education Association
   1201 West 16th Street, N.W.
   Washington, D.C. 20036

   The NEA has state and local affiliates accessible to teachers.

4. National Organization on Legal Problems in Education
   5401 S.W. 7th Street
   Topeka, Kansas 66601

   Publications: NOLPE School Law Reports (bimonthly), *NOLPE Notes, School Law Journal, Yearbook of School Law,* and *Annual Convention Reports.*

Glossary of Terms

Adversary system: System of law in America, where the truth is thought to be best revealed through a clash in the courtroom between opposite sides to a dispute.

Affidavit: A written statement sworn to before a person officially permitted by law to administer an oath.

Amicus curiae: "Friend of the court"; a person or organization allowed to appear in a lawsuit, to file arguments in the form of a brief supporting one side or the other, even though not party to the dispute.

Answer: The first pleading by the defendant in a lawsuit. This statement sets forth the defendant's responses to the charges contained in the plaintiff's "complaint."

Appeal: Asking a higher court to review the actions of a lower court in order to correct mistakes or injustice.

Beyond a reasonable doubt: The level of proof required to convict a person of a crime. This is the highest level of proof required in any type of trial, in contrast to *a fair preponderance of the evidence,* the level of proof in civil cases.

Brief: A written summary or condensed statement of a case. Also a written statement prepared by one side in a lawsuit to explain its case to the judge.

By a fair preponderance of the evidence: The level of proof required in a civil case. This level is lower than that required in criminal cases.

Cause of action: Facts sufficient to allow a valid lawsuit to proceed.

Certiorari: A request for review of a lower court decision, which the higher court can refuse.

Circumstantial evidence: Evidence which indirectly proves a main fact in question. Such evidence is open to doubt, since it is inferential, e.g., a student seen in the vicinity of the locker room at the time of a theft is the thief.

Civil case: Every lawsuit other than a criminal proceeding. Most civil cases involve a lawsuit brought by one person against another and usually concern money damages.

Class action: A lawsuit brought by one person on behalf of himself or herself and all other persons in the same situation; persons bringing such suits must meet certain statutory criteria and must follow certain notice procedures.

Code: A collection of laws. Most states have an education code containing all laws directly relevant to education.

Common law: "Judge-made" rather than "legislature-made" law. The body of law developed from judicial decisions based on customs and precedents, as distinct from laws enacted by legislatures and written in statutes and codes.

Compensatory damages: Damages which relate to the actual loss suffered by a plaintiff, such as loss of income.

Complaint: The first main paper filed in a civil lawsuit. It includes, among other things, a statement of the wrong or harm done to the plaintiff by the defendant and a request for specific help from the court. The defendant responds to the complaint by filing an "answer."

Criminal case: Cases involving crimes against the laws of the state; unlike civil cases, the state is the prosecuting party.

De facto: In fact, actual; a situation that exists in fact whether or not it is lawful. *De facto* segregation is that which exists regardless of the law or the actions of civil authorities.

Defamation: Injuring a person's character or reputation by false or malicious statements. This includes both *libel* and *slander*.

Defendant (appellee): The person against whom a legal action is brought. This legal action may be civil or criminal. At the appeal stage, the party against whom an appeal is taken is known as the appellee.

De jure: Of right, legitimate; lawful. *De jure* segregation is that which is sanctioned by law.

De minimus: Small, unimportant; not worthy of concern.

Demurrer: The formal means by which one party to a lawsuit argues against the legal sufficiency of the other party's claim. A demurrer basically contends that even if all the facts which the other party alleges are true they do not constitute a legal cause of action.

De novo: New, completely new from the start; for example: a trial *de novo* is a completely new trial ordered by the trial judge or by an appeals court.

Dictum: A digression; a discussion of side points or unrelated points. Short for *obiter dictum;* plural is *dicta.*

Disclaimer: The refusal to accept certain types of responsibility. For example, a college catalogue may disclaim any responsibility for guaranteeing that the courses contained therein will actually be offered since courses, programs, and instructors are likely to change without notice.

En banc: The full panel of judges assigned to a court sit to hear a case, usually a case of special significance.

Equity: Fairness; the name of a type of court originating in England to handle legal problems when the existing laws did not cover some situations in which a person's rights were violated by another person. In the United States, civil courts have both the powers of law and equity. If only money is represented in a case, the court is acting as a law court and will give only monetary relief. If something other than money is requested—injunction, declaratory judgment, specific performance of a contractual agreement, etc.—then the court takes jurisdiction in equity and will grant a decree ordering acts to be done or not done. There is no jury in an equity case. Actions at law and suits in equity involve civil cases, not criminal.

Et al.: "And others." When the words "et al." are used in an opinion, the court is thereby indicating that there are unnamed parties, either plaintiffs or defendants, also before the court in the case.

Ex parte: With only one side present; an *ex parte* judicial proceeding involves only one party without notice to, or contestation by, any person adversely affected.

Ex post facto law: A law which retrospectively changes the legal consequences of an act which has already been performed. Article 1, section 10 of the U.S. Constitution forbids the passage of ex post facto laws.

Expunge: Blot out. For example, a court order requesting that a student's record be expunged of any references to disciplinary action during such and such a time period means that the references are to be "wiped off the books."

Ex rel: On behalf of; when a case is titled *States ex rel. Doe* v. *Roe*, it means that the state is bringing a lawsuit against Roe on behalf of Doe.

Fiduciary: A relationship between persons in which one person acts for another in a position of trust.

Hearing: An oral proceeding before a court or quasi-judicial tribunal. Hearings which describe a process to ascertain facts and provide evidence are labeled "trial-like hearings" or, simply, "trials." Hearings which relate to a presentation of ideas as distinguished from facts and evidence are known as "arguments." The former occur in trial courts and the latter occur in appellate courts. The terms "trial," "trial-type hearing," "quasi-judicial hearing," "evidentiary hearing," and "adjudicatory hearing" are all used by courts and have overlapping meanings. See *trial*.

Hearsay: Secondhand evidence; facts not in the personal knowledge of the witness, but a repetition of what others said that is used to prove the truth of what those others said. Hearsay is generally not allowed as evidence at a trial, although there are many exceptions.

Holding: The rule of law in a case; that part of the judge's written opinion that applies the law to the facts of the case and about which can be said "the case means no more and no less than this." A holding is the opposite of *dictum*.

In camera: "In chambers"; in a judge's private office; a hearing in court with all spectators excluded.

Incriminate: To involve in a crime, to cause to appear guilty.

Informed consent: A person's agreement to allow something to happen (such as being the subject of a research study) that is based on a full disclosure of facts needed to make the decision intelligently.

Injunction: A court order requiring someone to do something or refrain from taking some action.

In loco parentis: In place of the parent; acting as a parent with respect to the care, supervision, and discipline of a child.

In re: In the matter of; this is a prefix to the name of a case often used when a child is involved. For example, *"In re John Jones"* might be the title of a child neglect proceeding though it is really against the parents.

Ipso facto: By the fact itself, by the mere fact that.

Judicial review: The power of a court to declare a statute unconstitutional; also the power to interpret the meaning of laws.

Jurisdiction: A court's authority to hear a case; also the geographical area within which a court has the right and power to operate. Original jurisdiction means that the court will be the first to hear the case; appellate jurisdiction means that the court reviews cases on appeal from lower court rulings.

Law: Basic rules of order as pronounced by a government. Common law refers to laws originating in custom or practice. Statute law refers to laws passed by legislatures and recorded in public documents. Case law are the pronouncements of courts.

Libel: Written defamation; published false and malicious written statements that injure a person's reputation.

Mandamus: A writ issued by a court commanding that some official duty be performed.

Material: Important, going to the heart of the matter; for example, a material fact is one necessary to reach a decision.

Misrepresentation: A false statement; if knowingly done, misrepresentation may be illegal and result in punishment.

Mitigation: The reduction in a fine, penalty, sentence, or damages initially assessed or decreed against a defendant.

Moot: Abstract; not a real case involving a real dispute.

Motion: A request made by a lawyer that a judge take certain action, such as dismissing a case.

Opinion: A judge's statement of the decision reached in a case.

> **Majority opinion:** The opinion agreed in by more than half the judges or justices hearing a case, sometimes called the opinion of the court.

> **Concurring opinion:** Agrees with the majority opinion, but gives different or added reasons for arriving at that opinion.

> **Dissenting opinion:** Disagrees with the majority opinion.

Ordinance: The term applied to a municipal corporation's legislative enactments.

Parens patriae: The historical right of all governments to take care of persons under their jurisdiction, particularly minors and incapacitated persons.

Per curiam: An unsigned decision and opinion of a court, as distinguished from one signed by a judge.

Petitioner: One who initiates a proceeding and requests some relief be granted on his behalf. A plaintiff. When the term "petitioner" is used, the one against whom the petitioner is complaining is referred to as the respondent.

Plaintiff: One who initiates a lawsuit; the party bringing suit.

Pleading: The process of making formal, written statements of each side of a case. First the plaintiff submits a paper with facts and claims; then the defendant submits a paper with facts and counterclaims; then the plaintiff responds; and so on until all issues and questions are clearly posed for a trial.

Political question: A question that the courts will not decide because it concerns a decision more properly made by another branch of government such as the legislature.

Precedent: A court decision on a question of law that gives authority or direction on how to decide a similar question of law in a later case with similar facts.

Prima facie: Clear on the face of it; presumably, a fact that will be considered to be true unless disproved by contrary evidence. For example, a *prima facie* case is a case that will win unless the other side comes forward with evidence to dispute it.

Punitive damages: Money awarded to a person by a court that is over and above the damages actually sustained. Punitive damages are designed to serve as a deterrent to similar acts in the future.

Quasi-judicial: The case-deciding function of an administrative agency.

Redress: To set right, remedy, make up for, remove the cause of a complaint or grievance.

Remand: Send back. A higher court may remand a case to a lower court with instructions to take some action in the case.

Res judicata: A thing decided. Thus, if a court decides a case, the matter is settled and no new lawsuit on the same subject may be brought by the persons involved.

Respondent: One who makes an answer in a legal appellate proceeding. This term is frequently used in appellate and divorce cases, rather than the more customary term, defendant.

Sectarian: Characteristic of a sect.

Secular: Not specifically religious, ecclesiastical or clerical; relating to the worldly or temporal.

Sine qua non: A thing or condition that is indispensable.

Slander: Oral defamation; the speaking of false and malicious words that injure another person's reputation, business, or property rights.

Sovereign immunity: The government's freedom from being sued for money damages without its consent.

Standing: A person's right to bring a lawsuit because he or she is directly affected by the issues raised.

Stare decisis: "Let the decision stand"; a legal rule that when a court has decided a case by applying a legal principle to a set of facts, that court should stick by that principle and apply it to all later cases with clearly similar facts unless there is a good reason not to. This rule helps promote fairness and reliability in judicial decision making and is inherent in the American legal system.

Statute of limitation: A statute which sets forth the time period within which litigation may be commenced in a particular cause of action.

Tort: A civil wrong done by one person to another. For an act to be a tort, there must be: a legal duty owed by one person to another, a breach of that duty, and harm done as a direct result of the action.

Trial: A process occurring in a court whereby opposing parties present evidence, subject to cross-examination and rebuttal, pertaining to the matter in dispute.

Trial court: The court in which a case is originally tried, as distinct from higher courts to which the case might be appealed.

Ultra vires: Going beyond the specifically delegated authority to act; for example, a school board which is by law restricted from punishing students for behavior occurring wholly off-campus acts *ultra vires* in punishing a student for behavior observed at a private weekend party.

Waiver: An intentional or uncoerced release of a known right.

Selected Bibliography

Fellman, David, ed. *The Supreme Court and Education.* 3rd ed. New York: Teachers' College Press, 1976.

Gee, Gordon E., and Sperry, David J. *Education Law and the Public Schools: A Compendium.* Boston: Allyn & Bacon, 1978.

Goldstein, Stephen R. *Law and Public Education.* Indianapolis: Bobbs-Merrill, 1974.

Hagerty, Robert, and Howard, Thomas. *How to Make Federal Mandatory Special Education Work for You: A Handbook for Educators & Consumers.* Springfield: Charles C. Thomas, 1978.

Hazard, William R. *Education and the Law: Cases and Materials on Public Schools.* 2nd ed. New York: Free Press, 1978.

Hull, Kent. *The Rights of Physically Handicapped People.* New York: Avon, 1979.

Journal of Law and Education. Jefferson Law Book Company, 646 Main Street, Cincinnati, Ohio 45201.

Kemerer, Frank R., and Deutsch, Kenneth L. *Constitutional Rights and Student Life.* St. Paul: West, 1979.

Levine, Alan H. *The Rights of Students.* New York: Avon, 1977.

Memin, Samuel. *Law and the Legal System: An Introduction.* Boston: Little, Brown, 1973.

Morris, Arval A. *The Constitution and American Education.* St. Paul: West, 1980.

Nolte, M. Chester. *How to Survive in Teaching: The Legal Dimension.* Chicago: Teach 'em, Inc., 1978.

Pepe, Thomas J. *A Guide for Understanding School Law.* Danville, Ill.: Interstate Printers and Publishers, 1976.

Peterson, LeRoy J.; Rossmiller, Richard A.; and Volz, Martin M. *The Law and the Public School Operation.* New York: Harper & Row, 1978.

Reutter, G. Edmund, Jr., and Hamilton, Robert R. *The Law of Public Education.* 2nd ed. 1976.

Rubin, David. *Rights of Teachers.* New York: Avon, 1972.

Schimmel, David, and Fischer, Louis. *The Rights of Parents.* Columbia, Md.: National Committee for Citizens in Education, 1977.

School Law News. Capitol Publications, Inc., Suite G-12, 2430 Pennsylvania Avenue, N.W., Washington, D.C. 20037.

Valente, William D. *Law in the Schools.* Columbus, Ohio: Charles E. Merrill, 1980.

Table of Cases

Index